Shakespearean Whodunnits

SHAKESPEAREAN WHODUNNITS

Edited by
MIKE ASHLEY

Special Edition for PAST TIMES® Oxford, England

Robinson Publishing Ltd
7 Kensington Church Court
London W8 4SP

First published in the UK by Robinson Publishing Ltd 1997

A copy of the British Library Cataloguing in Publication data
is available from the British Library

ISBN 1–85487–945-6

Printed and bound in the EC

10 9 8 7 6 5 4 3 2

CONTENTS

CONTENTS VII

ACKNOWLEDGEMENTS

The following stories are published for the first time in this anthology and are printed by permission of the authors.

"The Collaborator" © 1997 by Rosemary Aitken; "When the Dead Rise Up" © 1997 by John T. Aquino; "The House of Rimmon" © 1997 by Cherith Baldry; "Imogen" © 1997 by Paul Barnett; "A Midsummer Eclipse" © 1997 by Stephen Baxter; "Mother of Rome" © 1997 by Molly Brown; "Not Wisely, but too Well" © 1997 by Louise Cooper; "Serpent's Tooth" © 1997 by Martin Edwards; "The Death of Kings" © 1997 by Margaret Frazer; "Buried Fortune" © 1997 by Peter T. Garratt; "A Villainous Company" © 1997 by Susanna Gregory (printed with the permission of the author and the author's agent, A.M. Heath & Co. Ltd); "Toil and Trouble" © 1997 by Edward D. Hoch; "Cinna the Poet" © 1997 by Tom Holt; "A Sea of Troubles" © 1997 by Steve Lockley; "Murder as You Like It" © 1997 by F. Gwynplaine MacIntyre; "Star-Crossed" © 1997 by Patricia A. McKillip; "Who Killed Mamillius?" © 1997 by Amy Myers (printed with the permission of the author and the author's agent Dorian Literary Agency); "This is Illyria, Lady" © 1997 by Kim Newman; "The Shrewd Taming of Lord Thomas" © 1997 by Mary Monica Pulver; "A Shadow that Dies" © 1997 by Mary Reed and Eric Mayer; "The Death of Falstaff" © 1997 by Darrell Schweitzer (printed with the permission of the author and the author's agent, Dorian Literary Agency);

"The Banished Men" © 1997 by Keith Taylor; "An Ensuing Evil" © 1997 by Peter Tremayne, printed with the permission of the author and the author's agent, A.M. Heath & Co. Ltd; "A Serious Matter" © 1997 by Derek Wilson.

"Much Ado about Something" © 1994 by Susan B. Kelly was first published in *Crime Yellow*, edited by Maxim Jakubowski (London: Victor Gollancz, 1994), and is reprinted by permission of the author.

INTRODUCTION

Shakespeare's Mysteries

The premise behind this anthology is simple. Each author has selected one of Shakespeare's plays, taken certain key incidents and converted them into a mystery story. Each story remains faithful to Shakespeare's play. They take place in the same settings and time as the original and include many of the same characters. Occasionally a new character or two has been introduced, but nothing that would seem out of place. Some stories are contemporary with the original play, reworking events from a new perspective to show how things might really have happened: the stories based on *King John* and *Julius Caesar*, for example, both do that. Other stories take place a year or more after the original events and consider the consequences of actions in the play: the stories for *A Midsummer-Night's Dream* and *The Merchant of Venice* both show how the episodes described by Shakespeare set in train events that would lead to murder.

Each story stands on its own so you don't need to know Shakespeare's original plays in order to understand them. However, I have added details of the play in my introduction to each story so that you can refresh your memory if you wish.

Shakespeare's plays date from 1590 to 1613 so all of these stories are historical mysteries, but some are more historical than others! Shakespeare's plays are normally sub-divided into the historical ones, the tragedies and the comedies. The historical plays were a series he wrote about the English kings which include a complete sequence running from Richard II to Richard III, plus an earlier play about King John. Several of his tragedies also cover actual events, particularly *Julius Caesar* and *Macbeth* although both of these, and other such historical tragedies as *Coriolanus*, *Cymbeline* and technically *King Lear*, have less regard for factual accuracy. Strictly speaking *A Midsummer-Night's Dream* must have an historical setting, since it takes place at the time of Theseus, king (or duke) of Athens, but this is a fairy play which could be set at any time. The comedies were often based on stories known to Shakespeare, some dating from several centuries earlier, but most of them have a sixteenth-century setting. In selecting some kind of sequence in which to present the stories I have ranked the genuine historical plays first and placed these in chronological sequence, and then grouped the other plays together and placed them in their own historical sequence in so far as internal evidence suggests.

Not every play by Shakespeare is covered, there was not the space to do that. If there is sufficient interest in this volume, the remaining plays and other episodes involving Shakespeare and his writings can be incorporated in a companion anthology.

Of course there is a great mystery about Shakespeare himself: who was he and did he write the plays credited to him? One of our stories, "The Collaborators", takes this mystery into account. Many hundreds of books have been written on the subject and I do not intend to go into detail here, but for those interested, let me spell out certain facts and enticements. The generally accepted wisdom is that the William Shakespeare who is credited with the plays is the same Gulielmus Shakspere who was baptized at Stratford-on-Avon on 26 April 1564. His exact date of birth is not known. His father was John Shakespeare, a local farmer who became mayor of Stratford in 1568, but whose fortunes waned in later years. His mother was Mary Arden, a farmer's daughter. William was their third child, but the first to survive infancy. In fact he outlived all his brothers, and only his sister Joan survived him.

We know nothing of William's childhood, despite what some biographies claim. On 28 November 1582 there is the record of a marriage bond to William Shagspere and Anne Hathwey, and six months later the baptism is recorded of their eldest daughter Susanna. Twins, Hamnet and Judith, were born a little over a year later, and baptised in February 1585. Shakespeare seems to have stayed in the Stratford area for a few years, as he is named with his parents in a legal action with a neighbour over some land in 1589, but soon after he must have made his way to London. The legend states that Shakespeare was caught poaching deer and though punished he fled to London, but there is no official record of this. It's possible that Shakespeare became attracted to a travelling theatre company, the Queen's Men, which visited Stratford in 1587. One of its company was killed by accident and it has been speculated that Shakespeare took his place and served as an actor with the company for the next four or five years. It seems likely that during this period he began writing, no doubt initially in collaboration with other players. The first play generally acknowledged to include his hand is the first part of *Henry VI*, which may have been written as early as 1589 or 1590. Other plays dated to this period include *The Two Gentlemen of Verona*, *The Taming of the Shrew* and *Titus Andronicus*, though there is some general agreement that most or all of *Titus Andronicus* was by some other dramatist, with Christopher Marlowe cited as the likeliest candidate.

At quite an early stage Shakespeare's name was taken in vain by his contemporaries. Just before he died in 1592, Robert Greene, a much respected Elizabethan dramatist, wrote a scathing attack on Shakespeare, calling him an "upstart crow", and describing him as bombastic and something of a coxcomb. A later reference by John Weever refers to Shakespeare as "honey-tongued". We get the impression of a confident, sweet-talking, witty but rather unscrupulous young man, full of his own importance, gaining a reputation by stealing from others. Supporters of Shakespeare's reputation have never denied that he borrowed material from a wide range of sources for his plays – there's nothing strange about that, most writers, certainly the Elizabethan dramatists, have done so for generations. Greene's implication was that Shakespeare was passing off material written by others as if it were his own. His reputation became firmly established with two long narrative poems, *Venus and Adonis* in 1593 and *The Rape of Lucrece* in 1594. These were soon followed by his immensely popular play *Henry IV*, where the characters of Prince Hal and Sir John Falstaff, captured the public imagination. This play was probably completed by about 1595. In 1594 Shakespeare, along with Richard Burbage, Will Kempe, John Heminges and others, founded a new theatre company called the Lord Chamberlain's Men (which became the King's Men after the patronage of James I in 1603). They went on to establish the Globe Theatre in 1599.

The 1590s provide us with a limited but interesting perspective on the careers of Shakespeare of Stratford and Shakespeare of London. In August 1596, Shakespeare's son Hamnet died, aged only eleven. Soon after Shakespeare is recorded as defaulting on payment of five shillings tax and indeed there are further records of his failure to pay taxes and other debts. Yet in May 1597 Shakespeare bought a large mansion at New Place, Stratford for sixty pounds, and soon after a friend of Shakespeare's wrote to him for a loan of thirty pounds. Evidently Shakespeare had become prosperous during the 1590s yet was also a debtor. There was even a writ issued for his arrest in 1596 along with several of his colleagues, because of his threats to another person's life.

Despite family troubles and sorrows (his father died in 1601, his mother in 1608, and his brother Edward – who had followed him to London as an actor – died in 1607) the production of Shakespeare's plays and poems continued at a regular pace. Most of the formal records that remain of his life relate to debts (either his own, or suing others), land acquisition and involvement in lawsuits. Interestingly, of the very few signatures by Shakespeare that have survived, none are consistent, suggesting that the names were attached by the legal clerks. In fact many claim that Shakespeare could not write – his parents couldn't, and neither could his children.

The last plays attributed solely to Shakespeare were *The Tempest* and *All is True*, though he also worked on some plays with John Fletcher (1579–1625), such as the now lost *Cardenio* and *The Two Noble Kinsmen*, which were completed around 1613. Soon after this Shakespeare seems to have retired to Stratford where he died on 23 April 1616, aged fifty-two. He had made his will only a month or two earlier. He left most of his estate to his elder daughter Susanna, but to his wife Anne he left simply his "second-best bed".

The impression I get of Shakespeare from all I've read about him is that he was something of a rogue. Maybe he was a likeable one at times, but he had no concern about chasing others for debt and putting the frighteners on them, whilst ignoring his own debts. He seems to have pretty much abandoned his wife after their first few years of marriage, though there is no reason to doubt that he loved his children. His younger daughter Judith survived him by nearly fifty years. She died in 1662. She had married Thomas Quiney in 1616 but their first child, Shakespeare, died an infant, and two further sons, Richard and Thomas, barely made adulthood. Shakespeare's elder daughter, Susanna, had married John Hall of Stratford in 1607. She outlived her husband and died in 1649. Their daughter, Elizabeth, died in 1670. Though she married twice she had no children and was Shakespeare's last surviving direct heir. The only descendants of Shakespeare's parents still living are those descended from William's sister Joan, who had married a William Hart. The Hart family remained in Stratford for several generations, one line remaining in a house owned by John Shakespeare which they used as a butcher's until 1806.

Even while Shakespeare lived there was occasional doubt cast upon his authorship of the plays. Although he knew and was on reasonable terms with the great Elizabethan dramatist Ben Jonson (1572–1637), Jonson seems to blow hot and cold on the subject in his writings: sometimes praising Shakespeare, sometimes damning him. The lack of any hard evidence to link the Shakespeare of Stratford with the authorship of the plays has resulted in endless speculation about who the real authors were. Top of the list is Francis Bacon (1561–1626), a brilliant philosopher and statesman who certainly had all the knowledge and abilities to produce the plays, though there is precious little direct evidence to support that he did. The other two main contenders are Edward de Vere (1550–1604), the earl of Oxford, and William Stanley (1561–1642), the earl of Derby. Both of these, especially Oxford, have wide support and fascinating cases made in their favour. Others have suggested that the name Shakespeare was used either as a collective pseudonym for a variety of writers or that Shakespeare plagiarized the plays of others, promoting them under his name. Amongst those believed to have been wronged or disguised in this way are Ben Jonson, Sir Francis Drake, Edmund Spenser, Sir Philip Sidney, John Webster and many more. We can even throw Sir Walter Raleigh and Christopher Marlowe into the fray. It seems that there is scarcely an Elizabethan writer of note who hasn't in some way been linked to Shakespeare. If we are to make any sense of this at all then the likeliest outcome is that Shakespeare was used by others to adapt their work for the stage in circumstances when it was important that no questions were asked. Shakespeare was enough of an opportunist to do such a thing for money, but also enough of a professional on the stage to know what the audiences wanted, so that he could adapt whatever he was given, intermingle it with extracts from earlier plays and present it as an homogenous whole. This would certainly explain the inconsistencies in the structure and format of some of his plays, and also his ability to juxtapose moments of soaring eloquence with moments of rustic banter. It would also explain his extensive and virtually complete knowledge about almost everything. But if Shakespeare was being used in this fashion, who was using him? Ah, well, there lies the rub. Suspicion turns again to Sir Francis Bacon as the likeliest candidate, but we could almost imagine a conspiracy. If ever there was a time for such intrigue, it was during the Elizabethan age.

It is all fascinating and the type of literary mystery that I love, but the case for or against is yet to be proved. The fact remains that regardless of who wrote them, there is a collection of some forty or so plays which contain some of the most memorable and brilliant dialogue ever composed for the stage, and stand firm as the foundation of English drama.

It is those plays that have provided us with an opportunity to recreate a series of historical mystery stories. I hope you enjoy them and that they bring Shakespeare's work alive for you in a way that you might not have expected. Have fun.

Mike Ashley
May 1997

King John 🍒

WHEN THE DEAD RISE UP

John T. Aquino

The Life and Death of King John *was first performed in about*
1595. It is believed that Shakespeare may have adapted it
from an earlier anonymous play, The Troublesome Reign of
John, King of England, *which had been published in 1591.*
The play concentrates on King John's tenuous claim to the
throne and the opposition against him from the French king
Philip and from Falconbridge, the illegitimate son of Richard
the Lion-heart. Central to the play is Prince Arthur, the young
son of John's elder brother Geoffrey, who has a greater title
to the throne, and who is supported by the king of France.
John has Arthur imprisoned and orders his death. In the
play's most moving scene, Arthur pleads for his life with
his executioner Hubert de Burgh. Hubert spares him but
later Arthur, disguised as a ship's boy, dies when he jumps
from the prison walls while trying to escape. When Arthur's
body is discovered it is believed that John had killed him, and
Philip of France uses that as his reason to invade England.
That is Shakespeare's version. In the following story John
T. Aquino looks at what might really have happened. These
events take place about the year 1203.

* * *

"His majesty is mad," Richard Faulconbridge said under his breath as he left King John on his page-boy errand.

He had seen madness before – his foster father with his rheumy eye and foul whisky breath swinging at Richard and his own son Robert; Richard's true father and begetter of his name, King Richard of the Lion's heart, seen from afar, from far behind his mother's wool skirt, as the King ordered a city burned and the ground sown with salt and all because it would not bow to him; and now King Richard's brother John, short to the point of dwarfness, howling in Westminster Abbey for his mother in a voice like sleet on a tin roof. Richard knew the look of madness, and John had it.

"Find the barons!" sleet-voice had ordered him. "Bring them to me. I have a way to win their hearts again."

"What way, madman?" Faulconbridge thought as he raced from the room to follow his orders – he would have welcomed any orders just to be out of his presence. "They have run from you as I have because they think you killed Prince Arthur. They are seeking his grave! They will side with France. No, there is no way back to their hearts."

As he approached the Abbey's gate, Richard ran faster still and, in passing, clipped the shoulder of Cardinal Pandolpho who had come to London to crown John – again. The beadle-nosed, beady-eyed prelate nodded curtly, but Richard paid him no mind.

He startled the boatswain as he landed on the deck and walked to the bow to watch the rise and fall of the boat in an effort to clear his head if not his soul. For Richard knew that he had no choice except to honor his king. Whatever else he did, he was sure that when his spirit left his body to face the God of Job and Jacob, he could wave his honor as if it was England's flag. And at the sight of that banner, St George at least would run forward, bow to God, and speak for Richard. Honor was Richard's shield, his strength, his sanity, even if it meant protecting a mad king. And, as the vessel approached the Tower, he came to understand what had made John mad.

Arthur, young son of Geoffrey, King Richard and John's late brother, had the better claim to the crown. And, by all

that was apparent, as trained and berated and bullied to royal
thinking by his mother Constance, he would make a good king.
At least King Philip of France thought so and gave the boy his
support, which was why John had put Arthur in the Tower.
On returning to London from France and walking through
its crowded but lifeless streets, Richard had heard the rumors
of Arthur's death – some said that John himself had drowned
Arthur in France – and he knew John could, he surely could
have killed the young man.

Richard's road back to London had been rimmed with
reports of the wrath of heaven – five moons had been
seen in the night sky and the Pomfret prophet Peter had
predicted John's death on Ascension Day. Defying fate, John
had planned his second coronation. Even John's son Henry
had come to London for the first time to be with his father
on this joyous occasion. And yet, confirming Heaven's anger
at the king and kingdom, a messenger had given John a triple
dose of bad news. John's mother Eleanor was stone dead
in Aquitaine, and Constance, rumored to have gone mad
since Arthur's capture, was also rumored dead. There were
sightings of Constance's ghost shrieking in the Tower like a
banshee, searching for her murdered son. Lastly and firstly,
the French had invaded England. Even a strong man would
tilt toward madness at such tidings. Tiny John had leapt in
with both feet and kissed madness on the lips.

Before he knew it, Richard was at the Tower's yellow-brown
walls. Over a hundred years before, William the Conqueror
had built this castle on a site where a millennium earlier
Julius Caesar had created a fort. The present structure was
three times as high as the wooden dwellings around it and
dwarfed the city just as the barons and most of the court did
John. It had originally been William's home but soon became
a place for prisoners and exotic animals – lions and leopards –
that kings were sometimes given by visitors from foreign lands.
Richard climbed out of the boat and immediately heard the
leopard's whine and the caged lion king's wail. Then he saw,
huddled at the Tower's base, Essex, Bigot, Salisbury. He
gulped and bravely approached them, asking them to return
to the King. It was then that they saw the body.

Its feet in cracked, brown boots were sticking out from a Norman bush that protected the Tower's ancient base from erosion. As the knights hauled him out, they saw that the boy's hair and general size were Arthur's. Holding the lad's cold hand, Richard Faulconbridge heard the barons say that the Prince's mean clothes were a sign that he had been trying to escape in disguise when he was murdered. Richard was barely aware that Hubert, the Prince's homely jailer, rushed in, hale and hearty, to greet the barons. There were shouts that Hubert had killed the boy on John's orders and the clang of swords, and, through it all, Richard clung to the young boy's cold hand and thought of honor.

By the time Richard got up, the barons were gone, gone to join the French forces, he supposed, and he did not care. His eyes were on Hubert. "You were his jailer. Did you do this, fiend?"

"No, my lord," he said earnestly. "I left him well."

"If you did kill him, you are damned, and there is no hole so deep, no ocean wide enough to save you. You are a demon black from hell that would shame Lucifer himself."

"And let hell torture me if I harmed him," Hubert shouted at once. "I loved the boy!"

Richard stared into Hubert's face and absorbed it in his mind – the broken nose, the hair-lip, and eyes that were open to his soul. Richard nodded, accepting the ringing clarity of Hubert's voice as proof of innocence – for now – and turned back to the body. The burlap shirt, brown breeches, and broken boots, as the nobles had said, were mean, but the hair was blond, soft, and washed, the hands fair and unworked, though stiffening in death. The nose and forehead and right temple were smashed and oozed blood mashed with tissue. "The rumors of the road had him already dead, but it has not been an hour, I would hazard, since he brimmed with life," Richard noted, clinically. "What clothes are these?"

"They look like a cabin boy's. A likely enough disguise in this city. See, he has an earring in his right ear."

Richard bent down and touched the gold ring with its etched design of lines and circles that pierced the boy's dead flesh.

"Surely he fell, attempting to escape," moaned Hubert. "If only he had waited for me, talked to me – "

Richard tilted his head and took his eyes to the highest window of the Tower. "It must be thirty yards at least," he said. "Would even this boy in his teens think that he could jump from there and land safely? Where did he get these clothes and where were those who watched him? Who helped him? Was it you, Hubert?"

"No, my lord!"

"Then someone else. And if he had help for that, through bribes, why could he not purchase being able to walk down the stairs to safety? Perhaps the barons are right, Hubert. He was murdered. And if you did not kill him, who did?"

Hubert followed Richard doggedly through the streets jammed with shoppers and stalls as he walked directly to a tavern frequented by men of the sea. As Hubert caught up with him, he saw that Richard had found the corner where young men of Arthur's age were clustered. Surveying them quickly, Richard noted one whose clothes were much too large for him. He also saw that while the other boys wore earrings, this one had only two visible holes in his right ear lobe. "You," he said to the boy. "Come here for a sovereign."

When the boy hesitated, Richard snorted and said, "It is for talk only, lad." The boy looked into the man's face – gaunt and worried, preoccupied even, but handsome, unmarked, and not unkind. The boy trustingly came over, and Richard pulled him outside by the scruff of his neck. When he let him go, he looked the teenager up and down and confirmed that he was of Arthur's build and height.

"Whom did you sell your clothes to, lad?"

"Coo – how did you know?"

"What you wear is not your own and you lack your earring, son. He bought it all?"

"Down to my sweat."

"Did he say why?"

"No. He came in – a monk, he was – looked us over as you did, called me as you did, and then offered me a crown for me clothes."

"And you gave them up – "

"No, sir, me father did. He heard the man and whisked me to the back room and stripped me naked."

"Your father saw the man? Where is your father?"

"With the money, sir."

"I see." Richard Faulconbridge took two crowns from his purse and placed them in the boy's calloused hand. "Is there anything else you can tell me, son? Anything about the man? Where he was from? Where he went?"

"He went east, sir."

"How do you know that?"

"I ran to the window to see what was going on. I was naked, I couldn't go out. I saw the monk bring me clothes to another man dressed in red robes, and then the carriage rode off to the east."

"A man dressed in red robes? Like a cardinal?"

Cardinal Pandolpho was still at Westminster and seemed to have spent an hour removing his vestments after the Coronation Mass. It was almost as if he were waiting for someone. He turned as Richard entered the sacristy. "Ah, Sir Richard, have you come to hit me again?"

"It was an accident, Your Eminence."

The Cardinal's face showed surprise. "An accident? But I thought – "

"I see you have already heard of Prince Arthur's death," Richard said, walking forward. "And you suggest that it was murder. The accident I referred to was my bumping into you earlier."

"I see," the Cardinal turned away and murmured something in Italian that began with an "m".

"Why did you think it was murder?"

"It – it would only have been logical. It would be a move that a chessmaster or experienced politician would make. King John – "

"Would have killed Arthur for undisputed right to the crown. Or so it would be in the best interest of France for it to appear. You arranged for his escape, Your Eminence. A holy father was seen bringing you the cabin boy's clothes that Arthur was wearing when he was killed."

"An effort to help," said the Cardinal, shrugging. "Both sides, really. Arthur and France and also John – to prevent – "

"His killing Arthur? How kind of you to try. And yet with Arthur dead by John's hand, King Philip's invasion of England seems – somehow justified. And who is the better friend of the Church, dear Cardinal, Philip or John? Who pushed the boy out of the Tower window, Your Eminence? You? Or your monk?"

The Cardinal smiled with all of his Italian teeth. "Sir Richard, your mind is quick but mistaken. The Church takes no sides in these matters – politically. If we can assist both parties – as I told you I was attempting to do with the cabin boy and his things – then that is to the good. But I am not France's friend and England's enemy. Did I not come to crown John – "

"A second time, making the first time seem to have no effect, making Arthur's claim the stronger – "

"And did I not escort John's son Henry back to England this morning? A lovely boy, you can see the Plantagenet blood in his face – "

"I have never had the honor of meeting him. But being his escort would have been a fine excuse to come to this land to arrange Arthur's death!"

"We would never commit, let alone, condone murder, sir!" the Cardinal cried out. "Besides, if you look for a murderer, look to one of your own. Look to this Hubert, Arthur's jailer. At first, he told John that Arthur was dead, and then, when the barons left John and the King accused him of – how do you say – over-zeal, Hubert recanted. He recanted to save his own neck. But since the boy is indeed dead, what other proof do you need? Hubert is your murderer."

Richard left the sacristy and passed a confessional positioned in the shadows. Inside, he heard John's shrill, cracked voice confessing his sins. The center door where the priest would sit was empty. John was confessing to himself:

"It is always the curse of kings to have subjects take their slightest word and do an act that was mere and idle fantasy. That Hubert did it – after telling me Arthur was dead and then that he was alive. God, you are playing tricks on me

– Arthur lives when he is thought dead and dies when he is thought alive. Perhaps he will rise again, only to die again. I will have no rest. I will have no rest."

Richard's first plan was to charge back to Hubert and confront him with the Cardinal's accusation. But when he returned to the Tower, he saw the man sitting on the ground, staring into space. Richard sat down next to the jailer and, with him, stared ahead. "I saw her," Hubert said at last.

"Saw whom?"

"Constance. Arthur's mother."

"Ah, yes, I have heard she haunts the Tower."

"Do not laugh at me, Sir Richard. I have seen her ghost, screaming and screaming and rushing down the passageway that leads to the window where the Prince – fell."

Richard snorted and crooked his thumb at the sounds of the leopard coming from the Tower window. "You have heard the animals, Hubert, and imagined the rest. It is in your mind. You could just as easily have seen Julius Caesar's ghost."

"But Caesar was killed in Rome."

"And where did Constance die? Not here. She has never even been up there. If she haunted any place, it would not be the Tower. But – tell me, Hubert, is it true that you told the King you had killed Arthur?"

Hubert shook his head as if ashamed. "Only to buy Arthur time while I planned his escape. You know how John is. He ordered me to blind Arthur, and then to cut his throat. It was the only way I could save him."

"I see. Poor Arthur. Everyone tries to help him escape, and yet he dies." Richard reached down and yanked out a blade of grass. "And as for you, poor Hubert, you could not kill Arthur and you could not keep him alive. This case is full of paradoxes. Who could have murdered him, Hubert – if not you? The Cardinal – who knows all the chess moves but says he never plays the game? King John? Has he ever come to see Arthur?"

"Never! That is why he ordered me – "

"To kill Arthur for him, of course. He wanted to himself and could have in another time. But to look at him now, seeking absolution from an absent curate – he has not the focus for murder. You say you did not. What about the barons? I found Essex, Bigot, and Salisbury standing near the body. Arthur's death gave them a fine excuse to defect to France." Richard turned his head back to the wall as sounds came from the upper level. "It is as if the animals confirm my idea, Hubert, claiming those three as one of their own. And yet – " Again, Richard turned back to the Tower, "on the other hand, Hubert, that last sound was no leopard. And where exactly *did* Lady Constance die?"

The only way to the upper level of the Tower was a black staircase that spiraled up from the basement. Richard started up, slowly, since the torches at the upper level were going out – there being no guards on duty since there were no prisoners to watch. As he climbed, Richard saw, in what light there was, a figure scurrying across the upper landing. Richard pulled out his sword on the chance the leopard was loose and moved more quickly to try to match the beast's speed. As he cleared the stairs, a body threw itself at him, but, in an instant, Richard recognized it, tossed his blade aside, and caught the woman's arms before her nails could pierce his eyes.

Her hair was matted to points and dribble streaked her cheeks. Even with little light, her eyes shone red as if possessed by demons. But she did not seem capable of speech, so Richard shook her to force the sound out. "Lady Constance! Lady Constance!"

Her head tilted back like a child's doll, and syllables gurgled from her open mouth. "My – lovely boy – is dead."

"Who killed him? Who killed him?" he shouted, shaking her.

"I – I – I did."

Richard dragged her into the open cell that had once been Arthur's, threw her to the floor, and sat on her belly, holding her down. "Listen to me, Lady Constance. Listen to me! How did you get here? We were told you were dead – "

"I am dead!"

Richard shouted over her words. "How – did – you – get – here?"

"I had to see my boy – my lovely boy, my perfect boy, who has no foul moles, scars, or eye-offending marks," she began slowly. "He was perfect, perfect to be king. I spent every waking minute of his life rearing him for kingship. He was my life, my life! I could not bear to be away. But Philip kept me locked up – for my own good, so he said. But I tricked them. I set fire to my cell and escaped in the chaos. Chaos. I bribed an English officer on a mission to France with money and favors to take me back and came in darkness to the Tower. He brought me in, and the only place to hide was in a cell next to the animals. They screamed and roared and screamed throughout the three days, like humans turned to beasts by the ancient gods. I could see Hubert guarding him. I would wait for my moment. But the voices of the animals! At times, it was as if they were singing. They sang and sang, and I sang with them by howling, howling – "

"Lady Constance, Arthur, when did you see Arthur – "

"That night?" she murmured. "Was it that night? I thought I heard his voice. I left my cell and ran to his, but it was empty, all gone. I went down the stairs and outside, but the guards were there and the barons coming. I ran back up and saw him at the window. I screamed. I know now he was only trying to escape. But I screamed. He turned to me. He answered to his mother's voice, he turned to his mother, but lost his balance and – fell. I did it. I killed my son. I killed my son. I killed my son."

Richard Faulconbridge left the Tower and walked toward Hubert, who was still sitting on the grass, lost in remorse. "And so, that could explain it," Richard explained to him. "Cardinal Pandolpho sends him clothes and bribes the guards. Arthur starts to go down the stairs, sees his mother and – panics?"

"Perhaps he did not know it was she."

"Or perhaps he did. What we do not know is whether he thought she was a ghost or fled her in her madness. At any rate, he runs to the window to see if there was another means of escape, she screams, he turns to her, and he loses his balance and falls."

"It makes sense."

"Well, when the dead return to life, then other things make sense. I'll to the King."

"He has left for the field to meet the French. Prince Henry stays in court, with William Marshall as Regent."

"Then, I'll to the Prince."

Richard started to leave but then saw something in the bushes.

This time, Richard took horse rather than boat to Westminster. If John was meeting the French in battle, Richard would join him, as soon as he met with the Prince.

The Prince was in the sanctuary at the altar under the church's great peaked vault whose ribs were like the ribs of heaven. The young man was dressed in a cloak and gown of red and gold and stood in front of the altar with his back to Richard, head bowed, hands clutched and folded at his chest. "Your majesty," the Bastard bowed to the young man. "I was talking to Cardinal Pandolpho and he noted the resemblance you have to Prince Arthur."

Prince Henry turned and smiled weakly. "We are cousins, after all. Or were. What can I do for you, Sir Richard. My day, as you can imagine, has become very crowded."

Richard described his investigation into Arthur's death and his conclusion that he had been frightened by his mother's shouts and accidentally fell to his death from the window.

"I see. My father will be pleased to know that the death was no fault of his but rather a bizarre connection of incidents. Unfortunately, it does not matter now. The barons are gone. The rumor is out. And we or France will be triumphant. Thank you, Sir Richard, for looking into this."

"The only problem is that it did not happen that way, Prince Arthur."

Again, the young prince smiled, only now he seemed more embarrassed and nervous. "You are mistaken, sir. I am Henry, John's son."

"Hardly," Sir Richard said boldly, stepping forward. "The body of the young man that was found at the base of the Tower had a gold earring in his ear. And yet Arthur's mother says that his body had no wound or scar or blemish. He did not have his ear pierced before, and there was no sign that the cut to his ear was fresh. Yes, it is true that the cabin boy gave up his own earring with his clothes. But not only could the real Arthur not wear it but the cabin boy's was brass, not gold. All the other young men, mimicking the gold circles true sailors wear, had earrings of brass. If this boy's earring had been gold, his father would have drunk it."

"Suppositions, sir – "

"Not really. The earring the dead boy wore was not the smooth, round gold ring of sailors but had etched engravings designed by artists. It is the type worn by court dandies who have little to do – dandies like Prince Henry who idled his time waiting for the fateful day when his father would ask to see him. How did you do it, Arthur?"

"I am Henry, prince of – "

"Did Prince Henry come to visit you, his cousin, and did you bash in his head and change places with him?"

The young prince was silent for a moment. The light from the colored glass windows made his face seem as if from another world. "If – " he began softly, "if such a thing were to have happened, one would have been surprised by the other who might have mistakenly thought one was attempting to kill oneself. One might have pushed the other away, who, sadly, struck his head."

"Why did you have to seek escape through the window at all? Did not Cardinal Pandolpho buy your safe passage by bribing the guards?"

"Surely that would have been the case. But if one's mother, one's poor mad mother, suddenly emerged from the animals' cell, one could not let her spoil the escape. She would hardly have been of help," he added. "I started out the window to see if there was a ledge to hold me when Henry came at me from behind."

"And so you stripped poor, stupid Prince Henry's corpse or dying body, put on his clothes, and dressed him in your cabin boy disguise. And then you placed him in the window and let gravity pull him down."

"If that did happen, it would not have been easy. But if

one found the opportunity to escape from one's murderous, mad uncle forever and guarantee that one day one would be king of this land, that blood would indeed rule – "

"As your mother wanted?"

"And wanted and wanted – yes, if that opportunity had arisen, it would have been impossible to ignore."

"I see." Sir Richard snorted in derision and turned away, walking down the steps and throwing his words behind him. "You had scant chance of being found out with your mother and the King gone mad, your grandmother Eleanor dead, and your country at war with France. It is not impossible that the King will be killed in this war, and then his son, whom no one at court has ever seen, let alone met, will be crowned. You are a miracle, Prince Arthur," Richard's voice all but filled the abbey vault. "You are dead, you live, you die, you live again. England has earned such a miracle!"

"Sir Richard!" Arthur shouted after him. The knight stopped and reluctantly turned. The Prince stood in front of the altar and looked down to him. The gold on his cloak and gown stood out against the white altar linen, and he seemed taller and older than he was. "I have great work to do, Sir Richard. This abbey is a cottage today compared to the grandeur it will have when I rule. The Tower? It was meant to be a fortress, not a lighthouse. I will add three or five that can be seen from the water as a tower *block* of England's strength. It was for this my mother had and bred me. These things and more I will do. That is – *if* I rule. What will you do with this new knowledge?" asked the Prince, with sudden softness. "And when you answer, please lower your voice."

Sir Richard sighed, folded his arms, and leaned his rear-end against a pew. "I go to fight for the king. If I am lucky, I will die in battle. If I am not, I will return and kneel at the foot of the new king – you, Your Highness. Although I can play the chess game as well as Cardinal Pandolpho, the price is too high. After I pledge my loyalty to the new king, I will leave England – perhaps to travel to Italy to court young ladies with rich dowries and die in pampered obscurity. I have no doubt Pandolpho the chessmaster will give me safe escort. Goodbye, Your Highness."

As Sir Richard turned to go, he snapped his fingers as if remembering something. "Oh, by the way, Your Highness, as I came down from the Tower, having interrogated your mother, I saw what I thought was a bundle of trash in the bushes. But it was your mother's body, who evidently – as soon as I had left her – threw herself from the window from which she thought you had jumped. No doubt my obtaining her confession pushed her over the brink, but her son's death – or feigned death – was the true cause. Rule well, sire. As I said, the price of kingship is high. As we have seen, those thought alive will die, and those thought dead will rise. You may find that, next time, Lady Constance's ghost – and perhaps Prince Henry's as well – will be real. Addio."

THE DEATH OF KINGS

Margaret Frazer

The Tragedy of King Richard the Second *was another of Shakespeare's early historical tragedies, first performed in about 1595. Richard II, the son of the Black Prince (who in his day had been England's greatest knight), reigned from 1377 to 1400. He was only ten when he came to the throne and his uncle, John of Gaunt, served as the real regent, although he was never officially appointed to that post. In his teens Richard gave a show of his courage when he confronted Wat Tyler, leader of the Peasant's Revolt, and for a while he was something of a hero, but he soon sank into profligate ways and rapidly became unpopular. He ruled as an autocrat, appointing to the court his own personal favourites and banishing anyone who crossed him, including one of his loyal supporters, Henry Bolingbroke, the son of John of Gaunt. It is with Bolingbroke's exile that Shakespeare's play opens. Richard subsequently confiscates Bolingbroke's estates in order to finance his war with Ireland. Bolingbroke invades England in order to reclaim his land. Richard II returns from Ireland and finds his troops have deserted. Alone with just a few attendants and noblemen Richard waits out his fate at Flint Castle. Richard is subsequently deposed and dies in Pontefract Castle. Margaret Frazer has looked again at those days at Flint Castle when Richard*

*waited for Henry and ponders on why Richard suddenly
lost all of his support.*

The weather that had held against us all those Ireland days
– contrary winds and lowering skies that broke to weak
sunlight only to close again to rain those fatal days on end –
is turned – God's jest? – to days on end of burning gold. Gold
of sunrises pouring over the eastern hills, gold of noontides
under cloudless skies, gold of sunsets promising fair days to
come. Gold where the corn still stands waiting for the scythe
in the fields beyond the castle walls; gold of the stubble fields
where the harvesting is over.

A golden world all turned to dross for our lord the King
who, hardly more than a month ago, seemed more golden
than it all.

We've come by way of Ireland, by way of Conway, by
way of treachery, to Flint Castle on Wales's north coast
and now there's nowhere else to go and here we'll stay to
wait for Bolingbroke because there's no more use in going
anywhere. Everywhere is Bolingbroke's but here. Everything
and everyone are Bolingbroke's . . . Except my lord the King
and this last castle.

So here we wait, in the highest chamber of the highest tower,
made by my lord the King's royal great-great-grandfather for
his eldest son, the first Prince of Wales, who proved to be so
weak a man and poor a king he was deposed and murdered
by his wife and nobles.

Does my lord King Richard think of that as he paces,
paces here?

It's a room most nobly made for pacing. The tower is
round and so is this high room, with windows facing every
way – southward to the hills, northward to the estuary, east
and west along the shore. King Richard can pace around it
without let, seeing in every direction as he goes. Seeing all
the ways that Bolingbroke may come.

He paces, paces, paces away the golden hours. Window

to window, around and around, with sometimes a pause to look out, sometimes a pause at the head of the stairs as if he's listening for anyone to come. What is he hoping they'll say if they do? What does he hope to hear this late in this deadly game? That somewhere one of his lost armies has somehow re-formed and is hastening to his aid? That most of his nearest friends aren't disappeared or dead? That lightning has come out of the clear August sky and struck down revolting Bolingbroke?

No one is going to come. No one has come for a while now and no one will. Not any more. Those few of us here now are all there will be until the end.

All seven of us where a month ago two dozen in immediate attendance on our king would have been more likely, not to mention the 200 men and servants there would have been throughout the castle as a whole where there's maybe now two score all told. If there's even that many not yet fled.

And of the seven of us here, Jankyn and I don't count. A clerk and an esquire left over from that mostly vanished royal household because Jankyn has been too fear-witted to make a choice of where to go, and I . . . Well, here I am, my choices made, so let the worrying over it rest.

But besides us, there's my lord Aumerle, for what he's worth. Narrow and nervous, sitting picking the threads from an embroidered pillow cover, unraveling the pattern to pass the time and unable these past days to keep from again and again telling Richard, who doesn't listen, that he has to play for time, that time will bring friends and friends their swords, that there's hope yet against Bolingbroke. He's badly frightened, is my lord Aumerle, and not hiding well that what he's truly hoping for is time to be sure his father, the traitor-turned Duke of York, has assured a pardon for him for being King Richard's friend. And York will, because his only other son and heir is even less a pleasure than Aumerle is.

What Aumerle hasn't considered is how well, even if pardoned and alive, he'll fare under his cousin Bolingbroke. Especially when Bolingbroke hears, as he surely will if he hasn't already, of what Aumerle had to say at length and laughingly against him when Bolingbroke was powerless and gone in exile. No, I doubt my lord Aumerle has thought that far ahead. He only hopes to be somehow alive at the end of the disaster everything's become.

That's more than the earl of Salisbury hopes, I'll warrant. After he failed to keep the Welsh levies together long enough for King Richard to reach them, he should have gone to Bolingbroke, or at least had sense enough to disappear, to lie low and be nobody until everything was over. There's lords enough have done that, I think. Instead, he came to find his king, to tell him straight his best hope of an army was gone, and now he stands here beside my lord Aumerle, thumbs hitched in his belt, staring at the floor or watching from under his brows King Richard pace.

At least, unlike my lord Aumerle, he's mostly silent.

And then there's Sir Stephen Scroop, watching my lord Aumerle pluck the pillow plain and looking as if he keeps himself still only by force of will, his hands white-knuckled clutched to each other between his knees. He's as uselessly here as my lord of Salisbury, without even lost troops and shame for an excuse. Maybe, for him, it's simply that he can't bring himself to back off and run for it, despite how much he probably wants to. Or else he's counting on the hope that he'll probably come alive through whatever lies ahead simply because he's too slight a matter for Bolingbroke to bother with him.

That's where my own hope lies, that's sure. I'm no one worth Bolingbroke's bothering with. A landless esquire of no inheritance who's made himself a very minor place in the royal household, not to be ever particularly noticed except in the way a piece of furniture is noticed – as being there and sometimes useful. Stand to one side of everything with hands behind me, eyes down-held and face unchanging and I'm "not there". I can listen and no one cares, I can watch and no one notices. When the time comes, all I'll probably need do – and Jankyn, too, if he can stop being frightened enough to think of it – is slip aside into Bolingbroke's service where the other royal clerks and hireling esquires have probably mostly gone by now, because it's one thing to take a kingdom and another to run it. Whoever is king, we'll be needed. Do what you want

with the great lords but don't kill off the men who know how
the accounts are kept.

At most, my pay may be held back for this while
when, to Bolingbroke's reckoning, I should have remembered rats and sinking ships and suchlike, and already left
King Richard's coming night for my lord of Bolingbroke's
fair-dawning day.

The devil is more than welcome to take Bolingbroke and
his reckoning to the black-iced depths of hell.

A place to where, by the look of him, my lord bishop of
Carlisle is already well on his way, albeit for a different
reason.

Of all of those not able – or not willing – when the time
comes to slip aside to Bolingbroke, my lord of Carlisle is
likely going to have the worst of it. When King Richard goes
down, so will he. Not so far as Salisbury, not to the death
since he has his priesthood to keep his head on his shoulders,
but down enough. And the fool part of it is that he could slip
aside to safety like so many have and will, could have long
since slipped aside, but won't.

He was a Westminster Abbey monk for most of the
years he's been alive. The learned but nobody-of-importance
Thomas Merke is all he was until he somehow caught King
Richard's notice. Now, in not very many years, he's not
only left his monastery life behind him but come close
into the King's confidences, been put on the royal council
to good purpose, headed diplomatic missions with success,
and hardly two years ago was made bishop of Carlisle, well
on his way toward higher church preferments under King
Richard's great favor.

Not that all that would hinder his shifting to Bolingbroke
if he chose, so far as Bolingbroke is concerned. Bolingbroke
in his arrogant self-satisfaction has no trouble believing a man
will gladly shift loyalty from King Richard to him, given the
chance. It's those who don't choose to shift to him that he
despises and must needs destroy for their stupidity.

And therein lies my lord bishop of Carlisle's downfall-to-
come. All questions of wisdom, survival or stupidity laid aside,
regardless of the honors, preferments and positions he's been

given, more than being bishop, more than all he might yet hope to rise to – more than any and all of that – he's King Richard's friend. God help the man, he cares more for King Richard as Richard than for Richard as England's king.

It comes from their like turn of mind, I think. I've listened to them prowl around a thought together for the pure pleasure of it, prodding at possibilities, refusing to let it rest until they've followed it as far as they can go in as many directions as they can find. They're both forever looking deeper into things than it's comfortable to see, and the main difference between them only seems to lie in my lord of Carlisle having a quieter soul than does our king. Those years of monkhood, I suppose, all that time spent in silences and prayer while King Richard has been caught from childhood in a constant coil of lords, never willingly left in peace from one hour's end to the next. Among their ambitions and stupidities, he's done well just to keep his footing until now, let be finding any quiet in his soul. Yet, because of their improbable like turn of mind, he and my lord bishop of Carlisle are friends. And while it's one thing to desert a falling king in favor of a rising one – after all, what's that but only sense and following God's apparent will? – it's another matter altogether to desert a friend. At least for some men.

So, no, this change of kings isn't going to go well for my lord of Carlisle. Nor, unlike the rest of us here, does he make pretence of interest in aught else than watching King Richard. Standing the other side of the southward-facing window from where I'm standing, he can see King Richard wherever in the room he is, though just now my lord the King is here between us at the window, looking out into the golden day and mountained distances.

It's not a matter of whether Bolingbroke will come but when, so how can King Richard not keep watch? Or we keep from watching him while he does? Somewhere out there his doom is riding toward him and he knows it; and yet even so, even now, he's refusing to be what he ought to be. He's refusing to be broken.

He's afraid, yes, and well he should be, waiting to face, powerless, the man who's envied, hated, tried since their young manhoods to destroy him and now has the power to do it. And he's desperate, with his armies gone, his last chance of escape – to what? he well asked as he gave it up – gone, most of his friends dead, captive or, worse, deserted to his enemy and the few he has left as powerless as he is. And angry, though maybe "angry" is too mild a word for it. He's always been skilled at being angry but this is a deeper, darker, more abiding thing, as if fed out of his soul and on the years of hatred between him and his cousin Bolingbroke. It feeds his defiance, at any rate. For all the good defiance will do him, now that he has no power left to make it any use.

Frightened, desperate, angry, defiant, in quantities enough to confuse most men to breaking point, and yet despite them all, he's still one thing more, the one thing he's always been that's kept him from breaking despite everything his lords have done to him over the years. He's proud.

Fatally proud.

Proud not simply because he's King of England but because he's – Richard.

These last hard weeks have left him lean-faced, the soft flesh gone that had begun to grow on him these past few years. In fact, after this past month, there looks to be nothing soft left in him at all. He's all sharp edges and bitter truths, and he stands here at this southward window, gazing out with a distance in his eyes as if he's looking at far more than what there is for the rest of us to see, and says without looking over his shoulder at my lord bishop of Carlisle, "I've been lied to, Thomas."

They're the first words anyone has spoken here in more than an hour, and startled my lord of Carlisle says, "My lord?"

King Richard looks at him. "I've been sent this way and shouldn't have gone. Someone has done this to me and I've let them. All of these things have gone wrong since we came back from Ireland, there've been too many of them and all of a kind. Think on it, Thomas."

I doubt there's any of us here who've thought of much else but of how wrong things have gone. That isn't where my lord of Carlisle's question lies, and he says bluntly, "I don't understand."

King Richard looks away from him, outward again toward the southward hills. "No. Nor do I yet. I've only just begun to see it, but seeing it, I've begun to doubt the chance of it. It hasn't all fallen so ill merely by chance."

"No, not by chance," my lord of Carlisle agrees. "By choices. Men made choices. You made choices. It's been by choices, not by chance it's all come about."

"But how is it that every choice has gone against me?" King Richard demands. "EVERY choice!"

"Choices meant one way turn out another," my lord of Carlisle says. "You've made choices. We've all made choices." A slight movement of his head includes Aumerle, Salisbury, Scroop in that fatality. "If they haven't gone the way we meant them to, that's the chance of it."

"No." King Richard flatly refuses that. "It hasn't been choice and chance. Ever since we landed in Wales I've been robbed of my chance for choices."

"It was your choice to come here, to Flint," my lord of Carlisle points out. "Your choice to stay here. Your choice to . . ."

"All choices made by default! Where's been the single hopeful word needed to give me some other way to choose?" King Richard demands. "Everything I've heard has been only to the bad. Even allowing for my uncle of York's cowardice and Northumberland's treachery, how can there be no one left who chooses me over Bolingbroke? Why haven't we heard aught of them, only of who's deserted me? Where are my Cheshire archers? Come to that, where are YOUR men out of Carlisle? Why haven't I heard a single thing about any armies gathered to my favor?"

"There was Salisbury's," my lord Aumerle offers across the room.

Salisbury's head flinches up. He's whey-pale and rigid with with what looks like shame and hurting but King Richard doesn't see him, is saying savagely at Aumerle, "And where is it? Don't you see how that's part of it? When they should have been hearing I was returned from Ireland, they heard instead that I was dead and, most predictably, they dispersed and fled. How many other men heard I was dead and did the same?"

My lord Aumerle begins, "It had to be a rumor Bolingbroke began . . ."

"He's not that clever, is my cousin," King Richard snaps. "And beyond what rumors might have done, why haven't I heard anything – even one single thing – since landing in Wales that doesn't pile worse on worse until I don't have any choice which way to go or what to do? You!"

All unexpectedly, he's swung around on me, is looking at me, SEEING me. I've been listening too hard and I stiffen, hoping guilt doesn't show in my face, but even if it does, he's too far into his questioning to notice, demanding at me, "Since we've come here to Flint have you brought me even one message with any good in it? A single hopeful word on anything?"

That's something I can answer readily enough. I know exactly what he has and hasn't heard since we've been here in Flint. With the great lords dead or captive or traitors and the lesser lords lying low, hoping to stay below the storm and come out to safety when all is over, there's been no one to send sealed messages. What news there's been has all come by word of mouth from our own scouts, sent out to find out what they can and that's been precious little, and because there are so few of us left here around the King, I've had all the questioning of those that have come back. The few and then fewer who've come back. So I know exactly what word has come, what King Richard has heard and what he's not and, no, he's heard nothing to the good these few days past. With bowed head, I say, "None, my lord."

And he swings back on my lord of Carlisle with, "You see? None! How can there be NONE?"

"My lord . . ." the bishop begins.

King Richard cuts him sharply off. "I'm to believe there's no one left who chooses me instead of Bolingbroke? That everyone's turned traitor?" He turns around to point at me. "We sent out messengers to find men and tell them join me, didn't we?"

"Yes, my lord."

"But we hear NOTHING back and no one comes! How can that be?" he demands at my lord of Carlisle.

My lord Aumerle tries, "My lord, allowance must be made for . . ."

Not bothering to look at him, King Richard snaps, "Don't do me double injury with your flattering tongue, Aumerle. You don't know any more about it than the rest of us do." All abruptly, he turns his back on the room and everyone and slams his fists down on the stone sill of the window, insisting, "If I'd heard any good thing – ANY good thing, ONE good thing – I'd have had some thought which way to go, could have found SOMETHING possible to do. But there's been NOTHING. How am I supposed to act on NOTHING?"

No one makes him an answer to that. My lord of Salisbury is looking at the floor again, the rest of us at King Richard, who with one of those quicksilver turns of feeling that drive the less emotionally adroit among his lords to impotent fury, suddenly laughs softly and says as if it's infinitely amusing – or else near to heart-breaking miserable – "I've wasted time, believing lies, and now it's likely time will be the waste of me."

He bends his head and his hair falls forward, hiding his face. The slanting sunlight of the ending afternoon lays a warm golden sheen across his hair's darkness, reminding how, when he was a boy, his hair was as fine and fair as new-spun gold. It's darkened with the years until now only the strongest light can find its brightness: an allegory on his life, if you will. All the bright promise of his early years turned to this darkness at his end. And looking down at his hands still braced on the stone still, he says so quietly that probably no one but my lord of Carlisle and myself can hear him – and likely he's forgotten I'm there at all – "When this is all over, Thomas, when there's nothing left to show I ever lived but black scrawls on parchment and dead people's memories of me, when I'm not even dust in my own tomb, supposing I'm allowed a tomb . . ." My lord of Carlisle starts a small, protesting gesture at that but stops it uncompleted. He knows Bolingbroke too well not to know, as King Richard does, that that is a possibility. ". . . this stone will still be stone and I'll be . . . what?"

That's not a question good for a man to ask and maybe a worse question for a friend to answer. My lord of Carlisle, for

all that he's a churchman, doesn't try. Instead, across the room
my lord Aumerle stands up abruptly as if he can keep still no
longer but, about to toss the pillow aside, stops in the middle
of his gesture, frozen for a moment before saying in an odd
and strangled voice, "My lord," so that King Richard, Carlisle,
and the rest of us, even Jankyn and I, turn heads toward him
questioningly, to find he's staring past King Richard, out the
window. Almost as one we all turn back to look where he
is looking and see that in the little while that no one has
been watching for them, horsemen have come distantly into
sight. A dark cluster of riders with sunlight sheened on their
armor, riding fast this way under a banner too far away yet
to be read.

All went much as was expected after that. They were Lord
Percy's men, and Bolingbroke and Northumberland were not
much behind them. Richard, with small choice left to him,
gave himself up into his cousin's keeping and in a few weeks
more was "persuaded" to give up the crown.

Even then he didn't dance to the tune Bolingbroke meant
to set him. With all his traitor lords standing by to watch
him do it in Westminster Hall, he gave the crown, it's true,
out of his own hands into Bolingbroke's but did it with such
a raw contempt and heart-seared scorn and naked hatred
as made Bolingbroke's triumph a bleeding, ugly thing. And
when he'd done, he turned his back on Bolingbroke and all
of them and left the hall as if they were no more than dogs
that he despised.

One way and another, I doubt he'll live to see the
summer.

For Jankyn and me it's gone the way I supposed it would,
neither of us worth anyone's bothering about once the great
matters were settled. I still serve a king; I go on saying, "your
grace", "my lord", and "as you wish" and doing what I'm
told the way I always have and there's an end.

At least I'm still alive. That's more than Salisbury and some
few others have managed to be. Scroop has scraped away alive,
though, and so has the lord Aumerle, more luck to them. And
Carlisle still lives, though assuredly not through any fault of

his own. In Westminster Hall, in the waiting before Richard gave up his crown, with all the lords that still lived standing silent by to see it done, Carlisle rose up and told triumphant Bolingbroke to his face that his deposing of King Richard was a sin, an obscene deed, a treachery foul in the eyes of heaven, and in time to come, if he went on with it, English blood would flow to pay for it and children yet unborn cry out against him.

Most eloquent and quite possibly true, but not words that Bolingbroke, about to lay hands on the crown he's coveted all his life, wanted to hear. Nor a truth that anyone was inclined to act on at that late date.

In return for those words and other matters that he did, Carlisle will spend his life as Bolingbroke's prisoner. His priesthood keeps him alive but by the time Bolingbroke is done with him, his life is nearly all that he'll have left. So, on the whole and given a choice, I'd rather not have seen my lord of Carlisle again, to see exactly what has come to him.

But it's after all my business to go where I'm told to go, do as I'm told to do, and like or not, when I was told to go with papers for him to sign, I went.

I came to where he's being kept on a mid-February day that might have been designed for what was being asked of him. Gray, dark, and damp, the dreg end of winter; and for good measure the room he's kept in was as gray and damp and dark as the day outside. Supposedly how he's kept will better now he's signed away his rights and properties to the King's use. He'll not go free again but he'll be allowed to live out his natural years, they say. For what that may be worth to him. I think he agreed to give up whatever was asked of him only because he wanted them to leave him alone, and because none of it's worth anything to him any more. Not his life or where he's kept or all the wealth and power he had as bishop. Not now that Richard is deposed and as good as dead.

What surprised me was that he remembered me. When I first came in, he said my name and started to say something else, until he saw King Henry's badge on my shoulder and after all said nothing. Nor did I, only laid the papers I'd brought on the table between us and he signed them without reading them, clearly not caring what they said; but then, when he'd stood a moment longer, staring down at them or the pen he'd laid aside or maybe only at the tabletop, he raised his head. His gaze went past me to the narrow slit of window looking out on nothing but the gray, weeping sky and narrow castle yard, and in a level, almost-empty voice he said, "I've been thinking. About what he said that last day at Flint Castle. King Richard," he added, as if I might not understand whom he meant by "he".

"King Richard," I echoed, despite a man can die these days for being heard to use the title "king" on anyone but Bolingbroke.

Carlisle's gaze came back from the gray distance to look at me. "You remember what he said?"

I made a movement of my shoulders that might have admitted anything or nothing, though I remembered well enough.

Because I didn't say, Carlisle did, still watching my face. "He said he'd come to think that more than happenstance and Bolingbroke had had hand in everything that had gone so wrong that he'd been robbed of his chance for choices by more than merely chance."

"Yes," I agreed. I'd not been charged to listen to Carlisle, but neither had I been ordered not to; I wanted to see where he was going with this.

He drew a deep, long breath and asked, "What if he had the right of it?"

"My lord?" I asked back, with caution enough, I hoped.

Carlisle hesitated, then repeated, "What if he had it right?"

I made no answer. A mind with nothing but itself and despair to feed on can turn to gnawing after things best left alone; I didn't much like where Carlisle might be going.

He pushed away from the table, to pace impatiently away from me, but it was too small a room for pacing. A wall had already turned him back and he was across the table from me again, leaning over it to demand, while I was still trying to think what to say to him, "And if he had it right, then who did it to him? And how?"

This wasn't speculation I cared for but for sake of saying something, I answered, "If you had how, you'd probably know who."

"Just as if I knew who, I'd probably have how," he returned sharply and shoved away from the table again, to pace the little way away there was to the other end of the room, where he turned back on me with, "But, yes, it's the HOW that I've been working at to find the who. Because I had chance to learn things before I was shut up here, and from what I learned and from thinking on it afterwards, I've come to think that Richard had it right."

This time I kept deliberately silent. He needed no urging on, nor was he likely to stop now. He came back to the table.

"For a beginning," he said, "there were all those rumors that he was dead. All those convenient, fatal rumors."

"Rumors are likely enough, given what was toward," I pointed out.

"But they went exactly where they would do the most harm, exactly to everywhere we expected troops would be gathered awaiting Richard's return from Ireland."

"And nowhere else?"

Carlisle dismissed that with a gesture. "Other places, too, a few, and that's to be expected, given, as you say, what was toward. But they went like arrows' flight to EVERY place where there was hope of men gathering to Richard."

"That could have been Bolingbroke's doing. Northumberland and York had turned traitor. They would have known where . . ."

He cut me off. "York and Northumberland turned traitor before Richard came back from Ireland. Word of their treachery had spread even before the rumors did and that should have been enough to make people wary of what they heard. But almost everyone who heard the rumor that Richard was dead accepted it for true. Why? Where were the doubts there should have been? Given how things were, why did so many men accept without doubt a rumor like that?"

He didn't wait for whatever answer I might have made him

but went on, "And then there's why everything WE heard, when we heard anything at all, was only of how exceedingly against King Richard everything and everyone had turned. Why was that?"

That was easy enough to answer. "Because everything and everyone HAD turned against him."

"No! They hadn't! Bolingbroke is not so universally beloved as he likes to think he is. Among the things that I found out before . . ." He gestured to the walls he'd earned by plotting Bolingbroke's death. ". . . was that not everyone dispersed in despair when they heard the rumors, the way the Welsh did. There were men held on to hope. For one, hardly two days' ride away from us at Flint there was a small army of Cheshire archers who would have come if they'd heard where King Richard was. But they never heard. Why not? We sent out scouts and messengers enough!"

I didn't answer him. What was there to say? One of my duties from our last days in Ireland had been the royal messengers and messages.

"And come to that," Carlisle said, with the passion in him suddenly gone cold, turned measured and deliberate, "how did Bolingbroke's men come down on us so straight? There are half a dozen castles, at the least, in striking distance along that piece of coast. Why did damn Percy come to Flint first of all?"

Forcing myself to hold where I was, I offered, "Chance. It could have been nothing more than chance."

"There were too many 'chances' like that in those last days, and all of them against King Richard. When it was too late, he began to realize it. Now I've followed where he was going and, like him, I don't think it was chance that worked against him all that while."

"Then it must have been God's will," I offered. That was a possibility that Carlisle, as a churchman, had to be willing to accept; but the answering look on his face told me he didn't and I tried again with, more practically, "It need only have been that one of the scouts we sent out betrayed he was at Flint. Out of fear or hoping for reward. That's all the reason there has to be for Lord Percy finding him so quickly." I remembered something else. "And not everything we heard was lies. What Scroop brought in was true enough. About folk rising against Richard. Old men and women and beardless boys."

"True so far as it went," Carlisle said harshly. "What we didn't hear was that they weren't risen of their own will but were all Bolingbroke's own people, called off his properties to stir up others into revolt."

"Then you think Scroop . . ." I began.

"I think there's not that much complication in Scroop, to come up with lies and half-truths to his king's face. And how could he have spread the rumors of King Richard's death so accurately, have them be so completely believed? It was authority made those rumors believed and Scroop has never in his life had that kind of authority."

I held silent, as I might as well have held all along. Carlisle needed no answers of mine. He already had his own. "No," he said now, coldly, flat with conviction. "The rumors that Richard was dead were believed because they didn't come in the general way of rumors, vaguely out of anywhere, but directly from the royal household. When we sent out messengers with word of when and where he would return from Ireland, the word that went instead was that he was dead, and hearing it from his own messengers, men believed it. Didn't they?"

It hadn't been that simple. Nor, for that matter, much more difficult. In the haste of the return from Ireland, time wasn't taken with writing full letters of explanations and commands. The messengers were given only short, sealed notes saying that the bearer was to be believed in what he said. The rest of their message was by word of mouth and I was the one who passed on to them what they were to say.

With deadly quiet, Carlisle asked, "What exactly did you tell them?"

And because he had thought his way into it this far, I told him. "I gave them their messages exactly word for word as I'd been told to give them. Where and when men were to join King Richard. How many men he was bringing back from Ireland with him. That he was . . ." Deliberately, I broke my voice, stumbled on the word, ". . . well. That under no circumstances was any word of his . . . death to be believed."

Carlisle stared at me, rapidly working out the rest of it. "You said what you were supposed to say but you made it sound a lie. A lie that seemed the more real because of what you didn't say. The messengers passed your half-told lie along with the message. Maybe not directly to whomever they delivered the message but to others. It wasn't the kind of thing a man could keep to himself, even if he only half-believes it. And given the way men's minds work when they're afraid, the lie, being worse than the truth, was easier to believe, no matter what else they were told."

That was what I had counted on – that ill news runs fastest and that rumors, once begun, are nigh to impossible to stop.

"And at Flint Castle," Carlisle said, "you were the one charged with sending out the scouts and reporting back to Richard what they learned. How much of what you told us was simply lies?"

"Enough." Not all of it but enough to set King Richard deep into despair and keep him there. Enough to hold him from rousing into hope, from finding out he still had ways of striking back at Bolingbroke.

Enough.

"First the rumors that robbed him of men," Carlisle said bitterly, "and then the endless ill news that robbed him of hope, and finally the betrayal of where he was."

"I didn't do the last. Not in so many words," I said. I've found it's well to hold to the truth where you can.

"No. You wouldn't have had to do 'in so many words', would you?" Carlisle agreed, harsh with mockery and pain. "All you had to do was half-say something to one of the scouts or anyone else among us who looked near to breaking, about how grateful Bolingbroke was likely to be for word of where King Richard was, then leave their fear to do the rest. Was that the way of it?"

"Near enough," I granted. He's clever, is my lord bishop of Carlisle, for all the good it's done him. "Though it's possible

someone thought of it for themselves without me. I maybe
had nothing to do with it at all." Though I thought not. I'd
picked who I'd half-said things to, men who looked most
near their breaking point with fear. All I knew beyond that
was that the men I'd half-said it to had been among the
ones who hadn't come back towards the end. It seems to
take very little to bring men to betraying themselves. Give
them rumors they can choose in place of truth, help them see
their safety lies in treachery rather than in holding loyal, or,
as with King Richard, feed them despair when they're most
in need of hope.

Carlisle closed his eyes. Pain was etching grief more deeply
into his face with every moment as he said, to me or to God or
maybe just to the ceiling beams above us, "He had it right. It
wasn't chance. It was never chance. God help him."

Then he looked at me as if I'd turned into a fiend while
standing there, and I looked back the way my kind are never
supposed to look at his, full in the face. And he demanded at
me, "WHY?"

Why not? I nearly answered.

But I didn't.

Instead I simply dropped my gaze away, gathered up the
papers he had signed and without a word or look at him
again went out the doorway he couldn't pass without his
keeper's leave.

Let him keep his question. It will give him something to
turn his cleverness to in the years to come. The likely very
many years to come, because he's not so old a man he's likely
to die soon or easily.

Besides, what could I have said that would content him? I
never had a reason for wanting Richard dead.

Except that I could do it.

That's all there was in it. He could have been a worse man
or a better, it would not have mattered. What mattered was
that I had chance to bring him down and so I did. How
many men have chance to kill a king and go free of any
blame for it?

Because Richard's death will be as surely by my doing as it
is by Bolingbroke's when it comes. If it hasn't come already.

No one has heard aught of him for a while now; or else no one who's heard is telling what they know. But it can't be much longer, surely. Bolingbroke can't sit easy on the throne while Richard lives.

Not that Bolingbroke – His Grace King Henry IV, as I should say – will ever lose the throne the way King Richard did. He's a different matter than King Richard was and he'll not fall the way that Richard did.

And yet . . . I've watched their faces, those lords who now say "Your Grace" and kneel to our new king, and it seems to me there are some – my lord the earl of Northumberland for one – who aren't as glad of it as they thought they'd be. So I wonder how it will be in a while, when they've grown less pleased with their new king than they are now – as they surely will, given the kind of man King Henry is. I watch them and I can't help but wonder what a word half-said in certain ears might do when that time comes.

I wonder . . .

A VILLAINOUS COMPANY

Susanna Gregory

The History of Henry the Fourth *was first registered in 1598 but it is likely that Shakespeare wrote it around 1595 or 1596. It was an immensely popular play, mostly because of the humour associated around the character of Sir John Falstaff (or Sir John Oldcastle in the original version). Its success meant that Shakespeare had to put aside the sequel he was writing,* The Second Part of Henry the Fourth, *to write a play centred upon Falstaff and his cronies,* The Merry Wives of Windsor. *This first part of* Henry IV *takes place less than three years after the events in the last story. The new king, Henry, troubled by the death of Richard II, wishes to go on a crusade in expiation for his sins, but he is stopped from doing so by civil war that erupts in Wales and Scotland. Henry despairs of his wayward son, Prince Hal, who consorts with Falstaff, whilst his former ally, Lord Percy, the earl of Northumberland, and his son Henry Percy, known as Hotspur, change sides to support the Welsh rebel, Owen Glendower. The play leads to the inevitable conflict at the Battle of Shrewsbury in 1403. Susanna Gregory considers the relationship between Hotspur and Glendower in the days leading up to the Battle of Shrewsbury when a certain death threatens their alliance.*

*   *   *

A circle of people had gathered around the corpse that lay outside the tavern. The only sounds were the patter of rain on the muddy street, and the clink of Owen Glendower's sword against his armour as he knelt awkwardly to inspect the dead man. Near the back of the crowd, Lady Kate Percy sighed irritably as her husband, Hotspur, stood in front of her to try to shield her from the sight. Did he think she sat at home and hid from the world while he was away fighting his wars, that she had never seen a body before? she thought impatiently.

A heavy thump suggested that Hotspur's misguided chivalry would have better served their sister-in-law, Lady Mortimer – when Glendower eased the corpse onto its back to look at its face, she gave a gasp of horror, and fainted.

"My wife!" exclaimed Edmund Mortimer, gazing at her aghast. He turned quickly to his sister, relying on her for help as he had done since they were children. "Do something, Kate! She's deadly ill!"

"She's nothing of the sort," said Kate brusquely, elbowing her brother out of the way. "She has only fainted, and will recover in a few moments. Give me your cloak to protect her from the rain."

Mortimer fumbled with the clasp, but it was Hotspur whose steady fingers unhooked the clip and covered Lady Mortimer with the cloak.

"I thought the Welsh to be of stronger mettle than this," Hotspur muttered disdainfully, as he bent to tuck the edges of the cloak under his prostrate relative. "If Owen Glendower is to believed, Welsh women are almost as skilled in the arts of war as are their menfolk."

"My wife is a gentle soul!" objected Mortimer angrily, kneeling in the mud next to her. "And it is to her credit that she finds the sight of a dead man so distressing. So should any decent woman!"

"Let me know if you plan to be diving in the mud, Kate,"

said Hotspur drily to his own wife. "The cloth on that gown is expensive, and fighting the King in open rebellion has drained my finances somewhat. We cannot afford to be careless."

"It was you who insisted I wear it," said Kate, a little resentfully. "You said you wanted to create a good impression on our new allies."

"I needn't have bothered," said Hotspur, looking around him moodily.

The Welsh town of Bangor was little more than a village – a ramshackle collection of timber houses that dripped and ran in the rain, and streets that were ankle-deep in mire. Its inhabitants regarded Hotspur and his companions with open distrust. Wales had long been struggling for her independence from the iron hand of the Plantagenet kings of England, and the Welsh Prince, Owen Glendower, represented the brightest spark of hope her oppressed people had seen for 300 years. Although the Welsh accepted that they were unlikely to gain their freedom without help, it ran against the grain to trust too much in an alliance with an Englishman – even if that man were the great warrior Hotspur, son of the powerful earl of Northumberland.

"If I were King Henry, I would let Glendower keep this pitiful patch of sheep-infested mountain he calls Wales, and good riddance!" muttered Hotspur's uncle, the Earl of Worcester, shivering and tugging his fur hat further down over his ears. "Then, at least there would be one corner of his kingdom that isn't rebelling against him."

He looked disparagingly at the gaggle of ragged people who clustered around their prince. Kate winced, hoping that they would not hear him.

"That's true," agreed Hotspur with feeling. "I wouldn't be wasting troops and supplies over Wales. It hasn't stopped raining since we arrived, there's no decent land for crops, and the people are little more than savages!"

"Shh! They'll hear you!" hissed Kate, glancing anxiously at the silent townsfolk. Although no one appeared to be paying any attention to the Englishmen, Kate was uneasy that Hotspur and Worcester should be so openly disdainful of the people they hoped would join them in their fight to overthrow the tyrannical Henry IV.

"I would sooner trust these people than that evil usurper Henry," said Mortimer, hotly. "I risked my life fighting for him, and he gave me nothing in return! The Welsh are my people now, an alliance sealed by my marriage to Glendower's daughter."

He gazed down fondly at his wife, holding one of her hands in his, and chaffing it gently. She opened her eyes slowly, looking around her in confusion. Hotspur and Kate helped her to her feet, and she turned to Mortimer, burying her face in his shoulder. Solicitously, Mortimer led her away to sit out of the rain.

Kate was surprised. Lady Mortimer had not struck her as being frail – quite the reverse, in fact, and when they had first met, Kate had felt a pang of anxiety that her gentle, malleable brother should be in the hands of someone who Kate suspected was crafty and clever.

"I can't see that a marriage between those two will remain sweet once the thrill of the wedding bed has worn off," said Hotspur bluntly, watching Mortimer fuss over his wife. "He can't speak Welsh, and she doesn't speak English."

"Then at least they won't argue," said Kate, pulling him away to give the newly-weds some privacy. "Although I'm not so sure she's as alien to English as she would have us believe."

But Hotspur had already lost interest in his brother-in-law's domestic arrangements, and he and Worcester were moving towards Glendower and the corpse that had occasioned the fainting fit. Kate shook her head. There were many women who would envy her her husband – a strong, fearless warrior, admired by all. Yet for all his courage and honour, she often wished he had a little more common sense and tact.

"Poison, without a doubt," said Glendower, looking up from the body at the Englishmen. "See how the muscles are rigid, and yet he died only minutes ago. And this foaming at the mouth is far from natural."

"There are agues that cause foaming," Worcester pointed out.

"Perhaps it was a falling fit," said Hotspur. "A sickness. But we have a rebellion to arrange, Glendower, and time is too short to waste in idle chatter over the dead."

"Look at this stain here," said Glendower, ignoring him. "It smells of wine and something bitter that was spilled as he thrashed about in his death throes."

"Are you saying that there was poison in his wine?" asked Worcester, appalled.

"I am," said Glendower loftily. "I know a good deal about herbs and magic, and I am certain that this man was killed with a strong dose of henbane."

"You mean he was a victim of foul play?" asked Hotspur. "It isn't possible he took his own life?"

Glendower shook his head slowly, his black eyes never leaving Hotspur's. "Look at his face – his expression suggests death was an unexpected visitor. Since he did not take his own life, I can only conclude that else someone took it for him."

Kate saw what he meant. The face of the man who lay in the rain was stretched into a grimace that bespoke sheer terror: this was not a man who saw death approaching and welcomed it. She studied him. He had been a handsome fellow, in middle years, with a neat grey beard and a fine blue military surcoat that showed him to be a person of some wealth and standing.

"Who would do such a thing?" she asked softly, watching the rain run in rivulets down the corpse's waxen face. In a gesture typical of him, Hotspur swept off his own cloak, and bent to lay it over the dead man, covering the contorted features from view.

"That, madam," said Glendower coldly, "is what I intend to find out." He glowered around at the silent ring of people who watched him in the pattering rain, although his eyes lingered longest on Hotspur. "This man's name was Sir Robert Colville, and he was one of my most trusted advisers. Whoever struck at him was aiming to harm me."

That evening, Kate paced restlessly in the solar of the ancient timber house that had been provided for Hotspur during his negotiations with Glendower. In the hall below, angrily raised voices suggested that dividing up the country the rebels were about to wrest from King Henry was no simple matter. Earlier, over a supper of boiled mutton and coarse bread, Hotspur guilelessly had questioned Glendower over what he had discovered about Robert Colville's death, his armour-clad feet oblivious to Kate's warning kicks.

Glendower had turned on him, his dark eyes flashing with fury, and announced that he would not lie easy until the murderer had been caught and punished, threatening to call up all manner of spirits "from the vasty deep" to help him. Hotspur had made no secret of the fact that he thought Glendower a charlatan for his claims to be a magician, and they began to argue. Worcester and Mortimer urged Hotspur to keep his thoughts to himself, but Hotspur was not a man easily silenced, and Kate knew it would not be long before he pushed fiery Glendower's patience too far – perhaps, even far enough to destroy the uneasy alliance between them.

She sighed, and poked aimlessly at one of the wall-hangings that covered the damp plaster. Although it was summer, the evening was chilly, and the window shutters were closed against the soft tap of rain. Lady Mortimer kept her company, sewing in the unsteady yellow light of the fire. Kate studied the Welshwoman covertly. Could she really speak no English as Glendower claimed? Somehow, Kate did not think the Welsh leader would have neglected such an important aspect of his daughter's education, and could only suppose that she was pretending to understand nothing in order to spy.

Kate went to the table for some wine, but the jug was empty. Silently, and with a strained smile of apology, Lady Mortimer took it from her and went to fetch more from the kitchens. Kate watched her leave with relief, grateful for some time away from the Welshwoman's watchful eyes. Within moments the door opened again, making the flames in the hearth dip and flutter. With a start, Kate saw it was not Lady Mortimer closing the door so carefully, but a friar clad in the grey habit of a Franciscan.

"Who are you?" she demanded, alarmed.

"My lady," the man whispered, pushing back his cowl to reveal his face. "I mean you no harm. My name is

Sir John Colville, and I'm a knight who is loyal to your husband."

"Well, he isn't here," said Kate, gesturing round the empty room. "So, please leave. If Hotspur finds us here alone, he'll kill you where you stand – habit or no – and me as well into the bargain."

That was not strictly true – Hotspur, for all his bluster and impetuosity, loved her dearly and was not in the habit of killing people without just cause – but it made the knight blanch.

"I'm here as his friend, my lady. But we don't have much time. Lady Mortimer will return soon – when she has finished cavesdropping on the conversation in the hall below."

"So she does understand English!"

"Of course she does. Robert Colville, the man poisoned earlier today, was betrothed to marry her. Do you think my brother would have affianced himself to a woman who could not understand him?"

"The murdered man was your brother?" Kate's mind reeled. "He was betrothed to Lady Mortimer? But she's married to my brother."

"That marriage broke Robert's heart," said Colville, looking away. "But he took the affront to his honour with dignity, saying he wanted only what would best serve Glendower and Lady Mortimer, both of whom he loved."

"But what has this to do with me?" asked Kate, bewildered.

"Glendower is beside himself with grief and anger over Robert's death. No Welshman would have murdered him. The most obvious suspects, therefore, are the Englishmen."

"You think one of us poisoned him? But that's ridiculous! We had never even heard of him before today!"

"That's not true, my lady," said Colville. "Hotspur, Mortimer, and Worcester all knew Robert – it was Robert who carried messages between them and Glendower to arrange this meeting. And all three knew that Robert was betrothed to Lady Mortimer. Perhaps you don't know Welsh law, but it states, quite clearly, that a betrothal is as binding as marriage itself. There are those in Bangor who believe Edmund Mortimer

committed a grave crime by taking a lady already promised
to another man. Others will not acknowledge the marriage
at all – or at least, would not have done as long as Robert
had lived."

"But my brother . . ."

"Your brother knew that by marrying Glendower's daughter, he was breaking Welsh law. But love made him blind to
such niceties. There are rumours that it was Mortimer who
poisoned Robert, because now Robert is dead, his marriage
is legal in Welsh eyes."

"Not Edmund! He's too gentle even to consider such a
vile act!"

"Perhaps. Some people are saying that Hotspur and
Worcester killed Robert, so that your brother's now-legal
marriage with Lady Mortimer will strengthen the alliance
between them and Glendower."

"But that's even more absurd! Hotspur would never resort
to poison as a means of killing someone." Worcester might,
though, she thought, although she kept it to herself.

"Then there are those who suspect Lady Mortimer herself.
What woman wants her offspring declared bastards because
of a broken betrothal? So, there are four people – Mortimer,
his wife, Hotspur, and Worcester – who had a motive to
kill my brother. You must determine which of them is the
guilty one."

"Me?" asked Kate, aghast. "I cannot start an enquiry into
a murder behind my husband's back!"

"You must, unless you wish someone to slip a dagger into it,
instead. There will be four deaths to avenge Robert's murder,
unless you act."

"Then you investigate," said Kate, still horrified. "Robert
was your brother."

"I would if I could, but Glendower needs me to carry
messages south for him, and he will entrust them to no one
else. I set out within the hour. You must solve this riddle
before you leave Bangor, or your loved ones will not be safe
from Welsh arrows along the way."

"But Hotspur plans to go tonight!" objected Kate. "I cannot
solve anything before then!"

Colville raised his shoulders in a shrug, and was gone as quickly as he had arrived, leaving Kate alone and bewildered. Moments later, the door opened again, and Glendower entered with Lady Mortimer.

"Our business is done," he said, teeth glittering white through his black beard. "My daughter has promised to sing to us in the hall, and we should like you to join us."

Thoughts still reeling, Kate followed Glendower into the hall. Lady Mortimer flew into her besotted husband's arms, and began crooning to him in Welsh. While Glendower translated her words, Kate watched them narrowly, wishing she could understand the melodic tongue – for all Kate knew, the Welshwoman might be reciting a cure for flea-bites, but Glendower was a poet and his eloquent phrases had Mortimer reeling in dizzy delight.

Hotspur was making a nuisance of himself, shifting and muttering, and demanding that Kate should attempt to best Lady Mortimer by singing in English. Kate grew exasperated, longing to be able to observe her suspects in peace – for there they were, all four, gathered in the same room. She even threatened to break his head, but he persisted with his babble. In the end, bored by the singing and by her absent-minded replies to his bantering, he leapt energetically to his feet and went to pester the clerks to write faster, so that the agreement between the rebels might be signed and they could be on their way.

"Two hours," he flung over his shoulder as he left.

Two hours! thought Kate, appalled. What could she hope to achieve in two hours? As far as she was concerned, there was only one plausible solution to the crime, and that would involve the devious Lady Mortimer. Hotspur, she knew she could dismiss from Colville's list of suspects: God knew, he had dispatched a goodly number of souls to meet their maker, but all of them in the heat of battle, and he would never stoop to use as insidious a weapon as poison. Could she say the same for her uncle and her brother? She reflected, tapping a forefinger gently on her chin. These were dark and dangerous times, and who knew to what depths a man might sink in order to protect his own interests?

As she tried to decide what to do first, Glendower came towards her, offering an exquisitely worked silver goblet in which some sour, brown-coloured wine slopped incongruously. The spoils of some looted merchant's house along the Welsh border, Kate thought wryly, as she took it from him.

"Please accept my condolences for the death of Sir Robert Colville," she said. Glendower's expression hardened, and he looked away. "I know he was dear to you. To your daughter, too."

"Not to her," Glendower replied, bitterly. "Well, not since she set eyes on your brother. I would not have allowed her to marry Mortimer, but Robert insisted that the alliance between Wales and the rebels was more important than his personal happiness. Had I known that someone would kill him for his generosity, I would never have agreed to him breaking the betrothal!"

Kate sipped at the wine so that she would not have to respond. The marriage between Mortimer and Glendower's daughter was vitally important, because it meant the rebels and Glendower were now kinsmen. Yet it seemed that Glendower was not completely easy about the match, and might even resent the fact that his daughter had so readily abandoned Robert in favour of the dashing Mortimer.

"What kind of poison did you say he had been given?" Glendower looked surprised at her abrupt question, and she continued hurriedly. "A poultice of henbane helps my uncle Worcester's gout. Therefore, I'm keen to know more of the plant, so that I might treat it with the respect it so obviously demands."

"Then you are a wise woman," he said approvingly. "Although your husband despises the art of herb-lore. Henbane kills quickly, causing fits and rapid breathing. I recognized the smell of it on Robert's clothes, along with spilled wine."

"So someone put henbane in his wine," mused Kate. "He died outside a tavern, so I suppose the deed was done there."

"So it would seem," said Glendower uneasily, doubtless suspicious of her unseemly interest in the death of one of his people. "According to the landlord, Robert went to the tavern after mass and remained there until his death. He spoke only to one person, and that was a man swathed in a black cloak against the rain. The landlord did not see this man's face, but it was only moments after he left that Robert began to complain about feeling ill."

"So, it must have been this man who killed Robert," said Kate, relieved. "It couldn't have been Hotspur, Edmund, or Worcester!"

"Could it not?" asked Glendower, softly. "What grounds do you have for such an assumption? After we left the church, we were all at leisure until we met for the midday meal. Your husband claims he was in the stables checking his horses, but none of my grooms saw him there; Mortimer says he was with his wife, but she was hesitant in confirming his alibi, and I am not certain that she isn't lying for him; and Worcester maintains he was here, all alone, huddled by the fire. Who knows who did this evil thing?"

"But the alliance between you and the rebels is far too important for any of them to take such a foolish risk with it," reasoned Kate. "If you do not join your troops with theirs, they will never win this war against King Henry. And if they don't die in battle, they'll be executed as traitors!"

"I know that," said Glendower, fiercely. "And I cannot understand why one of them should commit murder when so much is at stake. But Robert lies dead, and he was killed by poison. Those are the facts. Now, you will excuse me, my lady. If I am to escort your husband and his retinue to the Marches – and he will not pass unmolested through Welsh lands without me – there is much I must do."

He bowed to her and left, although not quickly enough to hide the sparkle of tears in his eyes. A cold fear gripped Kate. If Glendower so loved Robert, who knew what vengeance he might take against those he considered guilty?

She approached Worcester. The older man smiled at her, drawing a furred collar more tightly around his neck. The hall was large and draughty, and Worcester was a chilly mortal, even in the summer.

"This man, Robert Colville," she said, taking his arm to lead him to the fire. "I hear he was betrothed to Lady Mortimer before my brother married her."

"How did you know that?" he asked, startled. "You mustn't listen to servants' gossip, Kate. It isn't becoming."

"Dear uncle," she said, smiling at him in her most winning fashion. "You know as well as I that servants often have better knowledge than their masters. Tell me about Robert."

Worcester sighed, and sat on a stool to warm his hands near the flames. "Robert was Glendower's most trusted messenger, and a good man. He and I shared a common affliction – gout. There's nothing that can make men friends like a shared suffering. He gave me this."

He held out a blackish lump for her to inspect. She took it cautiously. It was a leather pouch containing something moist and sticky.

"Pickled comfrey," he explained. "The next time I am in pain, I am to soak this in hot water and apply it as a compress to my feet. Then, if I say three Hail Marys, I will be cured."

"Really? Then how is it that Robert still suffered if he had this miraculous cure to hand?"

"It doesn't always work, apparently," said Worcester reluctantly. "Anyway, I gave him the poultice you made for me, so that he could try it next time the gout attacked him."

"What else do you know of Robert, other than his medical history?"

"Nothing much. He is brother to Sir John Colville, a knight whose life Hotspur once saved. The last I saw of Robert was this morning, after mass. Hotspur stopped to pass the time of day with him – you remember, Kate, Hotspur had to run to catch us up again, and he stumbled over that dog and almost fell in the mud."

He chuckled, a deep rumble inside his chest. Kate did not smile with him, although she had laughed until she had cried when it had happened. Hotspur had indeed lingered at the church, and she recalled glancing round to look for him.

She also recalled, with a cold, sick feeling, that Hotspur had someone pinned to one of the pillars by the neck – someone wearing a fine blue surcoat, like the one Robert had worn. Hotspur's face had been dark with anger, and she had heard him shouting. She had thought nothing of it at the time, thinking it had been an errant servant, but now she realized that it had been Robert. Had she misjudged her husband? Was he the kind of man to don a cloak and slip poison into a goblet of wine in a tavern? More to the point, did Glendower think so?

Or was the killer Worcester, who hunched near the fire, stretching his bony hands towards the flames? Of all of them, he was the one most likely to take a warm black cloak on his summer travels, and he had no one to corroborate his whereabouts at the time the murderer was passing his deadly brew to the hapless Robert. Or was it Mortimer, whose alibi in his wife was dubious, and who had every reason to rid himself of a man who might later be the cause of his children being proclaimed illegitimate? And, of course, there was Lady Mortimer herself, a woman who lied to the man she claimed to love about her language abilities, and who, like Kate, was tall enough to pass for a man if disguised in a heavy cloak. Had Lady Mortimer fainted from genuine shock at seeing a former suitor so ruthlessly slain, or from guilt at seeing the result of her handiwork?

All four had a motive; all four had the opportunity. The evidence was slightly stacked against Hotspur, in that Kate herself had seen him arguing with Robert shortly before his death. And the means? Henbane was a common enough thing: Kate had some in her own bags with which to salve Worcester's gout. Any apothecary would have it, and would sell it with no questions asked if the price offered were high enough. She sighed, and glanced at the hour-candle. It was almost midnight, and they would soon be leaving. And before they did, Kate had questions to ask of some of the servants about the whereabouts of her relatives that morning, and confirm her suspicions about Robert's corpse in the chapel.

Riding wearily along darkened lanes, with water dripping into her eyes and down her neck where the seam had weakened between hood and cloak, Kate cursed the restless spirit that drove her husband. They could just as easily have travelled at dawn, when she would at least have been able to see the soggy branches and leaves that slapped at her, drenching her further with showers of droplets. A long twig caught against Lady Mortimer who was riding in front of her, and whipped back to catch Kate a stinging blow on her cheek. Her cry brought a spiteful smile from her sister-in-law, and Hotspur galloping back from the front of the party in alarm.

"It's just a scratch," he said, cupping her face in his gauntleted hand. Since she had heard him describe some quite serious battle-wounds as scratches, his words held little reassurance.

"I don't feel comfortable in this deep valley," she said in a whisper, holding a patch of clean linen to the cut. "Glendower grieves for Robert, and I keep expecting to feel a knife between my ribs."

"I doubt Glendower thinks you killed him, Kate," said Hotspur drily. "If my page is to be believed, I am at the top of his list of suspects." He hesitated, and then plunged on. "I argued with Robert, just before he died."

"What about?"

Hotspur swallowed hard. "I thought he might have read some of the messages I entrusted to him for Glendower. Glendower said the seals had been tampered with, you see. It would go badly with us if our plans were passed to the king's forces in advance. Henry could have us executed for treason before an arrow was ever fired."

"But by all accounts, Robert loved Glendower so much that he was prepared to give up his marriage plans to secure Welsh success against Henry. Why should you suspect him of betrayal?"

Hotspur shrugged, wearily. "I don't know, Kate. But you can see that Glendower believes me to have a powerful motive for wanting Robert's death."

But if that were true, then so did Glendower, thought Kate, if he found one of his most trusted advisers had turned traitor. She was about to say so, when there was a sharp singing sound.

Even while she tried to imagine what it could be, Hotspur had drawn his sword, and was yelling a warning to the others that there was an ambush. While they milled around in confusion, he was off into the woods that lined the dark park, his battle cry echoing through the trees.

It was all over in moments. The ambushers were nothing more than starving villagers whose homes had been burned by English raids, and who mistook their prince and his entourage for easy prey. Three of them lay dead before Glendower was able to call Hotspur back and send his subjects away with a furious reprimand and a saddle-bag of food.

"I thought that might have been your retribution for the death of Robert," said Worcester shakily to Glendower.

"I would have been more careful," said Glendower, watching Hotspur sheath his sword. "I only wish Robert's killer to die, not all of us, and especially not me!"

"I can tell you now who that killer is," said Kate, smiling at the startled faces that turned to her. The last piece of the puzzle had fallen into place.

They stopped at the next village, and ordered breakfast in a shabby tavern. The rushes that littered the floor were alive with vermin, and the walls were splashed with the remains of meals eaten long before Kate was born. She shivered, declining to sit on the greasy bench near the fire that the obsequious taverner offered her. Her suspects were all there, waiting with mixed curiosity and unease to hear what she had to say.

"And now we are sitting comfortably," said Glendower, raising his dark eyes from his ale to gaze at her, "we will have your tale, madam."

"It's really very simple," said Kate. "There are five people with a motive for killing Robert – Lady Mortimer, Hotspur, Worcester, Mortimer, and Glendower." She waved Glendower's startled objections away with an imperious hand. "The marriage uniting the rebels and the Welsh is vital to the success of your plans – to overthrow King Henry and obtain independence for Wales. Robert's life would be a small price to pay to ensure that no previous betrothal could mar the legitimacy of the marriage.

But all of this is irrelevant, because none of you killed Robert."

There was a sudden babble of voices, as everyone tried to speak at once. Only Hotspur did not join in. He watched her with a faint smile, stretching his hands towards the fire. Kate continued.

"I was very thorough in talking to the servants – unlike you, my lord Glendower. A lowly scullery maid, whom no one had bothered to consult, can confirm Worcester was huddled by the fire when Robert was killed. A falconer, not someone who usually frequents stables and so also not questioned, is proud to say that he passed the entire morning discussing hawks with Hotspur. Meanwhile, my brother and his wife spent their time going through Glendower's household jewels, watched by a clerk who was later too afraid to admit what he had seen."

Lady Mortimer exchanged a guilty glance with her husband, a glance that would not have been exchanged had she not understood completely what was being said. Kate wondered how long it would be before the same thing occurred to her brother.

"That's why you were hesitant to say where you were," said Glendower, a smile tugging at the corners of his mouth. "My household jewels! Did you see anything you liked?"

"So, Lady Mortimer did not faint from guilt for Robert's murder, but from the shock of seeing a former suitor dead so unexpectedly," Kate went on. "And finally, Glendower spent all morning with his steward. Despite the fact that all of you had the motive, none of you had the opportunity after all. Now, Robert, like Worcester, suffered from gout, and so they exchanged cures. Robert gave Worcester a poultice of comfrey, but Worcester gave Robert a poultice containing henbane."

"I didn't kill him!" exclaimed Worcester, outraged and standing so abruptly, his chair crashed behind him. "You have just proved my innocence! I was seen all morning in the hall!"

"I know," said Kate, soothingly, putting a hand on his shoulder. Hotspur picked up the chair, and gestured for his uncle to sit again, while Kate continued with her analysis. "But did you tell Robert what to do with this poultice?"

"Of course not," said Worcester indignantly. "Any fool can see you slap it on the afflicted part. Why should I tell him something so obvious?"

"Then I think Robert was indeed a fool," said Kate. "I inspected his body in the chapel before we left, and when the priest looked inside his mouth – on my instructions – he found a sprig of lavender. I use lavender to try to mask the unpleasant smell of the poultice. The conclusion is obvious: poor Robert dissolved the poultice in his wine, thinking it had to be swallowed, like a medicine. He was not murdered, and his death was nothing more than a silly, wholly regrettable accident."

"And the man in the black cloak?" asked Hotspur softly.

"No one with a role in this tale," said Kate, smiling. "A chance traveller wrapped up against the weather, whose presence merely muddied the waters for a while."

Glendower rubbed his temples tiredly. "I have done you a grave injustice, my friends," he said, standing and offering his hand to Hotspur while he laid his other arm around Mortimer's shoulders. "I suspected you of the most foul of deeds. But all is well now. This clever lady has saved me from dishonour and our cause from failure."

Worcester eased himself out of his chair, and offered Glendower his cup. "Then let us drink to our success, my lords. Here's to a kingdom at peace, sealed and sanctified by the marriage of Glendower's gentle daughter to the noble Mortimer."

The rain turned to sunshine as the day wore on, bathing the craggy Welsh hills in a golden light. On the horizon, however, the clouds were leaden grey, and there was a distant rumble of thunder. Kate was content, feeling the heat of the sun on her shoulders, and breathing in deeply the scent of wet earth. She began to dawdle, enjoying the peace of the countryside and the warm, proud feeling following the successful discharge of Sir John Colville's mission. Soon, only a groom was behind her, a sullen soul who wore his hood over his face against the sun.

Hotspur left his place at the head of the column, and came to ride near her, edging his mount close, so that their legs touched.

"So, Kate," he said quietly, lifting his face to the sun with his eyes closed. "It seems I married a lawyer. Your logic was impeccable."

"And what would you know of logic?" she asked impishly. "You know only about battles and fighting."

"And killing," he said in the same soft tone. "I know about killing, too, Kate. And I knew Robert. He no more drank Worcester's poultice than I can sprout wings and fly."

She gazed at him, but his eyes were still closed, his face tilted towards the sky.

"What are you saying?" she asked, confused. "That I was wrong?"

"Oh, I think we both know that, Kate." He gazed at her suddenly, his eyes sad. "I looked in Robert's mouth, too, when I thought Mortimer or Worcester, or even I might be accused of his murder. I saw no lavender, and I looked before you did."

"So, someone put it there to deceive me?" she asked.

"Enough, Kate!" he said, sharply. "I liked Robert. He was a good man and a loyal friend . . ."

"But you told me you suspected him of passing secrets to the enemy," protested Kate. "I saw you arguing with him about it."

"I was arguing with him because he wouldn't take my advice and leave Bangor. I knew his life was in danger, but he felt he could best serve our cause by staying to take Glendower's messages to our supporters. I grew angry, and even threatened him, but still he refused to go. Foolish, misguided man!"

"But the secrets!" insisted Kate.

"He opened no letters of mine. I lied to you about what we discussed."

"You lied?" asked Kate, bewildered. "But why? I don't understand. You don't lie! You prize honesty and hate untruths!"

"I have had to learn the art of deception," he said, bitterly. "And what better teacher than my wife? I lied to you because it was you who killed Robert, Kate. It was you who slipped into the tavern swathed in a black cloak and put the henbane in his wine. The rest of us might have had alibis at the time of the murder, but no one thought to check yours – except me. Your maid told me you were gone an hour, and that you came back wet."

"I went for a walk in the garden," protested Kate. "Ask the cook. She must have seen me."

"Believe me, I did. She saw nothing, and the garden is far too overgrown for walking. So, alone of us all, you had the opportunity."

"This is nonsense!" she said, laughing suddenly. "Why would I kill Robert?"

"Your motives are obvious. First, you love your brother dearly, and you do not want to see his happiness spoiled because of some Welsh law that says his marriage is illegal. Second, the marriage between Mortimer and Glendower's daughter is a vital link in the alliance between us and the Welsh. If Glendower does not lend us his troops, then we are doomed – we will either be overwhelmed in battle, or we will be executed as traitors. You know that no one can be allowed to stand in the way of the alliance – especially a man like Robert, whose betrothal to Glendower's daughter might be seen to render null Mortimer's marriage."

Kate said nothing, and Hotspur went on.

"Perhaps this is my fault because I talked too much about the importance of the marriage to our plans. I thought someone might try to harm Robert – but I didn't think it would be you, Kate. Your mistake, of course, was that you didn't know what Robert meant to Glendower: by acting to strengthen the alliance, you actually placed it in the gravest danger."

Kate still said nothing, and stared at the gathering thunder-clouds in the distance.

"And as for the means?" continued Hotspur. "Well, none of us had access to henbane, but you were quite open about the fact that you carry some to make salves for Worcester's gout."

She was about to reply to his accusations, when there was

a sudden heart-broken sob from the groom behind them. Kate glanced round, and saw his face for the first time.

"It was you who sent Sir John Colville to me, Hotspur," she said in sudden understanding, nodding to where the knight wept. "When you realized I had killed Robert, you saw that the best way to keep the identity of the murderer from Glendower was to let me come up with an alternative solution that Glendower would accept." She nodded in begrudging appreciation. "And you lied to me about Robert betraying you so that I would think Glendower had you on the top of his list of suspects. You used my love for you to spur me to produce a solution more quickly than I might otherwise have done. That was clever."

"It was cunning and deceitful, and I am not proud of it. But I have no wish to see my wife hanged as a common killer any more than I want the alliance with Glendower to flounder. You left me with few choices, Kate."

"But the alliance is secure now," she said, reaching over to take one of his hands in hers. It was cold and limp, like that of a corpse, and she dropped it quickly.

"It isn't secure," he said. "The taverner told Glendower that the 'man' in the black cloak might have been a woman. He suspected his daughter, but it won't be long before he begins to turn his thoughts to you – especially when he discusses your 'solution' with her."

"With Lady Mortimer? But how can anything she knows make a difference?"

"She can read English as well as speak it. You left that recipe for Worcester's poultice lying around for her to see. Glendower knows about herbs, and he will see that the amount of henbane you use in it isn't enough to kill, even if Robert had been foolish enough to eat it all. Oh Kate! Why did you interfere?"

"Because I was frightened for you! You were so offensive to Glendower, mocking him for his beliefs in magic, and then arguing with him about the way he planned to divide the country once you took it from the King. I was afraid he would use his daughter's betrothal as an excuse to annul her marriage, and back away from supporting you."

It was Hotspur's turn to remain silent.

"I see now I made a terrible mistake," she said unsteadily. "But I did it for you and for my brother. Glendower must support you when you go to war against King Henry!"

"When we first agreed to join forces, Glendower said he could raise ten thousand men in three days. Yesterday, after Robert's murder, those three days became fourteen. I don't believe I will have Welshmen fighting with me against the King."

"What have I done?" cried Kate in horror.

"You have killed me, Kate, just as surely as you have killed Robert."

Postscript

On 21 July 1403, after the meeting of Glendower and the rebels in Wales, Hotspur and his supporters fought King Henry IV at the Battle of Shrewsbury. Glendower's troops were not present, and Hotspur was killed during the bloody hand-to-hand skirmishing.

THE DEATH OF FALSTAFF

Darrell Schweitzer

The Life of Henry the Fifth *was the last of the straight historical plays by Shakespeare. It was written and first performed in 1599. Henry V was one of England's most popular kings. Gone are the days of his youthful indiscretions as Prince Hal with Falstaff in the two plays of* Henry IV*. Henry V rebuilds the English territories in France lost by his forebears and becomes the heroic victor of the Battle of Agincourt in 1415. One of the sub-plots of the play refers to the apparent death of Sir John Falstaff whilst he is resting at Mistress Quickly's tavern with all his former cronies preparing to travel to France with the King. All we know is that Falstaff dies, but we don't know how. Darrell Schweitzer uncovers the past.*

The King was in Southampton that night.

Everyone had left me but the day before: Nym who was once to be my husband, though I had little liking for him, and Bardolph, whose nose glowed like a lantern, and the boy, and even my own Pistol, who was my husband. Off they were, to France, in their country's service, for God and gold and glory, but mostly for the gold, if you take my meaning. Now the tavern was empty and silent, as all those who had made merry in it had gone away, with even my own husband saying, "Sweet Nell is such a clever one. She will take care of everything."

So they left me, even my husband, to clean up after them in more ways than one.

And with poor Sir John still lying in the bed upstairs. It was I who was to attend to that, who would send for the undertaker and clean up the remains of Sir John's life as if I were wiping a tabletop.

Trust Mistress Nell. She can look after things.

A lot more happened on that night than just myself sitting around in the dark, mourning for Jack Falstaff, though I shed many a tear, and I sat by him in the dark, I did, looking at his dim shape in the dark, his nose all sharp and his fine, round face shrunken like a winter's apple. I wasn't afraid, being with a dead corpse, because it was only Sir John and I didn't fear his ghost.

"Oh, Sir John," says I, "I hope you're in your green fields now – "

And then there was a thunderous knocking at the door. I let out a cry and dropped my little candle. I groped around and found it, but couldn't relight it, so I felt my way to the door.

Still the thundering, as if to knock the whole house down.

"Anon!" I cried. "Anon!" And to Sir John I says, "If that be the Devil come for your soul, I'll just tell him the tavern is closed and send him away."

But it wasn't the Devil at the door, instead a tall, fierce-looking fellow, richly clad, and beside him a man in arms, who might have been a soldier. I couldn't quite tell in the dark, but the one had on a black coat, like velvet, and the other wore a steel cap on his head and a sword at his side.

"Mistress Quickly?"

"Aye."

"I am called Doctor Peake."

"Well, whatever you're called, what is your business?"

"Does the body of Sir John Falstaff lie within this house?"

I could not deny that it did, but before I could have any whys or wherefores, this Peake and his bully-boy brushed me aside and come in. They showed me a paper, which they said was from a Higher Authority, but of course I couldn't read it.

There was something strange. I knew they came not from the watch, or from the sheriff; and the thought hits me like a thunderbolt, *My God! They are from the King!* But why? The King did not love Sir John in the end. He broke his heart, and of that broken heart Sir John died. So what would the King care now?

I did as they bade me. I lit my candle from the embers and led them upstairs, then fetched a lamp when it was called for, and the one in the black coat, he that called himself a doctor, he examined Sir John most closely, peering into his eyes and ears with a kind of glass, poking and touching as if a dead man were not a dead man plain to see.

"He is beyond all physick now," says I, but the doctor just growls and says, "Silence, woman," and goes on with his prodding and poking. The armed man looked at me, then at his master, but his master said nothing more, so I was allowed to stay.

I stood there, in the dark by the door, wringing my hands in silence.

At last he was done, and Doctor Peake said to his man, "It is as I had feared."

I didn't ask him what he feared, other than that Sir John Falstaff was dead, and I didn't understand why he would be afraid of that.

The other fellow nodded and hurried downstairs and out of the house. I heard him galloping off.

"And now, Mistress," said the doctor, "if you will fetch some refreshment while we wait, here's a gold noble for you."

My eyes lit up at that, you can be sure. I snatched the coin before he changed his mind and told him for that price he could have King Solomon's Feast; but he only wanted some wine and some cold mutton and cabbage, downstairs in the common room, of course, for to eat upstairs was to invite Sir John to rise up and ask for some, as he always did enjoy his victuals.

But also, for that amount of money, Doctor Peake wanted other things of me, first my swearing my silence, and then he wanted to know divers things about Sir John, his comings and goings and who he met, especially in the last days of his life.

I told what I knew, how the King had broke Sir John's heart, and how Sir John had called for sack and drank so much you'd think he'd drown in it, and how he ate enough for five huge fat men. Yet still there was no comfort for him in it. He tried to be merry with his old friends, but he could not.

The doctor waved his hand impatiently.

"Enough of that. Did he meet with other than his usual associates? Did he take any stranger aside and speak in a whisper? Did they mention the names Cambridge, Scroop, and Grey?"

"Why sir, if they was whispering, how would I know what names was mentioned?"

I saw rage in his face then, a flicker, light lightning far away on a summer night; but he was a hard man, and in control of himself.

"Then there *were* such persons? Agents? Conspirators? Speak plainly, woman! There are those who'd have your tongue out for this!"

I was all a-flustered then, and didn't know what to say for those were names of great men, the Earl of Cambridge, Lord Scroop of Masham, and ... I didn't know who Grey was, but he must have been great too, to keep such company. But when do such quality as those come to an Eastcheap tavern to talk with John Falstaff?

"You *said* there were conspirators – "

"Oh no, sir, if I may be so bold, sir. *You* said it. I but asked if they was whispering, how I could hear what was said."

Then the doctor was angry again, for just an instant, and he let out a long sigh, like the wind escaping from a bag, and he says, "I have been told, by one who knows you passing well, that you have a better wit and a more observant eye than one might expect from ... your kind. Here's a silver groat if you will but tell me with whom Sir John Falstaff did converse this past week or so."

I snatched the coin quick, but all I could tell him, to be truthful was, "He did go out alone, just before he took sick, and he did say it was to meet an old friend over a matter of some money. 'So you are going to pay what you owe me?' says I. Quoth he, 'What? I owe *you*? After such custom as I have given you? I have brought such honour to your house.

You've had a prince under your roof because of me.' Meaning Prince Hal, he did, and God save him who is now our lord the King. But Prince Hal then. I think there was a tear in Sir John's eye then, because his heart was broke, but he had his little joke on me and I got never a shilling. Out he went, and he came back with his face all flushed and red, like Bardolph's nose, and his speech was slurry, so Pistol my husband and the boy that was Sir John's page helped him upstairs. Soon after Sir John was sick, and sooner after dead. That is all I know, Sir, in God's honest truth."

"Then you know enough to have perhaps come to the same conclusion as have I, that Sir John Falstaff's death was not natural, but that he was murdered."

"Jesu Christ have mercy!" I put my hand to my mouth.

"There are definite signs of poison on his body. Now the matter darkens, Mistress Quickly, and your tact is required, for this is *the King's business*."

I let out another little cry, and for an instant you could have knocked me over with a feather, all a-swoon was I, sorrowful and afraid, for he had said this was the King's *business*, which is very close to the King's *doing*, and Oh, what a terrible thing it had to be, how it must be the very work of the Devil, that Prince Hal, who loved Falstaff, became King Henry the Fifth, who did not, and that King, to save himself the shame of his former life, found it politic to have Sir John *murdered*.

If that were true, I did not want to live.

But no, I could not believe it. I prayed to God and promised to repent my sins, and Sir John's too, if it were not so.

Doctor Peake said nothing to comfort me, but only said we should wait.

"What are we waiting for?"

"For another, who has been sent for."

So we waited. That was all there was to do. I didn't feel like idle talk, so I busied myself, tidying this and sweeping that, and I put some wood on the fire to give us light. The doctor just sat waiting too, drumming his fingers on my tabletop like the patter of rain.

Then past ten of the clock there came hoofbeats in the street outside, and thunderous knocking again.

I went to the door but the doctor got there first, and he opened the door to let in his armed man, who he'd sent away before, and another, whose face I could not see because of his hooded cloak. I think there were more men in the street outside. I heard metal clank and clink, and heavy footsteps. The doctor closed the door swiftly.

I could see that the newcomer was a young man, tall and strong. He had a mailed sleeve, and I saw the ring he wore, even in such poor light.

Once more I crossed myself, and repented my sins, lest I die that night.

"Is it true, then?" This stranger asks the doctor.

"Sir John is murdered, my lord," says the doctor. "There is no doubt of it."

And the other one's voice trembled a little, and he said, "But *why* would someone kill a harmless old clown who couldn't conspire his way out of a cup of sack?" He was speaking from his heart, and that surprised me, and I watched him careful, like.

"Begging your pardon, lord," says I, and I curtseys. "But if you want to go up and see him – "

It was reckless of me to say anything at all, but I was crazy with fear and grief and my thoughts all a jumble; and all the other things I wanted to ask him I couldn't find the words for, not then.

The hooded man nodded to me politely, as if I were a real lady, and said, "Your pardon, Mistress Quickly."

He held out his hand, and if he had not stopped me I would have knelt down and kissed his ring, though at that instant if I knew why I dared not admit the reason, even to myself.

"Oh no," says he. "If anyone is to ask, say only that you were visited by a gentleman this night, whose name was Henry Le Roi, while the King was in Southampton, preparing for his French war."

The doctor said, "I have purchased her silence, lord."

"Nell always knew a good bargain, though it is not in her nature to be entirely silent, as I well know," said Sir Le Roi. I didn't ask how he knew. To me he said, "Hostess, if you will lead the way."

So I lit my candle and led them upstairs, the three of them, Sir Le Roi, who still hid his face beneath his hood, and Doctor Peake, and the soldier.

We stood before the bed where Sir John lay. I bethought me that I ought to cover him up, but they'd want to see him, so I did not.

"Poisoned, my lord," said the doctor.

"Poor old, fat, drunk, rascally fool," said Sir Le Roi. "He once said that sack would be his poison."

"But not here, sir," I said. "He got no poison here, though he drank overmuch, and did not always pay for it."

"That was in his nature," said Sir Le Roi.

"It would seem he was poisoned elsewhere," said the doctor, "and returned here to die."

"We must discover the murderer then," said Sir Le Roi, "and within but a few hours, too, for I have pressing business, as you well know. *Damn!* But for more time!"

"We can hardly search the whole city in a few hours, lord. Even if we knew what the criminal looked like."

"We must make him come to us. But how to get word to him? He could be anywhere."

"Likely in his bed at this hour," said the doctor.

"I think not," said Le Roi. "I think not. But let me think further. Let us plan our stratagem . . ." He began pacing back and forth, clinking and clattering beneath his cloak. "If this rogue wants Sir John dead, and thinks he *is* dead, then he'll feel a sense of relief that the task is completed and the tongue he wanted silenced *is* silenced, and this murderer, being a low fellow, will celebrate his exploit in a low manner. I think he will be in a tavern, with his comrades, saluting the completion of their enterprise. He'll be drinking a toast, which I swear will slake his thirst all the way to the gallows."

"That still does not find him, lord."

Le Roi stopped suddenly. He struck his hand with his other fist. His ring flashed in the candlelight. "I have it! Imagine the fright the fellow would have if he were to learn that *Sir John Falstaff is not dead!*"

"But sir," I broke in, amazed, "why there he is, cold and dead as you see. You cannot bring him back!"

Sir Le Roi said softly, "In Arthur's bosom, so I hear – "

"Sir!" I said, much alarmed, wondering if this Le Roy might be the very Devil, who could read my thoughts.

He turned to the doctor, to the soldier, then back to me, as if to include all of us in his council. "Hark you then. Pray to God this works."

To the soldier he said, "Station the men all about the street, out of sight, so our quarry may enter the house but not leave it."

"It shall be done, lord," said the soldier, and off he went.

To the doctor, he said, "We must conceal ourselves. Where?" He looked about the room. There was a trunk, but barely big enough to hide a boy in it.

He turned to me.

"Mistress Quickly, is there a curtain?"

"What, sir?"

"A drapery. A hanging of some sort."

Befuddled, I could only say, "There's just the sheets."

"It will have to do. Take you a sheet then, and hang it up on the wall like a curtain, as if to cover a window, for all there's no window there. In the dark, he'll never notice."

"Never notice what, sir?"

"But do as I instruct you."

I did. The doctor was the taller and helped. I stood on a stool by him, and we two nailed a sheet up at the ceiling, so it hung down behind the bed, like a curtain.

Then Le Roi and the doctor hid behind the sheet.

Now this made no sense at all, and they looked like a couple of lunatics, hiding in the room from a dead man, as if this would conjure up who murdered him. I might have laughed, were I not so afraid. But if these were lunatics they might murder *me* and wrap me up in that sheet, and it was no laughing matter.

Sir Le Roi came out from behind the sheet and directed me downstairs, into the common room. The doctor remained where he was, hidden.

"Mistress," says he, in a low, secret voice, "would you undertake an adventure tonight – for gold?"

"I might," says I, not knowing what he meant.

"Would you do it for love of Jack Falstaff?"

"I would, for I did love him, for he was a most merry gentleman and a true friend – "

"So did we all love him," says Sir Le Roi beneath his hood. Very much I wanted to push that hood back and see his face, but I dared not.

"We?"

"All who loved him, for who did not love him?"

I couldn't contain myself any longer. Call me a fool, but I broke down into tears and cried like a baby, and I spoke my mind clearly, not caring of the result. "No, sir, not *all*. First there was the murderer, who did not love him at all. But also there was the King, and God strike me dead for saying so. Prince Hal, who *seemed* to love Jack, did not and proved false to him when he became King, and he broke Jack Falstaff's heart when he turned him away and said he knew him not. And, sir, it may even be that the King so wanted to quit Jack's company that he made Jack do the quitting – "

"What do you mean?" says he, and his voice was very grim, but my fire was up, and I spoke on.

"I mean that maybe it was the King that caused Sir John to quit this Earth."

There I had said it, and strike me dead.

But it was Sir Le Roi who staggered back as if struck, and he let out a little cry of, "Oh," and then "Oh no," and his voice was trembling and I think he wept. I think I could see just a glint of a tear, by the light of the fire.

He took me by both my shoulders and peered into my eyes out of the darkness of his hood, and said, "Mistress, how could you make so monstrous an accusation? It is treason, you know."

"If I hang for it, I hang for it," says I.

"Upon my honor as a Christian, you shall not hang," says he. His voice stumbled, but then gained strength. "The King is in Southampton tonight, as you well know – "

"I know it, lord. Getting ready for the wars. My husband Pistol is with him."

"May he prove a good soldier."

I doubted he would, but didn't say so.

"What I mean to say, my dear lady," said Le Roi, "and may

I be damned to Hell if I lie, is that I am a close companion of the King, and I know his mind, and I swear to you that the King still loved Jack Falstaff, for all that he, in his office as king, could not keep such company. But he provided him with a purse to buy him drink and keep a roof over his head, and, most assuredly, the King wished the old man *no harm.*" Now he let go of me and began to saw the air with his hands, and pace about, like a hound on a leash, straining to run. Once his hood fell down, but I turned away, and he put it up quick. "What the King desires, more than anything in this world, is that Falstaff be avenged. Therefore Mistress Quickly, justify your name, and go quickly to all the other taverns in the neighborhood – and I have the King's word for it that there are many – and proclaim to all that Jack Falstaff is *alive* and has begun to recover his senses, and speaks in his feverishness certain names. God willing, this will frighten the murderer to coming here to finish his work, and we'll *have* him!"

I gaped in amazement.

"Will you do this, for sweet Jack Falstaff's sake?"

"Oh yes, lord! I will!"

And I went out, fast as I could, to every other tavern that was open that night. I told it to people in the street too, to anyone and everyone. "It's a miracle!" I shouted. "Jack Falstaff is alive!"

Oh, they laughed at me. They asked if Jack had changed his name to Lazarus. Somebody threw beer in my face and said I hadn't drunk enough yet. But I told the story, all excited and breathless like, of how Jack Falstaff had begun to recover from his illness – I didn't say from his poison, for that would have given the game away – and now he was back from Arthur's bosom after all and asking after some rogue who meant him harm.

"What rogue?" says they.

"It's just the fever. He's talking nonsense," says I, "but praise God, he is alive!"

When I was alone again, I cried bitter tears, wishing it were so, though I knew it was not.

And past midnight, when I'd cried and proclaimed my throat sore, and thought to drink a little sack myself for the soothing of it, I returned to my own house.

It was dark when I went in, Sir Le Roi was waiting at the foot of the stairs.

"Is it widely proclaimed?" says he.

"Aye."

"And well done," says he, and he went upstairs to hide behind the curtain.

I soothed my throat, and soothed it a bit more. I sat in the common room, soothing it, and perhaps I slept some, and dreamed of Sir John Falstaff and Prince Hal and the Devil all sitting around that table making merry, like in the old times.

Then there was a light and stealthy rapping at the door.

I took up my candle.

"Who is it?"

"A friend of Falstaff's. He wants to see me. Urgent."

I opened the door a crack. There was a big, ragged man outside, with an evil look to him, no friend of Sir John's that I ever knew.

"Is it true that Falstaff's upstairs and he's recovered?"

"It is, but he is weak and old, and cannot have visitors disturb his rest, so if you will just come back in the morning – "

I had to make myself convincing, for if I'd said, *Sure, come right up and see him*, when I was supposed to be harboring a sick man who'd almost died, the rogue would have smelled a rat, or the rat a rogue, or whichever.

Instead he shoved his shoulder against the door and came crashing in. Quick as a snake he caught me by the hair, gave a good yank, and had a dagger pointed at my throat.

"I think Sir John will see me now," says he.

"You're not his friend," says I.

"Maybe I lied. But he *will* see me. Lead on."

I didn't have to pretend to be afraid, because he could have butchered me like a sheep right there and found his way upstairs by himself, but I led on, and up we went, and he stood by Jack's bedside for just a moment and said, "Sir John Falstaff, Roger the Bear has come to settle an old score," and he plunges his dagger into poor Falstaff's dead heart.

Then I screamed and Sir Le Roi and Doctor Peake jumped out from behind the hanging sheet and there was some scuffling in the dark. Doctor Peake went to the window, threw open the shutters and shouted, but by then Le Roi had wrestled Roger the Bear to the floor and it was all over.

Le Roi's hood came off then and I saw his face clear in the moonlight, the shutters being open. Our eyes met. He seemed to be saying, without any words, *The King still loved Falstaff*. And I knew that it was true.

But I am sworn to say that the King was in Southampton that night, preparing for the war.

And that is all there is to tell, though I do not even know the ending, really, because the house was suddenly filled with armored men and they hauled Roger the Bear away all trussed up like they was hunters that had caught a bear indeed.

I heard someone say, "This is no conspiracy, but some trifling matter of an old insult."

And Sir Le Roi, Henry Le Roi, him that knew the King's mind so well, though the King was in Southampton, said, "My conscience is clear."

I can only tell you what I overheard, that Roger the Bear got his name from his sheer ugliness, though I suppose he was like a wild, murdering beast. He was but a common cut-purse and cut-throat, the low, evil sort of fellow Sir John sometimes kept company with, when it was his humor, and the more his grief it was.

I can tell you that it's the way of things, histories and the doings of kings sometimes all turn on little happenings, or nothing. We is but on this world for a little time, and the leaving of it can be just a chance, like somebody stumbles and hits his head, or there's an old grudge and Sir John dumped a cup of sack over Roger the Bear when he tried to collect some money Sir John owed. Sometimes the great is small and the small is great, all mixed up, and it doesn't mean anything at all.

Sure, no comet blazed for the passing of Falstaff.

The King was in Southampton that night, as all the world knows.

But I can tell you this, too: that as they dragged Roger the Bear down the stairs and out of my tavern, the armour Henry Le Roi wore beneath his cloak rattled like the thunder of a gathering storm, and just a little while later, that storm broke upon France.

Henry VI 🍎

A SERIOUS MATTER

Derek Wilson

The three plays that make up Shakespeare's study of the reign of Henry VI (and which are now rather boringly known as Part One, Part Two *and* Part Three*) are amongst the earliest of Shakespeare's works and may not all be entirely by his hand. Dating them has proved difficult and there is no reason to believe the three were written in sequence. In fact the second part, originally called* The First Part of the Contention, *a title that refers to the start of the Wars of the Roses between the houses of York and Lancaster, seems to have been in existence as early as 1590. Shakespeare then seems to have gone back to the start of Henry's reign with* The First Part of Henry VI, *first performed in March 1592, and finished the sequence with* The True Tragedy of Richard Duke of York *which was probably written soon after, and published in 1595. The third play ends with the death of Henry VI in 1471, in a final confrontation with Richard of Gloucester. But was Shakespeare's version of events correct? It is that which Derek Wilson explores here.*

GLOUCESTER: *I'll hence to London on a serious matter;*
Ere ye come hence be sure to hear some news.

CLARENCE: *What? What?*
GLOUCESTER: *The Tower! The Tower!*
        Shakespeare, *King Henry VI Part Three*, V, 5

In Dei nomine Amen. In the year of our Lord a thousand,
four hundred and seventy-six, on the Feast of St Michael and
All Angels [29 September], I Fra Michael de Hampton of the
Order of St Dominic set down this statement of events that
have recently occurred in this troubled Kingdom of England
as also in the lands of France and Anjou, calling upon Our
Lady with St Michael, my patron, and all the host of heaven
to bear witness that this account of my enquiry into the blessed
martyrdom of King Henry VI is true.

On the Feast of the Epiphany [6 January] in this same year,
as I performed my duties of prayer and instruction in the
Royal College of St Nicholas [King's College] in Cambridge,
there came to me, in secret, one from beyond the sea with a
message bidding me repair to the Lady Margaret of Anjou.
I obtained leave from my superior to make pilgrimage to
the shrine of St Martin of Tours, and so, with the Lady
Margaret's messenger for guide, made a stormy crossing
of the English Sea, traversed the lands of King Louis XI
and Renée, Duke of Anjou and came, at the beginning of
February, to the aged castle of Dampière on the banks of
the Loire.

As we approached along lanes whose frost-hardened ruts
made the horses stumble, our hoods drawn close about our
faces against the frozen wind, I could only reflect upon the
vanity of human pomp. The fortress, upthrust from the
lifeless fields like the broken, blackened tooth of a cadaver,
was topped by jagged battlements which proclaimed neglect.
No coloured standards flew proudly above the entrance
tower. Desolation spread its cloak over all. Thus are the
great humbled. I remembered the last time I had seen the
Lady Margaret – not "Lady" then but triumphant Queen
of England. I was in her entourage when she marched into
the town of St Albans at the head of a Lancastrian army
brandishing the spoils of victory. The people cheered, the
mayor and council prostrated themselves in the dust beneath

her charger's hooves and everyone who could fashion a red
rose out of cloth or parchment wore it on his breast. There,
for seven days, she held court in the name of King Henry.
It was in St Albans that I took my leave of their majesties
to follow a life of poverty and holy reflection. All that was
fifteen years ago. Now Henry was dead and his consort the
châtelaine of a semi-neglected castle which she occupied by
gracious favour of King Louis.

Our dinner that afternoon was not frugal by convent
standards but there were no delicacies such as sometimes
find their way to the lower hall from courtly tables and few
attendants were there to share it. Of the castle's mistress there
was no sign. The Lady Margaret, I was told, seldom ate with
the rest of her household. In fact, she led a solitary life withal.
After the meal she summoned me to her privy chamber.

The gloom of waning day had penetrated the room but no
lamps or candles were lit. Lady Margaret sat in a high-backed
chair drawn close to the fire. I made obeisance but she laughed
a cracked laugh and gestured to me to rise.

"Enough of that, Brother Michael. No man kneels to
me now."

As I rose and looked at her closely I saw how ill the passage of
time had used her. She was, by my reckoning, in her forty-first
year, but in the firelight she looked two decades older. Still
she had the erect posture of one used to command but the
body within the woollen dress was frail. Her cheeks and eye
sockets were hollows where deep shadows lurked.

She sensed my scrutiny. "Yes, Brother, I am no longer the
young woman with peachdown skin who sat in the orchard
listening to recitals of the lives of the saints and begging you
to read Signor Boccaccio instead. Now, books are my only
companions – books which tell tales of the death of kings."

"Madam . . ."

She seemed not to hear me. "In the olden days how often
you chided my frivolity and urged me to meditate on mortality.
You would find me a more apt pupil now. I think of death all
the time. Princesses are not born to penury, nor, like friars,
can we easily embrace it. My daily prayer is that God will
release me from this . . . empty . . . life."

"Say not so, madam . . ."

She ignored my protest. "But he tells me that there remains one service I must perform before he will grant my desire." For the first time she looked at me squarely. "And that is why I have sent for you, Brother. Come, sit here and warm yourself. Soon we can chatter of old times but first I must entrust you with a solemn mission."

I took my place on a low stool opposite the Lady Margaret and thankfully held my hands to the blazing logs. "Anything I can do for my queen I will readily do."

"And for your king?"

"Madam?"

She laughed at my bewilderment. "Oh I do not mean that swag-bellied lecher – I hear he has grown very fat – who calls himself Edward IV. Your true king."

"I say daily mass for his soul, madam."

"As you are bidden by the statutes of the college he founded."

"As I do in loving memory, madam. His majesty was very good to me."

"Good?" She sighed. "Yes, that is the best word for poor Henry. 'Henry the Good' – is that how men will remember him, I wonder?" She stared into the fire, muttering again more to herself than to me. "Good men make bad kings. Kings should be strong. Poor Henry; I had to be strong for him against the scheming rabble of Nevilles, Montagues, Mortimers and . . . They say miracles are performed at his shrine. Do you believe it, Brother Michael?"

"No doubt of it, madam. So many people flock to his tomb at Chertsey Abbey to invoke his blessings and healings that King Edward has forbidden all pilgrimage thither. Men and women have been thrown in prison for speaking of the cures wrought by the martyr. Why, madam, I could tell you wonderful stories . . ."

"Later, Brother, later. It is not of his spirit that we must speak but of his body – cowardly and brutally done to death."

The image flashed vividly into my mind. The catafalque in St Paul's, the King's corpse lying upon it with the face uncovered. I had kept tearful vigil beside it for many hours as it lay awaiting burial. "Dead from grief over the loss of his son in battle" – that was the official story. But grief does not bleed. I had seen the blood on the pillow beneath his head – and the confusion among the members of the royal guard when it was pointed out – and the hasty changing of the pillows.

Lady Margaret's voice broke into my sombre remembrance. "Find out who killed him, Brother Michael. That is the charge I lay upon you . . . that God lays upon you."

I looked up in alarm and saw her eyes staring at me with that majestic intensity that had once commanded ministers, humbled enemies and sent soldiers willingly to death. "Madam . . . I . . . it is commonly believed . . ."

"That Richard of Gloucester did the deed." She scoffed. "An easy scapegoat! Richard is dark and secretive. He lacks his brother's easy charm and has never courted the people. So he is not popular. That suits Edward very well. Whenever he has committed or ordered some shameful act that sets his subjects murmuring, he only needs to spread the rumour 'Gloucester: the culprit; the king knew nothing of this'."

"It is reported that Richard went to the Tower the night . . ."

"Aye, he and several others."

There was a silence of two paternosters' length disturbed only by the sounds of crackling flame and a rising wind beginning to howl in at the narrow casement.

"So," the Lady said at last, "you will do this thing; this last service for your king."

"You repose too much confidence in me, madam. The deed was done five years ago. To discover the truth now . . ."

"That is why I have chosen you, Brother Michael. No one has a keener mind or a deeper loyalty than you. Many men followed Henry and Margaret when our way lay downhill and across fresh-mown meadows. You were among the few who were still there on the forest tracks and the craggy mountain slopes. You will do this thing." Was it a statement or an order?

"It is a heavy and bloody business . . ."

"It is the business of justice."

"Suppose that I were able to find out . . . to discover some proof . . . what use would you make of the information?"

The lady glared with a measure of her old hauteur. "That concerns only me and such other faithful servants as I choose to instruct."

Though we talked together long after candles were lit, there was no further mention of the matter. When I left Dampière the next morning I had made no spoken promise to the Lady Margaret. There was no need.

Having prostrated myself before the relics of St Martin and besought his aid with my quest, I returned to England. The day after my arrival in London I called upon Father Bartholomew Mauclerc, a meeting I approached with dread. The priest is a likeable fellow – with, in truth, little enough of holiness to make him an austere shepherd of souls. It was the place where he and his flock lived that caused my feet to drag as I approached it.

A light, cold rain hung in the air as I emerged from the shelter of All Hallows. There, in the centre of the open space between city and Tower was the new, permanent gallows set up by our gracious sovereign, King Edward. Beyond it, masons and carpenters were working on the Bulwark, an additional fortification thrust across the moat from the fortress – symbol of further royal intrusion into the liberties of subjects. I had to clamber over a jumble of stone and timber in order to reach the main gate, where a surly guard demanded a penny before he would send word to Father Bartholomew of my arrival.

The stocky little priest greeted me warmly, announcing what a pleasant surprise it was to see an old friend after so many years. We had, in fact, never been more than acquaintances but it suited me to encourage his familiarity. It would soon enough be put to the test when he learned of the reason for my visit. We went to the alehouse within the inner gate and swapped gossip about court and university.

At last I approached the purpose of my coming thither. "Barty, you know of my devotion to our late master."

"Yes." He looked at me warily over the rim of his beaker.

"All of us in Henry's college are bidden to pray daily for the repose of his soul."

"As do I," Father Bartholomew observed, crossing himself.

"Many of our students ask me about the old King. The young know little, eh?"

He nodded. "I am sure you can satisfy their curiosity. You were closer to poor Henry than most men."

"Aye, but not at the end. I never visited him here in his last months. I did come to London in hope to see him five years ago – and arrived too late."

"Ah, yes, the end was very sudden. When he heard of the death of the Prince it broke his heart."

"So I believe. It grieves me that I could not reach him in time to offer spiritual comfort. But I am sure you urged upon him the consolation of religion."

He nodded emphatically. "Aye, he made a good end, well shriven." The man drained his beaker and could not meet my eye.

"I would consider it a great boon to see the chamber where Henry spent his last days – the Wakefield Tower, was it not?"

My "friend's" attitude changed abruptly. "Why would you want to go there?" he gasped.

"The better to inform my prayers and those of my students."

He lowered his voice and leaned forward across the table. "I cannot help you with that – and you were well advised not to pursue the matter. The King . . ."

"Has nothing to fear from an aged friar. What harm can it do to satisfy my holy curiosity?"

The priest frowned. "Wakefield is occupied."

"Even so? By whom?"

"By a truculent Lancastrian nobleman who will not make his peace with the King and so must soon make it with God."

"Perhaps together we may persuade him from his treacherous stubbornness."

It took every argument I could summon but, at last, I overcame Father Bartholomew's very obvious fear. We left the inn and he hurried me almost furtively the few yards to the base of the round tower opposite the watergate. The priest held a rapid conversation with the jailer who came to the door. The fellow, whose leather jerkin stretched tightly over a well-filled belly, shrugged and led the way to an inner staircase. On the first floor he opened a heavy door and, when the three of us had passed into the room beyond, he turned the key in the lock behind us.

The chamber was high-ceilinged and paintings of St George, St Catherine and St Nicholas decorated its curved wall. It was sparsely but adequately furnished with bed, table, chairs and a large wooden coffer. A small arbour set in the thickness of the wall held a small altar and a statue of the Virgin. This, then, was the narrow world in which King Henry had been confined for his last months. It was but yards from the palace buildings where he and his court had lived in royal splendour – where now wanton Edward frequently cavorted with his whores, flatterers and cronies.

Father Bartholomew busied himself with the occupant of the prison, a young man in once-fine clothes, who either would not or could not rise from his truckle bed. Torture bruises were very obvious on his bare arms. When I had seen all there was to see – which, in truth, was very little – I stepped across to the doorway to talk with the jailer.

"This is a responsible job you have, friend."

He sniffed and spat on the floor rushes which were grey and brittle and obviously had not been changed for months. "Bred to it, Brother. I come from an old Tower family."

"Then you have seen many sad and merry comings and goings over the years."

"It's all one to me. I'm like the Tower itself. I just stand here and watch fine ladies and gentlemen rise and fall. One day over there." He nodded in the general direction of the palace. "Feasting on venison, capon pasties, fresh pike, jellies and I know not what all. The next delivered to me and grateful for any crusts and scraps I can sell them."

"Better, then, to be a humble jailer or friar than a nobleman or king."

"Aye, Brother, true enough, true enough. You talk of kings,

well 'twas in this very chamber the old King died. I'll warrant you knew not that."

I feigned astonishment. "Here? In this very room? Where exactly did you find his body?"

He shook his head. "Not I, Brother. My father, that died of the sweat two years' since, he had charge of Wakefield then. Though, in truth, he never saw Mad Henry's body neither."

"How so, if he was in charge?"

"We was all given a feast that night – all the Tower servants. Roast meat and ale flowing free – by order of the King, to celebrate his victory at Tewkesbury."

"The King was here, then?"

"No, he was celebrating at Westminster."

"Richard of Gloucester, then, was here?"

I saw from the man's suspicious frown that I had pressed too far. "You show strange interest in old stories, Brother."

"I am curious by nature – I confess it. There are so many rumours abroad about the old King's death and I am glad to learn the truth of it. I deplore unchristian gossip."

There was a groan from the far side of the room. As I looked across I saw the prisoner roll over on the bed to face the wall. Father Bartholomew turned from him and I knew my chance to discover anything from the jailer had gone. I tried one last question. "What do people say here in the Tower about King Henry's death?"

"Nothing! We know better than to speak of these things," the man muttered curtly. "Anyway, one king's as good as another and we had a more important death to worry about. Finished, Father?"

"Aye, there's no helping the fellow," the priest said.

Whereupon the jailer unlocked the door and showed us out.

As we walked back towards the main gate I asked Father Bartholomew what the jailer had meant by "another death". He shrugged and shook his head. "I know not. Some relative perhaps."

"I suppose most of his family is here in the Tower."

"Yes, almost all the people who work here are intermarried.

They . . . we . . . are a very close community. We are not loved by Londoners, nor by any who fear what happens within these walls. So we have learned to be cautious of others – especially of people who come among us asking questions. I know not what your purpose here is, old friend, but I assure you you will learn nothing from the people of the Tower. What I will tell you is that on the night of King Henry's death the palace apartments were locked up. There was no one here from the court. The King, his brothers, the Woodville clan – all were at Westminster. While they celebrated the death of Henry's son, the end of his line, he, poor sad soul, pined and died."

We had reached the outer gate. As Father Bartholomew grasped my hand I acknowledged that he was right. The Tower keeps its secrets. I thanked the priest for his time and was turning away when he said "The Constable's man . . . Plowland . . . Dick Plowland."

"I do not . . ."

"It was Dick Plowland, Tom, the jailer's, cousin . . . I remember now. He was the one who died that same night . . . fell from Tower Wharf in a drunken stupor . . . making too free with the King's ale."

We said goodbye and the next morning I began my journey north with a heavy heart. Gladly would I have unvowed the silent vow made to the Lady Margaret. There seemed no chance of completing my commission for her. Yet I had promised and only when I had tried every possible source of information could I absolve myself. Thus I had to make the long journey to Northumberland to see a man bearing the fatal name of Neville.

There were only a few of the Kingmaker's clansmen and supporters who had survived the Yorkist triumph. One was George Neville, the earl's brother and Archbishop of York. He had been Henry's keeper during the last few months and shared the old King's imprisonment in the Tower when London fell to Edward. Though eventually pardoned, he kept himself well away from the court. I had a slight acquaintance with his grace but doubted whether that would gain me an audience. However, for the sake of my vow, I had to try.

Divine favour blessed my journey with sunny days and good roads. So I came in good time to the remote manor of Blyth at the end of April. As I approached the Archbishop's gatehouse I was prepared to argue my way in but as soon as news of my arrival was sent to his grace word came back that I was to be admitted. To my surprise I was conveyed directly to the Archbishop's bedchamber. A sad sight greeted me there.

The darkened room reeked of incense. Around the large canopied bed was a cluster of priests and physicians ministering to the pallied figure who lay upon the pillows. Archbishop Neville was weak and harrowed nigh unto death. Yet his mind had lost no vigour for he saw me as soon as I entered and whispered to a page who came to bring me to the bedside. I knelt and kissed the ring which was loose upon the shrivelled hand clutching feebly at the counterpane.

The sick man spoke in a rasping whisper. "I recognize you, Brother Michael. It is kind of you to come all the way from Cambridge to visit a dying man. All our other old friends keep their distance."

"Your grace, I am sorry to find you like this."

"You should not grieve at my imminent release from the pains of this life. But . . ." His body was shaken by a spasm of coughing. Two attendants helped him to sit up. One held a pewter vessel to catch the discoloured sputum. The other applied a damp napkin to the Archbishop's face. When he had recovered, he looked at me again. "You see how little time there is, Brother. We must talk quickly of the subject that brings you here – the death of our late sovereign."

I was shaken. "Your grace, how could you . . ."

"Dying men are often given the gift of prophecy." He looked around the circle of anxious faces. "Now, all of you go. Leave us. Brother Michael and I have private matters to discuss."

After the others had withdrawn, the Archbishop looked at me imploringly. "Tell me, Brother, these stories of miracles; do you believe them?"

"Some seem well attested, your grace."

"So I think, also." He moaned and closed his eyes. "Then I have murdered one of God's saints and, of all men, stand in need of your prayers."

"*You* murdered . . .? I cannot believe . . ."

He frowned impatiently. "Listen, Brother, and do not interrupt. I must tell you what I can before the coughing comes upon me again. At the end of 1470, when my brother drove Edward of York out of the capital, he brought King Henry from the Tower and placed him in my charge. For five months he was my guest in my palace in London. God forgive me, I took him for a shuffling simpleton, frightened even of his own freedom. To my blinded eyes there was no evidence of holiness."

His brow was moist with the sweat of anxiety. I pressed one of the damp cloths to it. But he went on, ignoring my ministrations.

"In March my brother took his army into the Midlands to face Edward. I was left as the main buttress of Henry's authority. I tried to maintain the people's respect for him. I *did* try." He looked at me appealingly. "I paraded the King through the streets. I ordered the Lord Mayor to keep the gates of the city closed against Edward. But the citizens were in no mood to risk lives and property for Henry and I could scarcely blame them. Men say that I should have put up more resistance but when Edward's host reached St Albans I knew they could not be stopped. I should have got the King away to safety, but coward that I was, I surrendered him into Edward's hands. I surrendered him to his death."

"If Henry was murdered on Edward's orders you cannot blame yourself."

The emaciated hand fluttered impatiently. "I have not yet told all. I knew Edward would return his rival to the Tower. I had made . . . arrangements . . . for his safe custody. My brother had appointed a new Constable of the Tower."

"Baron Dudley?"

"Aye, John Dudley, an old and trusted servant of the Lancastrian cause."

"But one who had made his peace with the Yorkists."

"He is a powerful lord. He was trusted and needed by both sides. Edward was sure to retain him in charge of the Tower. I knew that Dudley would be able to prevent harm befalling Henry. Alas, I was wrong."

"What then happened to Henry?"

"We were both lodged – separately of course – in the Tower. I visited his majesty daily. He was in good spirits. In that small chamber he felt secure. He had no worries, no concerns of state, no decisions to make. It was I who broke to him the news of his son's death. He seemed not very distressed. I am not sure that he knew who I was talking of. I sent reports to the Constable through his man in the Tower."

"Was that Dick Plowland?"

"I do not recall the fellow's name. He was just a messenger. He brought Dudley's orders from the court and made sure that Henry was provided with every possible comfort. I thought that in time the old King would be allowed to go into exile with his wife. But . . ."

Tremors began to shake the Archbishop's body, heralding another coughing fit. He clamped his eyes tight shut and I watched him make a great effort to prevent the spasm.

At last he was able to continue. "On 21 May they made a feast in the Tower by order of the King. While everyone was busy eating and drinking someone entered poor Henry's lodging and bludgeoned him to death – God rest his soul."

"But who?" I tried not to shout in my eagerness.

"What does the name matter? It was I who put him at the assassin's mercy. I told the Constable as much. He came immediately he heard the news, furious that his reputation had been damaged because a royal prisoner in his care had been done to death. He questioned everyone in the Tower. If he learned the murderer's identity he said nothing to me. He simply conveyed Edward's order that everyone was to say the old King had made a quiet, Christian end."

"He must have been angry also about the death of Dick Plowland, his messenger."

"Was that the lad who was drowned? I doubt that concerned him much."

The Archbishop was tiring and the words came now with difficulty. I stood up to take my leave. "You must rest, your grace. It has been extremely kind of you to see me."

His eyelids were flickering. "Promise me . . . your prayers . . . Brothers."

"Of course, your grace, and I beseech you not to reproach yourself." I doubt whether he heard my last words.

I returned here to Cambridge where, in the middle of June, news arrived of Archbishop Neville's death. I have been true to my promise to pray for him. He was a good man, more fitted for church or university than for court or council chamber. He was as open and uncomplicated as his brother was scheming and devious. The Archbishop believed the best of all men and that faith finally broke him.

As for my voyage of discovery, it had but one more port of call. I hesitated long about making it. Lord Dudley is an important man, a member of the King's council and often abroad on foreign embassies. Constable of the Tower of London is just one of his many offices. I doubted greatly that he would make time to talk with me. Perhaps there was nothing that he could tell me. The more I thought about the night of 21–22 May 1471 the more likely it seemed that only Dick Plowland had known the truth. I found it difficult to accept the coincidence of his supposed accident within hours of King Henry's death. Was it not more likely that he had been silenced before he could report to his master?

Deterred by all these doubts it was not until St Thomas's Day [3 July] that I wrote to Baron Dudley, begging him, for the love he once bore King Henry and Queen Margaret, to grant me audience. But two days since I received a reply. His lordship is to keep the Michaelmas feast in Cambridge and will be graciously pleased to receive me. Thus, I look to know within hours all that can be known about the death of the blessed martyr, King Henry.

Editor's note

This manuscript, which recently came to light among the muniments of King's College, Cambridge, ends at this point. Search among college records has produced but a few references to Fra Michael de Hampton. It seems that he was a master of arts and a senior of King's from 1467 to 1476. What is interesting is that his academic career came to a sudden end, for the last reference to him informs us that "he was drowned in the River Cam on the Feast of St Michael and All Angels in the year of Our Lord one thousand, four hundred and seventy-six."

A SHADOW THAT DIES

Mary Reed and Eric Mayer

The Tragedy of King Richard the Third was the sequel to The True Tragedy of Richard Duke of York and was probably completed around 1593. It describes the events from the death of Henry VI in 1471 and the succession of Edward IV, through to Richard III's rise to power and his death at the Battle of Bosworth. Shakespeare's portrayal of the hunch-backed villainous King Richard has remained our image ever since, regardless of its veracity. Amongst Richard III's most notorious alleged crimes was the death of his nephews, the famous Princes in the Tower. In the following story, Richard reflects over the events and seeks to solve their murder himself.

"A dream. That's all. Look, the damp earth of Bosworth Field lies undisturbed at the entrance to my tent. Had these midnight accusers trod upon other than my imagination the mud would be churned as if by the passage of an army.

"Yet it did seem my departed brother Clarence returned. And the Lords Hastings and Buckingham. My poor wife, Lady Anne. Even the young princes, my nephews. And others.

All accusing me, as if Richard, single-handed, had populated the Kingdom of Heaven. All of them bidding me to fall this coming day to the sword of my foe Richmond.

"No. Nothing but a dream. The candles burn brighter now, golden and mortal, yet I thought, when I woke, they glared cold and blue, such as the lights travelers see betimes in northern skies. Curtains of God, I have heard those lights called by the superstitious. Do they not also whisper that, when the spirits of the departed are abroad, lights burn blue?

"But why then would my nephews appear among my accusers? Even they think me a villain? When it was I who delivered them from the Tower? Should they hate me for keeping them there for their own safety? Their father the King had already been murdered. I promised them it would be no more than a day or two, and wasn't I as good as my word?

"I can understand how some might have misunderstood my words to Sir James Tyrrel, when I asked him to deal with my two enemies in the Tower, before drawing him near to whisper him my instructions. I was speaking for a shadow. Is it here, even now, that shadow? Yes. The candle trembles at its cool breath.

"What was I saying? Tyrrel reported the butchery had been done by those bloody dogs, Dighton and Forrest, though Forrest wavered when he saw how innocent they were, those sleeping babes.

"But didn't Tyrrel tell me that he had seen the princes dead, and that the chaplain of the Tower had buried them, though he knew not where? Do you hear, shadow? He saw them dead.

"Have I said I am a villain? I am not. I lie. Yet, there is a murderer here. You are here, aren't you?

"If I die on the battlefield, will no soul pity me?

"But, courage, Richard. Are you to be unmanned by wine-dreams on this very eve of victory? Curses, omens, are these not only phantom shadows woven from the fabric of our dreams? And yet, did not such nonsensical fripperies serve their place in all your schemings, twisting those trusting hearts with horror?

"Remember when our brother, the Duke of Clarence, unwittingly gave us this weapon, when he told me – on his way to the Tower! – that the King heeds such omens? And didn't the King act upon them, imprisoning his brother, our brother, because his Christian name is George? And why, because a drunken soothsayer said 'G' would be the initial of the man who would depose him. Is it not a marvel that an illiterate peasant's drunken ramblings would set state affairs on such to path to bloodshed?

"But, my brother, we alone know the truth of it, do we not? For who would dare to think that poor, lame, twisted Richard, the prince with less than a beggar's form, had in him the iron soul of true kings? Hunchback Dickon, they all called me in their dark corners, hardly bothering to lower their voices. And your sweet poisonous words, dropped in the ears of royal advisers at frolic in the stews – a masterly masquerade it was. Who among that band of noble fools would dream to suspect the pronouncements of a squat parody of a man – less of a man even than I – acting out the loyal subject and telling everyone about his troubling night visions? The jackanapes hardly stopped fondling the wenches!

"I see you are surprised. Did you not see me in the alehouse shadows? Oh, there was no danger, little possibility of discovery, for I stood straight and tall, watching my plot – our plot – set in motion. I have since heard slanders abroad in which I see your cunning touch. To persuade the king to execute that miserable toad of a publican, the bloated owner of the Crown, because the fool proclaims, in his cups, how his son would be heir to the Crown! But I soon realized this was calculated not only to rouse the rabble's passions, but also to protect me, had I been recognized while you were spreading poison in the guise of a drunken fortune teller. A masterly stroke.

"It is passing strange how often people will pay more heed to ill omens if the prophet is deformed. Yet all my life there have been none who would accept ought I said as true, or love me without fear. Not my nephews, the princes, who owe their very lives to me. Not even the Lady Anne, my reluctant bride, so lately gone from us.

"I thought of marrying only to protect her. She called me a devil. I told her I did not kill her husband, but she refused to believe the truth. So I admitted I had helped send him to a better world, thinking to gain some credit for my honesty. Of course, I could not explain how unwitting my help had been.

"I think her heart was not in the marriage. And, then, when you told me she was ill ... but am I to be held accountable for fate? It is true I feared she might betray me, once she discovered how I was formed, but marital beds conceal more than one secret, and tapers can be quenched before passion is slaked. And may priestly tapers shine on that upstart dog Richmond's coffin before too long!

"But I see you smile, my brother. Your thoughts run in similar channels to mine, perhaps? After all, more than one marital bed conceals a secret. That was why our own mother, proud Duchess of York, came to despise us both, her supposed blessing not completely formed, like you and I. Had we been as fair of limb and face as our siblings perhaps we might have been allowed more, instead of being the butt of jests, and half-concealed whispering.

"You suffered the most, being even more ill-favoured than I, and made into the court jester, forced to conceal our proud lineage. Oh, it rankled, I know. And yet ... and yet, having mightily considered it this long night, it comes to me that perhaps truth is spoken in scandal as well as in jest, or indeed curses. But we are stronger than all three. All the curses laid upon our heads, Medusa-like, would make the common herd knock knees and wither away in a fortnight.

"Well, I am already partly withered, it is true, but when I revealed to my minion Buckingham that our paternity was not as the world knew, but that we were in reality sons of the King, then did our mother reap the bitter harvest she and he had sown while our father was at war. He believed me. Mayhap it was the persuasive evidence of my withered arm, pointing to truth.

"Oh yes, of course, we knew it was a lie, a foul slander, but a necessary evil, mother or not. And after all, we suffer, rotting fruit, living, alas, in bodies as twisted as the olive tree, yet with none of its peace. There can never be olive-branches between our mother and us, for to acknowledge, however begrudgingly, the unfinished but more complete son, and ignore the other, denying maternity – yes, yes, we have often talked of suitable punishments for our proud mother, when we are kings.

"When we rule I will send mirrors into exile. Ours will be a kingdom without reflection. Still, though mirrors are banished from my own residence, I see my stooped form in those who cringe at the sight of me.

"You were always the stronger spirit, were you not, my brother? When I saw you humiliated, your very life denied, I promised you – my flesh and blood – the use of this body of mine, poor thing that it is. And you promised we would rule together. When King Edward died, I thought fate, for once, had allied herself with justice. But was it fate? Then there was Clarence. I should have known what you intended. I should never have assisted you. But, when it was done, you swore to me his death would be the last.

"My Anne . . . you brought me the news that she was ill. It was so sudden. She was ill, wasn't she, brother?

"And then you told me the princes were threatening our plans.

"But dawn approaches, I see the field of battle revealing itself, emerging from a mist as cold as the kiss of a succubus – enough to sap a man's courage. I have played the part you wrote for me. I am an actor, not a villain. Go, now. Play your own part. Act the slave one last time. Prepare my weapons. Caparison my horse.

"You vanish so quickly, as if you were never here. Like a shadow that dies when the sun is at its zenith. When we rule I will bring forth the proof of my innocence, those two young innocents, the princes.

"Did I not arrange it all with Tyrrel? For after I blustered and bid him rid me of my enemies in the tower, never knowing what shadow might be eavesdropping, did I not whisper to him my true instructions? 'You'll see they are well taken care of,' I told him. 'Only let me hear you report them as dead.' For their own safety, I meant. Was I not plain enough? And the evidence is that he carried out my wishes and spared the boys. Why else would he claim not to know where they were buried?

"Could he have misunderstood, and in truth engaged those two murderers Dighton and Forrest to do the deed?

"Wait. Is that the wind brushing the sides of my tent? Are you back so soon, my brother? What's that you say?

"Let no man whisper that Richard and his brother Gloucester were base cowards and would not bloody their own hands. Were we not quick to act when those assassins Dighton and Forrest pitied the babes?

"What do you mean, Tyrrel's report was only partly true, that the villains fled, leaving our work undone. Surely not.

"Yes, we did hurry to the Tower, you riding under my cloak as always. Who would notice another deformity on one as ill favored as I? I am scarce half a man, and you even less. But together, we will make a king.

"You said you wanted to see that the boys were . . . gone. I distracted the jailer with princely demands after you clambered down off my shoulder, crept from beneath my cloak and made your way to their empty cell.

"How can you say it wasn't empty? How can you say you found the princes where the cowardly villains had left them, and smothered them?

"But the cocks are trumpeting and through the mist I can see a ghostly sun surmount the horizon.

"Detestable creature! Only one of us will live to see the sunset. I will cut you loose, shadow brother, before we ever engage in battle.

"The candle is blue and guttering. The air feels cold. Brother, come, climb up on my back, and I shall shroud you in my cloak, just as I always do when great deeds are to be wrought. But soon enough, oh, yes, soon enough, when we rule, all the realm will see you by light of day.

"You have honed my sword, then? And seen my saddle tightly cinched? For on this battlefield to be unhorsed would mean certain death."

MOTHER OF ROME

Molly Brown

In addition to his standard sequence of historical plays, several of Shakespeare's tragedies also make use of historical characters and settings, though Shakespeare's understanding of some of these more distant times is uncertain to say the least. Coriolanus, though one of Shakespeare's later plays, written about 1608, and the last where he used a Roman setting, is nevertheless the earliest in his Roman sequence. It takes place in the fifth century BC (around the year 493 BC) in the early years of the Roman republic. In this dawn time of Roman expansion Rome's closest enemies were the Volsci, who lived south of Rome in the towns of Antium and Corioli. Caius Marcius, one of Rome's patricians, helped defeat the Volsci and thereafter he was given the nickname of Coriolanus. From hero he rapidly turns into villain. Rome is struck by famine and Coriolanus refuses to distribute corn to the starving plebeians. This leads to a confrontation between Coriolanus and the Tribunes which results in Coriolanus deserting Rome. He joins forces with his old enemy, Tullus Aufidius, the Volscian general, and leads an army against Rome. He spares the city only after a confrontation with his mother, Volumnia. This is seen as a betrayal by the Volscians and Coriolanus is killed. There the play ends and the following story begins.

*   *   *

I stormed through the streets of Antium in a fury. Coming upon the house, I kicked the door to the ground, roaring the murderer's name: "Aufidius!"

No one answered my summons; no servants came running. The house was dark and silent. I strode forward into the gloom, the fact there was no one to resist me only increasing my rage. "Aufidius!"

I searched from room to room until at last I came upon a solitary figure, slumped on a couch in front of the fire, an empty cup on the table beside him, an overturned jug on the floor. He raised his head slowly, squinting at the doorway where I stood. "So the news has reached Rome, at last. I have been waiting for you. Or someone like you. Your name, soldier?"

"Titus Lartius."

"Titus Lartius," he repeated, leaning back to rest his head. "I have heard of you, Lartius. Caius Marcius spoke of your courage, a quality he too often found wanting among the Romans, I believe."

"Dare you speak to me of Marcius?" I crossed the room in two strides, raising my sword to his throat. Tullus Aufidius made no move, merely looked at me, his face wan and tired.

"You hesitate," he said. "Why?"

I shook my head in disgust. I had come to kill the general of the Volscians, the warrior Marcius had described as a lion he was proud to hunt, not some haggard slug who would not even rise to defend himself. I lowered my sword.

"I remember the night Marcius came to me," he said. "It was here, in this very room. I did not recognize him at first. Then he unwrapped his cloak, revealing the face of him I hated more than any in the world. He said he had no care to save his life, or he would never have come to me, his sworn enemy. Then – I remember it so well – he sat himself down before me, threw back his head and offered me his throat . . .

or his service. I chose to take his service, a decision I shall regret until my dying moment. Now, Titus Lartius, I do not offer you my service, but I offer you my throat. I advise you to take it." He lay motionless upon his couch, waiting.

Once more I raised my sword and once more, I lowered it. "I am a soldier, not an executioner."

He rose up from the couch, sighing. "If your honour demands it, then I will die standing, my sword in my hand."

This did not make sense. Tullus Aufidius did not speak of fighting, only of dying. I watched dumbfounded as he picked up his sword, then placed himself before me, the hand which held the blade hanging loosely at his side. In the dim light of the fire I thought I saw a look of pleading in his eyes. He *wanted* me to kill him, "What is this?" I asked him.

"I saw to it that Caius Marcius was buried with every honour, with arms and jewels and a stone tablet listing his ancestry and his accomplishments. All I ask in return is: let me have a soldier's death. Let it be known that I died at the hands of a man skilled in battle. Let it be known that I died with honour."

My fist tightened round the handle of my sword. How dare this cur speak of honour! He who had murdered my friend in cold blood! I raised my hand to strike, then stopped, a series of memories flooding into my mind.

I had gone to visit the lady Volumnia the morning after she re-entered Rome in triumph, having succeeded where all others had failed, in persuading her son to make peace and spare the city.

I had met the lady before, many times – the first being seventeen long years ago, soon after the first campaign in which Marcius and I served together, fighting for the republic against the ousted King Tarquin. I was then a young man of twenty, hardened – I thought – by service in previous battles, while Marcius was barely turned sixteen. They said he had been raised alone by his widowed mother, and his large eyes and curved lips seemed more suited to the face of a woman than a man. This was no soldier, I told myself on first seeing him within my ranks, but a mere pretty boy who will flee at the first sound of alarum.

I could not have been more wrong. Never in my life did I see such a one born for killing. There was no fear in him and no pity. He strode across the field trampling on the dead and dying as he chopped and sliced, oblivious to screams and burbling death rattles, his sword dripping the blood of all who fell before him. For this he was crowned with the oaken garland.

I accompanied him to his mother's house on our return to Rome. Volumnia was in those days only a year or two over thirty, with black hair and gleaming dark eyes. As mother and son faced each other, I was struck by the resemblance between them, as if one person had been split into two halves, male and female.

"Oh my brave boy, my brave and honoured boy," Volumnia exclaimed, embracing Marcius. Then I remember her examining his injuries. "Mark this one," she said, finding a deep gash on his left thigh. "This one must surely leave a scar – a useful testament in years to come."

Marcius looked up at the ceiling as she cooed and fussed over each and every wound. "Mother, please."

Volumnia finally turned her attention to me, though only to ask if, in my opinion, her son had the makings of a soldier.

"He has a fierceness in battle unlike any I have ever seen," I answered truthfully.

She laughed and clapped her hands. "That's *me* in him. He got that fierceness from me; he sucked it as an infant from my breast."

Marcius was by now staring at the floor, his face burning red. "Mother . . ."

"If I had been a man, I would have earned my own glory," Volumnia went on, "but as the gods made me a woman, I must be content with the honour accorded my child. And great honour he will bring me, I know it." She grabbed Marcius by the waist, pulled him close and kissed him on the lips.

I looked down at my feet, feeling like an intruder. "I must be going," I said.

"Nonsense," Volumnia said. I looked up to see mother and son facing me, their hands intertwined. "You shall join us for a feast tonight, to celebrate the victory you have won for Rome."

I was about to thank her when Marcius said, "Not victory for Rome, Mother, but for you. For you are all Rome to me."

When I first heard those words, it never occurred to me that seventeen years later plebeians and patricians alike would be united in saying the same. Yet on the morning I went to pay my respects to Volumnia, I passed a crowd gathered in the marketplace, cheering her as "Mother of Rome", until one man among them shouted, "No, more than that. Volumnia *is* Rome!"

"Yes, yes!" another shouted. "Volumnia is Rome!"

They were all at it after that.

It was only a few minutes' walk from the market to the house where Caius Marcius had dwelt with his mother. A servant conducted me into the room where Volumnia received visitors.

I was amazed by her appearance. She looked younger than she had in years. The lines of care and worry that had been so pronounced during the period of her son's disgrace had vanished. She wore a bright red stola fastened with golden clasps, her face and lips were painted, her hair twisted into a cascade of ringlets.

"Titus Lartius," she exclaimed as I bowed to her from the doorway. "Sweet Titus, how good of you to come."

We spent several moments in polite conversation, I expressing my gratitude and admiration for what she had done, she telling me of the many prominent visitors she had had and the promises they had made. "The senate have agreed as one: they are going to build a temple," she said, "to whichever god I choose. And a statue!"

"And what news of your son?" I asked her.

The sudden harshness of her expression shocked me. "Gone with the Volscians, I expect. His allegiance is to them now, and we'll see no more of him in Rome."

"I am sorry to hear it. I had hoped . . . I mean . . ." I found myself sweating under the woman's hard gaze, not knowing what to say.

She must have noted my discomfort, for her expression softened. "The people may cheer me in the streets, they may pay for temples and statues, but they will never grant my one most dearly held wish: to repeal the unjust banishment of my only child."

"I am sorry," I said.

"It is a sorrow I will bear to my grave. But thank the gods I have my grandson. I tell you, Titus, I have such plans for that child. His shall be a greater name than his father's ever was."

"And how does Virgilia fare?" I asked, enquiring after Marcius's young wife.

"Unwell," Volumnia replied. "She has taken to her bed with a fever and is too ill to see anyone."

Virgilia had been well enough to travel to the Volscian camp the day before. Though the delegation that had gone to plead with Marcius had also consisted of his wife, his son, and the gentlewoman Valeria, Volumnia's was the only name being cheered in the streets. I couldn't help wondering how much Virgilia's illness owed to her mother-in-law's new fame. "I pray she may recover soon," I said.

"As do I, Titus. As do I." Her expression changed to one of annoyance. "Yes?"

I turned to see a servant enter, apologetically bending forward to whisper in his mistress's ear.

Volumnia rose and begged my pardon as she must attend to an urgent household matter. I said I would take my leave of her, but she insisted I stay. "I will only be a moment, and I should like to speak to you further. I hope you don't mind me saying this, but now Marcius is gone away, I look to you as another son."

"Then I will gladly wait."

I hadn't been alone more than a minute when I thought I heard someone screaming. I hurried along the corridor towards the source of the sound, then stopped beside a window looking out upon the atrium. In the middle of the courtyard, a small boy was laughing as he chased a large yellow butterfly. I shook my head to think I could mistake a child's laughter for a shriek of fear.

I recognized the boy at once – it was Marcius's son. He was a fine-looking boy, with sparkling eyes and a mop of dark curls. My mind wandered briefly to thoughts of his mother, Virgilia, lying alone in a bed somewhere within these walls. I forced myself to concentrate on the boy. I couldn't help smiling at the way he squealed with pleasure as he caught the flapping insect in his chubby little hands. The smile faded from my lips as I watched him rip its brightly coloured wings to shreds, screeching the word "die", over and over.

I turned at the sound of footsteps and saw Volumnia walking towards me. She stood beside me at the window, gazing fondly at the boy. "Thanks be to the gods, Titus. I have been given a second chance to mould a child and this time I will not make the same mistakes. I will teach my grandson more than strength of the body; I will teach him cunning, the one trait my darling son lacked. My poor boy was too direct, Titus; he could never grasp the concept of expediency." She turned to face me. "That's something *you* have no trouble with, I'll wager."

Before I realized what I was doing, I found I had taken a step backwards. "I'm not sure I know what you mean."

"Don't you?" She smiled and patted me on the arm as if I was a child. "Now, there is something I would like you to do for me."

The senator Menenius Agrippa greeted me cordially enough, but the old man looked weary and ill. I explained that Volumnia had asked me to call upon him; she had heard nothing from him for days and was concerned for his well-being. "She asked me to tell you that of all her friends, you are the one she longs to see more than any other."

Agrippa gestured for the servant who had poured us each a cup of wine to leave the room. We sat facing each other on carved stools, the flickering light of an oil lamp creating strange shadows in the folds of the senator's toga. "I do not wish to see her," he said at last, his voice trembling slightly.

I wrinkled my brow, confused. Menenius Agrippa was an old family friend of the Marcii. When Volumnia's husband died, the senator became like a second father to the infant Caius Marcius, doting on the boy as if he was his own flesh and blood. Because of his close relationship to Marcius, Menenius Agrippa had been one of the first to enter the Volscian camp to plead for Rome. He had said little upon his return, only that Marcius was now as different from the boy he had known as a moth from a caterpillar.

I wondered if it was possible that the old man might be jealous of a woman's accomplishment where he, a senator of Rome, had failed, but I could hardly believe that was likely. Menenius Agrippa had been every bit as devoted to Volumnia as he was to her son. "I don't understand," I said.

He sighed. "How can I resist a summons from the Mother of Rome? Tell the good lady I will call upon her soon. Now, if you will excuse me, I am very tired."

As I stood to leave, the old man grabbed hold of my arm. "I could almost pity the Volscian general, you know."

"Pity Aufidius? Why?"

"It does not matter. Just promise me this: remember Caius Marcius as Coriolanus. Remember him as he was, not as he became."

Three days later, news reached Rome of Caius Marcius's death at the hands of Tullus Aufidius.

The Volscian stood motionless before me, willing me to end his life. This was not what I expected; it did not seem right.

"What happened to Caius Marcius Coriolanus?" I demanded. "How did he die?"

"You know how he died or you would not be here."

"I want to hear it from you!"

"I alone was responsible for his death. I killed him." In the dim glow of the hearth-light I saw his eyes dart to one side, unable or unwilling to meet my gaze. He was lying.

"I was there when Caius Marcius took the city of Corioli single-handed. It was my testimony that earned him his third name of Coriolanus. How many times did Marcius vanquish you in the field? How many times?"

The Volscian's eyes flashed briefly, but he said nothing.

"You could never defeat him in battle and I do not believe you could have killed him."

"I could have," Aufidius shouted, "and I did! He betrayed my trust and the cause of the Volscian people, and in my wrath, I came upon him unawares and murdered him for the traitor he was."

"Menenius Agrippa said he could almost pity you. Why is that, Tullus? Why should you deserve an old man's pity?"

"Enough!" Aufidius screamed, raising his sword. We fought for a minute or two, but the Volscian's heart wasn't in it and I soon had him backed against a wall, my blade once more to his throat.

"You didn't kill Coriolanus, did you? What really happened to Caius Marcius?" I demanded. "Why are you so willing to take the blame for his death? Who are you protecting?"

Aufidius spat in my face. "Kill me."

I threw my sword to the ground and walked away, shaking the dust of the Volscian's house from my feet.

I found my friend's tomb in a burial ground outside the city. Aufidius had told the truth about one thing at least: Caius Marcius Coriolanus had been buried with every honour.

I reached up to touch the cool stone wall of the sepulchre. Coriolanus did not belong inside that cold rock structure. He should have been consul in Rome, if only he had not been so honest and outspoken that he managed to offend nearly everyone who might have come to his aid when his enemies conspired to charge him with treason against the people.

I was one of those who stood beside Marcius as the rabble crowded into the Forum for his trial. The day was hot and still, the air thick with the smell of perspiring bodies as the multitude pressed in around us.

Menenius Agrippa stepped forward to plead on Marcius's behalf. "Good people, I beg you, listen to me. You have only to look at the wounds on Coriolanus's body to see how bravely he has served you all his life."

The crowd's murmur of approval was quickly silenced when the tribune Sicinius Veletus asked Marcius what had become of the spoils from Corioli.

Marcius stiffened. "I came here to address the populace of Rome, not to answer insinuating questions."

"Why were the spoils not distributed among the people?" Sicinius's confederate, the tribune Junius Brutus demanded.

"You did not fight at Corioli! What right does a coward who remains safe behind Roman walls while others risk their lives, have to question *me* on spoils?"

"Marcius, no," Agrippa whispered. "Remember you must speak mildly to appease the people."

"Appease them? I will not dissemble to please the filthy herd! I will speak to them honestly or not at all."

"The filthy herd?" Sicinius repeated. "Do you hear what he calls you? His own disdainful speech condemns him as a traitor."

The tribunes' agents began moving openly through the crowd, inciting them to chant: "Take him to the rock! Take him to the rock!"

"Good people, pay no mind to Coriolanus's rough speech. It is only his way as a soldier," Agrippa tried to explain, his voice drowned out by a cacophony of hoots and jeers. "Caius Marcius refused his own rightful share of the spoils from Corioli."

". . . to the rock! Take him to the rock!"

"You flock of honking geese who know nothing of valour or service, dare you call *me* a traitor? The fires of hell take you!"

"Is this how you keep your promise to speak mildly? I pray you, be careful!" Agrippa urged him. "You are falling into their hands!"

"Hear how he addresses you?" Sicinius asked the crowd. "What does he deserve but a traitor's death? Take him from here to be flung head first from the Tarpeian rock!"

"The rock!" the crowd roared in approval, as guards closed in around us. "Take him to the rock!"

The tribune Brutus raised a hand to silence the rabble. "No, wait! In light of his past service to Rome, I propose we show mercy and reduce the sentence to one of perpetual banishment."

"Mercy? From *you*? I would rather be flung from the rock!"

"Too proud for mercy?" someone shouted. "Then let him die!"

Menenius Agrippa raised his hands in a gesture of conciliation. "Please, please, good people. I beg you, hear me – "

"No more hearing," said Sicinius. "His sentence is pronounced: perpetual banishment."

I will never forget the look on Marcius's face at that moment. For one instant, his features twisted and contorted; the next his face was a mask of placid calm. He almost smiled as he surveyed the hostile throng. "You unwashed curs. I banish *you*."

A mob of jeering plebs followed him to the gates of the city. Menenius Agrippa and I were among the small group of patricians who walked beside him, doing our best to shield him from the missiles and taunts of the same people who only days earlier had greeted him with cheers and kisses on his triumphant return from Corioli.

Virgilia and Volumnia were waiting at the gate, both bent over double with sobbing. At Marcius's approach, Volumnia wiped her face and straightened her back. "No tears," he chided the women. "No tears." Then he left alone, taking nothing with him.

My friend had begun that day as the most honoured man in Rome and ended it the most hated. I traced one of the carvings on his tomb with my finger, musing on how a man's fate might hinge on the events of a few short hours.

I heard footsteps. My Roman garb hidden beneath a long cloak, I turned to see a man walking towards me along the path, his short tunic marking him as a soldier.

Like my late friend, I have never been fond of deception. Unlike him, I have learned that in certain circumstances it can be useful. "I know you," I said, moving forward to greet the Volscian. "We served together in the recent war against Rome."

He paused, looking confused. "Did we?"

"Didn't you fight in the war?" I asked him.

"I did."

"Didn't you take part in the siege?"

"I did."

"I *knew* it was you!" I clapped him on the back. "My, you do look well!"

"As do you," he said. "Forgive me, but I don't – "

"If only the damned generals had not made peace, Rome could have been ours," I interrupted.

"Rome *should* have been ours," the Volscian agreed, his doubts about me gone. We were now the best of friends.

"For victory to slip from our grasp like that, for the sake of a woman! It makes me angry just to think of it."

"Three women," the Volscian corrected me. "And a child. I saw them come into the camp."

"Did you?"

"And I saw them leave again as well. They were behaving very strangely, if you ask me, considering they'd got what they came for."

"How was their behaviour strange?"

"They were weeping – or at least two of them were, anyway. Sobbing as though their hearts were broken."

"And what about the third woman?" I asked him.

"She seemed in a hurry to leave."

On my return to Rome, I called again at the house of the senator Menenius Agrippa. The old man seemed even more tired and ill than at our last meeting. I asked him to tell me more about his unsuccessful mission to the Volscian camp.

"Titus, you swore you would remember Marcius as he was. I beg you, leave that memory intact."

"But would you have his murderer go free?" I persisted.

"What can be done while we remain at peace with Antium?"

"His murderer is not in Antium. Tullus Aufidius did not kill Marcius."

The senator nodded. "You are right. I will tell you who killed him."

I leaned forward, holding my breath.

"We did," he replied, looking me in the eye. "We all did."

I let my breath go. "Oh."

"We should have defended him more strongly, Titus. We who were his friends should never have allowed him to be banished."

"But it would have meant civil war," I reminded him.

"We should not have stood by, even if the streets of Rome had flowed with blood," the old man said. "Marcius died that day in the Forum. Though I did not realize it at the time, the man we accompanied to the gates was already dead."

"I don't understand."

"The stillness, the smile, the quiet acceptance of his fate: these were not Marcius! What we mistook for calm was an anger so deep-seated and intense it acted in his belly like a poison."

The senator shivered as if he was freezing. "The day I went to the Volscian camp to speak with Marcius, it was like meeting a hostile stranger. I was searched for weapons, then a guard led me into a tent where I found Caius Marcius and Tullus Aufidius sitting side by side. It was Aufidius who spoke first, to ask me what I wanted. I explained I had come to speak to Marcius on behalf of his many friends in Rome, to which Marcius replied, 'I have no friends in Rome.'

"'What about your family?' I protested. 'Your wife? Your child? Your mother?'

"Then Marcius fixed me with a stare . . . Titus, I cannot describe it except to say that it chilled me. There was a strangeness in his eyes, unlike anything I had ever seen.

"'Family?' he said. 'I have no family. No wife, no mother, no child.' Then Aufidius clapped his hands, ending the interview, and I was escorted from the tent.

"I cradled Marcius on my lap as an infant, but I was afraid of him that day. If he had led the attack on Rome, there would have been no hope for any of us. To him there was no distinction between friend and enemy; he would have killed us all alike. There was no more hope of mercy from him than of milk from a male tiger."

"Yet only two days later, the women – " I began.

"No more," the old man interrupted, tears welling in his eyes. "No more, Titus, I beg you."

My next call was on the young widow, Virgilia. The servant who came to the door told me Virgilia could not see me as she was ill. I walked past him into the atrium where Virgilia was sitting beneath a tree, a black shawl draped around her shoulders.

She was as beautiful that day as the first time we met, perhaps a month or two after her wedding to Marcius. I must admit it, I envied Marcius his bride, with her delicate features and hair that shone like burnished copper.

She was seventeen when she came to live in the Marcii household, and what an odd family grouping they made: the warrior, the girl and the ever-present mother. Marcius only married at his mother's bidding, to produce an heir, but I sometimes think that if it had been I, I would have needed no bidding from anyone to marry Virgilia. (I must stop this; I have said too much. Marcius was my beloved friend, and Virgilia his devoted wife.)

"Titus," she said, "I am glad to see you." She beckoned me to sit beside her.

"I have been concerned for you. Volumnia told me you were ill."

"Did she?" Her eyes were red from crying. Though the day was warm, she pulled her shawl tight around her body, trembling. "I am a little weary, perhaps. I find it difficult to sleep . . ."

"That's to be expected," I tried to assure her.

"No, it's . . ." She hesitated, glancing nervously about the courtyard. "Forgive me, I must not . . ."

"Must not what?"

"There are many things I must not do, but chief among them is: I must not cry. Everyone always tells me, your tears are no use to anyone, if you would ever accomplish anything, you would turn those tears to anger." She tugged at her shawl again, though I did not see how it could possibly wrap any tighter. "But it's hard. Being angry all time is hard."

"The loss of a husband like Coriolanus must be difficult to bear."

Her reaction both surprised and alarmed me. She laughed, a harsh little barking sound without a hint of mirth.

"Virgilia, are you all right?"

"You speak of *my* loss? There was only one woman in my husband's life and that woman was his mother."

"He was always close to her," I admitted. "But surely that is to be admired."

"Admired? I shudder to think of the hours they spent alone, lingering over his wounds. It was unnatural."

"His wounds were a source of pride," I said. "Each one the mark of an enemy's grave."

"What does it matter now? Forget I ever spoke," she said, looking over my shoulder.

I turned to see Volumnia at the window.

"Titus Lartius!" Volumnia called. "I did not know you were here!"

"When can I speak to you alone?" I whispered to Virgilia.

"Don't you understand? It's impossible."

"But it's important we speak about Marcius."

Virgilia turned away. "My husband never loved me. What more is there to be said?"

Then Volumnia was upon us, accompanied by two servants. "Virgilia, dear," she clucked, "you should not have left your bed." She gestured to her accompanying servants, shaking her head as they led Virgilia away. "The poor child; I am worried about her, Titus."

"She is grieving for the loss of her husband," I said. "Surely that is only natural."

She turned to me sharply. "As I grieve for the loss of a son. Come into the house with me, Titus."

She poured me a cup of wine and bade me sit down. "Virgilia has been behaving strangely these last few days, Titus. The truth is, I fear for her mind."

"Her mind?"

"One moment she seems perfectly calm, the next she flies into a rage. I don't know what to do, except to keep her

safe indoors, away from anything or anyone that might
upset her."

It was late afternoon when a servant ushered me into the room
where the gentlewoman Valeria sat sewing beside a window,
dressed in black mourning. Her face was covered in a thick
layer of chalk powder and her head was crowned with a mound
of false curls taken from the scalp of a slave girl. She smiled
and raised a finger to her lips. "Titus Lartius, isn't it?"

I nodded.

"You were with Marcius at Corioli," she said. "I remember
seeing you at his side as he approached the city gates, crowned
with the oaken garland. I thought you looked very handsome,"
she added, giggling.

"And I saw you at Volumnia's side on her return from the
Volscian camp."

"Ah, yes." She rubbed her forehead and looked down at
her sewing. "Marcius was a dear friend to my late brother;
we both knew him from childhood and Volumnia thought
my presence might be some help."

"And did your presence help?"

"I doubt it."

"What happened in the camp that day?"

She shrugged, her eyes still on her stitching. "I'd rather not
talk about it."

"Why not?"

"Perhaps I fail to see the benefit in damaging the reputation
of a childhood friend."

"Caius Marcius joined with the Volscians to destroy his
own city. What could anyone possibly say to damage his
reputation further?"

She hesitated, pursing her painted lips into a pout. "But I
promised."

"I can understand the value of such a promise while Caius
Marcius was alive, but surely you see that his murder changes
everything?"

She looked up from her sewing. "It's Virgilia I feel sorry
for. When I think how badly he treated her that day . . ."

＊   ＊   ＊

I spent a day and a night alone, thinking, before I went to see Volumnia once more. "I know who killed Caius Marcius Coriolanus."

"Everyone knows that, Titus. My son was killed by Tullus Aufidius on his return to Antium."

"I have spoken to – "

"Valeria," she interrupted, smiling. "I know all about it; she told me everything." She lay down on an upholstered couch. "Valeria has always been fond of you, Titus. I believe she might say anything to please you."

"I found nothing especially pleasing about her words."

"How disappointing for you both." She rolled onto her side, propping her head up with one hand. "Well then? What did she say?"

"I thought she told you everything."

"Maybe I like the sound of your voice." She nodded towards the couch opposite hers.

I sat upright, keeping my feet on the floor. "Menenius Agrippa told me that Tullus Aufidius was present throughout his interview. According to Valeria, he was also present during yours."

The low table between us held a platter piled high with fruit. She selected a single grape for herself, then pushed the platter towards me.

"Marcius would not listen to the entreaties of Agrippa, the man he had loved like a father, and he would not listen to yours," I said, ignoring the proffered fruit.

"He was stubborn at first, I admit it."

"It was more than stubbornness. Valeria said that when his wife tried to kiss him, he pushed her away."

"My son never cared for tears, it was strength he admired, and the wretched girl would not stop grizzling."

"She said Aufidius averted his eyes in shame as Virgilia fled the tent in tears, taking the child with her. Meanwhile, you continued to argue and cajole, warning your son that if he went through with this attack on Rome, his name would go down in history as one to be abhorred. But nothing you said made any impression. At last you rose up from your knees and said, 'So it ends. You would burn Rome and kill your own mother. I have done all I can to sway you; now on your own head be it.'"

"That is not what I said." She waved her free hand in a gesture of dismissal. "But let it pass."

"You told Valeria to wait outside, saying, 'This cruel stranger was once my child, so let me embrace him one last time.' Or do I misquote you?"

She waved her hand again. "It does not matter. You have the gist of it."

"She said they waited for you close to an hour."

She pushed herself up to a sitting position. "I wanted to talk to my son alone. Even then, it took some time to make him see reason."

"Was it your son who at last saw reason," I wondered aloud, "or was it Tullus Aufidius?"

"I don't know what you mean."

"I believe you did stay behind to embrace Caius Marcius once last time, but hidden inside your cloak was a dagger or some similar weapon. It was this you used to kill your son, thus preserving his name and your own reputation."

"You are forgetting Tullus Aufidius," she said.

"I have not forgotten him. He had the decency to look away as Virgilia fled weeping from his tent. Would he not do the same for a mother's last embrace?

"It must have been a great source of shame to him. No one in his command had thought to search an old woman for weapons, while he himself had stood by with his eyes averted, unknowing and unseeing until the deed was already committed.

"The most feared general of all the Volscians had been too slow to stop a feeble woman. Aufidius could never allow this to become known, so he did not dare have you arrested for the murder. Also, he did not wish the death of Coriolanus to become public knowledge, lest the Volscians lose their advantage in making a peace treaty; the death must only be revealed *after* the peace was concluded on the Volsci's terms.

"It was eventually agreed between you and Aufidius that

you would carry the news back to Rome that your son had been persuaded by love of his mother and he would take credit for the death of his long-time foe. Is that not the truth of it, Volumnia?"

Volumnia looked at me a long time before she answered. "It had to be done. He was no longer my son. He was a mad thing set on vengeance, with no drop of love or feeling in him. He would have destroyed Rome. I tried to reason with him, to make him see sense, but all to no avail. He would have killed us all, Titus. Unless I, who gave him life, took it upon myself to take that life away.

"You must understand, I did what I did out of *love* for my son. I saved his name for posterity as one who showed mercy out of family love, and sacrificed his life for that love.

"And what about you, Titus? Did you not love Marcius? Do you not wish to preserve his family name and his honour? Or perhaps you care less for my son's memory than his sworn enemy, Tullus Aufidius?"

I am a soldier, a plain man given to plain speech. I have no love for politics or dissembling. But I know when to keep silent.

And a city needs its heroes.

The next morning, I passed a group of workmen laying the first stone for Volumnia's temple. They bade me good day in the name of the Mother of Rome, and I bade them the same.

BURIED FORTUNE

Peter T. Garratt

From Coriolanus *we move on about eighty years to the time of the Athenian leader Alcibiades at the close of the fifth century. This is the setting for* Timon of Athens, *one of Shakespeare's later and less successful plays. Its origins are a little unclear but it is possible that Shakespeare helped Thomas Middleton (c. 1580–1627), an up-and-coming playwright, rework an earlier play of his about Timon into the current play. This may have been about 1604 or 1605. The earliest recorded performance was in 1607. Timon is really a play about human nature and its plot is quite simple. Timon is a rich and generous Athenian who, through his largesse, loses his money. Those who were his friends now desert him and Timon becomes a misanthrope. He turns his back on his ex-friends after humiliating them at a banquet and leaves Athens to live like a hermit in a cave. Here he discovers a pot of gold and his sudden return to riches brings his old friends back to him. Timon has, however, sided with the exiled Athenian general Alcibiades, and Timon's wealth helps finance Alcibiades' victorious army. Soon after these events Timon dies unexpectedly and the play ends with many matters unresolved. So the following story begins, seeking to bring together the final threads and solve the mystery of Timon's wealth and death.*

*   *   *

"So! It seems Timon is not only dead, but already buried, though no one will admit to knowing exactly when he died, or more importantly, how!" Alcibiades, the new Strategos of Athens, looked at me with a mixed expression. I felt he would trust me if he could, intimidate me if he had to. "You're educated, Apemantus, and you've got a reputation for blunt speaking. Too blunt, but I'm one of the few who never minded that in the old days."

I had resolved to be less outspoken, at least with important people. It went against my nature, but too much of my income came from teaching philosophy for me to offend anyone who might point pupils my way. My creditors were numerous, and a summons, couched as an invitation, to renew my acquaintance with Alcibiades, had been welcome. We had not quite been friends, but had known each other well. I consider few men worthy of real friendship.

His questions took me aback. I didn't have a correct answer, but felt I should provide something, so I said: "No one seems to know. It's another mystery. When I think about it, it's one of many. I don't know where Timon got his money in the first place, let alone why he spent it all in such a profligate manner. Then, just when everyone had written him off, he seemed to come into more money, or at least gold."

Alcibiades' face showed a hint of embarrassment. His house was richly furnished, with busts of Pericles and Solon, urns decorated with recent scenes of battles against the Spartans, all new. His family wealth had been restored since his exile. He now lived as well as ever, though the place had a musty smell, as if new wealth could not purify the atmosphere years of emptiness had given it. Timon, of course, had ended his days in a hut in the woods. Alcibiades shook his head. "And then, with his fortunes improving, he died. How does your philosophy explain that, Apemantus?"

I shrugged. However many questions politicians ask philosophers, they use the answers only if it suits their politician ends, narrow as the ram of a trireme, shallow as the crowd's loyalty. They never use one's advice to learn to think logically, only to spout persuasive rhetoric in the Assembly. Still, I shouldn't upset him. The mood in the city was getting uglier, the supposed Athenian tolerance of serious thought and discussion more of a sham than ever. For now Alcibiades's military record gave him power and popularity, and as the would-be successor of Pericles he felt the need to pretend an interest in learning, and to protect philosophers. I said: "I believe the humours of the mind can affect the humours of the body. Timon for most of his life was over-sanguine. Then, when even he could not deny the folly of his previous opinions, he rushed headlong into an angry, choleric mood which was excessive. And physicians say choler causes many diseases in the body, some of them almost instantly fatal."

The Strategos looked unimpressed. "In other words, he just died of his moods. That could happen to anyone. Why Apemantus, you've been excessively choleric for longer than Timon was alive, and your health is as rude as your manner!"

I said indignantly: "My health is due to a healthy balance! I have learned to subdue my urge to be sanguine, which leads to disappointment and melancholy, without giving way to the choler appropriate to the disillusioning behaviour of the Athenians who surround me!" I forced myself to say: "Though it's true their political judgements have got a little more sensible lately!"

Alcibiades smiled thinly, and I thought for a moment I had been too honest. People say I often am. But he himself was in essence a sanguine type, and he said: "It doesn't add up. He wasn't a bad man, or an old one, or unhealthy. He got gold from somewhere when money was short, then he died. I want you to find out what really happened, whether any of the tenth-raters who kept me out of the city for years were involved. In politics you can never know too much about your enemies. You'll be looked after."

Curiosity got the better of me. Knowledge and understanding are my only real cravings, but they are urgent. I understand men too well, but Timon had been among the

least corrupt, and his downfall was sad. For a moment even
I, whom men call bitter and unfeeling, had to blink unfamiliar
tears. Then we stood and shook hands . . . quite a contrast, I
imagine. Alcibiades was no further into his forties than I, but
despite his continued military activity, he was greyer and a
bit stouter than in his years as the rising golden boy. Men
say my appearance changes no more than my opinions, that
I will always be lean and dark, with a face creased from
concentration and realism.

As I crossed the courtyard, I reflected on my new position.
It was mid-morning, the sun was blazing as if annoyed by
the blueness of the sky, and it wasn't just the heat that made
me uncomfortable. Every politician has an investigator to
ferret things out, usually discreditable material about his
opponents. It was a sign of good taste in Alcibiades that
he chose a real philosopher like myself for that job. Most
chose human sewer-dogs fit only to catch rats. I argued with
myself that for me, to support Alcibiades was the least bad
option. He was more intelligent than his rivals, and though
almost as corrupt, was free of the self-deceptions and lapses
into indignant frenzy which have so degraded the Athenian
polis. While Alcibiades lasted, I would have power as well as
pay, but he had been prominent in Athens before, and had
never ruled for long. The last time he had been forced into
exile, ironically at a time when he wasn't at fault. If I made
enemies in my new job, I myself would have to visit foreign
schools of philosophy at short notice.

Timandra arrived as I was leaving. Unlike some *hetairae*,
she made no pretence at respectability. She had been walking
through the city in a dress so flimsy it might even have been
comfortable in that heat, her body burned bronze by the
sun. Oddly, this didn't make her look like a peasant, perhaps
because she protected her face with so much white paint it
could have been the theatrical mask of a ghost. With her
were two guards, who showed the locals that, though in
theory available, she was in practice out of their reach.
I liked Timandra. Though able to lie and dissemble very
convincingly, she used that ability only to advance her
interests, or those of her friends. She was thus more reliable

than most Athenians, who are so used to deceiving themselves that out of habit they lie to others in gross and absurd ways. Timandra said: "Good morning, Apemantus! Could you be sullying your hands with political business? It's surely a bit early for even you to come just to insult us!"

"Why should I want to insult you? A courtesan may be no more than a whore with more than her share of good looks and intelligence, but what are your respectable married sisters but kept women with no sense of adventure?" I stopped abruptly, having fallen into my old habit of over-blunt speech.

"My married sisters are kept by me, as are their husbands!" she snapped, then mellowed: "What is a philosopher, but a politician whose arguments only convince a few? What is a teacher, but one who holds forth about professions he cannot earn a living from?"

I said: "My new profession is investigator. I am to look into the death of Timon, and the source of his last fortune."

She brushed the sweat off her brow with a movement that made the gold bangles rattle all down her brown arm. "Ah, Timon. You know, he helped me out with that last fortune, the one he said he found in the woods, as much as from his first. I was the oldest of a family of starving sisters. It was find a rich patron or earn my living the hard way in the porna-house. Timon ordered his servants to give me food, but never . . . asked anything . . ." From her eyes I saw that Timon's unrewarded generosity had meant more to her than to anyone else. She said: "It was lucky really, Alcibiades is so much more practical. But Timon was always loyal . . . even with his own troubles he helped me right up to the end."

Like most of Alcibiades's friends, she regarded loyalty to him and to the city as one. I said: "You mean, by helping you, Timon was helping Strategos Alcibiades?"

"Oh yes. It's expensive to travel round incognito, suddenly turning up and mixing in well-heeled circles." She was sharing with me what I already guessed, that she had acted as a secret agent for the exiled Alcibiades. I feared she would regard a rival source of information with suspicion, but she said: "You and I must compare our thoughts. Come early for supper."

It might seem wrong for such a woman to so command a

philosopher, but I am used to worse injustice. Let's face it, she had subtler methods of getting information than I. She could seduce the figurehead of a ship into telling her the captain's secrets: I never had the knack of dissembling my contempt for the stupid and the dishonest.

I walked slowly through the streets, reviewing my knowledge of Timon, looking for a theory to test by argument. Timon had been a landowner, though not from a well-known family. His estates were among those damaged by the Spartans early in the war, so he had another source for the wealth he eventually squandered. Perhaps he had been a trader in the short-lived peace negotiated by Nicias. He had travelled, but never talked about where or why. He must have served in the war, but I'd heard nothing of his achievements or failures. Nor had he been active in politics. He was just a very generous man, whose parties echoed with stimulating conversation, but were so lavish that by the end sensible men like myself became worried that his generosity was a symptom of folly. Of course we were proved right. Around the time Alcibiades was exiled on obviously false charges, Timon left the City hounded by creditors and lived in a hovel in the woods. Some people said he owned the wood, one of the few near Athens, and made a bare living selling timber, but it wasn't big enough for him to have lived well.

Beyond the market I could see the Acropolis, dominated by the marble and gold temple of Pericles . . . that is, Pallas Athena. It was a beautiful building, but I fancied the politician needed to impress the people with his genius more than the Goddess did.

I had reached no conclusion by the time I reached the Agora. In his munificent days Timon had only had friends, temporary ones: but I wasn't aware he'd had real enemies. Meanwhile, I wanted to see if any politician was out canvassing support for the next Assembly, who might be disposed to talk. Most would be enemies of Alcibiades.

The market was crowded. Alcibiades' naval victories had freed the trade routes, and goods had come in from places we had at times been out of touch with: ivory, for instance, which must be from Egypt or Carthage, wines from Gaul and

Spain. People browsed but bought with caution, though their clothes were threadbare: twenty-five years of intermittent war, often unsuccessful, had taught them some prudence when they weren't thinking as a mob.

It was getting hotter: soon people would head to taverns for their noon meal. I saw Cleophon was out, a big, bluff man with the coarse features of an artisan and the fine clothes of a merchant. He toured the stalls and bought overpriced knick-knacks almost everywhere, odd extravagance for one who posed in his speeches as a poor lyre-maker, defender of the yet-more-poor. It was true that his lyres were poor tuneless things, but he had many other business interests, and had done well out of his own policy, which was to continue the war with Sparta whatever the cost to the City as a whole. I nodded to him, then to a couple of his young followers who hung around him like pupils in the shameful art of the demagogue. I said: "Made any good liars lately?"

"Business is terrible, since that playboy Alcibiades was allowed back!" he sneered. He was sober, and evidently considered it beneath his dignity to reply to candour.

It was time to get on with my new job. I said: "It's a shame the City wasn't as generous to Timon as it's been to Alcibiades."

Cleophon looked puzzled. I didn't attach importance to that: he was false to the depths of his soul, so the natural connection between his true emotions and those in his face had been totally eroded. He said: "Timon . . . I don't recall a vote of exile in his case . . . didn't he go and live in the woods for his own reasons? He was outside the walls, but not an exile."

"The state wouldn't help with his debts."

"Well, why should it! He was just a fool, like all these landed types, born to too much and easily parted from it. Mind you, I did hear that as soon as Timon's creditors had forgotten him, he conveniently found some more money of his own!"

"Interesting. It was odd that he found money buried in the woods. You think it was his all along?"

"If he found it at all. There're tales about Timon and his

parties, but honest folk were never invited, so if you want the story from the whore's mouth, it's not me you should tap up. Try that lot over there, if you can get a word in edgeways!"

He gestured toward the expensive end of the market, presumably meaning a group of young nobles, some with political connections on the aristocratic side. Critias was holding forth, of the rest I only recognized Plato, one of the few with any real brain, though there was an older man just out of sight behind the group. They moved forward and I was not surprised to glimpse the still-vigorous stride of Socrates. Cleophon turned away dismissively, and I moved towards this slightly more congenial group. Socrates nodded to me, stroking his beard as he did so, and the others fell silent. He said: "Here's a man whose opinions I value, though I've never quite pinned them down. Your views on the weakness and corruptibility of our democratic regime are of interest, but I find that you don't advocate a return to a traditional, aristocratic system!"

I shrugged. "Why should a small corrupt group be any better than a vast corrupt crowd? Why should men who lack wit or education be any worse than those who have both but seldom bother to use them, except to rationalise their own interests?"

Socrates began to reply, but Critias interrupted, the only one of that group who would. He was tall, sour-faced, not heavily built but still physically impressive. He said: "Probably Apemantus has suddenly noticed the economy of having but one corrupt ruler, to judge from his new visiting habits. But doubtless the whole crowd who used to meet up round at Timon's will soon be back in favour!"

I started, hoped no one noticed. Timon was already in this discussion, and I hadn't had to mention him! On the other hand, news of my relationship with the new Strategos had reached the Agora faster than I could walk there. I didn't like politics! But I had an opening, and I said: "I'll discuss philosophy with anyone, as you will, Socrates. I spoke of it to Timon, not that he listened. But I have little interest in politics, and Timon had less. Why, now I think of it, I never heard him discuss it. I never saw him at the Assembly, or heard of him standing for office."

Socrates, however, did not want to discuss Timon. "What arguments, Apemantus, can you advance against the superior virtue of the educated mind, the mind that is, which has sought education and made good use of it?"

This was irritating. Usually I didn't mind arguing with Socrates. He had one of the most sharp and inquisitive minds in Athens, though as he seldom wrote his views down, I suspected that he changed them subtly to suit the prejudices of different admirers. But he had a single great weakness, an obsession with abstract speculation about the nature of the soul, which distracted him from observing the reality. I said: "I reserve my greatest scorn for those who are given education by their parents, and presumably some kind of wit by the Gods, yet fail to use it. Take Timon. He could talk very entertainingly on all kinds of topics. But he would never listen if I explained to him that those who surrounded him were unacquainted with gratitude . . ."

"Ah!" Critias interrupted smugly. "So you do agree that Timon surrounded himself with worthless men! Like for instance, Alcibiades, the blasphemer and ally of the Spartans! What . . ."

"Just a minute!" Our philosophical argument was taking place in an area where swordsmiths and other metalworkers displayed their wares. A crowd had been looking them over, but some of these were making no secret of listening to us, and one shouted: "There's been quite enough badmouthing of the Strategos! Enough lies!"

Someone else shouted: "While he was away we lost! Now he's back we win!" This was of course true. The metalworkers, several of whom had jugs of wine on their stalls, shouted their agreement, and so did most of the crowd. Critias opened his mouth to disagree, and someone flicked a nutshell into it, and he half-swallowed it, his neck muscles convulsing as he tried to stop it going down. He looked amazingly stupid, standing there trying to decide what it was and whether it was dangerous. Everyone burst out laughing, including some of the young philosophers. Critias finally managed to spit the broken shell out: realizing his dignity could not be easily restored, he turned on his heel and strode away.

This was frustrating! Critias was the only person I had met so far who actually wanted to talk about Timon, and he was being chased out of the market. I wondered if I should follow him: as I began to move, I noticed that several of the angry metalworkers were looking after him, and I stopped without really beginning . . . perhaps an omen for this difficult investigation! Luckily, the mob calmed down and moved off to the tavern, chuckling over this small victory for the forces of democracy. I was relieved as well as disappointed . . . I could never have reasoned with such men, had they threatened actual violence, which I suspected they were capable of.

Meanwhile, Socrates was saying: "There are many ideas to be tested by argument which stir fewer passions, and perhaps we should repair to the widow Phillia's and go on to one."

Phillia ran a large and exclusive tavern on behalf of her son. There was a roof garden with excellent views: up to the Acropolis, white marble almost burning the eye in the noonday sun, and down to the Agora, where even the most dedicated canvassers and salesmen had retreated under shelter. There were palms growing from huge urns, and Socrates, Plato and I managed to sit under one. There was also a large striped tomcat, whose task was to ensure that birds didn't roost in the trees and discomfort the patrons, but he was asleep.

The wine had scarcely been poured before Socrates offered a new topic: "I see the argument has again been raised that private performances should be encouraged of plays which won prizes at the Festival. I know of no argument against that myself, but as you are against most things, Apemantus, I would welcome your opinion."

I felt uncomfortable. In my younger days, I denounced the lavish praise heaped on the artificial excitements of the drama: but I had begun to see that it had its virtues. I said awkwardly: "In my view, if a tragedy adequately portrays the punishment of vice, or a comedy is rigorous in lampooning the hypocrisy of self-important men, there is no objection. In which case, it is a shame the rules of competition only allow a play to be seen once."

Socrates nodded, but glanced at the young Plato, who at once said: "Drama can be too powerful! It should be controlled by strict rules. Everyone agrees that the business of the republic should be settled by argument: but a poet has the accursed ability to load his arguments with emotion on one side only, so spectators can be moved to excesses of grief or anger, even of guilt, by unfair means!"

Socrates said calmly: "Some people argue it's unfair that Euripides thinks it's too dangerous to live in the city. They want to raise funds for him by performing one of his dramas, his 'Oedipus' perhaps."

Plato looked agitated. "But that's a dangerous drama even by the standards Apemantus just set out. It argues that Oedipus didn't intend to do any harm, and unlike the other versions, it slyly argues that his downfall was as much to do with his political enemies as Fate or the Gods."

I wasn't that interested in his criticism. People do spend so long picking over the fine detail of things that never actually happened! But I was fascinated by the way people allow themselves to be influenced by plays and poems, and it was a wide-open secret that Euripides used traditional stories to comment on modern themes and characters . . . something he wouldn't have been allowed to do openly. That was why he had left the city . . . too many people upset for other than literary reasons! I cut in: "It's an interesting theme, that he didn't intend harm. One could equally argue that a man like Timon never intended any harm, but harm came to him."

Socrates looked at me quizzically. He would have noticed my interest in Timon, and be wondering about it. But he only said: "Of course, Oedipus at least tries to serve his city, but Timon, after a good start, took very little interest in public service."

I realized I still didn't know enough about Timon's life in the period before he started inviting me to his lavish parties. I said: "Just what service did he get started on?"

"Military at first, but he didn't like it. He was with Nicias when they negotiated that treaty with the Spartans."

We continued drinking, and discussing issues which usually interested me, but the others rapidly moved on from Timon.

I was preoccupied with the mystery: I made my excuses and went to my house intending to think further, though in the end I went to sleep. I had to harass the one slave I keep to deal with matters that could distract me from philosophy, to not be late for my meeting with Timandra.

She received me in her own part of Alcibiades' house . . . an airy upper room which overlooked the courtyard. Unusually, there was also a small window overlooking the street. She wore a scanty outfit of a diaphanous blue material more suited to posing for a sculpture of Aphrodite than receiving guests. I guessed she was a little older than she looked, tiny lines just visible on her face, but she had kept her figure and her skin had not been damaged by her habit of walking in the sun half-dressed. Though her arms and shoulders were bronze as a statue, her face was pale and delicate, protected I suppose by the mask of white paint she used outside.

I reported: "Most of the people I spoke to were philosophers, no serious interest, but Critias dabbles in politics, doesn't he? He's stirring up trouble against Alcibiades . . ."

"Nothing new!"

"He seemed to assume Alcibiades had been a leading member of Timon's dinner-party circle, though I only ever saw him there a few times. That was enough to give him a grudge against Timon!

"Cleophon was out too. He didn't think much of Timon, but I didn't expect him to. He wasn't very interested and didn't sound familiar with the details. Of course, he could be lying."

"Of course!" She nodded knowingly. I wondered at that knowing look. For a second the thought poured over me that anyone could lie, anyone conceal what they knew. What if Alcibiades himself, or one of his associates like Timandra, had had their own reasons for wanting Timon out of the way? I couldn't imagine what such reasons could be, but why did they want me to investigate a crime no one else thought was a crime? Could it be to deflect suspicion if someone hiding somewhere knew there had been a murder, and was preparing to say so? I shuddered and felt sick, and wondered if I would be able to face the dinner, which no doubt would be more smothered with spices than Timandra was with perfume.

I swallowed, and asked for a cup of watered wine. I drank slowly and tried to calm down. To fear that I had attached myself to diametrically the wrong party didn't make a lot of sense: yet the fear was real, and my suspicions were all too seldom wrong.

Timandra was almost looking through me, as if she knew my thoughts from my expression. Perhaps she did, for in her profession such knowing must be important. But she said nothing, and after a moment I went on: "I did hear that Timon was involved with Nicias in negotiating the fifty-year treaty."

"The one that lasted for three years? It makes sense. He was away a lot in those days, but not in the army."

"You knew him back then?"

"Yes. Oh yes, I have always known Timon. He used to come to see my mother . . . I was a child then, and he a very young man. I think she was his first . . . courtesan. His father had recommended her. When she died, she didn't leave enough silver for me to be fully grown before starting . . ." Timandra rose and went to look out of the street window. I could not see her face. "I went to see him. He had inherited some money, but nothing like what he had later. Though I was little more than a child, I could see he was tempted . . . but he gave me food and a little money and never did anything. We had long talks though . . . did you know his mother was a Spartan?"

"No!" I was amazed to hear it.

"So was mine . . . but in our case it didn't matter much, in our business you can go anywhere. I think my mother had known his . . . they would have been distant relatives, if we had relatives at all. His mother was respectable." She stopped again, and I wondered what her relationship to Timon's family had really been. Timandra went on: "They have different rules there. All the girls exercise naked in the Gymnasium . . . I think men are supposed to be excluded, but Timon's father was on a visit there . . . this was well before the war . . . and managed to find a way of peeking at them. He fell for one of the girls, scraped an introduction, and they eloped. They did get permission to marry in Athens, it went right to the Assembly, but there was a scandal, and she was kept out of sight."

Most Athenian wives were, of course. Timandra continued: "I think she died about a year before the war started. It would have been around the time he first came to our house . . . he was very young then. There had been no contact with her family for years, and Timon decided to go to Sparta and tell them. I think he was expecting a hostile reception, but after all that time they were prepared to let bygones be bygones. In fact they welcomed him . . . I think that was why he hated the war so much . . ."

I thought quickly. "Could Timon have been a major go-between, between Nicias and the Spartans?"

"It would make a lot of sense . . . he bought a lot of clothes which didn't look Athenian, and I remember he used to entertain merchants from neutral cities which still traded with both sides . . . of course the people who most wanted peace were landowners like Nicias and Timon himself. Our army couldn't stop the Spartans destroying their estates, but people with interests at sea rely on the navy to look after them, even in wartime!"

I nodded: "Sounds like Cleophon and his mob are the suspects . . . they gain from the war, or think they do!"

She shrugged her shoulders. "But why so long after? If they knew about it. By then, Timon had given up on thinking everyone was his friend and hated us . . . hated us all equally. Do you know the first thing he said when he saw me in the woods with Alcibiades? 'Are you Timandra?' as if he couldn't stand his hungry little girl succeeding at the one profession I'm allowed! He was no more an enemy to Cleophon than to everyone else!"

For dinner, Alcibiades had invited only friends I had to assume were to be trusted. I told him how far we had got, and Timandra helped, though avoiding full credit for her rather large contribution. I decided her mind was as remarkable as her body, and briefly wondered how she would respond to an approach. After all, she wasn't actually married. She was next to me, and I was starting to find her perfume a lot more enticing than the spices over-used by Alcibiades's cook. Usually I trust women even less than men, but this unrespectable beauty had liked . . . had hinted she had loved, notwithstanding her profession . . . my one friend Timon.

I looked around the table. All were looking at Alcibiades for his comments, though the men stole sneaky glances at Timandra, and the other *hetairae* envious ones. No one was interested in my contribution. As usual I was alone. I admitted to myself that though I say I have few friends, what I mean is none. Timon was the only man I would have wished as a friend, and the wine of his decency was too little watered by wisdom for me to admit it, though I often sought him out. As for women, I had scorned them more than men. I had not learned their ways, had no idea how one approached the *hetaira* of one's patron, except with extreme caution. Her profession might allow it, but her position wouldn't.

Meanwhile, Alcibiades was saying: "Cleophon's a swine, but I doubt if he would have acted without an immediate reason. And I don't much trust the crowd on the other side, Critias for instance." He turned to me: "Critias hated Timon and thought he was my ally?" I nodded, and he went on: "I knew him, but he lost any interest in politics . . . yes, it was around the time of the Treaty. I did keep seeing him, but mainly because he invited everyone round. It *was* around then he really started spending money."

Timandra said: "Perhaps the landowners clubbed together to give him a secret reward for his mediation. Now I think about it, the people who used to talk about Timon's great service to the city without saying what it was, were all from that party!"

I frowned, feeling bewildered. The only real evidence that Timon had been murdered was his premature burial, though it seemed that no one knew who had buried him, or composed the epitaph on his tomb. How could that be connected to a treaty several years earlier, years in which he had played no part in public life? I racked my brains for an answer: not finding one, my usual scepticism overwhelmed me, and forgetting my new job, I said: "It seems there are no witnesses to his moment of death or how he came to be buried. So unless someone confesses . . ."

"Hardly likely," Alcibiades said. "He'd have to get really carried away." The others nodded, like a chorus.

"Just a minute!" A plan did come to me, and I had to organize it. "Yes! Plato was saying today, how people do get emotionally carried away during dramas, and he was opposed to them being performed outside the Festival!" Timandra snapped her fingers with delight as I said this, and the extraordinary thought raced through my head that a woman's mind could be as sharp as a man's. But it wasn't the time for that discussion. I hurried on: "There's a controversy at present as to whether Euripides' *Oedipus* could be put on as a benefit for him right now. I wonder if it could be performed in a way which would make Oedipus sound like Timon!"

"You remember the play?" Alcibiades asked.

"Yes." I had also read it. Books of plays were one of my few extravagances. "What I think you should do, is to announce a rehearsal of the play, to which all the leading political figures will be invited, so they can decide if the public should see it!"

"We'll serve them wine!" Timandra exclaimed. "From Naxos, none of this rubbish from Gaul! Then we'll see who reacts!"

Before I left, Timandra made a strange request: "Do you have a portrait of Timon?"

"On a serving plate," I said grudgingly. I didn't like to admit to having once prepared to hold dinner parties. When I could afford them, I could never think of anyone to invite. "In theory it shows the dinner after the Peleus' marriage to Thetis, but you can see that the faces are of Timon and his guests."

She shook her head impatiently. "No, there was a full-face portrait on board." She named an artist. "Timon never paid for it."

The painter she named lived in a small house cluttered with decorated urns and dishes. A few were unfinished, but most would be unsold work from the hard years earlier in the war

when even the Athenians realized they could spare no money
for fripperies.

He admitted reluctantly to having the portrait. Perhaps he
knew he had erred in keeping it from a ruined man who had
once been so generous. He enquired for whom it was being
bought. When I said Timandra, his face lit up, then took a
guarded expression. While he rummaged in an old chest for
the portrait, I couldn't help noticing a series of plates decorated
with scenes from the life of Helen. The model had obviously
been Timandra. He noticed my interest: "These are for sale,
if your *patroness* is interested."

"I'll ask. But the main interest is the Timon."

"She was never vain," he said sadly. "She had an interest
in the art for its own sake." I realized he had been in love
with Timandra. There was a painting on the wall of the nine
muses, each modelled by her, which had not been for sale.
But despite her love of art, and his for her, he asked a high
price for the Timon.

I looked at it carefully. It showed Timon clean-shaven,
barbered and good-looking, but prettified: indeed I could
see that he had still been thinking of Timandra when he
did it. "It's a high price, for an idealized picture of a man
no one now idolizes."

"Yes, but they idolize Alcibiades. For the moment."

"It's still an absurd price."

"I'd give it you for the chance to paint him as Theseus,
if I thought he'd last. But Alcibiades appoints too many of
his friends to positions where they make mistakes. Last night
I heard Critias denouncing the Strategos' captains. No one
disagreed."

"So! His friends are no better than Timon's friends?"

He smiled sourly. "Look. As a favour, if you get me the
price, I'll throw in a sketch I did when I went to that hut he
had in his wood. Maybe it can serve as a funeral portrait."

This last picture of Timon was very different. It was the
work of a man who loved art as much as silver. Timon was
still clean-shaven . . . for some reason he had scraped off
his beard even in the woods . . . but he had deep lines of
disillusion on his face.

Timandra loved it. She saw it had more merit than the first.

The day of the rehearsal was another hot one. I arrived as Timandra was instructing some younger courtesans in the art of anointing their skins with oil as well as perfume, to get away with wearing the sort of outfits which would please the guests. There were as many hangers-on as senior figures, though most of these did attend. They came on time, clearly eager not to miss a minute of the action they might decide no one else was to see. Wine was served by the oiled courtesans before the first of the three parts had begun. I tasted a little, it was good quality, hardly watered, but Timandra pointed Alcibiades and myself to a separate jug, which was heavily diluted. There were sun-awnings over the seats, but even so people were drinking thirstily as the drama began.

The first part wasn't controversial. It showed Oedipus reaching Thebes, and contrasted his humane wisdom with the icy intelligence of the Sphinx. During the choruses, Socrates expounded to his group that this did support his view that the soul was perfected by knowledge, while ignorance was a form of sin. Plato listened attentively, while Critias looked distracted and irritable. On the other side of the theatre, Cleophon's gang were mainly concerned to attract the attention of the young women with the wine. Timandra stayed on the aristocratic side, serving the men with deep bows which swung her breasts almost out of her low-cut dress. I noticed . . . well, I was meant to look in that direction . . . that she wore odd jewellery: a necklace threaded with rare gold coins which rested on the tops of her breasts and slapped against them as she came out of a bow. It was gaudy and extravagant by her standards, and there was something else strange about her: her mask of white face-paint made her resemble the prettified image of Timon.

After the first part, we consulted. No one had acted oddly, but they weren't yet expected to. It was so hot, we took longer than usual to restart. During that time, the guests took their noon meals, washed down with seemingly inexhaustible supplies of wine.

The second part was more interesting: Oedipus discovered his identity and put out his eyes. It was soon clear that it was controversial: Creon, in most versions depicted as loyal, was shown plotting against the Tyrannos. The leader of the Chorus in this part had a distinct lisp: and he pronounced the name "Creon" as "Cleon". By the third Chorus, the conspiracy was under way. Cleophon leaped to his feet: "How dare you let them insult Cleon!" he yelled. Cleon had been his predecessor as leader of the war party, and some people thought he owed his own popularity to the similarity of his name to that of the dead demagogue. Even so, most of the audience, even some of his own men, looked appalled. The actors, who were returning to the stage, stopped in their tracks.

People started shouting all round the theatre. Critias yelled: "Afraid of the truth, ignorant lout!" Now all of Cleophon's followers united to yell back. Alcibiades ran to the stage and vaulted onto it, looking a little surprised that he could still do so. He raised his hand for silence, then whispered to the Chorus, pushing the lisping leader unceremoniously into the ranks and indicating another to take his place. Then the courtesans hurried out with more wine: the last section was repeated with correct diction, and Cleophon's mob began to cheer.

The action went on to the usual disaster, but the audience had only just settled down enough to be moved. During the interval, I saw Timandra strolling over to observe Cleophon, and followed. However, he and his followers no longer seemed at all disturbed. They were chanting: "Cleon! Creon! Cleon!" as if attending a chariot race and those were the drivers they had backed!

Timandra did not serve Cleophon: she disappeared behind the stage for a few minutes. She came back with a fresh jug and went to Critias. As she filled his cup, he stared at her breasts and she into his eyes: I thought he was about to speak to her but instead he wrenched his eyes to one side and shouted: "Thus, Socrates, are virtue rewarded and ignorance punished! Thus!" though whether he referred to the play or the audience I could not tell.

In the third part, Oedipus arrives at Athens, and is made to stay in a hut in woods outside the walls. He is in exile, an old blind man polluted by sins he did not intend, much punished for an ignorance he could not have avoided. Usually, the Athenians are glad to see him, and he dies peacefully of natural causes. But here they were shown debating whether to grant him refuge, and unable to decide. I dragged my eyes from the play, and looked round. People looked upset, but not angry. I guess none knew how they would themselves react if such an issue was put to the Assembly.

After the third Chorus, King Theseus was shown with his closest advisors. The situation was impossible, he said. Athens cannot be seen to welcome the involuntary sinner, or to turn him away. As Oedipus was old and tired of life, he had to be helped to die.

This was a scene of immense power, diluted in the first part by the snores of Cleophon, who had no other reaction than to sleep off his wine. One of his followers jogged him awake, and he had the decency to pretend to be watching and listening as intently as the rest, but he showed no detectable reaction from then on.

I looked around and saw that Timandra was standing near Critias, staring at him. I saw she had altered her face make-up. On the white paint, she had traced the exact bitter lines from the last portrait of Timon, so now she looked even more like a ghost in the theatre. Critias's eyes were flickering wildly between her and the stage. "Theseus" pronounced the words: "His virtue is an illusion, inimical to the state!" and then Critias leaped to his feet and yelled: "Why are you doing this! Why are you saying this! You!" He pointed angrily at Timandra and shouted: "Why are you wearing those!" He lunged at her as if to grab her necklace of gold coins, but she ducked out of his reach. He yelled so loudly that the actors stopped in mid-scene: people started moving towards them. I myself went forward, so did Alcibiades. Meanwhile Timandra held up the necklace of coins for all to see. We crowded round the two of them, and she said: "Are these not good Athenian gold?"

"No!" he spluttered. "Those are," and he pointed to the two which had been on her right breast, "but those are forgeries, Spartan fakes which the traitor Timon got for the unendurable terms he brought us in the treaty."

"Ah," she said. "So you think I got these from Timon? Well, this one I did." She held up a coin which indeed looked larger and coarser than the rest, puffy round the edge, as if made with a copy of the Athenian stamp. "But this one," she held up another possible fake: "You gave to a friend of mine for a night's favour! So you call Timon a traitor, and you had his gold!"

Critias looked wildly around. "So, what if I did!"

"So perhaps you killed him, and stole his gold!"

Critias seemed to shrink: "Not for the gold. Not the gold. There was no virtue in letting it waste as he would have." A shocked murmur ran round the theatre, and he pulled himself together. He seemed to grow and gain dignity, and he shouted: "Timon may not have intended treachery, but he betrayed his own intelligence, as well as Athens!" The crowd fell silent, and he went on: "Timon and Nicias brought peace terms which sounded good, but didn't last." Cleophon laughed hollowly, but someone shushed him. Critias went on: "Then, Timon announced his belief in the good nature of all of humanity, he was so pleased with himself in those short years of peace. He wasted his money, at least what the Athenians had given him. Then, he went to the woods, and dug up his bribe from the Spartans. Lived like an animal with no virtue!

"Last year we got the upper hand again, and the enemy sent secret messages." Cleophon's men jeered, but Critias yelled on: "They offered better terms than before, better than Nicias got. Terms which might have lasted. But they would only speak to Timon. He alone they trusted.

"So, I went to the woods, and approached Timon. Would he at least go to them, see what they did offer? Would he?" Critias glared rhetorically round the crowd. Now no one contradicted him. "No. He was so sunk in his own personal misery, his abject betrayal of his supposed virtues, that he refused to help at all. He was busy cursing the world and writing his own epitaph! And yes, I killed him, and took his Spartan gold. And if anyone says I am the traitor and the criminal, let them prosecute me!"

Many of the people on his side of the theatre broke into applause. Even Cleophon's men were silent: they didn't want peace, but wouldn't touch anything contaminated with Spartan gold. I did not think Critias would be prosecuted, and I wasn't surprised that when he turned and strode out of the theatre, no one impeded him.

The rehearsal was not resumed. A public performance was allowed, but the author remained in exile. As for me, I suspected that Critias's star was rising, despite his crime, and soon the mob would propel him into power.

When that happened, I intended to be visiting foreign schools of philosophy.

CINNA THE POET

Tom Holt

Julius Caesar is probably the best known of Shakespeare's Roman plays. It was written and first performed in 1599. The play is really in two parts. The first shows Caesar's success after his defeat of Pompey and the distrust amongst the republicans who believe that Caesar has designs upon kingship. The result is Caesar's assassination led by the conspirators Cassius and Brutus. After Caesar's death we witness the tragedy of Brutus as he reconciles himself to his actions and of the resultant civil war between Brutus and Cassius on the one side, and Mark Antony, Octavius and Lepidus on the other. This second part of the play does not concern us here. Tom Holt has focused his attention on the riots that happened following the death of Caesar and on the unfortunate fate of Cinna the Poet.

> *When beggars die there are no comets seen;*
> *The heavens themselves blaze forth the death of princes.*
> Shakespeare, *Julius Caesar*, II, 2

I'll be honest with you; I didn't recognize him. There wasn't really anything to recognize.

Curious; he was, after all, my son. I'd known him for thirty-seven years. I was there when he had the fall from the apple tree that left him with the scar on his shin. I was the one who measured him every year against the frame of the back door, cutting a little nick in the wood for every finger's breadth he'd grown. I should have been able to recognize him, even in that state. But I didn't.

They brought him back on the morning after the riots, the morning after Caesar was killed. I have no idea to this day who they were; four grey-faced men knocking at my door in the early morning, carrying something blanket-wrapped on a door. One of them spoke my name.

"That's right," I said. I was worried, of course; frightened. Naturally enough; there had been an assassination, riots. And there was the embarrassment of my name. "Who wants to know?"

None of them said anything. They put down the door and walked away. I knew what the thing under the blanket was; no divine inspiration there, what else is that size and shape? But I didn't recognize him. I stood there like a fool at my own front door, wondering what in perdition was a smashed-up dead body to do with me?

And, more to the point, what was I supposed to do with it? A hundred and eighty pounds of fresh meat, all in a hell of a mess, and in these troubled times – passers-by were staring, and I suddenly realized how it must look, so I told the kitchen boy and the houseboy to get the horrid thing inside. I was taking a last look up and down the street before going in myself when my brother Quintus came scurrying round the corner, head muffled up in his gown (bloody fool!) –

"Have you heard?" he panted. But he always says that. Pompey's dead – the Tiber's in flood and we're all going to drown – anchovies two sestertii a medimnus, what will become of us all? It's always been "Have you heard?" ever since we were boys, and he's never once had anything interesting to say. Not up till then, anyway.

"Go away," I replied. "It's not safe on the streets," I added, because he's the world's worst coward and completely self-centred. "If I were you I'd bolt the doors and the shutters and stay indoors till it's all – "

"You haven't heard, have you?"

"Brother – " I hesitated. Quintus always looks a complete idiot when he's trying to be serious; big fat lips puckered up into a thin line, dimples in his cheeks you could hide your thumb in. "Quintus, what's going on? You look dreadful."

"You haven't heard," he repeated. "Publius. He's dead."

My first reaction was to say *Don't be absurd, Quintus, of course he isn't*; and then it occurred to me that yes, people do die, people get killed in riots and at times of civil disorder, that I hadn't actually seen my son since – when was the last time I'd seen him? And then I thought of the body, the horrible mess that four strangers had brought to me on a door.

Of course, he was a very bad poet. A dreadful poet. A father's love for his child untimely dead can't make up for the fact that my son Publius Oppius Cinna couldn't write his way out of a shallow bucket. But for all that he was still a poet. That's all he ever was, poor fool.

Accordingly, as soon as I was myself again I went to the little temple of Apollo, the rather tatty and run-down one three blocks away from my house. It's always quiet and empty, peaceful enough if you don't mind the smell of rancid oil and leftover offerings. Besides, it seemed an appropriate place to ask the god for revenge for my son who was, let's not forget, a loser.

I kept it short and to the point. "Apollo," I said, "we both know about gods, you and I. We both know that you aren't better than us, only bigger and stronger, and I know what it's like to be someone's big brother. Help me find the men who killed my son and I'll be grateful to you. I won't ask where you were when this happened."

That was enough of that; I left the laurel chaplet he used to wear when he was giving recitals, and a copy of his precious book (embarrassingly many of those in the back pantry; he couldn't give 'em away, poor little bastard) and went home.

Getting home took some time. I was, of course, well behind

with the news, so I didn't know that Brutus, Cassius and a few of the other conspirators had fled the city, others hadn't been so lucky, there had been more riots and more looting and disorder and general high spirits, *et cetera*. I was probably the only man in Rome who didn't know. Didn't care much, either. I suppose I wondered at the back of my mind why there were so many people standing around in the streets looking as if they were waiting for something to happen, or why several shops looked like they'd been broken into. A few details didn't escape me; I noticed the fairly new and (in my humble opinion) rather ugly statue of Caesar near the portico had had its head smashed off and then rather clumsily glued back; it was a hot day, and I think I noticed the foul smell of the hide glue, mixed with the scent of a garland someone had put on the wretched thing. I noticed it, but I didn't think anything of it. Politics, I'd have muttered under my breath, and carried on. Somehow, I couldn't seem to find any enthusiasm to spare for politics that day.

When I got home, Quintus was back. Marvellous, I thought. And then something occurred to me.

"Quintus," I said, cutting him off before he could start blethering sympathy at me, "how did you hear about it?"

He blinked at me in that half-witted way of his. "Syrus told me," he said. "He was there."

Syrus. I could tell it was going to be one of those days.

Let me tell you about Syrus. He's a head shorter than me, solid as an oak-tree, bald and probably the most unsavoury human being I've ever met. His real name is some foreign gibberish; my brother, of course, tried to learn it until I told him quite firmly that since he came from Syria, Syrus would do fine. I found out later how much my idiot brother paid for him; gods be thanked our father wasn't alive to hear it.

But the thing about Syrus is this incredible knack he's got of being in the wrong place at the wrong time, of always doing the wrong thing and always getting caught. Actually, I don't think he's unusually dishonest for a houseboy; they all thieve scraps from the table, wood from the woodpile, odds and ends that we think we must have dropped or put somewhere safe but can't remember where. But Syrus always gets caught.

Likewise, if there's a shower of rain, Syrus is always out in it and always gets soaked to the skin. If someone empties the slops out of a high window, you can bet your life Syrus is waiting underneath at precisely the right moment to get the whole lot on his head. Which came first, his incredible bad luck or his revolting personality I wouldn't care to hazard a guess. The two are obviously related, but it could be either way round.

"Syrus saw it all," I repeated. "Did he recognize the men?"

Quintus shook his head. "I don't think so," he said.

"You don't *think* so?"

"No. Syrus didn't say anything, and I'm sure he'd have mentioned it if he had."

Congratulate me. I kept my temper, I didn't even shout. "Quintus," I said, "go home and fetch that pathetic waste of food and clothing and bring him here now. Do you think you can do that?"

"There's no need to be rude."

"I wasn't. Rude's when something's offensive and untrue. Tell him – " I closed my eyes and then opened them again. "Tell him that if he can tell me anything useful, anything at all, I'll give him twenty sesterces."

Quintus drew a deep breath; he was going to lecture me on how unwise it is to allow slaves to get into the habit of expecting to be rewarded for doing what they're told. Fortunately for both of us, he didn't. "Very well," he said, and left.

"I didn't get a clear look," Syrus said. "Like, it happened quick, you know?"

Yes, of course I knew. Things do. I remember one time when I was walking in the Subura with a friend of mine, and he pointed something out on the other side of the street, and I turned my head to look; and then I heard this *thwack!* And when I looked round there he was, flat on his face with the back of his head smashed in, and bits of the loose roof-tile that had fallen off and brained him scattered all over the place. Yes, things do happen that quickly, and anybody could be looking the wrong way at that particular moment. But not today.

"Syrus," I said, putting a hand on his shoulder, "I think you probably saw something. I think you don't realize that what you saw was actually quite important. I'm absolutely certain that you don't realize what I'm going to do to you if you don't tell me something that'll help me find the men who killed my son. Now think."

He started to whine, so I grabbed his jaw between my thumb and forefinger. I have big, strong hands, like my father's.

"There was a man in an apron," he said.

"An apron," I repeated. "What kind of apron?"

He looked up at me with that it's-not-fair expression of his. "I don't know," he said. "Just an apron, that's all."

I shook my head and tightened my grip. "No it's not," I said. "For a start, was it leather or cloth? Brown or white?"

He thought for a moment; I could have sworn I could hear the water in the mill-race and the slow grinding of the stones. "Leather," he said at last. "I think."

I nodded. "That's better," I said. "A leather apron could be a smith or a shoemaker or a stonemason – "

"Or a lime-burner," Quintus suggested.

"Quite," I replied, "except there aren't any lime-kilns in the City. So what else did you notice about this man in an apron?"

Syrus pulled an ugly face, as if he was trying to give birth to something large and sharp. "He was a big man, black hair, short beard." Further unpleasant effort; then he added, "And he had a pierced ear. I think."

"Very good," I replied, pleasantly surprised. "So, an ex-slave, a tradesman, big, black hair, short beard. And he was the man who was actually – " Stupid, that; I couldn't bring myself to say it. "That was him, then?" I finished lamely.

"No," Syrus said. "But he was standing next to one of the men, and I think he was talking to him, before. Or after."

People tell me I have a temper, that I can be abrupt and impatient. They should have seen me then. I was as sweet as milk.

"I see," I said. "And this man our tradesman was talking to. What can you tell me about him?"

Syrus shrugged. "Nothing," he replied. "All I saw of him was his head. And his arms," he added, "later."

"Later?"

"When he was stabbing – when he was doing it."

"Stabbing," I said. "What was he stabbing with?"

Syrus scratched his shiny, sweaty head. "Shears," he said at last. "A big pair of shears."

"You mean scissors."

"No, shears. The sort with a spring in the middle."

I smiled. "That's better," I said. "Now we know he was tall, because you could see his head over the top of this other tall man in the apron, and he was carrying a pair of shears, and he seemed to know the man in the leather apron. That's very good," I went on. "Syrus, you're a very intelligent and observant individual, you know that?"

Syrus blinked at me like a suspicious sheep. "Oh," he said.

"Yes indeed. And here's your twenty sesterces," I went on, thumbing the coins out of my purse, "and there's ten more for you if you can remember anything else. And if you make anything up just to get the money," I added, "I'll personally geld you with a hot iron. Understood?"

Syrus nodded. "I can't remember anything else," he replied.

"Pity. Not even where any of this happened?"

He blinked again. "In the Via Nova, just past the temple of Saturn," he replied. "Didn't I say?"

"Not in so many words. Would you recognize them again, do you think? Bearing in mind what I said about the ten sesterces and the hot iron?"

He gave me a look that would have scythed rawhide. "I suppose so," he said. "Anyway, I think so. I can't promise anything."

"No, of course you can't," I replied. "Now then, you're going to take me to the exact spot where it happened."

Needless to say, my useless brother insisted on coming as well, so there were five of us; myself, Quintus, Syrus and two big, brutal lads from the forge across the way. I'd given them ten sesterces each and told them to bring a big hammer.

There was a lot of politics going on in the streets. There were men standing on the steps of the temples or the pedestals of statues, spouting a lot of stuff to crowds of gawpers. I think they were trying to recruit soldiers to fight for one lot or the other; Marcus Antonius, or Brutus and Cassius. Probably both. There were more trashed shops, some burnt out; when history's in the making, there are plenty of opportunities to sort out any unfinished business you may have with your neighbour. There were even a couple of bodies lying around, though whether they were dead or just dead drunk I don't stop to look. Above all there was still this general feeling of waiting for something to happen, and an accompanying sense of frustration because nothing was happening. My guess is that all the people who'd been busy and missed the show while it was on were out waiting for someone to put on a second performance for their benefit. That's another problem with history in the making; it happens fast, usually on the other side of town, and by the time you get there it's over.

"Here," Syrus said, pointing. "I think."

"I believe you," I replied, as I knelt down and tested one of the marks on the paving stone at my feet with the tip of my finger; my son's blood, already dry, already most of it scuffed away by the feet of people going about their business. It was just a brown stain, hard to associate with my son, that fool Publius.

(I knew he was dead, but I didn't really believe it. You don't, under such circumstances, not until much later. Hint; the best way to deal with it is to cram your mind with other things for as long as possible, until somehow or other the idea *he's dead* has quietly taken the place of the idea *he's alive*. If you're lucky, it can happen without you even noticing, at the time.)

"Didn't see a thing," they all said, as they explained that they'd been too busy hiding or frantically closing the shutters or getting the stock into the back room. I believed them; they were shopkeepers, tradesmen, people with property and a livelihood to protect and a riot going on in the street outside. Some of the people I talked to had been in the crowd, but at the back, where you can't see anything and all you can hear is muffled shouting and the voices of the men next to you talking about something else, such as the weather or the price of olives.

I suppose I could have dragged a few bits and pieces out of them, if I'd had all day and a platoon of the Guard to make them hold still while I questioned them. But an old man asking questions in the middle of the day, when there's history going on and work to be done for those who haven't the time or the inclination, is a pest. I gave up after a while, and we held a staff meeting on the kerbside, much to the annoyance of the carters.

Maybe it was Apollo helping us out, the way he's supposed to help mortal heroes in the stories; maybe not. Maybe Luck is also a goddess, though usually I wouldn't belittle her by calling her that. In any event, we were sitting there talking it over when a man who was leading a team of mules stopped and looked at us for a while. I noticed him and looked back.

"Couldn't help overhearing," he said. (Liar, I thought.) "The man who was killed here yesterday."

"My son," I replied. "Were you there?"

He nodded. "I take my team through here about this time every day," he said. "Got held up in the crush yesterday, of course. Quite some day that was, too. Of course, I never liked the man myself, but it was a hell of a way to go. A hell of a way."

It took me a while to realize that he was talking about Caesar. I was in no mood to talk about Caesar, but I managed to keep my temper. "So what did you see?" I asked him.

"Nothing much," the muleteer answered. "I was stuck in the road behind a bunch of people, couldn't really see much. One minute we were moving slowly along, then suddenly we stopped, and I was asking the man next to me if he knew what was happening; and then there was someone shouting and yelling, and some people laughing, and then a lot of screams and more shouting. And that was it, really."

"Ah," I said. "Thank you."

"Thing was," the muleteer went on, "and this stuck in my mind, I don't know why. It's odd the way some things do, isn't it? One of the men, up at the front, I think he was one of them doing the shouting; he had this long bit of red cloth wrapped round him, like this – " He stopped and demonstrated a piece of cloth coming over the right shoulder and under the left arm, then wrapped once round the waist. "And I reckon I know what that was. It was one of the flags."

I frowned; this was all a bit much. "Flags?"

"That they were hanging up on the statues up along the Aurelia. There was that fuss about them, remember, what they're saying sparked it all off." I must have looked as befuddled as I truly was, because he went on, "People putting flags and stuff on Caesar's statue, and the tribunes taking them down again."

I forced myself to be patient and actually listen to what he was saying. "Thank you," I said. "That's very helpful."

"No problem," he said. "Hope you catch them, eh?"

I smiled, very thinly. "I hope so too," I said.

We found the statue. Someone had taken a hammer to it, but hadn't really connected; one arm was off, the nose was gone and the paint was scratched. There were still tatters of red cloth lodged between the splayed fingers of the imperiously raised right hand. You could be melodramatic about that, I suppose. If Publius was still alive, he'd make some awfully trite comment about them being the blood on Caesar's hands. And I'd have told him no, dry blood isn't red, it's brown. Trust me, son, I'd have said; I know about these things.

Then we walked about for a bit, asking questions here and there, following directions from one shop to another, until we found what we were looking for.

"He's not here," said the woman who answered the door at the first place we went to. An unsavoury old bat she was, presumably the man's mother. "What d'you want him for?"

I told her some lies about needing my shutters fixed; riot damage, I said.

"You're not the only ones," she replied, with a grin. "He's out on a job right now. Say what you like, that Caesar getting killed's been good for business."

"It's an ill wind," I replied. "Mind if we wait?"

She frowned at me. "You can't come in the house," she said. "Isn't fit for visitors. You can wait there in the shop," she conceded, "if you must. Don't touch anything."

I smiled. "Actually," I said, "I've got another call to make and then I'll come back. If he comes home before then, ask him to wait."

She grunted and slammed the door. I poked about for a few minutes, and then we crossed the street. It wasn't far to walk.

He was sitting under the awning outside his shop, with a half-finished sandal on his knee; a thin man, unusually tall. He looked up and gave me a pleasant smile.

"Morning," he said. "And what can I do for you gentlemen?"

A pity; he seemed a pleasant enough fellow. I nodded, and the two thugs I'd brought with me darted forward and grabbed his arms. He started to protest, but I smacked him round the face so hard that his upper teeth came through his lip.

"Quintus," I said, "find his shears. They'll be hanging up, I expect; there, with the rest of the tools."

There they were, sure enough. They'd been cleaned, but not well enough to remove every last trace. Blood is tricksy stuff that way; it gets in the hinges of scissors and shears, and if you leave it a while before you clean up, it won't wash off, it has to be scrubbed.

"I think I've got this straight in my mind," I said, "but if I've got anything wrong, you tell me. Yesterday morning, you and your mate the carpenter from across the way joined the mob who were putting up the flags on Caesar's statue, there." I pointed. "The tribunes took them down again, and then the news came that Caesar had been killed. You and your friend and some others I don't know about decided to go and watch the fun, and you took the flag with you. And these," I added, waving the shears under his nose. "Well, you found some excitement and had some fun, and maybe things were starting to get out of hand. That's the way it can be, I know; everybody gets a bit full of himself, everybody acts a little bit crazy. It's just human nature, after all."

He tried to say something, but his mouth was full of blood and broken teeth.

"Anyway," I went on, "there were quite a few of you by now, and then you came across this lanky-looking type mooning about; bloody comical he looked, I'll bet, with his laurel wreath and his Greek gown. Was he carrying that little gilded harp?"

The man looked up and me and nodded. I smiled.

"He couldn't play it, you know," I said. "I don't think it could be played, even. He just carried it around because he thought it made him look the part, because he was a bloody fool. Anyway," I went on, "you and your mates said a few things, all good-natured fun, and then maybe he said something stupid back; I don't know, I wasn't there."

The man mumbled something. I didn't catch it, so I made him say it again.

"He said his name was Cinna," the man said. I nodded.

"That sounds plausible enough," I replied. "You thought he was Cinna the conspirator. Or some of you did, and the others joined in. That right?"

He dropped his chin, which I took to mean yes.

"Fair enough," I said. "Anyhow, the long and the short of it is, you stabbed him. With these." I drew the point of the shears down his cheek, drew blood. "Then everyone piled in, and that was that. Am I right? Syrus, do you recognize this man?"

Syrus nodded. "That's him," he said. "I think."

There was a little crowd gathering, but nobody seemed the slightest bit inclined to interfere. Too much history being made locally over the last couple of hours, I suppose.

"That's all right, then," I said. "I knew I had to look for a shoemaker and either a smith or a carpenter – shears and leather apron – and I knew I'd find them near the statue that got decorated with flags. I am right, aren't I?"

The man made a little gurgling noise, then nodded. "Thank you," I said; then I stood back and dipped my head in his direction. One of the smith's boys slashed his throat open with his own shears. I'd have thought I'd have looked away at the last moment, but I didn't. I've been a soldier in my time, of course; I was with Sulla's men in Numidia, though we never saw any action where I was posted.

We were just about finished with him when the carpenter came home. He had a little boy with him; his son, presumably. He watched while we killed his father, then ran into the house screaming for his granny. The sound of her cursing and screaming followed us all the way down the street and into the square.

What the hell; she was entitled. He was her son.

IMOGEN

Paul Barnett

Cymbeline *is one of Shakespeare's oddest plays. It was probably written in 1610 and first performed later that year or early in 1611. Like the events in* King Lear, *Shakespeare drew upon episodes from the* Chronicles of Raphael Holinshed *which told of the early history of Britain.* Cymbeline, *known elsewhere as Cunobelinus, was a High King of southern Britain in the years before the Roman conquest. Historically we know little about him and much of what Holinshed wrote is based on legend. Shakespeare's play concentrates on the relationship between Cymbeline's daughter Imogen and his adopted son, Posthumus Leonatus. Incensed by their marriage, Cymbeline banishes Posthumus who seeks refuge in Rome. There he befriends the scheming Iachimo who wagers he can test Imogen's love and seduce her. He fails to do so but by his wiles he finds out things about Imogen that only a lover might know. When Iachimo feeds this back, Posthumus plans to kill Imogen and sends word to his servant Pisanio to do the deed. Pisanio won't but sends a bloody cloth to Posthumus claiming Imogen's death. In the meantime Cymbeline has remarried and his new queen plans the death of Posthumus in order that her son, Cloten, can marry Imogen. Imogen escapes to Wales, disguised as a boy under the name Fidele, and becomes a page to the general Belarius. She is pursued by Cloten who plans to rape her but Cloten is killed by Guiderius, one of the lost sons of Cymbeline. Imogen is taken ill and is believed dead. She is left in a cave alongside the headless corpse of Cloten who was dressed in the clothes of Posthumus. When Imogen recovers, she believes the body is that of Posthumus. The Roman army invades and is defeated by Belarius, though Posthumus is taken prisoner. Imogen is still disguised as Fidele and serves as the page of the Roman general Lucius. Lucius pleas for Fidele's life, which is spared by Cymbeline. Iachimo is forced to confess his scheme whereby Posthumus realizes that Imogen had remained faithful. Imogen now reveals her real self to her father, and all ends in happy reconciliation. To say that the play is contrived is an understatement. Its strength lies in the character of Imogen and it is that and her reflection on her life and the truth behind the events that Paul Barnett explores in the following story.*

At the very last she retreated to the cave.

She felt as if this were a new birth, more real to her than any memories of childhood. It was here that she had discovered her brothers, here that she had discovered the love she felt for her father despite his harshness, and here that she had discovered herself for what she was.

Imogen. Daughter of Cymbeline. Wife of Posthumus Leonatus, the man her father had first adopted and then, because of the illicit marriage, banished. All had for a time been reunited and reconciled, but Posthumus and Cymbeline had never known the truth of it all.

The cave was cold, and water ran from its walls. She gathered long grasses and made out of them a bed on which she lay each night listening to the Welsh wind swirl around the mountain, reminding her of her age. As the grasses rotted the bed became more comfortable, but at last they began to stink, so she threw them out of the cave and gathered more. Winter was coming, and

soon she would have to find some other form of bed-
ding.

In the daytimes she often looked at her hands, seeing the
liver-spots and the creases. She had never intended to live
this long.

She had never intended to do most of the things she had
done during her life.

Each day Imogen lit a fire, sparking flints over dry leaves
and then adding kindling and finally dead branches foraged
the day before. After warming herself by the blaze she
went naked to the stream that emerged further down the
mountainside and washed both her body and her clothes. She
ran from the stream on her old, old legs back to the fire, using
its heat to dry first her flesh and then her frayed garb.

The days were all alike, except that some were windier
and colder than others. After a time, she began to forget
that they were passing, her only knowledge being that the
sun was lower and whiter in the sky than it had been, so
that the cold season was nearly upon her.

Sometimes she forgot her name, believing herself to be
called Fidele and believing herself to be a man. Then she
would feel her breasts, or discover that she lacked a penis
and remember that, yes, once upon a time she had posed as
a man. Pisanio had persuaded her to do this, and it had been
as a man that she had become the page of Belarius and then
the slave of the Roman general called Lucius . . .

Then came the snows. She had been wise enough to store
leaves and wood at the back of the cave, and these gave her
warmth for several days. With the last of her fuel, she dried
out more wood, but it was becoming increasingly hard to
find any amid the deep drifts. She stopped bathing herself:
there was no one else here to be offended by the smell of an
old woman growing older.

The thick layer of snow made it harder to find food as well.
Most of the time she subsisted on vegetables stolen from the
scanty fields of the farmers who tried to make a living on
the rocky soil further down the valley. Sometimes she took
a sheep, running after it and clapping her hands until the
terrified animal fled from her into the cave, where she could

capture it and cut its throat. Those were good times, when she had meat to eat; when the carcase began to decay she could throw the remains onto her fire, so that everything sizzled and spat and filled the cave with a cooking smell that seemed to fill her belly even if she had eaten nothing. She felt she should do something with the wool – perhaps add it to her bed – but always much of it was bloodstained after her clumsy execution of the beast.

Once she found a dead hare, which she skinned and gutted and cooked. The taste was a delight after weeks of turnips and occasional mutton, but the following day found her too ill to move except as far as the cave-mouth, where she uncontrollably and simultaneously vomited and shat and piddled, blemishing the snow.

Once she had been a king's daughter. No, she was still a king's daughter – nothing could take that away from her – but she was also the humblest of any savage in all the land that her father ruled.

What she recollected most about the war was the noise.

The Romans, believing themselves invincible, had sent an army into her father's land, imagining it to be an easy conquest. But the Romans had been defeated, largely because of the bravery and cleverness of those whom Cymbeline had banished: the lord Belarius and Imogen's husband Posthumus. Her father, believing Posthumus to be a Roman and Imogen to be the servant of one, had come close to having her and her husband executed out of hand. It was the discovery that he had almost slain his own daughter that had given him a wisdom he had never before possessed.

But Imogen rarely let her mind rest long on that. The war brought noise. It brought screams and the clash of metal on hide, and the particular sort of noise that is one's own fear.

Looking out of the cave-mouth she could see nothing but whiteness interspersed by a few skeletal trees. She hugged her arms around herself, trying to stop shivering. The wind was a constant scream, and sometimes it swung around to batter her chest. There was enough fuel in the cave for her to

have a fire today, she thought, but not enough for tomorrow.
She couldn't bring herself to leave the cave to look for more
wood. The cold was great enough that the half-sheep she still
had would remain edible for days.

Then she saw the wolf.

The wolf was very large and very black – looking even
blacker against the snow. It was sitting about one hundred
yards down the slope from her and watching her.

So this was to be the end of it – the final sentence of the
scroll of the things she had done.

Dying would be a pleasure. Anything would be better than
the life – not life, just existence – that she was leading in
the cave. She made a small bow and fluttered her hand in a
beckoning movement to the wolf.

It raised itself, stretched its rear legs and then its fore legs,
rolled over a couple of times in the snow, shook its head and
came up towards her.

At last I can die, she thought.

The wolf was moving more quickly through the snow now.
She lowered the top of her tunic to make her throat a more
attractive target for the beast's attack.

But the wolf merely took her hand very gently in its jaws
and led her back into the cave. After some misunderstanding
it was able to persuade her to sit down by the embers of
yesterday's fire, then it fetched fresh wood from the pile she
had built up.

The wolf smelled of excrement and old sweat and many
other things, but it also smelled of friendship. The animal
would not approach the fire closely, instead dropping branches
by Imogen's side so that she could toss the wood onto the
flames. Each time the animal did this she ran her hands
through the coarse hair on its head; once she tried to pull
its muzzle towards her face, but this seemed to frighten it
and it ran away from her and out of the cave-mouth. Later,
however, it returned: shuffling with its rear-legs, it presented
to Imogen several branches and half a rabbit, then watched
her use the former to cook the latter. Her half-sheep could
wait. She had been given a gift.

"You have a name," she said later to the wolf.

The wolf was snoring loudly, half-wrapped around the fire but not too near to it. She could see that it was not an "it" but a "he".

"You have a name that is very appropriate, and even if it weren't I'd give it to you anyway." She reached forward a hand and laid it on the flank of the wolf. "You're called Cymbeline."

As soon as she said the name she wished she hadn't.

Her father. What he had done to her.

And what in the end she had done to him.

It was too late to change her mind, because by her act of naming the wolf had been defined; it had been given its position not only in her world but in the world as a whole.

Despite the heat of the fire, she shivered.

Then, after a while, she began to cease regretting her impulse. Her father had been an old wolf, defending himself through rage against the young wolves among the pack that surrounded him – the Catevellauni pack. He had been unable to understand that age must make way for youth, and even more unable to understand when one of the bitches he had sired, Imogen herself, had disobeyed him – had, as he saw it, rebelled against his gods-given primacy, his natural entitlement to command each and every member of the pack.

For some reason, she trusted the wolf. Had it wanted to kill her, it would have done so by now. She lay down beside it, curling her body around its back, holding it as close against her as she had ever held a lover. Soon she slipped into sleep, and dreamed dreams that made no sense, although her father was there, and Posthumus was there, and Iachimo was there, and Lucius and Belarius too.

In the morning she awoke to find the fire dead and the wolf gone, but her dreams continued, and now they were sorting themselves out into rationality. She wished that all of her life had been a dream, because a nightmare could be forgotten within days and the acts one performed in it were guiltless, being unreal. True memories were different: they were inescapable.

Outside the cave she could see the tracks of the wolf in the snow, and she followed them. They took her through the frozen air to the stream, where the wolf was waiting for her, its breath steaming even more than her own.

With a stone she hacked through the ice so that the animal could drink. After it had finished it watched her as she cupped her trembling hands and put water to her lips. She wasn't able to drink much. The dreams were still lingering, as if she were enduring two realities at once.

Pisanio – loyal Pisanio, servant to both her husband and herself – is saying: "Your husband wants you dead."

"But why?" says Imogen, horrified.

"Because of your adultery with the Italian scoundrel Iachimo. Iachimo told Posthumus about it. He gave him evidence." The servant looks shamefaced, as if this is something that should never be mentioned. He also looks a little frightened: should she wish to, she could have him killed, although he knows her as a merciful woman. "He took your bracelet. He says you have a mole on your left breast, which I know to be true. Posthumus has sent me a letter from Italy telling me of all this, and has instructed me to kill you for your infidelity."

"Iachimo? He tried to seduce me but he failed. My heart is true to Posthumus."

Pisanio shrugs. "I believe you." It is clear that he is lying, but she doesn't feel any anger towards him.

They are in the Great Hall of her father's house. It is early in the morning. Wind whips through the room, making the hangings flap against the walls as if they were alive. She feels that the hangings are listening to their conversation.

"Does my husband believe more in Iachimo than he does in me?"

"It seems so, yes."

"Then," she says, looking at the hem of her blue skirt, "it seems that I have very little to live for. Kill me, Pisanio. I'd rather be dead than doubted."

The servant, daring, touches her hand. "I won't kill you, lady."

"I've asked you to. I have ordered it."

"I disobey your orders."

She looks into his eyes, and sees the compassion there. She sees that the man is devoted to her, and will never raise a hand to harm her, however much she asks him to. For a moment she is angry with him, but then she relents.

"Lady Imogen," he says, "I cannot see you die. I will not *let* you die."

"You're more arrogant than you are permitted to be," she says, not meaning the words. She moves to the unglazed window of her father's house and stares out over the woodlands below. The tops of the pine trees are moving like hands in the wind. She smells the stench of the farm animals directly beneath her: it is a good stench, reminding her of life.

Pisanio is once again beside her.

"If I decline to kill you, at Posthumus' order, someone else will – and likely kill me as well because of my disobedience."

She draws a deep breath. "Then kill me," she says with a shrug. The matter is not important to her. "He has told you to. I have told you to. If you have the affection for me that I just saw in your eyes, Pisanio, put an end to my life."

Once, among the pine needles in the forest down the slope, she and Posthumus made impetuous love, yipping with pain as the dead brown-grey needles stabbed into their bodies. At the time the pain had almost added to their pleasure, because it was shared between them, a secret thing. Now she wonders if the thrust of a dagger into her chest would hurt any more than the pine needles did. Tears come to her eyes. Posthumus' accusation – that she has betrayed him – is in itself an act of betrayal.

"Kill me," she repeats in a whisper.

"No," says the servant.

Suddenly he is a master whom she must obey. She has no will left of her own. He leads her out of the Great Hall and down long stone corridors that smell of suet. She must have been in this part of her father's house before – as a child she explored every nook and cranny – but now she cannot remember these walls, these floors.

"My room," says Pisanio at last.

It is a bleak place, containing nothing but a cot and a pot, which he has not emptied this morning. On the bed are trousers and a shirt.

"Wear these," he says. "The cook will have to kill a pig today, and I will soak one of your garments in the animal's blood and send it to Posthumus as proof that I have done what he required of me."

She is unselfconscious as she undresses in front of him: he has seen her naked often before as he has bathed her. Imogen no longer seems to have any will of her own – strange for one who has always been so wilful. Pisanio helps her strap her small breasts to her chest, and then she puts on the surprisingly foreign-seeming clothing. The garments, although clean, have a faint smell of manhood in them. Although simply changing her clothing ought to make no difference, the trace of odour makes her feel like the young man she sees when Pisanio holds up the mirror to her.

"Quick," he says. "Come and sit here. I'll crop your hair. You can choose yourself a name while I'm working with the blades. What does your man-self want to be called?"

She sits, and the tiny soft hairs on the back of her neck start to prickle, not unpleasurably, as the servant shears away a great fistful of her locks.

"Why are you not loyal to your master?" she says.

"I am being loyal to him. Hold your head stiller. In a few months or years he'll remember how much he loved you and the crime he had forced me to commit. He's in a fury at the moment, but his fury will soon die. Do you think he's been entirely chaste in Italy?"

"Yes," she says without thinking.

The servant makes no reply. He is concentrating on making her look like a slender, small young man. This is clearly the only reason why he makes no reply.

"He and I are supposedly faithful to each other," she says. "So I'll call myself Fidele."

That night, as they sat on either side of the fire eating turnips that were acridly black on the outside and

almost raw in the middle, the wolf began to talk to
her.

"How much can you really remember?" it said.

"Everything of importance. My memory's not so clear as
it was, but I'm not yet old." She paused. "Yes, I *am* old, but
I'm not in my dotage. Yet."

The wolf looked at her without expression. She suspected
that later, after she had fallen asleep, it would go out into
the night, and catch some creatures to eat. Or maybe it would
gnaw at her half-sheep. But at the moment, out of pity or some
other emotion alien to her, it was making do with these vile
turnips which she'd dug up out of the snow with her bare
hands from some poor farmer's land.

"I've just lied to you, and I didn't realize I was lying," she
said suddenly. "I *can't* rely on my memory. I think sometimes
it . . . deceives me. I remember the things I did during my
life as if they were dreams, and maybe that's all they are.
Maybe my life was entirely different. Maybe I've never truly
lived at all, but am just a creature that has learned how
to dream itself up a past where it was the daughter of a
king. I could be an elemental – I could have come from
Faerie and lost myself in the fogs of mortal delusion. All
the dreams I have could be born out of the fact that I
am in the wrong world. Do you think this could be true,
Cymbeline?"

"No."

The wolf spoke the syllable so curtly that it was as if she
had been slapped.

"Why are you here?" she said.

"To help you find out what you did and why you did it,
so that you can reconcile yourself with yourself."

"What have I done?" She wasn't hungry any more, and
threw the rest of her turnip into the fire; there was a chorus
of complaint from the flames and then, almost immediately,
a reek that had her dragging herself away across the cave-floor
until she was out of its direction.

"That was a foolish thing to do," said the wolf.

"I've done many foolish things," she said. "More of them
than you can imagine."

"But I want you to *remember* what you've done, not just to dream it."

She put an arm around the wolf's shoulder and at last, after a first reluctance, it rested its heavy head against hers, almost as if they were sweethearts gazing into the fire.

There were castles among the flames, and there were also caves. One of the caves was this one, where now she sat beside a wolf that was irrevocably called by the same name as her father.

The heat lulled her.

Fidele wakes to discover a headless corpse at his side, and he shrieks, putting his knuckles into his mouth. For a moment he thinks it is the body of the wolf: no, this is a human, a man. Posthumus. Fidele remembers knitting the jacket this dead thing wears.

Fidele turns away from the dead thing and weeps – not for Posthumus, who wanted Pisanio to stick a dagger into Fidele's heart, but for himself. He sees that there is blood on his soft hands, but only after he has tasted its salt and smeared it across his face.

A man shouldn't weep like this. Fidele's tears are those of a woman.

The remains of his illness gnaw at him, as does his hunger. Through his tears he looks out over the hillside, and memories begin to come back. Living in the cave. Being the servant of Belarius and Guiderius and Arviragus, all the time keeping from them a secret.

A secret.

He has kept it so well that, in his delirium, he has managed to keep it from himself. Only now does he gather the strength to try to discover in his mind the truth of that secret. And at last it comes to him.

His womanhood.

Fidele touches his groin, and remembers the time when he was Imogen. Yet his inner sense is telling him that he is a man – though a man still weeping a woman's tears.

"Madness took you," said the wolf.

Imogen had been almost asleep, leaning against the mass of the beast. She sat upright, moving slightly away from it, putting her hands to her cheeks and discovering that fresh tears had flowed down her cheeks.

"Yes," she said. "Always there was madness. I was wrong to say that I've done a lot of foolish things. They were *mad* things. And I don't think the madness has left me. I'm sitting in a cave on a Welsh mountainside having a conversation with a wolf. Rational people don't do that."

"A rational person wouldn't have slept with Iachimo."

There it was: out in the open. The flatness of the way the wolf spoke the words made the truth all the more painful.

"I was rational enough to lie about it afterwards," she said, before being engulfed by a further wave of sobbing.

"I don't attach any blame for either act," said the wolf. "You were a woman who had only just discovered the joys of lovemaking, and then your husband was banished. You might never see him again. You were like a furnace that was eager to devour coal. You took Iachimo to your bed not out of any fondness for him but just because you needed someone to be there. And then afterwards you lied so well to Pisanio and all the others that you convinced yourself that it had never happened."

Once again Imogen put her arm around the wolf and stared into the flames. The animal seemed to know more about her past than she knew herself.

Iachimo had been suave and attractive, and he had used every weapon in his armoury to seduce her. No one else in her father's court would have dared try, because they pitied her situation or because they feared her father's ire. How she had damned their pity! Waking up in a cold and lonely bed each day had been like the plucking out of her eyes, as if the gods had selected her to be cursed. She had wanted Posthumus to be there, to feel him running his fingers through her hair or to listen to his silly jokes.

But Posthumus had been in a faraway land, and would likely never return. So she had allowed a surrogate Posthumus to come to her chamber – not once but many times – so that in the mornings she would feel warm breath against her neck and a hand caressing her stomach and breasts.

For that the price of Iachimo's somewhat hasty and careless intercourse had been one worth paying.

"You might have had his child," said the wolf.

"That, too, would have been a price worth paying," said Imogen. "Because of my father and his accursed stubbornness I was barred almost entirely from the simple pleasure of the touch of another human being."

"Pisanio bathed you."

"That made it worse. Don't you understand? It wasn't until far too late that I realized that Pisanio, in his own way, genuinely loved me: at the time I believed that he performed all his servantly deeds because he had no alternative. It was only when he disobeyed Posthumus' order to kill me that I began to know the truth. Before then, Pisanio had been part of the furniture, but each day, with his ministrations as I lay in my bath, he unknowingly aroused me."

"I thought it wasn't arousal that you were looking for," said the wolf. "I thought it was merely affection."

"I *didn't* want the arousal," replied Imogen sleepily. "It happened despite me. But I would have slept with Pisanio rather than Iachimo had I known his fondness for me."

"Iachimo was not an entirely bad man."

"No," she said. "He did me one great act of kindness."

"And what was that?" said the wolf. It shuffled around until it was lying on its side, its head in her lap.

"He lied."

"About what?"

"When my father insisted he tell the truth about the ring, he lied. He pretended that all he had done was spy on me when I was naked."

"The ring?"

The bet. Her husband, Posthumus, bragging about her virtue and probably drunk, had wagered her chastity against a diamond ring. All this she had discovered too late, long after she had fled her father's house.

He had treated her as if she were a common whore, an object.

And, she told herself, because she wanted affection she had become much like that common whore.

"Was it your fault or Posthumus'?" said the wolf.

"Mine," said Imogen firmly.

"Are you so sure?"

No, she wasn't sure. Her adultery – her various adulteries – had all come about because of that wager. It was strange that men felt they could bet about the bodies of women, even the women they had told they loved.

"He made me what I am – what I have been," she said. The wolf fetched more wood for the fire, giving it to her as gently as a parent would have. She threw the branches onto the redness. Some of them were green, and sizzled alarmingly. She smelt the death of their resin.

"So why do you blame yourself for it all?"

"My adulteries were petty crimes. They don't matter. Lucius thought I was a boy when he ordered me to his room, but was just as glad when he found out that I was a woman: all he wanted was someone who had no choice but to obey his commands. He turned out to be the most tender of all the lovers I ever had. Posthumus was clumsy and Iachimo was efficient in attaining his own pleasure, but Lucius stroked me until the whole of my body sang, and only then would he move into me. I believe he loved me – yes, I *know* that he loved me, because he lied as well."

"To you?"

"Never to me."

Imogen reached out a foot as close as she dared to the fire.

"He loved me enough to make sure that I was, in one way or another, returned to my husband," she said. "To do that he had to lie – he had to pretend that he knew me only as his page, Fidele."

"So many lies," said the wolf.

"My life has been built on lies," said Imogen. "That was why, even in the early days, I was enslaved by the madness. Even now that I'm telling you my memories, Cymbeline, I can't be certain that they're the truth. Maybe I'm lying to you without even knowing it."

"Maybe I'm a lie as well."

"I can feel the weight of your head against my thighs, father."

"Are you sure that you can?"

"I'm too sleepy. Let's talk again tomorrow."

They didn't talk tomorrow, or for the next few days after that. Father Wolf, as she had nicknamed the beast, became skittish and uncertain of her, and wouldn't allow her to come near it, let alone touch it. It seemed to have lost its powers of speech, although at night, as she drifted into an inevitably fitful sleep, she could hear the wolf dragging fuel into the cave for the next day's fire. Sometimes it would bring her food as well: always the neatly bitten-off half of an animal or a bird. It was sharing with her. More often they had no food. The mutton was long gone, and she was too listless to chase for more. The wolf could have caught and killed a sheep, but for some reason it never did.

Hunger and the relentless cold of the days were driving her into a pit of despair that seemed to have no bottom. This was the place where she had been so ill so many years ago that Guiderius and Arviragus had assumed she was dead. Perhaps she *had* died, then, and everything she thought had happened to her since was an illusion.

She left the cave only to piss and shit. Sometimes, when the cold was particularly cutting, she pissed in a corner of the cave, knowing that the meatish smell would soon dissipate.

She hoped for death. She wished that she had indeed died here decades ago. It would have been better.

Then, one night, the wolf spoke to her again.

"You killed him, didn't you?"

"Killed who?" She was confused, both by the question and by the sudden speech.

"Your husband."

"I . . . I don't know. Perhaps I did. He deserved to die. He tried to have me killed."

She did her best to remember, but all that would come to her mind was the sensation of her lethal little bronze dagger hacking at the throat of her sleeping stepmother. Despite

Imogen's pleas for clemency, Cymbeline had executed a dozen men most brutally on the grounds that one of them might have committed the murder; it had never occurred to him that a woman would have used the assassin's knife so adroitly.

The Queen. The woman Cymbeline had taken as his second wife and who had wanted to foist her doltish son Cloten on Imogen as her husband, when Posthumus had been her husband. The Queen had betrayed Imogen and Posthumus to Cymbeline, telling him of their marriage. Yes, she, too, had deserved to die. But Imogen could recall nothing of her husband's death – even though she knew that he was long dead.

"Your stepmother," said the wolf. "I hadn't known about that."

"Aren't *any* of my thoughts my own?"

"Any word that you speak becomes shared. Why should thoughts be any different?"

The beast moved – still with the old wariness – around the fire and came to settle itself against her as it had done in the early days after she had found it, or it had found her.

"You're right," it said, its breath redolent of the squirrels it had caught for their supper. "She tried to destroy your life with her silly little schemings, so it was justifiable that you destroyed her. It was *not* justifiable that your father had those men killed."

"How was he to know who had murdered her?"

"If he had thought about it – or if he had ordered someone to do his thinking for him – he could have uncovered the truth."

"But he was the king!" Although the wolf was physically very close to her, she felt at the same time that it was far away.

"And they were men. They had the same right to life as he had. As you had." The wolf's voice was very quiet.

"*Would* he have discovered what had really happened?" she said.

"If he'd wanted to – if he'd tried to. Oh, he was probably too much of a fool to do so himself, but there were some clever men about him: he could have directed one of them to use his natural powers of detection to find out who had killed the Queen."

"And Posthumus, you say, was murdered?" She hardly knew that she was speaking. Since the wolf seemed able to read her thoughts, it was often difficult to know whether or not she'd spoken them.

"I believe he was. I believe you were the one who murdered him."

"Are you certain?" She still had no memory of the act.

"Perfectly."

"Why are you so sure?"

"Discovering the truth of past deeds is always, to be trite, a matter of probing memories: who saw what happened and where, and piecing together the jigsaw of all the pieces that seemed inconsequential to them at the time. But detection of guilt can work in another way, for not everyone *knows* their own guilt. You don't, as yet. Even if you hadn't been in the suffocating embrace of your madness you might not have known."

The wolf nudged her with its head in a curiously affectionate way. Yes, she had been right to call him Cymbeline, and also Father Wolf, because this was the kind of fondness and understanding that she'd always sought in her father, but never found. She had loved him so much, even after he had banished Posthumus, but he had been too tangled up in the duties of kingship ever to notice her.

Or perhaps he had.

"So to discover the truth of a crime you must take memories, which are elusive things, and put them all together," said the wolf. "Sometimes people take the memories of others and weave them until they make a tapestry which is the truth of what occurred. In your case, Imogen my daughter, you have only your *own* memories to explore. You must uncover your own crimes."

"You have fresh blood on your hands, and on your riding-gown," says Fidele.

"Nothing that will not wash away," says Imogen. She strips

the garment off over her head, unembarrassed by her nudity in front of Pisanio – no, this is Fidele – though at the same time wishing that her body did not bear the all too obvious marks of having borne Posthumus' children. It is little wonder that Posthumus has come to her bed only rarely these years, and then usually with an expression of grim duty on his face. Equally, it is little wonder that, as is common knowledge in her father's house, he was taking his pleasures elsewhere. Fidele told her this long ago; everyone else conspired to try to keep it a secret from her. "Come down to the river with me. You can bathe me, if you like, just as Pisanio used to do."

"The gown will never come clean," says Fidele. "You'd be better to burn it, or bury it."

"No," she says. "I need the blood still to be there when I return to my father's house, as I shriek and wail and tell them all how thieves set upon my husband and stole the pouch of coins he wore at his belt and the diamond ring from his finger and then slit his throat. After they had gone his loving wife took him in her arms and held him, even though his life had ebbed away by then. What must be hidden is not the gown but the pouch and the ring – and the dagger. Would you do this for me?"

"We can only do it together," says Fidele, looking across to where the horses are tethered. The animals are nervous, trying to distance themselves from Posthumus's motionless, prostrate form.

Fidele.

Her perfect lover.

The one who has always been faithful to her. The only one who has not simply tried to use her, in some way or another.

Together they take the pouch and the ring and the dagger down towards the riverbank. She smiles at Fidele, and he smiles back at her.

"Swim out into the river," he says. "I'll swim by your side."

He takes off his doublet and hose, then squelches through the mud of the bank ahead of her and dives ungracefully into the water. She laughs at him, with him, and they laugh again when she performs the manoeuvre with equal awkwardness.

The water is sweetly cold on their skins after the heat of the noonday. Both of them take a mouthful of it as they swim to the centre of the river.

"Here?" says Fidele. He has in one hand the dagger and in the other the pouch.

"Yes, here."

He lets the objects loose, and they vanish into the darkness of the river. Perhaps one day the sluggish current will carry them to the sea.

Imogen waits a little longer before she sends the diamond ring to the same destination. It was her loving-gift to Posthumus, but he used it as the wager in a drunken bet he made with a schemer. She, who loved him, was the basis of a bet. Yet she is reluctant to let it go, for it reminds her of how much and how purely and passionately she did love him, once. Before she became something for him to bet on. Before he destroyed her body and aged her with the children. Before he began to make love with her only because it was expected of him by the court, so that every time he made love with her it was as if he were hurling abuse in her face.

She has hated him for many years. Her revenge has been overdue.

"Hiding the ring is the only way to lose your misery," says Fidele, floating easily in the water, moving his arms and legs just enough to counter the current.

"Yes," she says. "You're right."

She is crying, but she drops the ring from her hand.

And then suddenly there is no more crying. She feels as if her body has become lighter, so that the water hardly needs to support her. She flips over on her back, and Fidele does the same. Now the warmth of the summer sun is like a hand stroking her – and she opens her eyes to find that it is indeed a hand.

Fidele's hand.

"You asked me to bathe you," he says.

"We shall bathe each other," she replies. "Then afterwards, perhaps, we can make love before I must re-don my gown and make the pell-mell ride. The thieves would have raped me, you know. Even though I'm a king's daughter, the wise-wives will look for evidence."

"I cannot give you that," says Fidele, washing each finger one by one, and then kissing them. For a reason she does not understand, she is attending to each of his fingers as well, as if there might be blood on his hands too. But it wasn't he who lured Posthumus away from the court for a ride through the country together, and it wasn't he who steered them towards a glade in the forest where they once made love on pine needles, and it wasn't he who chose that spot as the place where, as her husband despised her nostalgia, she plunged the wicked dagger into his throat.

Later, after both she and Fidele are clean, they do indeed make love on the riverbank, and then she puts back on her bloodied gown and, with Posthumus's horse following behind her, rides home.

The afternoon sun is cooler.

"I killed him," said Imogen wearily. "Fidele helped me."

The wolf shifted against her.

"Fidele helped you in so many things," it said.

"Did I kill my father as well?"

"No. Your father is still alive, just. But you took all his will to live from him. It might have been kinder if you *had* killed him."

"How do you know this?" Despite the heat of the fire, she was trembling with cold.

"Because I *am* your father."

"Father Wolf?"

"Cymbeline."

"You've known all along. Everything about me. But you've never told me that you knew. Always you've pretended that I was just some bit of household goods – as if I were a ham hanging in the kitchen or a jester dancing in the Great Hall."

"I'm a king. It is the duty of kings to create heirs, not to nurture them."

The wolf abruptly moved itself away from her. It looked

at her as if it wanted to kiss her. She turned her head and gazed into its eyes. There was love visible there.

"No," she said. "You're not my father."

"How can you tell?" said the wolf.

"Your eyes. You love me."

"I'm an old and ailing wolf."

"You love me."

"Perhaps."

"Don't lie."

Imogen closed her eyes in weariness, then opened them again.

There was no wolf in the cave, only the shadows that the fire made on the furthest wall. They had made – they had been – the wolf that had for such a short time befriended her.

Yet she still felt that the wolf had loved her in a truer way than anyone else.

It had loved her. The other Cymbeline, her father, had regarded her as a possession.

She wound her body around a fire that for days had been nothing but ash, shut her eyes, and begged the cold of the night to take her forever from the things she remembered.

And it did.

SERPENT'S TOOTH

Martin Edwards

The character of King Lear will be found in Geoffrey of Monmouth's History of the Kings of Britain, *where the name is usually spelt Leir or even Llyr, and is almost certainly based on the Celtic sea-god who was widely venerated in pre-Roman Britain. If he had any historicity at all then he must have existed three or four centuries* BC, *but Shakespeare's treatment of him makes him seem almost contemporary, or at best a few centuries before Shakespeare's time, which is why I've placed this story at this point in our journey. Shakespeare wrote his first version of the play around 1605 but revised it more than once over the years. In some adaptations and interpretations* King Lear *stands out as Shakespeare's greatest study of the human condition, and it may be seen as his darkest and most poignant tragedy. Nearing his dotage, Lear wishes to share his kingdom with his three daughters. His youngest daughter, Cordelia, refuses to share in the public display of affection for her father which cuts Lear to the quick as she was his favourite. He disinherits her, sharing the kingdom between her sisters Goneril and Regan. Cordelia marries the King of France and goes to live there. Lear finds that living with his daughters and their husbands is insufferable and he flees to the countryside where he suffers a mental breakdown. The Duke of Gloucester befriends Lear and helps him escape to Dover*

*where he is reunited with Cordelia and regains his sanity.
For his efforts, however, Gloucester is tortured and blinded
by Cordelia's sisters. Gloucester's illegitimate son, Edmund,
orders the deaths of Lear and Cordelia. Although Edmund is
defeated by his legitimate brother, Edgar, it is too late to save
Cordelia. Lear dies of a broken heart. There is just a glimmer
of hope at the end of the play that Edgar, along with Goneril's
husband, the Duke of Albany, will restore some sanity to the
land. Martin Edwards moves on a generation in order to look
back at the events and find out what further dark secrets remain
to be uncovered.*

The boy on the edge of the cliff closed his eyes. Overhead
the gulls were shrieking, as if to warn him of the danger, but
Tristram paid them no heed. He could not rid his mind of
the memory of the screams of terror as his father plunged
his sword into Aldfrith's body.

It was *his* fault that Aldfrith was dead. Guilt hurt him like a
dagger thrust. Why had he not held his tongue? His curiosity
had always been insatiable; now it had provoked Osric into
murdering a faithful servant. Although the King's moods had
become increasingly erratic of late, Tristram had not foreseen
the consequence of asking his father if it was true that he had
inherited his sword from King Lear. As the words left his lips,
Osric had flown into a rage that was terrible to behold.

"Who told you that?" he had demanded, seizing his Tristram
by the throat.

"I can't recall."

Osric tightened his stranglehold. "*Tell me!*"

"It – it may have been Aldfrith, sir," Tristram had gasped.
"But . . ."

It had been enough to seal the servant's fate. The memory
of Aldfrith's cries had tortured Tristram as he blundered out
of the castle grounds and along the path through the forest.
A low branch cut his face and nettles stung his hands and
legs as he stumbled along the track. Blinded by tears, he had

fallen over the root of an oak and cracked his head upon a jagged stone, but the pain meant nothing. He had kept on in the direction of the path that led to the sea. Once or twice he had sensed that there was someone – or something – behind him, but he had not looked back. Savage beasts roamed here, wolves and wild boar. Yet there was no reason to be afraid, when you were ready to die.

As he filled his lungs with misty air, he began to tremble. Despite the chill, his blood-streaked palms were moist with sweat. The waves that would swallow him were roaring over the rocks below. Did death offer peace at last – or nothing more than a different form of torment?

"Stop!"

His whole body shuddered as he let out his breath. The old man's voice was muffled by the fog that shrouded the coast-line, but he recognized it at once. He turned and peered back down the muddy path. A stooped figure was hurrying towards him, arms outstretched.

"So I am not too late!"

The boy's throat was parched and he struggled to form his reply. "How – how did you find me, Fulk?"

The old man approached him, strands of white hair flapping over his hollow cheeks. He was wheezing with the exertion and his eyes were bloodshot. "I saw you leave the castle. I followed as fast as I was able. You see, I was afraid of what you might do."

"You should have let me be. After what we witnessed today, I wanted to think in solitude."

Fulk touched the boy's arm with a bony finger. "If you wished to be alone, you could have retired to your chamber. This is no place for a prince. The cliff is sheer, the path treacherous. One false step – and you would be no more."

Tristram gazed at his mentor. "Would that be such a terrible thing?"

"For Britain, yes. As for your father – it would break his heart."

Tristram bit his lip. "Did you see his face as he struck the blows that killed Aldfrith? I no longer believe he has a heart."

"That is where you are wrong. Osric still cares for you. He always longed for a son, an heir to the throne. He fought long and hard to gain this kingdom. You have often heard him say that it was his destiny. If he lost you, he would lose his mind."

The boy gave a harsh laugh. "Has he not lost it already?"

Fulk shivered and pulled his cloak more closely around his frail shoulders. "You were shocked by Aldfrith's death. It is understandable."

"My father murdered him – because of me."

"Why do you say that?"

"You know that lately I have become fascinated by the history of our land. I have heard tell of the valour of King Lear and of the rift with his daughter Cordelia. As far as I can ascertain, they died at the same time, but I have found it impossible to discover the circumstances of their deaths. The mystery has begun to nag at me. Why so much secrecy? You have evaded my questions and no one else has been willing to speak. At length, I decided to press Aldfrith."

"He was always a notorious gossip," Fulk said grimly.

"Yet even he was reluctant to talk. Finally, he muttered something about my father's sword. He hinted that it had once belonged to Lear himself. At once I decided to challenge my father, hoping to catch him off guard and thereby to learn the truth."

Rubbing the neck that still felt tender, he described Osric's frenzied reaction. "I yielded Aldfrith's name under duress. Yet the slaying will lie on my conscience for ever."

Fulk sighed. "The fault is mine. I taught you to crave knowledge, but I did not mean to encourage inquisitiveness where no useful purpose is served. To question Osric about Lear – or Cordelia – will drive him to fury beyond reason."

Tristram said hoarsely, "I saw Aldfrith's head, you know. The mouth was curved in a dreadful grin."

He turned back to face the sea and retched. The old man put a restraining hand on him and said, "I saw it too, Tristram. It was a sight to sicken any man. Yet there have been many violent deaths in my time. I have witnessed many horrors."

After a little while the boy said in a muffled tone, "How can you bear it?"

"Because there is no choice." Fulk tightened his grip on his pupil. "To sacrifice your own life because of revulsion at your father's behaviour would be to betray your countrymen as well as yourself. Come, soon there will be icicles on my beard. Let us return to the warmth of the castle."

Tristram listened once more to the crashing of the waves against the shore. "Very well," he said after a long pause. "But I still wish to solve the puzzle of King Lear. Unless I have solved it already."

"What do you mean?" Fulk demanded.

Tristram took a deep breath. Now was the moment to put his shameful theory to the test. "When Lear died, my father was a young soldier. If his sword once belonged to Lear, I can only surmise that he claimed it after killing the King. Is it true that he gained the throne through regicide?"

"No!" Fulk exclaimed. "Lear was not slain. He died of a broken heart. Besides, you are forgetting that after Lear's death, Kent and Edgar ruled jointly for a time."

The boy swore in frustration. It was as if Fulk was relieved that he had guessed wrongly. "Then tell me this. Once my father was a great warrior, renowned for his courage in the heat of battle. I was proud to be his son. More than that, I adored him. But now he has become a vicious tyrant. What is the explanation for his dark moods, Fulk? Why does he lock himself in his chamber and rant behind the bolted door? Why does he turn on a loyal servant and kill him without good cause?"

"You ask too many questions."

"But there are some answers you prefer me not to hear, are there not?"

Fulk grimaced. "I do not mean to treat you like a child."

"Then will you be frank with me?" Tristram moved closer to the old man, so that they were almost touching. "If I am to rule our kingdom, do I not deserve to know how that came to be? I need to learn how my father took possession of the sword and what it is about the events surrounding Lear's reign that tortures him."

Fulk bowed his head. "Throughout my life I have quested for truth, but one thing above all I have learned. Some mysteries are not meant to be solved. There are times when to know too much is dangerous. Yet if you insist, I cannot deny you. But for now, I am tired and cold. If we do not return soon, then I fear that I shall not see the castle again. Here, take my arm. We must make haste before night falls and the wolves scent our presence."

"Where did you go to this afternoon?" Osric said suddenly that night. "I searched for you, yet you were nowhere to be found."

Their meal finished, Osric had invited Tristram to drink with him in his private chamber. Tristram hoped that he might be able to persuade his father to talk and offer some clue to the change that had crept over him, turning him into a despot dreaded and despised in equal measure. Osric's trusted sword, a fearsome weapon made of welded strips of iron, leaned against one wall. Aldfrith's blood had been washed from it and the King had made no mention of the slaying of his servant; it was as if the man had never lived.

Osric was in excellent spirits, his mood reminiscent of the days that the boy could now but dimly recollect, days when his father had taught him how to hunt and ride a horse. Tristram's mother had died within a year of his birth; women servants had helped to rear him and Fulk had been his teacher, but Osric had always inspired in him a mixture of awe and devotion. In recent years, however, the King had become increasingly reclusive, prey to melancholy and sudden bouts of anger. Yet this evening it had been as if the years had rolled back and the pair of them were bosom friends again as Osric strode up and down, telling stories about the battles of yesteryear.

The question took the boy by surprise. He stammered, "I – I needed time to think, sire."

"What?" his father roared. The jovial humour had vanished. "What need have we of thinkers? Contemplation is an old man's pastime – and a dangerous one, to judge from the cuts and bruises on your forehead." He spat on to the floor. "When the time comes for you to succeed me, you will need to be bold. If you spend your days in idle reflection, enemies will seize the chance to strike, depend upon it. Our people expect deeds from their ruler, not fine thoughts."

Tristram inhaled the thick smoke from the peat fire. "I am not certain that Fulk would agree with you, sire."

"Fulk?" the King demanded, with a loud belch of contempt. "What does Fulk know? He is a stranger to the battlefield. He bears no scars." He banged his cup down on the table, then touched the thick line of ridged tissue which stretched across his leathery cheek from the ear to the corner of his mouth. He had never spoken about the campaign of which the scar was presumably a legacy, but Tristram guessed that the enemy who had inflicted it would have suffered an unspeakable fate. "You should not attend to what that foolish old man says. I have half a mind to banish him."

Tristram's stomach lurched. "You cannot do that!"

"I am the King," Osric said stretching out his hairy, muscular arms. He was tall, with broad shoulders, and although his shaggy hair and beard were now liberally flecked with grey he remained as physically powerful and intimidating as in his prime. That very afternoon he had, before Tristram's eyes, proved that he was strong enough to decapitate a man. "I can do as I please."

"But he is wise and these past thirty years, the King of Britain has had no more trusted subject." Tristram moistened his lips. "He taught the children of Kent and Edgar and before them, the daughters of Lear. Goneril, Regan – and Cordelia."

Osric started. It seemed to the boy that his father cast a quick, uncertain glance at the large chest in the corner of the room in which he kept his most precious treasures of conquest. But the moment passed and Osric smashed his fist down on the table, knocking the flagon over and spilling the beer on to the floor. "Have I not told you before? I do not care for history lessons!"

Tristram flinched and, by instinct, took a step backwards. He had seen too many of his father's rages end in violence to relish a confrontation, yet he could not let the matter rest. "Sire, what is it about the death of King Lear that causes you such dismay?"

"Dismay? Dismay, you say?" Osric made a stabbing gesture with his forefinger. "Why, you impudent young pup! Perhaps I need to whip some sense into you."

"I do not mean to be impertinent," the boy whispered. "You are my father as well as my King. I have no other wish than to see you enjoying peace of mind. If something troubles you, then I would wish to know it."

"Nothing troubles me!" Osric's face had turned purple. "Do you hear me? I said nothing!"

"Yet – "

"Enough!" Osric leaned forward and seized Tristram by the wrist, causing the boy to cry out with pain. "If any other person teased me thus, I would treat them to the same fate as Aldfrith. Now be off with you, whilst I still remember that you are my son. And never mention the old king and his daughters again!"

Tristram slept fitfully and rose at cock-crow. It was another bleak February day. There had been a hard frost overnight and the skies threatened rain. As the boy walked out of the castle and across the mound, he winced at the bite of the wind which was coming in from the sea. A few men in a group were talking in whispers and he could feel their gaze upon him. He sensed that the brutality of Aldfrith's death had alarmed even Osric's most loyal subjects. He looked around, trying in vain to conquer his despair. Even the horses and cattle had a sullen look today, as if they could bear subjugation to the whims of man no longer.

He caught sight of a familiar bent figure shuffling along in the shadow of the palisade. He ran after Fulk and hailed him. "You promised that we could talk!"

His mentor turned and sighed. "I see that you are indeed your father's son. There is no denying you. Very well, shall we take a walk? At this hour we are unlikely to be disturbed if we visit the circle of stones up on the hillside."

As they walked together through the main gate, Tristram said, "Last night my father said he did not care for history lessons. Yet it seems to me that I must endure them, if I am to uncover the secrets of the past."

"Already you know that, until your father seized the throne, ours was a nation in turmoil. There was a desperate need for a leader who could quell the factions seeking to tear the country apart. We would have been easy prey for predators from the west and the north as well as from across the sea. Not since Lear's power was at its height had Britain seemed secure."

"Lear was a great king?"

Fulk's eyes were filled with infinite sadness as he inclined his head. "Oh yes, Tristram, be assured of that. Yet even before his death, the struggle for succession had begun. Goneril and Regan were ambitious but selfish. Following their death, it seemed as if the throne might be in safe hands after all. Edgar and Kent ruled together and dedicated themselves to healing the wounds sustained during the last few years of Lear's turbulent reign. Yet all too soon, Edgar and his family succumbed to the plague whilst Kent was murdered by a retainer discovered in the act of theft from his master. A civil war began."

"That was when my father came to the fore?"

Fulk nodded. "He had been a soldier from boyhood. Whilst Lear was still alive, he began to rise through the ranks and in time he became recognized as a brave and remorseless warrior. He was nakedly ambitious and many distrusted him on that account. Tales of his supposed barbarity began to circulate, but his craving for power served the country well. During the interregnum which followed Kent's death, he defeated Hrothgar and warded off the challenge led by Curan. With his opponents in disarray, he was able to seize power for himself. Thereafter he suppressed every hint of insurrection. People feared him, but they were grateful for the stability that he brought."

They were at the foot of the hill, following a way which wound up the slope through brambles and bushes to an ancient stone ring at the summit. Tristram said, "You once told me how Lear divided his kingdom between Goneril and Regan because of the affection they professed for him, at the expense of Cordelia who refused to flatter him. I know that his mind was by then diseased and you once hinted that his folly culminated in the deaths of them all. Yet you have refused to say more. It is as if my father ordered that the story should be forgotten."

Fulk sighed. "I warned Osric long ago that the truth cannot be hidden for ever." He closed his eyes, as if about to recite a tale he had rehearsed. "Goneril poisoned Regan and then took her own life. The bastard Edmund had captured Lear and Cordelia. He – he ordered one of the captains to kill them. Cordelia was hanged, but Lear slew the captain and escaped. Edmund was killed by his brother Edgar, but Lear died soon afterwards, stricken down by grief."

Neither of them spoke for a little while. Fulk's breath had become laboured as he struggled up the hillside and the boy grasped his arm to guide him up the last part of the journey. Finally they arrived at the grassy ridge that was their destination. A dozen rough-hewn upright stones had been set in a circle to mark the place as holy. People had worshipped here for many years, although their prayers for peace had often gone unanswered. The old man leaned against one of the stones and closed his eyes.

"Are you sick?" the boy asked urgently.

"You must not worry about me, Tristram. My life is nearly done. My sole concern now is that your life should not be destroyed by the evil that has corrupted your father."

"He is deranged, is he not?"

Fulk kept his eyes closed. His voice had become a croak. "I have seen the madness cast its shadow over him for many years. Osric has seen it too and fought it desperately. To no avail. This is one enemy who refuses to die. To this day, your father enjoys intervals of rationality, but the clouds grow darker all the time."

"What can I do?" the boy cried.

Fulk shook his head. "You have been a good son to him. I recall his despair when your mother died, but at least she left him with someone to whom he could entrust his kingdom. That was his heart's desire."

"So my mother was expendable as long as she produced a son?" Tristram asked, unable to suppress his anger.

"I have said it before. Unless you realize that, for your father, securing the throne meant everything, you will never understand him."

"I understand that he is a brutal dictator who lacks all conscience. Perhaps I need to know nothing more."

Fulk's breath was coming in shallower gasps. "You are wrong," he said faintly. "Osric has a conscience. Perhaps it is his conscience that has finally cost him his sanity. As for Cordelia . . ."

A cold dread clutched the boy as he stared at his mentor's pallid features. "Fulk!"

The old man slumped to the ground and gave a muffled grunt. Tristram bent over him and hissed into his ear. "Tell me!"

"In the chest he keeps within his chamber . . ." The words faded away.

Horrified, the boy gazed into Fulk's dim eyes. "Please," he implored. "Speak!"

But when he sought for a pulse in the skeletal wrist, he found nothing.

Fulk was buried with honour. At Osric's command, he was to be interred in a cairn of the kind which otherwise was the last resting place of the most distinguished soldiers or members of the king's family. Osric had so far forgotten his threat to banish the old man that he led the mourning. He spoke to the assembled gathering of his respect for Fulk's learning and wisdom and of the debt he owed to the old man for his devotion to the heir to the throne.

Tristram found it too much to bear and seized the chance to steal back into the castle. He squatted on the floor of his own room, wondering what he should do. Fulk's death had shocked him but he told himself that now, more than ever before, he needed to think clearly. Another idea had begun to form in his mind and although it appalled him, he knew that he would never be able to rest until he had ascertained whether or not it was wild imagining.

His decision made, he hurried to the kitchen and picked up an axe that was lying on the table. Its blade was smudged with the blood of a deer. He hid it under his tunic and made his way along the passageway which led to his father's quarters. Taking his courage in his hands, he gave the guard a curt nod and was allowed to pass unchallenged. With a quick glance over his shoulder, he entered the chamber and heaved shut the oak door.

He remembered his father's guilty glance at the chest of treasures when Cordelia's name had been mentioned. Surely Fulk had been trying to tell him that it contained the answer to the mystery?

The chest was locked and Tristram knew that Osric carried the key on the chain which hung around his neck. It never left his possession. There was no other course but to break open the chest. It would be impossible to conceal what he had done. Osric would regard it as an act of treason. Tristram guessed that even their blood tie might not suffice to save his skin.

He took a deep breath, then lifted the axe high in the air and swung it down on the lid of the chest. One strike. Two. Three. The lid was strong but it began to splinter. He swung again, possessed of a strength he had never known before. The lid was breaking. He threw it open and plunged his hand into the treasures that the chest contained. There were gold coins and silver trinkets. Valuable perhaps, but Tristram did not believe they would help him to solve the mystery.

At the bottom of the chest, his hand came upon a small bundle wrapped in a cloth. He opened it to find a small bejewelled bracelet. It bore an inscription: the name *Cordelia*. With it was a lock of fair hair with ragged ends. It was no lover's token: he could see that it had been hacked roughly from the head. He sank to his knees and began to weep. He had been hoping all the time that he might have been mistaken. If so, it would have been worth facing Osric's wrath. But now all hope was gone.

He heard footsteps running along the passageway, but he no longer cared. He did not even look up as the door was thrown open and the guard said breathlessly, "My liege, it is as I told you! The intruder is your son!"

"Tristram!" his father roared. "What is the meaning of this?"

His head buried in his hands, Tristram said, "I might well ask the same of you, sir."

"What are you talking about?"

The boy hauled himself up so that he could look his father

in the eye. It required an immense effort, for his legs felt as if they would give way at any moment. Osric's face was red with fury. In his hand he held his unsheathed sword.

Tristram held the bracelet and hank of hair aloft, as if to ward off a blow. "Is this why you turn pale at the mention of Cordelia, father?"

Osric gave a roar of pain like a wounded bear.

"My liege?" The guard was frightened by his king's anger.

"Leave us," Osric said harshly.

"But . . ."

Osric raised the sword above his head. "Leave us, I say!"

"Yes, my liege."

The guard shrank back into the passageway. Osric slammed the door and then turned to point the blade of his sword at his son. "Why did you have to meddle, Tristram? You are the King's son, you occupy a position of privilege. Why could you not be grateful for that and accept me as I am?"

Tristram took a step backwards. "You have kept a terrible secret from me, father."

"Cordelia was hanged by a captain on Edmund's orders," Osric said fiercely. "Lear killed the wretch for his trouble. One of the courtiers witnessed it."

Tristram shook his head. "Lear was an old man, sick of mind and body. How could he have slain a young active soldier?"

Osric advanced towards his son and said, "Have a care about what you say. Your life depends upon it."

Tristram snatched the axe from the floor and clutched it to his body. "I reasoned it thus," he said urgently. "Edmund sent an ambitious soldier to kill Lear and his daughter. As he hanged Cordelia, Lear found the strength to break free of his shackles, attack the captain and drag the girl's body away. He struck the captain a terrible blow, but it was not mortal. It gave him heart to think that he had killed the captain, but he was deceiving himself, as he had done so many times before. When he realized that Cordelia was indeed dead, it was too much for him. He had no reason to continue living."

Osric touched the scar on his cheek. "And what was the captain's fate?"

"Lear had wounded him, but he was young and strong. He managed to escape, taking with him three trophies. The girl's bracelet and a lock of her hair, together with the sword that Lear had left behind. Having killed the daughter of the King, he convinced himself that his destiny was to take the throne."

Osric said thunderously, "I have warned you before, Tristram. You do too much thinking."

"I made a mistake in thinking you killed King Lear," the boy said. "It was the defenceless daughter who was your victim, was it not? Cordelia."

As he uttered the name, Osric let out another roar and lunged at his son with the sword. In striving to avoid the blow, Tristram lost his footing. As he lay sprawled on the floor, Osric raised the sword above his head and began to bring it down. Tristram shut his eyes and waited for the blow that would kill him. It did not come. He opened his eyes again and saw that the sword was suspended in mid-air. His father was staring down at him, an expression of horror on his face. It was, Tristram suddenly realized, a moment of self-knowledge. As Osric hesitated, the boy scrambled to his feet and retrieved the axe.

"You do not yet know everything," Osric said slowly. "You said I believed it was my destiny to become king. That is not the whole truth. It was my *right*."

"How can you say that? You were not born to a noble family."

"What do you know of my family?" Osric demanded. "Nothing. And that is because I was denied the right to a family. Denied it by my father, who abandoned my mother after a single night's pleasure, unaware that he had left her with child. As she often said to me when I was your age and younger, had he been a man of honour, I would have been his acknowledged heir."

Tristram's eyes opened very wide. "Lear was your *father*?"

"Perhaps now you may understand why I was embittered by his betrayal of my mother and of me. Lear's punishment was that he had only daughters to carry on the line. I became determined to prove my courage in battle, but too soon his mind began to wander and I realized that I could not win the throne through earning his respect. His judgement had gone. The absurdity was not lost on me when I heard him railing against the ingratitude of his children. I was ready to seize the chance of revenge when Edmund gave it to me. Edmund was ruthless, but I had some fellow feeling for him. He too was a bastard who believed he had been mistreated."

Tristram could not conceal his revulsion. "You hanged your own sister!"

Osric glared. "You look at me as though I were mad."

"You are!" the boy cried. "And you know it!"

Osric grunted and swung the sword again. But this time Tristram was ready. He swayed to one side and thrust the axe forward. It struck the King on the neck and felled him to the ground.

Tristram trembled as his father bellowed in agony. Blood began to stream from the gaping wound.

Osric tried to say something and the boy knelt by his side in the hope that he might hear the words.

"Well, Tristram," Osric murmured, "why should I not be mad? My own father lost his mind. My fate was not just to take the throne. It was to succumb to the same insanity that killed King Lear. Like father, like son. Now I can see the pit of darkness that lies ahead for me."

A sickly rattling noise came from his throat and then he lay still. Tristram's stomach heaved and he let out a wail. An eerie sound, a lament for the dead – and for himself.

A commotion began outside. The door was flung open and the guard burst in, followed by a group of soldiers. But whilst they gazed in astonishment at the body lying on the ground, Tristram began to laugh wildly, the tears streaming down his cheeks. As they turned to him, he spread his arms.

"I can read your thoughts." Suddenly he felt ice-cold, as if the pit of which his father had spoken were opening up in front of him as well. *Like father, like son.* "This – is madness."

TOIL AND TROUBLE

Edward D. Hoch

"The Scottish play" is also one of Shakespeare's best known, doubtless through many performances in schools. The play was probably written around 1606, though the surviving text includes later adaptations, some of them believed to be by Thomas Middleton, who added more to the episodes with the witches, a subject in which the new king, James I of England (James VI of Scotland) had much interest. According to Shakespeare's version of history Macbeth and Banquo are the generals of King Duncan who rescue him during a rebellion. Macbeth is confronted by the three witches who predict that Macbeth will become king. Macbeth is prepared to let fate take its course, but his over-ambitious wife, Lady Macbeth (whose real name, incidentally, was Gruoch), compels Macbeth to kill Duncan and contrives that the blame falls on Duncan's sons Malcolm and Donalbain who flee from Scotland. The witches had also prophesied that Banquo's children would inherit the throne and this begins to play on Macbeth's mind now he is king. Although he succeeds in arranging the murder of Banquo, his son escapes. Macbeth seeks out the witches and is reassured that he will remain king until Birnam Wood comes to Dunsinane Castle, which seems almost impossible. However, Duncan's son Malcolm, along with the powerful thane Macduff, raises an army which they camouflage with

*branches taken from Birnam Wood. Macbeth's fate is thus
sealed, and he is killed by Macduff. That's Shakespeare's
story. But what was the witches' perception of events – the
real story?*

They often met Hecate on moonless nights by the crossroads.
The dogs would be with her, as they always were in those
early days, great howling beasts that always frightened poor
little Artemis. It was Selene, the bravest of them, who would
step forward to confront her.

"How are the dogs this night, dear Hecate?" she would
ask.

"Darker than the hounds of Hades," Hecate answered, her
voice hissing the final esses.

Artemis, who loved moonlight on the heath, shrank back
in terror when she saw the serpent coiled around Hecate's
neck. Persephone had to step between them to protect the
poor girl. Those were not their real names, of course. Hecate
had named the sisters Selene, Artemis and Persephone the first
time they'd ever met on the Scottish heath. "You are like me,"
she'd told them. "You are parts of me. I will name you thus
and you will always be at my call. The weird sisters." She told
them the letters in their names had numerological significance,
and like the letters of her own name they offered protection
from harm.

The sisters found a cave after that, and a cauldron to set
in the middle of it. Selene had taken the lead, as she always
did, gathering wood for the fire and tiny creatures from the
heath to add to the bubbling pot. Hecate came to them there,
without dogs or serpents, and she was pleased with what she
saw. "You three will do my work, and I will be mistress
of your charms. Noble lords will come to learn the future
from you."

Selene had taught them a chant to use around the fire, and
she led them in it now. "Double, double, toil and trouble;
Fire burn and cauldron bubble!"

Hecate clapped her hands with pleasure. "O, well done! I commend your pains. And what will make it bubble best, dear Artemis?"

Youngest and shyest of the weird sisters, Artemis thought of herself as the second witch because she was the second one that Hecate had named. "A ray of moonlight, perhaps?"

"No moonlight, you foolish girl! You need fillet of snake, eye of newt, toe of frog! Wool of bat and tongue of dog! Lizard's leg and owl's wing!"

"I – I will gather them," Artemis promised with some trepidation.

Hecate turned to Persephone. "Keep an eye on your younger sister. She has much to learn."

When she thought about it, Selene was bothered by the manner in which Hecate seemed to have taken control of them for her own purposes. There were times when she worried about her sisters and wondered if Hecate really was some goddess of the underworld.

One day, after the three had been practising their spells and predictions like actors at a pageant, Hecate came to them and said, "Your fame has spread across the countryside. It is important that you arrange to encounter Macbeth and Banquo, the generals of King Duncan, as they ride across the heath today. Tell Macbeth, Thane of Glamis, that he will soon become Thane of Cawdor, and then King of Scotland. Do you understand?"

"We understand," Selene agreed reluctantly. She watched Hecate depart from the cave and told her sisters, "Come, let's make haste away from here. She'll soon be back again."

It was Persephone with her sharp eyesight who first spotted the two horsemen riding across a remote part of the heath. "They are coming from the direction of Macbeth's castle," she observed. "No doubt it is Macbeth and Banquo, out riding as Hecate said they would be."

The three sisters hurried to reach a large flat rock that overlooked the route the two horsemen were following. As they waited, dark clouds were forming on the horizon and a peel of thunder shook the morning air. The one they knew as

Macbeth spoke as the riders approached. "So foul and fair a day I have not seen."

It was Banquo who noticed them first, and called Macbeth's attention to them. "What are these, so withered, and so wild in their attire?"

"Speak if you can," Macbeth called out. "What are you?"

"All hail, Macbeth!" Selene responded. "Hail to thee, Thane of Glamis!"

Artemis joined in with her weaker voice. "All hail, Macbeth! Hail to thee, Thane of Cawdor!"

And Persephone: "All hail, Macbeth, that shalt be king hereafter!"

Macbeth was startled and seemed almost afraid at their words. As the weird sisters turned away he shouted, "Stay, you imperfect speakers, tell me more! I know I am Thane of Glamis, but how of Cawdor? The Thane of Cawdor lives, a prosperous gentleman. And to be king stands not within the prospect of belief."

But the three hurried away before he could question them further, vanishing into the underbrush.

Within days word reached Selene and the others that Macbeth had indeed become Thane of Cawdor by appointment of His Majesty, King Duncan. The news was not welcomed in the cave as they fired up the great cauldron. "We are only poor simple folk," Persephone told them. "We have no magical powers to predict the future. What say you, Selene?"

A shrug. "We must take what life gives us."

Later that same day Hecate visited them once again. Poor Artemis was actually frightened of their visitor and tried to hunch out of sight behind the giant cauldron. "The first part of your prophecy has come true," Hecate told them. "But the most important part is yet to come. Macbeth will soon be King of all Scotland."

"How is this to be?" Selene asked.

"King Duncan comes to spend the night as a guest at Macbeth's castle. Be assured that the Thane and his Lady will not let such an opportunity pass."

"I know of Lady Macbeth," Artemis said, coming out from behind the cauldron. "She is a kind-hearted person."

"Not where ambition is concerned," Hecate assured them. "If Duncan dies, the line of succession will elevate Macbeth to the throne. Be prepared. He may come to you again."

But Macbeth did not come then. Dire events took place on the night Duncan visited the castle, events which would change the future of the entire country. Persephone learned the bare facts some days later from one of the castle servants who was her friend. "Great King Duncan was slain in his bed," she told her sisters later, "stabbed to death by his own grooms. When Macbeth found them bloodied and asleep he slew them in a fury. The noble Macduff was there too, shocked and horrified by what he saw."

"And now Macbeth is to be King, "Selene mused, "so soon after our prediction when he rode this way in the company of Banquo."

"It troubles you," Persephone said. "I see it in your eyes."

Selene nodded. "Let us make haste to Macbeth's castle, separately and in disguise, to see what we can learn from the servants and grooms. We will meet back here at sundown."

Selene dressed herself in the garb of a beggar woman, and walked with a stick up the long hill to the castle entrance. Beggars and servants were directed to the rear, and it was there that she fell into conversation with a scullery maid named Roseanne. "I hear talk our king is dead and Macbeth doth take the throne," she said, opening the conversation while the maid brought her some leftover food.

The girl nodded. "A terrible crime upon the country! Two grooms stabbed their master while he slept. Macbeth found them bloodied and asleep and slew them both."

"Did you see the room in which it happened?"

"I helped to clean both rooms with these very hands. The bodies of the two grooms were bloodied everywhere from Macbeth's dagger, yet the wounds of the King himself barely bled at all."

"How is this possible?" Selene asked. "Is it enchantment? A sign from heaven?"

Roseanne lowered her voice. "Duncan's sons have fled the country, fearing for their lives. Malcolm is in England, raising an army. Some say Macbeth did kill the King, and then his lady didst smear the grooms with the bloody deed."

Selene returned to the cave with news of what she had learned. Artemis and Persephone had heard much the same from other servants. There was fear in the castle, Artemis reported, and rumors that Lady Macbeth, tormented and maddened by guilt, had been observed sleepwalking in the night. Persephone, attempting to determine the course of events on the night of the King's killing, had learned that a servant woman named Theeca took the King his nightly wine shortly before he retired and found him in the company of his two grooms. Yet no one believed them to be guilty of the crime.

It was Selene herself who brought more bloody news in the days that followed. Banquo had been slain, apparently on Macbeth's orders. Selene decided it was time to stir the pot and utter again their lines of enchantment. "Double, double, toil and trouble; Fire burn and cauldron bubble!"

It was then that Hecate entered the cavern. "Macbeth cometh to you again, sisters. It is said he imagines the ghost of Banquo, so recently slain, doth haunt his dining table. All this is because you dared trade and traffic with Macbeth in riddles and affairs of death. I was never called to bear my part or show the glory of our art."

"We followed as you led!" Persephone protested. "You bid us encounter Macbeth and we did so."

"Now follow my command," Hecate said. "If King Macbeth asked who can conquer him, tell him he cannot be killed by any man born of woman. Tell him he will not be vanquished until Birnam Wood comes to Dunsinane. Will you remember that?"

"We will remember," Selene assured her.

Hecate moved off, leaving them alone by the bubbling pot. "What wants she with us?" Persephone wondered. "I find her actions strange to behold."

They sang and danced, feeding the cauldron with tiny creatures gathered from the heath, until suddenly Artemis paused, hearing a sound. "By the pricking of my thumbs, Something wicked this way comes! Open locks, whoever knocks!"

It was Macbeth who entered, alone this time. "How now, you secret, black and midnight hags? What is it you do?"

"A deed without a name," they answered, all at once.

Then Selene spoke alone. "Gaze into the cauldron, O Great King, and see your future there."

"My eyes are blinded by the steam!"

"Macbeth, Macbeth! Beware Macduff," a voice spoke.

And then another. "None of woman born shall harm Macbeth."

And a third. "Macbeth shall never vanquished be until Great Birnam Wood to high Dunsinane Hill shall come against him."

"That will never be," Macbeth said, visibly relieved.

The sisters seemed to retreat from the cavern as Lennox, one of Macbeth's noblemen, arrived with urgent news. Macduff had fled to England! Listening from her hiding place, Selene heard Macbeth ponder this surprising development, then order an attack upon the castle of Macduff to murder his wife and children.

"Killing, killing, it never stops," Selene told her sisters later. "When he learns the fate of his wife and children, Macduff will raise an army against Macbeth. In England he might even unite with Duncan's son Malcolm. We have not seen the end of bloodshed here."

The sisters used their disguises to visit the castle of Macbeth again during the following weeks, hiking up Dunsinane Hill to learn the latest news of his foes. Word at the castle was that Macduff had indeed joined forces with Malcolm and their armies were drawing nearer.

"They are almost to Birnam Wood," Persephone reported. "I will go there to learn what I can."

It was Selene herself who was at the castle the following day, when the crying of women announced the death of Lady

Macbeth, her mind and spirit crushed by the foul deeds of which there seemed no ending. Selene crept up the stone steps to where Macbeth did rage and mutter at the news. "Life's but a walking shadow, a poor player. It is a tale told by an idiot, full of sound and fury, signifying nothing!"

A messenger soon arrived, so short of breath he could barely speak. "As I did stand watch upon the hill, I looked toward Birnam and thought the wood began to move!"

"Liar and slave!" shouted Macbeth. Uttering curses, he rushed out to witness for himself what had transpired.

When Selene returned to their cavern she found Persephone in a highly agitated state. Artemis tried to calm her and she was finally able to pour out her story. "I saw a woman speaking with the slain king's son Malcolm. She seemed to know him. Then, as the soldiers passed through Birnam Wood, Malcolm ordered each man to cut a leafy branch and advance on the castle screened behind it."

Selene felt a sudden stab of fear. "The woman – "

"It was Hecate!"

Selene pondered this news at length. She stared at the glowing embers beneath the cauldron, trying to read some great truth there. Finally she spoke. "It was Hecate who instructed us what to tell Macbeth. But how did she know what course events would take?"

"Her powers are frightful," Artemis whispered, trembling at the thought.

"Or else – " Selene broke off in mid-sentence, saying instead, "We must now await the outcome of the battle. Remember the other part of the prediction Hecate gave us – Macbeth cannot be killed by any man born of woman. Let us see what wonders this day brings."

The three sisters heard about it the following morning, when all was silent at last and the banner of Malcolm flew in the breeze over the castle. Macbeth and his followers had come down from Dunsinane to meet the attackers on the field. When Macbeth faced Macduff, still believing he was safe from any man born of woman, he learned that Macduff had been from his mother's womb untimely ripped. With their clash of swords, the battle raged on until Macbeth fell beneath Macduff's blade and was beheaded.

"So it is over," Persephone said.

"Yes," Artemis agreed. "Let all the killing be over at last!"

"Not yet," Selene told them. "Hecate will come again now."

"To harm us?" poor Artemis asked, the blood draining from her face.

"We shall see."

It was the following day, when they had returned to the cavern after searching the heath for treasures, that they found Hecate waiting beside the cauldron. She had started a fire beneath it, and was fanning the flames with her cloak. "Always keep the fire going," she told them as they entered. "Fire is good. It keeps the pot boiling."

"What befell King Macbeth?" Selene asked.

"Killed by an enemy," Hecate answered, "the same as the King before him."

"And Lady Macbeth too is slain?"

"She died of madness and guilt. There was too much death for her to bear."

"First King Duncan and then Banquo, and Macduff's family. Lady Macbeth and the new King himself, not to mention all those brave men killed in the battle. Are they on your conscience, Hecate, or do you even have a conscience?"

"What do you mean?" Hecate asked as the sisters surrounded her, taking courage from Selene's words.

"It was you who caused this misery, Hecate. Macbeth did not murder King Duncan. You did."

Hecate threw up her hands. "Begone, foul sisters, begone! Only the Devil could know this thing!"

"The Devil or a fertile mind." Sensing victory, Selene moved in for the kill. "It was you who told us what predictions to speak for Macbeth, and Persephone saw you with Malcolm before the battle, no doubt telling him to cut the leafy branches from the trees in Birnam Wood. You know him from the castle, as you know Macduff as well."

"I am not of the castle," Hecate insisted.

"I think to differ. A castle resident with a sharp ear might have heard of Duncan's plan to name Macbeth Thane of Cawdor. The dagger wounds inflicted by Macbeth bled hardly at all, because good King Duncan was already dead. You had killed him earlier, in fear that Macbeth's courage might fail him at the last moment. In the dark he never saw that he was stabbing a dead man. That was your plot, because you wanted Duncan and Macbeth removed in a manner which could not be blamed on Malcolm or Macduff. Macbeth played into your hands, as you knew he would, and even ordered Banquo killed as a bonus to your scheme."

"How did she kill Malcolm?" Persephone asked.

"By poisoning the wine she brought him at bedtime. Hecate has another identity, that of the castle servant Theeca, whom you mentioned to me, Persephone. Remember Hecate's telling us of the numerical importance of the letters in her name? Surely for such an important mission she would not choose an entire new name but would merely rearrange the letters of her existing name. Thus Hecate and Theeca are one and the same."

"It is Theeca whom I really am," the woman told them. "I chose the name Hecate, goddess of the lower world, to lure you poor sisters into my plan. I needed your predictions to lull Macbeth with a false sense of confidence. And it worked, better than even I expected. Lady Macbeth went mad with guilt, and it was a simple task to poison her also when the time was proper."

"Why?" Selene asked. "Why did you perform these awful acts?"

"Because twenty-five years ago I was the nurse to Macduff's mother. I saw her dying, and it was I who so untimely ripped the babe from her womb to save its life. I made a bloody promise then that someday this babe would rule over all the land. Now he is second to King Malcolm, and my promise is one short step from fulfillment."

"She is mad," Persephone whispered to the others, and they had only to look upon the face of Hecate to know the truth of those words.

Hecate uttered a final growl of contempt. "Away, all of you! I created you and I can destroy you as easily!"

It was little Artemis who rushed forward then, shoving at Hecate with both her hands, toppling her into the boiling cauldron.

Later, much later, the sisters who had been Selene, Artemis and Persephone left the cavern and walked together in the sunlight. They never went back again.

A SEA OF TROUBLES

Steve Lockley

Hamlet *must rate amongst Shakespeare's most quoted plays, although I suspect that many who quote it are less sure of the full story of Hamlet, Prince of Denmark. Shakespeare probably wrote the play about 1600, but made several revisions to it subsequently. The story is based on a Scandinavian legend which dates from at least the twelfth century and probably earlier. Shakespeare's version, which added several features, including the ghost of Hamlet's father, is a murder mystery in its own right, though with rather more bodies than good detective work. Hamlet's father (also called Hamlet) dies and is succeeded by his brother Claudius, who marries the King's widow Gertrude. Denmark is under threat from Fortinbras of Norway and Hamlet, seeking to avenge his father, tries to undermine Claudius's authority. Hamlet sees the ghost of his father who tells him he was poisoned by Claudius, but Hamlet is not entirely sure of the ghost's honesty and sets out to prove Claudius's guilt himself. Hamlet tries a variety of subterfuges to test his stepfather, including feigning madness, though as the play progresses Hamlet begins to fear he really is mad, especially when he kills his friend Polonius by mistake. Hamlet no longer seems in control of affairs and events snowball to their final tragic conclusion. In the following story Steve Lockley tries to*

unravel these events and see who was really pulling the
strings.

The journey from Wittenberg had seemed longer than on
any previous occasion that Hamlet had travelled. Longer
because he did not want to arrive. His father the King
was dead, his body barely cold in its grave, and yet his
mother already remarried. Not to some stranger who had
captured her affections, but to his uncle. His father's own
brother trying to take the place of a man he was not even the
shadow of. There was no longer anything for him at Elsinore,
only unanswered questions.

The ship was still some way from the harbour but Hamlet
had been able to see the castle for almost an hour. At first it was
no more than a vague shape in the hillside, unrecognizable to
anyone who did not know it as home, but his eyes knew it
for what it was.

In the stretch of water between the ship and dry land a small
rowing boat approached slowly until it drew alongside.

"My lord Hamlet?" called the boatman.

"Horatio?" A friendly face at least.

"Yes my lord. It saddens me that we have to speak in such
circumstances."

"Why have you come to meet me?"

"I have to speak to you before you go to Elsinore. There
is something you must know."

"What is it?"

"I would rather not shout. This is something for your ears
alone."

Hamlet worked his way around the ship until he found a
rope ladder coiled on the deck, one end already secured.

"We will be ashore in less than a quarter of an hour, my
lord," said the captain who came down from the upper deck
as Hamlet threw the rope over the side.

"Then perhaps you will arrange to have my things sent on,"
said Hamlet. "It appears transport has been provided."

Horatio heaved on the oars, pulling the small boat away from the ship, almost as soon as Hamlet had balanced himself in the barely stable craft.

"Why so much secrecy, Horatio?"

"The King has ears everywhere, my Lord, and I would prefer they were not to hear."

"The King? The King is dead."

"Not your father, but the new king. Your uncle, Claudius."

"Claudius. Now I understand," said Hamlet. "If you have something to tell me about my uncle then I am not surprised you should be afraid of being overheard."

"There is a rumour about the castle that your father's death did not come about by natural causes."

Hamlet watched the other man's eyes, not surprised by the news. His father had many enemies, his past was littered with rebellion and conquests. Names and faces leapt into his mind, any of whom could have been responsible; Claudius stood to gain the most, or perhaps his mother Gertrude but there were others. Many others.

"Murder? Do these rumours say who killed him?"

Horatio shrugged and Hamlet knew his friend dared not voice his suspicions even after taking the precautions he had.

"Was the Prince of Norway here? He has made no secret of his desire to find a kingdom of his own."

"Fortinbras? No, he has not been seen at Elsinore for some time, certainly not since your last visit. He has family problems of his own."

"Yes, I have heard he and his own uncle are not exactly in agreement."

Horatio looked over his shoulder, gauging the distance to the shore, only the creak of oars in the rowlocks breaking the silence.

"There is something else you need to know but I would prefer that others were with me to confirm what I have to say."

"And I thank you, my friend," Hamlet said. "If you can not tell me at this time then I will not press you. I suspect you have already taken a great risk but fear the knowledge will not be an end to it. This is something which may need to be resolved by more devious means."

"My lord?"

"Nothing, but I will not rest until I have found my father's murderer. All I ask is that you do not mention this meeting."

"Whatever you say, my lord. I am your servant."

"No, Horatio, you are more friend than servant."

As he walked up the hill towards the castle Hamlet did not turn to look back. Murder? Somehow he was not shocked at this news, only surprised his father had been careless enough to let someone close enough to him. If Fortinbras was not responsible then it had to be someone already in his confidence.

The main hall of the castle was crammed with the members of every high-born family in Denmark, and many from beyond its boundaries. Some were already starting to leave, having paid tribute to their new King, when Hamlet entered. Insisting on entering unannounced he crept into the back of the hall in silence, preferring to watch the fawnings of others. Although a few of those crowded at the perimeter of the activity acknowledged his presence, they were of little importance, and did not even seem to realize who he was. Had he been away from Elsinore so long?

The crowd had thinned to little more than a handful when his presence was acknowledged by his mother and new-found stepfather.

"Hamlet," his mother, Gertrude, said with what seemed like surprise. "Welcome home."

"My son," added Claudius, extending a hand.

Hamlet ignored it, recognizing the tone was not surprise. It held more concern than that. It was fear. For a moment he considered that perhaps they feared his reaction to his uncle taking the throne he could so easily have claimed as his own. And yet he had made it plain many times he had no great ambition in that direction. All he wanted from life was the opportunity to learn.

"My lord," he said, lowering his head in a show of deference although it pained him to do so.

"No need for such formalities, Hamlet. You are with your family."

"Laertes," Claudius continued, turning his attention back to the man he had been speaking to before Hamlet had been recognized. "What are your plans?"

"With your blessing I would like to return to France shortly. I am needed there."

"If your father agrees then you go with my blessing. What do you say, Polonius?"

"He goes with my blessing too," said Polonius who had been standing silently to one side. His position as Lord Chamberlain seemed unassailable, no matter who commanded the throne.

Hamlet watched Laertes as he turned to face him before leaving the room. Blue eyes seemed to pierce his soul.

"Take care, Hamlet."

Take care? What did he have to take care of? Was his own life in danger? Laertes had much to gain by the death of the King and his ambition was undoubted. A step closer to the throne certainly, perhaps within a sword's length of it. But cold-blooded murder?

"And you, Hamlet," said Claudius, pulling Hamlet away from his thoughts. "What are your plans?"

"Plans? I have no plans."

"Stay Hamlet," said his mother. "Please do not return to Wittenberg. Surely your time at University is at an end. You are needed here. Please stay."

"I hope you will stay too," said Claudius. "But let us go, my dear."

Claudius had not changed. If anything his new-found position had made him even more arrogant than before. Now he could come and go with barely an acknowledgement to those left behind.

The room emptied within moments. Without the light of the King the room held no attraction for those who remained, still waiting for an audience. Left alone Hamlet found his thoughts pondering on what Horatio had said. Then, as if his very thoughts had summoned him up, Horatio entered the room. Following him were two other men in the dress of the castle guard.

"Horatio," he said in mock surprise, remembering his own warning not to mention their previous meeting. "What brings you to Elsinore?"

"I came for your father's funeral."

"I suspect it was my mother's wedding."

"It is true they were close together."

"There is something I have to tell you," said Horatio, stepping closer. "Something of grave importance."

"What is it?" said Hamlet, preparing himself for a repetition of the previous day's conversation. Did he think these guards were spies for Claudius?

"I have seen your father."

"Seen? What do you mean?"

"Last night I stood watch with these good men, Marcellus and Bernardo. We saw a pale figure walking slowly along the battlements. When he drew close there was little doubt that he bore your father's likeness."

"Did you speak to it?"

"I did, but it did not reply. It raised its head as if to speak but then a cock crowed to signal morning and the figure disappeared."

"This was the third time I had seen it, my lord," said Marcellus. "It has appeared in the same spot on each of the last three nights."

"And are you on watch again tonight?" A hoax, a cruel joke, it had to be. But if that were not the case he had to hear what the figure had to say. He had to be sure.

"Indeed," said the two guards in unison.

"Then I will join you."

The sea mist had rolled in to envelop the castle by the time night had fallen and the chill air was enough to freeze muscle to the bones of guards who stood watch that night. Sound barely carried in the stillness of the damp air, and in the silence Hamlet began to doubt the ghost would appear. How could he have believed so easily such a fantastic tale. Yet Horatio supported the claims and it was his testimony that had convinced him to brave the cold night.

"What time is it?" Hamlet asked. He felt no great desire for the information, but needed to break the silence.

"Still a little short of twelve," said Horatio.

"No," said Marcellus. "Midnight has already struck."

"We should not have long to wait," said Horatio.

Then, from out of the mist, a swirling figure whose whiteness made it hard to discern, approached them.

"Hamlet!" said Horatio, pointing. "It is here."

"Father?"

The ghostly form shifted in the mist and raised a hand, seeming to beckon Hamlet to go with him.

"Don't go, Hamlet," said Horatio. "I fear for your safety."

"It will not speak here, my friend," said Hamlet. "If that were so then surely it would have spoken on previous nights. I must go with it. And besides, why should I be afraid. When life is held in such little value there is not much to lose. I have no choice but to follow."

"You cannot go with it," said Horatio, his hand gripping Hamlet's sleeve. "Who knows where it may take you."

"Let go of me, Horatio, I will do what I must. Follow me if you will."

The creature of mist moved away slowly, without looking back. The spirit held no terror for Hamlet. If there was any fear it was that he should lose the ghost in the mist which camouflaged it.

"Where are we going?" he called. When no reply came he shouted again, this time louder, "I will go no further. Tell me where we are going."

The ghost turned and despite the mist Hamlet could see there was no doubt. This was indeed the spirit of his father.

"*Pay attention, I have little time to speak before my time comes again.*" said the ghost.

"Then speak quickly. I must hear what you wish to say."

"*Revenge my murder, Hamlet. I cannot rest until this has been put to rights.*"

"Murder? Then it is true?"

"Murder most foul. Avenge me, Hamlet my son."

"But who?"

"The man who stole my life also stole my crown."

"My uncle."

"While I slept the adulterer poured Hebenon into my ear. Fast as mercury the poison curdled my blood to end my mortal life in moments. Avenge me, Hamlet, but do not allow yourself to become as corrupt as he, and leave your mother to heaven. The morning is now almost upon us and I must say goodbye. Remember me."

As the ghost faded and returned to the mist from which it had formed Hamlet fell to his knees and wept. Not from the confirmation of his father's murder; not because he was now sure his uncle was the culprit, this too came as no surprise. Claudius had gained the double prize of the crown and a new wife. What had broken him was having to say goodbye to a father he thought he would never see again. Drained he fell to his knees and let out a blood-curdling scream which echoed eerily through the mist.

In moments Horatio and the guards were by his side demanding to know what he had seen, but the words would not form. But as he kneeled, gibbering, a plan began to take shape.

The morning mist had been burnt away by the early sun and from a window at the end of a passage Hamlet could see the calm waters of the bay and a single boat lying idle in the harbour. Further out on the water a smaller boat was hauling in its net. A solitary gull swooped around it, emitting the occasional shriek. This was real life, not the secrecies and intrigue of court. Perhaps this was what he was missing. It had been three days since he had seen his father's ghost and in that time he had changed his habits to convince the members of the court that his mind had become unbalanced. At night he wandered the castle, ignoring anyone he came across, and by day he ranted on the battlements. The whispers about his experience during that mist-laden night had been spread despite his pleas that it be kept secret. It was perhaps this reluctance to break the news that had made it so potent.

Hamlet heard voices coming from the room closest to him as a door opened. He pressed himself to the cold stone wall beside the window and concealed himself behind drapes.

"He wanders here for hours sometimes." A man's voice. Polonius?

"That is true," his mother said, talking about him behind his back. "Do you think he is truly mad?"

Polonius spoke again, but this time his words were difficult to distinguish no matter how hard Hamlet strained to catch them.

"We will try it." Claudius? Were all three of them conspiring against him? Were they all implicated in his father's murder?

Light from the room threw shadows into the corridor as the door swung inward. Should he hide? Or should he reveal himself? In the instant he saw the swirl of his mother's dress emerging into the passage he flipped open the book he had been carrying and walked slowly towards the door.

In his peripheral vision he could see Claudius and his mother as they realized he was approaching. He heard them whispering but maintained his steady stride. Keeping his head bowed he swung past them into the room.

"Hamlet?" said Polonius.

"Yes?" he said, without lifting his gaze from the page.

"What are you reading?"

"Words," he said, flicking pages quickly. "Words, words, words."

"Do you know who I am?"

Hamlet raised his face and glanced quickly into the familiar face. "Of course," he said. "You are the fishmonger."

Was he going too far? Was his plan doomed to fail, before it had passed its first real test?

"Not I," said Polonius.

There was silence as the two men looked into each other's eyes and Hamlet could feel some sort of unspoken test taking place. If he could convince Polonius his sanity had left him and was no longer a man to be feared. If it worked then Claudius would have no reason not to believe the same.

After almost a minute of silence, Polonius smiled then left

the room without saying another word. He was soon replaced by two of Claudius's toadies, Rosencrantz and Guildenstern. Two men neither he nor his father would have trusted more than was required. Their allegiance changed with the wind and it seemed no secret that they favoured whoever could assist them most.

"My lord Hamlet," they said in unison.

He acknowledged them both with as wide a smile as he could muster, embracing each in turn like long-lost friends. They were here on their master's behalf, there could be no doubt about that. But perhaps they had a greater part to play in this entrapment, perhaps they also carried confirmation that he was one step closer to success.

"We have good news, my lord," said Rosencrantz. "Something which may raise your spirits after your tragic loss."

"Good news? What good news?"

"The players from the city, my lord," he said. "You once mentioned that you admired the players and would like to be entertained by them again."

"I did," he said.

"They are coming here to Elsinore. It seems your wish is to come true."

Of course it was, but not by luck as these two seemed to think. Loyal Horatio had succeeded in delivering the message he had imparted to him. There could be no turning back now. No way he could stop the momentum.

Trumpets sounded in another part of the castle and echoed around corridors and stairwells.

"The Players," cried Guildenstern. "They have arrived."

Hamlet let out a whoop of delight, and dragging the two men with him he charged out of the room. He hoped this uncharacteristic display of energy would help spread the talk of his derangement. It was essential for his plan that the rumour of his madness should continue to spread. Without it he may not have sufficient latitude in his actions.

There was an element of relief when Hamlet saw the troupe assembled in the Great Hall. The leader of the players was the same grizzled man he had met before. The man bowed deeply to him with his back to Claudius and Polonius who were fussing around the other players, picking at masks and pulling at costumes. Hamlet winked at the man as he rose and the player returned the signal. Horatio had indeed succeeded.

Away from the confusion of the troupe Hamlet spoke softly to the actor, outlining the performance he wanted to see. The player seemed to grasp the requirements without difficulty and it was all Hamlet could do to stop himself from sharing the entire plan with the older man.

"Does this please you, Hamlet?" said his mother, gesturing to the players as they prepared for their performance that evening.

"Does it please you, mother? If it does then it pleases me."

"We are both pleased," said Claudius weaselling his way into the conversation.

When Hamlet spoke to his mother alone he could almost forget for a moment what had happened to his father, but every word that poured from his uncle's mouth only served to remind and reinforce his anger. Tonight he would see. Everyone would see him for what he was.

The room fell silent as the lead player took centre stage and addressed the assembled audience. Hamlet was not listening, instead he whispered into Horatio's ear.

"Watch the King," he said. "Do not take your eyes from him for one second. Tell me how he reacts. The play is called *The Mousetrap* but perhaps tonight we will trap a rat."

The play began with a mime but Hamlet watched Claudius and his mother more than he did the action. Beside him, Horatio too spent all his time scrutinizing Claudius as he had been requested.

On the makeshift stage a king and queen appear and embrace. After a few moments the King lies down to sleep. The Queen seeing him asleep, leaves him. Another man enters, removes the King's crown and kisses it before pouring poison into the sleeping man's ear. When the Queen returns she finds her poor husband dead and is beside herself with grief. The poisoner returns and consoles the Queen as the body is dragged away. The poisoner showers the Queen with gifts and although she seems unwilling at first, she soon relents and accepts the poisoner's love.

"Did you see?" Hamlet whispered to his friend. "Did you see how Claudius reacted?"

"I did. The play has rattled him for certain. He wipes his sweaty palms on the arms of his throne and his face is flushed. When the poison was delivered he almost leapt out of his chair. There can be no doubt."

"Do you think he suspects me?"

"He has not looked this way during the entire performance."

"Watch him well, my friend. Watch him well."

The play continued although Hamlet paid little attention. Claudius had given himself away and already Hamlet felt vindicated in confronting him. Should he do it before the rest of the court? No, he would wait and seek his revenge in private. Above all he had to protect his mother from the matter.

The play ended and the actors took their places on the stage to take their bows. Almost before the echo of the applause had died away Claudius had risen and taken his queen's arm to lead her away. A smile emerged unrestrained on Hamlet's face.

"The trap has been sprung, Horatio," said Hamlet standing with the rest of the audience.

"What will you do now, Hamlet?"

"Do? I will do what has to be done," he replied and after nodding his acknowledgment to the leader of the players he followed Claudius from the room.

Stopping outside what was once his father's chamber he found the door ajar. Inside, Claudius was praying.

"Damnation," Hamlet hissed unable to keep his curse inside. He could no more take a man's life while he was praying than if he were asleep. And besides he could not allow the murderer to leave this earth in a state of grace and find the gates of heaven open to him. His father had been denied this fortune and he did not wish his enemy to achieve a better death. No, he would wait to choose his time, to strike in a moment of argument or anger.

He paced for a while, convincing himself he had made

the right choice, but could not let the grip of his sword alone. Inside his head his blood pounded a driving tattoo that seemed to exclude all other sounds. Had the madness he had been feigning taken hold in reality? Could he shake himself of it until he had ended his torment?

There were voices along the corridor as he walked back towards the King's chamber, this time coming from his mother's room. When he entered he found her alone.

"Hamlet," she said. He thought he detected surprise in her voice.

"Were you expecting someone else?"

"I was expecting no one," she said.

"Did you enjoy the play?"

"Enjoy? I don't know whether enjoy is the sort of word I would use to describe the entertainment. It was so, so . . ."

"Disconcerting?"

"Perhaps."

"Or perhaps a little too close to the truth."

"*Do not forget me, Hamlet. I will be avenged.*"

Hamlet gasped in surprise as he saw the ghost reappear in the corner of the room.

"Hamlet," said his mother. "What is the matter?"

"Don't you see him?"

"See who? You stare into empty space and ask me if I see someone."

"My father. Don't you see him."

"Of course not, Hamlet, your father is dead."

"Dead perhaps, but he still speaks to me."

"*I will be avenged, Hamlet.*"

"There is no one there, Hamlet. I fear your father's death has taken its toll on you. Let me fetch Horatio."

"Do you think I am mad too? I can see him, there. Will I ever be rid of him?"

"You should rest," she said taking his hand.

"Rest? How can I rest?" The ghost started to fade but even as it did the sound of his father's voice was still ringing in his ears.

"*Do not forget me.*"

No, he would not forget, could not. He would kill

Claudius at the first opportunity, if only to be rid of the spirit.

There was movement behind the arras and Hamlet sensed his opportunity. Claudius; it had to be him hiding, spying on him. This was his moment. Hamlet snatched his hand from his mother's and drawing his sword, drove it into the yielding shape behind the arras.

"A rat!" he cried and let out a shout of victory before withdrawing his blade from the dead weight which had fallen into him. The body fell face down to the floor taking much of the arras with it.

"He is dead," he shouted in triumph then bent down to look at his victim's face. But it was not the battle-weary features of his uncle that pressed to the floor, but those of Polonius. The wrong man.

"What have you done?" his mother screamed, her voice just short of hysteria. "How has this poor man ever wronged you?"

"He has not. I was mistaken."

"Mistaken? Then who did you intend to kill?"

"My father's murderer. But then perhaps I was not mistaken, perhaps it was the hand of God that guided my hand to reveal the true culprit," he said half to himself. He stared at the sword still in his hand, its blade stained red. Guided by God.

One of the storerooms near the kitchen was almost empty and had been left unlocked. Hamlet managed to drag the body inside without being discovered and waited there to gather his thoughts. Claudius would understand his own life was now under threat. His mother would be unable to keep the news of the murder from her lover, even to protect her own son. But her loyalty no longer seemed to matter.

The sound of voices and heavy footsteps echoed around the castle and Hamlet half expected one of them to belong to his father but the ghost did not appear. Had he really seen him in his mother's room or had it been a figment of his imagination. A manifestation of his madness. He no longer felt he was acting a part, but that it had overtaken him.

Hamlet sat on the stone floor of the storeroom, his

arms wrapped around his raised knees and rocked himself
backwards and forwards. Would the ghost of poor Polonius
now come to haunt him too? Would his spirit rise from its
body as it lay there wrapped in the bloodstained arras? He
had never intended to harm the man, and would not have
wished him dead. How could he have thought him a murderer
even in his moment of anger? Claudius was the murderer, his
father had told him so.

The door swung open and a weak light crept in from the
corridor beyond.

"Hamlet. Are you there?" A familiar voice called softly.

"Horatio?"

The door closed and the room was plunged into darkness
again. "The King is looking for you."

"He knows then?"

"The Queen has told him, but I can get you out of here. I can
get you away from Elsinore and out of Claudius's reach."

"No, my friend, I must finish what I set out to do. It can
be delayed no longer. This thing must be put to rest."

In the Great Hall Claudius and his mother were waiting.
Beside them stood Laertes, his rage obvious.

"Where is my father?"

"I suspect he is in hell, unless he was fortunate enough to
see the error of his ways before his hour arrived."

"Then it is true. I will have my revenge, Hamlet, and it
will not be swift."

Claudius raised a hand to silence them both. "I have first
claim in any trial by combat. I believe you have been maligning
my name, Hamlet. I had hoped you would have been as good
a son to me as you were to your father."

"But you are not my father."

"And you are not my son."

"Then we are agreed. I accept your challenge with pleasure,"
said Hamlet, relieved he would have the opportunity to take
his revenge in a fair fight.

"I choose my champion," said Claudius.

"Champion?" said Hamlet. "I accepted the challenge of
trial by combat with you not with any champion."

"I choose Laertes, but this is not to be trial by combat.

Let this be settled in a more friendly manner. Settle your differences in a fencing match."

Claudius swept out of the room half dragging Gertrude behind him despite her obvious wish to speak to her son.

"One hour, Hamlet," said Laertes. "Make your peace with God."

"And you, Laertes. My heart is already clear." He knew his opponent had no intention of this being a mere fencing match. But he was no longer certain who was the killer. Could it have been Laertes? He now seemed so eager to see him dead. Was this more than the desire for the death of his father? If he had been leaving for France how could he have been recalled so quickly unless his departure had been nothing more than an elaborate ruse. Had he been planning to kill him all along even if this opportunity had not arisen?

Perhaps he had been acting on instruction from Claudius. That would make sense. Why did it have to be one person? Would it end if he managed to kill both Laertes and Claudius or was there more to be put right? Had his father misled him about his mother? Was she involved too? So many questions flooded into his head that the pounding returned. All he could do was to press his fingers to his temples to drive away the pain.

The Great Hall was full of noise when Hamlet returned. Horatio had tried to reassure him but Hamlet knew he had to beat Laertes. If he lost, Claudius would escape the punishment he so richly deserved. Laertes the brave, Laertes the warrior, Laertes the wronged and Hamlet no more than a sporting fencer. Laertes could kill him with impunity and Hamlet felt there was little he could do to prevent it. All he could do was his best even if he was doomed to fail. He had to try.

Claudius set a golden cup down on a small table before the two contestants. "Wine for the victor," he said. "Now let the duel begin."

The first few clashes of steel were little more than child's play, but Hamlet felt the hidden power behind his opponent's strokes. Laertes was toying with him like a cat playing with a mouse. His opponent dropped his guard momentarily and Hamlet lunged, missing by no more than inches but realized too late that it had been deliberate. Laertes slipped his blade through Hamlet's own defence and tore through his sleeve. Hamlet stepped back out of reach and touched his hand to the wound, pulling it away stained crimson.

"Come now Hamlet, are you beaten before you begin?"

"Not I," he replied and attacked once more, this time the venom of his strike caused them both to drop their weapons. Hamlet was first to the nearest blade, not realizing at first that it was Laertes' sword he had recovered. His opponent scrambled across the floor to reach the other weapon, even though Hamlet had no intention of attacking him unarmed.

Again and again Hamlet attacked, but Laertes' skill was more than a match for his own.

Laertes stepped forward with a powerful lunge but Hamlet skipped out of the way and raised his sword beneath his opponent's attacking arm and drove in as deeply as he could. Laertes was smiling as he lay dying at Hamlet's feet.

"It is too late, Hamlet," he said, blood frothing from his mouth.

"Too late?"

"The blade was poisoned," he whispered. "A single scratch would have been enough to prove fatal. It will not be long before the end for both of us."

Behind him Hamlet heard his mother cry out, but as he turned around he saw her start to swoon. Claudius rose to her assistance, but Hamlet thrust him back into his chair in order to get to his mother's side. In the few strides he took he dropped his sword and grabbed the golden wine goblet from the table. With her head in the crook of his arm he pressed it to her lips until she started to drink.

After only a few sips her eyes grew wide and a silent scream choked in her throat as her whole body flew into spasm. Hamlet looked over his shoulder at Claudius who was standing again, and saw the horror in his eyes.

"That was meant for me, wasn't it?" said Hamlet. "Just in case I beat Laertes."

He let his mother's limp body slide to the ground and rose to his feet.

Claudius took two steps back then opened his mouth and screamed, all signs of his arrogance disappeared. Before the sound had died away Hamlet had retrieved the poisoned sword. With his teeth clenched he drove the blade into his uncle's chest, and hugged him as tightly as he could. He only let the limp body fall to the ground when he was sure all trace of life had disappeared.

"Do you hear me now, father," Hamlet called as he slumped to the floor himself, feeling the poison coursing through his own veins.

"It is over. Let Fortinbras take the throne. It is better that he should take it now to save any more bloodshed."

"I'm sorry, Hamlet," said Horatio, kneeling at his side, mopping his brow as the fever raged.

"Horatio, my one true friend and ally through all this. What do you have to be sorry about?"

"Using you."

"Using me? How?"

"Laertes was innocent of any crime beyond wanting the same revenge for his father's death that you desired yourself. Claudius convinced him to carry the poisoned sword. But he would not have done it without my encouragement."

"Yours?"

Horatio lowered his head and Hamlet felt a tear fall onto his own cheek. "I gave Claudius the Hebenon to poison your father and then did all I could to encourage you to take your revenge."

"But why?"

"I am not proud of what I have done, Hamlet, and never thought it would lead to this. I only wish you had left Elsinore when I offered to help you escape."

"No, Horatio. This had to be finished. But why did you do it?"

"For money, and power. Isn't that the root of all betrayals?"

"But what do you stand to gain?"

"Perhaps only the crumbs from my master's table, but I have been promised much more."

"Your master?" Hamlet grimaced as the pain increased inside him, burning every sinew. He almost missed his friend looking up at the figure of Fortinbras himself.

"Leave him now," said Fortinbras without approaching. "You have done well, Horatio. Your future is secure."

"I'm sorry, Hamlet," said Horatio. "Truly sorry."

Hamlet tried to answer, to show his anger at betrayal when the ghost appeared again in the midst of the concerned onlookers.

"*I had to do it, Hamlet. Even in death there is no guarantee of truth. I hold no enmity for Fortinbras, he only did what I would have done when he cajoled my brother to murder. It is better he holds the crown you never could. Now it is finally ended.*"

A MIDSUMMER ECLIPSE

Stephen Baxter

Although technically A Midsummer Night's Dream *takes place in about 1200* BC *its setting is as contemporary as Shakespeare's other comedies. It is one of his most popular plays. It was probably written around 1594 though the earliest known performance was in 1596. The central plot concerns Hermia and her love for Lysander. Hermia has, however, been ordered by her father Egeus to marry Demetrius with whom she is not in love and who, in any case, is madly in love with Hermia's friend Helena. Theseus, the Duke of Athens, who is about to wed the Amazon queen Hippolyta, supports Egeus's orders with the result that Hermia, threatened with execution, flees with Lysander and they meet up with Helena and Demetrius in a wood outside Athens. The wood is the haunt of the fairies. Oberon and Titania, the King and Queen of the fairies, have argued over the care of a changeling boy. Oberon, with the help of the mischievous Puck, acquires the juice of a magic flower which, when dropped in the eyes, makes that person fall in love with whoever they first see. As the result of Oberon and Puck's intervention, Lysander and Demetrius both fall in love with Helena, while Titania falls in love with Bottom, the weaver, who leads a group of craftsmen rehearsing a play for Theseus's wedding ceremony. Puck has transformed Bottom's head into that of an ass.*

Oberon manages to secure the care of the changeling boy and thereafter he and Puck repair all the confusion they have caused so that everything ends happily ever after. What whodunnit could we possibly make out of that, you might ask? The following story takes place shortly after the events described above when all of the couples have been married but, as Stephen Baxter reveals, not all lived happily ever after.

It was as if a bite had been taken out of the disc of the sun.

The shadow of the moon swept across the forest, and as the eclipse deepened, the light at the base of the trees became a grey, muddled twilight. Bird song was stilled, and the air adopted a preternatural clarity.

It was, thought Puck, as if night had come to this midsummer day: as Phoebe, the moon, embraced the sullen carcase of Phoebus Apollo, the sun. He shivered in the greyness, scarcely daring to move.

And in the moment of maximum eclipse there came a noise from the heart of Athens, a dismal howl that chilled Puck further. It was the hounds of Theseus, bred for their musical bark; but today their cries were discordant, redolent with distress.

Even when the eclipse began to pass, the light remained subtly changed, Puck thought: midsummer was barely gone, and yet already autumn tinged the air.

The eclipse was almost over when Hippolyta came striding into the wood.

She wore a tunic of buckskin – cruder than the customary garb of the Athenian aristocracy, but following the fashion of the northern Amazons from whom she had come – and Puck could see, from the hang of the skin, the emptiness where her breast had been cut away.

In the renewed sunlight, Hippolyta stood in a clearing. She glared about suspiciously. She was a tall, proud woman, and despite her abduction by and forced betrothal to Theseus,

Duke of Athens, her enduring strength radiated from her posture, and the set of her powerful limbs.

"Sprite?" she snapped. "I know you are here. Come before me."

Puck, watching, was startled. Nervously, he assumed the shape of a toad, and crept forward into the clearing, croaking deeply.

Hippolyta's warrior face turned to him immediately. "I see you, sprite. Do not attempt your tricks on me."

Puck's humour immediately deserted him. He felt his mask fall away, the costume of a poor actor shredding in the fire of her gaze, until he was exposed.

He straightened up and stood before her, trying to match her fearlessness. "You know me, mortal?"

Her eyes narrowed – but there was an odd softness about her mouth. "Yes, I know you, Goodfellow. And I know the circumstance of your birth."

Puck frowned, disconcerted anew. His birth was a mystery to him. He had known no father or mother – although he had once endured a dream of the true nature of his parents: a human woman and a he-faerie . . . But he had woken in the cold dawn, and the vision had fled.

He said, "What do you want of me?"

"Did you hear the hounds?"

"When Phoebe engulfed her nephew Apollo – "

"During the moments of eclipse. Yes. The hounds were distressed, Goodfellow. They had good cause. There was a fire, in the heart of Athens. A house was destroyed. A life was taken."

"A mortal life?"

"It was Lysander – a young man who recently married Hermia, the daughter of the sage Egeus." She glared at him. "All this after the confusion of your sprite tricks, Goodfellow."

Puck did not have to feign distress. "To die, so soon after such a happy wedding day! Whatever the cause, it is a tragedy."

She snorted. "We mortals live close to death, sprite. That is not the issue. The Athenians are saying the fire was an act of the gods – at the moment of their rage, signified by the eclipse."

"Rage?"

"Perhaps over some abomination performed by Lysander. So they say. Lysander recently returned from a visit to the Oracle at Delphi. He has spoken to no one since."

Puck nodded. "Then that is your answer. The anger of the gods was made obvious by the eclipse, engulfing the whole world – "

"The gods," she said heavily, "needed to burn a man to death? I think not. Goodfellow, I do not think this death was the work of god or faerie – or even a simple accident. *I think it was caused by human action.* The eclipse was used as a distraction, while the deed was done."

"You think that Lysander was murdered? By whom? And why? And what of the eclipse? What mortal could control the flight of the moon herself?"

"I anticipate hearing your answer."

"My answer?"

She smiled thinly. "Goodfellow, you are a malicious imp, but you are no fool. Half of you is human; the other half has sprite cunning. I want you to leave this desolate wood, to come with me to the city, to resolve this crime for me." She waved a hand. "I will introduce you as a Trojan merchant. Assume some appropriate form. Other than that, none of your damaging tricks, sprite. You will use your intelligence, and that alone."

"Queen – why are you doing this? What is your purpose?"

She stiffened. "That is not part of your study. Come with me, sprite; if we hurry we will reach the house of Lysander before its embers have cooled."

And she turned and stalked off, towards the walls of the city, so confident in her authority that she forbore to look back.

Puck, as if bewitched by her command, followed.

Athens was bustling and populous, the centre of a web of roads thronged with foot-travellers and jostling two-wheeled chariots. Dominating the city's heart was the Palace of

Theseus, its circuit wall and huge Lion Gate overshadowing the houses clustering at its feet – as, thought Puck, Theseus, Duke of Athens, overshadowed his subjects.

Puck was uncomfortable here. Athens was built of straight lines and walls and enclosed spaces, hard and real in the too-bright daylight. There was no softness here, no room to dream – save of a future of conquest and control.

This was not his place.

He knew that this Athens was only a shadow of the glories that would come. These mortals, unlike the faeries, were embedded in time: doomed to die, every one of them. And yet this very rooting in time gave the mortals a chance to learn, to grow, to change.

And not always for the better.

Hippolyta led him direct to the house of Lysander. A number of citizens were clustered here, most of them unfamiliar to Puck. None of them gave him a second glance. He needed little sprite trickery to achieve his anonymity; their own distraction and fear, on this ill-omened day of eclipse, was enough to fill their minds.

Hippolyta pointed out Hermia: short, dark and intensely beautiful, now cast in the role of grieving widow, she wept in the arms of her father, Egeus. The sage was a tall, stern man, bald-headed and beak-nosed, who stared at the wreckage of his daughter's home with an expression Puck could not read.

The house was of the usual *megaron* plan, with mud bricks piled neatly over a stone footing. It had been roofed over by wooden beams, thatch and pitch – but the blaze had consumed the roof, which had fallen in, and the neat brickwork was stained with charring.

Hippolyta led Puck through the open door, and he walked along a short hall – now open to the summer sky – to the main room. The hearth had largely survived the blaze intact; Puck saw that it was piled neatly with firewood which was, ironically, unburned. The floor was littered with fragments of the burned-out roof, some of which still smoked. Remnants of wood and thatch crackled under Puck's feet, giving off a stink of ash. The falling roof had smashed the furniture here.

Puck saw a number of clay tablets on the floor, most of them cracked beyond decipherability; evidently Lysander had been an enthusiastic reader.

On the walls, Puck noticed, the oil lamps remained, intact, evidently spared by the fire. That struck him as odd, and he made to remark on it to the Amazon. But Hippolyta led him to a still shape, half-buried in the rubble of the roof.

Here, there was a stink of charred meat.

Hippolyta glared down at the body of Lysander, grim but not afraid; this was, Puck remembered, a warrior, a woman who knew death. "I asked that he not be disturbed by the priests until you had a chance to inspect him."

Puck knelt in the ash and, with care, scraped away some of the roofing. Although there was some charring of the clothing – a nightshirt – the flesh itself was not too badly burned; Lysander's handsome face was easily recognizable.

"It is evident that he was not killed by the fire itself," Hippolyta said. "Perhaps the smoke consumed him."

"Perhaps." Puck ran his hand over Lysander's face. The flesh was cold. The front of the young man's scalp was shaven smooth, without stubble. "He made an offering of his hair to the Oracle."

"Yes," the Amazon said. "As is the custom. The fore part only, in the style of the Abantes introduced by Theseus – "

"When did he visit Delphi?"

"He would have been there three days ago. His servant, Nick Bottom, tells me he returned yesterday."

"Bottom? The weaver?"

"Another victim of your malice. He was a poor weaver; Lysander, taking a liking to the man after he performed as Pyramus at the wedding, offered him employment."

"I would like to speak to him."

She frowned. "To a servant? For what purpose?"

Puck shrugged. "Servant he may be. But this Nick Bottom may be the last man to have seen Lysander alive."

"What else?"

"The doctors should examine this body."

"The doctors? You mean the priests. The funeral preparations will – "

"No, with respect, madam: the doctors. I should like them to establish that fire, or smoke, was indeed the cause of death of poor Lysander."

Her face was a mask of anger. "Are you mad, sprite? What purpose will that serve? Is it not obvious – "

"Nothing here is obvious, Queen. If it were, you would not need my help."

Growling, she acceded to his request.

He was glad to leave the burned-out house. The gritty reality of broken bricks, ruined roof and twisted corpse in this harsh Athenian day intruded on him, making him long to return to the dreamy dark hollows of the forest.

Hippolyta led him to the home of Philostrate, Theseus's Master of the Revels. Philostrate's home was handsomely appointed, adorned with gold masks and fine painted pottery and a handsome replica of Theseus's famous bronze sword, all of it testifying to the wealth of his master, the Duke. Philostrate had grown fond of the young couple during the wedding preparations, and had offered his home to Hermia until her distress eased and her affairs were reconciled.

Here, in the presence of Hippolyta, Puck questioned Nick Bottom.

The poor servant was confused and distressed. "I don't know, your worship, I don't know – "

"Never mind. My questions are simple; just answer them one at a time. Now. Your master, Lysander – "

"Oh what a destitute day this is! What tragedians we have become! Oh, oh – "

"Yes, yes. But Lysander. He returned home from Delphi yesterday."

"Yes. Before the sun set. So I was told."

"So you were told?"

"I had already prepared the house for his return. I swept the hearth and – "

"Yes. Who told you of his return?"

Bottom frowned, struggling to remember. "It was the Lord Egeus, father of my lady Hermia. My lady was staying with her father. He – Egeus, I mean, not Hermia, what a fool I sound! – he said I should fix the house, and then retire to my quarters before my master's return, for Lysander would be tired after his journey and would require no attention, rather repairing to bed."

"So you did not see Lysander? You have not seen him since he set off for Delphi?"

Bottom's broad face creased. "Why, I, yes, no. Do you know, I believe I have not. And now I will never see him again, except in his mound!"

"Control yourself, man. We are almost done."

"Thank you, sir Trojan – "

"The lamps."

Bottom looked up, and Puck was aware of Hippolyta's sceptical eyes on him.

"The lamps, your worship?"

"The oil lamps in Lysander's home. Did you fill them for your master? Is that part of your duty?"

"Certainly I did, sir. My master was wont to read the records of the Council, every night, before he slept."

"No matter how fatigued?"

Bottom looked blank.

"I mean, even if he was very tired?"

"He always read, sir, even if he had been fatiguing all day."

Puck smiled.

When Bottom had gone, Hippolyta glared at Puck. "I hope this trivial business you pursue, of lamps and servants, has some bearing on the issue."

"At the moment, Queen, all I have is questions. And I must ask that you hold to your patience while I seek answers."

"Then," she said sourly, "how will you try that patience now, sprite? I presume you will speak to the widow – "

"Not yet. I would like to meet her father, Egeus."

Despite Hippolyta's growing restlessness, Puck questioned Egeus in general terms about his life and business. Egeus was cautious, but – in the presence of the Amazon Queen, now married to Theseus himself – he answered Puck's questions reasonably openly.

Egeus, Puck learned, was a man of learning and no small influence. He served Theseus, tyrant and deity, as *lawagetas* – a leader of the people, chamberlain to the Duke. In this role Egeus advised Theseus on matters of law and the economy. He was also a natural philosopher of some grasp, Puck learned.

"For instance," Egeus said rather immodestly, "I advised the Duke on the river diversion which enabled his army to pass a fortified town during his invasion of the Amazon country in the north, which – "

"I concede you are a scholar, sir," Puck said. "Equally as well versed in the law and affairs of state as in medicine, mathematics, and astrology."

Egeus frowned. "I have a little understanding."

"In your capacity as *lawagetas*, you are a careful record-keeper. A disciplined mind is never at rest. I imagine you apply your record-keeping to other issues: your study of the sky, for example."

"Of course. The Oriental astrologers, whose methods I have studied, follow a similar practice. How else is one to predict the motion of the planets and other lamps of the sky without full and proper records? Even you Trojans should understand that."

Puck bowed his head. "We can only acknowledge the superior wisdom of you Athenians. Sir, can you tell me where you were at the moment of eclipse?"

He frowned. "Where I was? I was before the Duke himself, supervising an audience with a *basileus*, a tributary chieftain from a remote province, who – "

Puck smiled. "But you Athenians are superstitious people. The eclipse was an awful omen. Was the business of the court, and other public institutions, not suspended as the moon's shadow crept across the face of the sun?"

"It was. That is our custom in times of ill omen."

"Then you were still in the court, before Theseus, when the eclipse began?"

Egeus glared at Puck; his thin mouth worked. "In fact I left a little before. I had other business."

Puck nodded. "Now, as to – "

Egeus turned to Hippolyta. "Oh, enough of this. Madam, must I endure more of these absurd questions from this – this foreigner?"

"Of course not." She waved a hand. "Egeus, you may go with my apologies."

Egeus stood, glared at Puck, and departed, haughtily.

Puck sighed. "My lady Hippolyta, if I am to resolve this sad affair, you must allow me to conduct my study in my own manner."

She shouted, "By offending one of our most respected citizens with your ridiculous, inconsequential questions?"

"My lady, is there anyone in Athens with a comparable knowledge of astrology?"

"None," she said through her anger. "But what of it?"

"It is odd," said Puck quietly, "that citizen Egeus appears to care so little about the death of his son-in-law, and the distress caused to his daughter. His dominant emotions were irritation and vanity – "

Hippolyta's anger grew. "What do you know of human emotions, Goodfellow? And what next? Will you wish to badger my husband, brave Theseus himself?"

"No. I would speak to the daughter: the widow, Hermia."

"It is about time," snapped the Queen of the Amazons.

Hermia's face was swollen with crying.

"I don't know what I can tell you," she said. "Our love seemed blighted from the start. I loved Lysander, and he me; but my father opposed the match. He proposed I should marry another, called Demetrius. My father even took me before Duke Theseus, who threatened our love with the sharp law of Athens, even up to a sentence of death for me if I did not obey my father."

"What did you do?" Puck asked, knowing the answer.

"We resolved to elope. My darling Lysander and I. We would run to the woods, and from there proceed to the house of his aunt, far from Athens, who would shelter us. But Demetrius followed us, as did a girl, Helena, daughter of Nedar, who loved Demetrius – though her love was not returned . . ." She wiped her tear-crusted eyes, and looked bewildered. "What a night we had of it! Something about the wood – the moonlight . . ."

"What happened?"

"We became – confused. Lysander started to protest his love for Helena. And so did Demetrius! I could not understand it. I thought Helena had stolen my Lysander, and we argued, and the men prepared to fight over Helena. But then – I think we slept, it was a strange night – we somehow came to our senses. Lysander loved me once more – even his memories of his infatuation with Helena were muddled, he said – but still Demetrius clung to his affection for Helena.

"We were discovered by Duke Theseus himself, who relented in his sternness at seeing our joy, and he invited the four of us – myself and Lysander, Helena and Demetrius – to join his own wedding party at the Temple. My father's opposition to my match with Lysander remained strong, although he acceded to the Duke's instructions, but his anger was a minor note in our happiness we *were* happy, sir – but then Lysander left to visit the Oracle, and I never saw him again – not alive – "

The girl's voice fragmented and she lapsed into inconsolable sobbing. Puck felt his heart go out to the girl. Her emotions – her love and loss – so clearly possessed her, in stark contrast to the clipped, peevish iciness of her own father, Egeus the sage.

Pitying the girl, he released her.

Hippolyta stood over him and hissed, "What was it you used to confuse them? Love-in-idleness, I'll wager. And you left poor Demetrius under the spell, under the illusion of his love for Helena. Do you expect such artificial love to sustain a lifetime of marriage?"

She began to pace, her powerful legs thrusting. ". . . But perhaps this meddling of yours – the crossed lovers – the quarrel in the forest – is the key to it all. Perhaps some lingering jealousy over the girl Helena led Demetrius to massacre the man he saw as a rival. Or perhaps it was Helena herself? Women are capable of murder and high passion too, as I should know. I hear the girl Helena has always envied the finer looks of Hermia, and perhaps she resolved to rob her at last of the one prize Hermia wanted above all, her husband, Lysander . . ."

Puck sat quietly as the Queen continued in this fashion, spinning out ever more fantastic hypotheses of love thwarted, of envy and fear, of passion boiling into murder.

There was a knock at the door. A servant admitted the doctor whom Hippolyta had instructed to examine Lysander's cadaver. The doctor – elderly, a little bent – was holding something in one liver-spotted hand. It was a small triangle of a dull grey metal; it was coated with dried blood.

It was an arrow-head. And it had been found in Lysander's heart.

"Iron," said Puck. "Is a new age of iron, of hard grey metal, about to sweep over you mortals?"

Hippolyta dismissed the doctor. "By all the gods," she said. "Why would anyone stick an arrow into a corpse?"

"But it was not so," Puck said evenly.

But she was not listening. "You see what damage you do with your sprite meddling, Goodfellow? You see what it has led to?"

"It was a jest," said Puck wearily. "A dream, of a summer's night – "

She said severely, "You mock us: you, who are alien to human emotions. You are a monster: you and your dwarfish king!" Her face twisted with genuine, and surprising, anger as she referred to Oberon, King of the faeries.

Puck watched curiously.

He said, "If that is how you feel, it is well that you may now release me from this assignment and allow me to sink back into the undisciplined woods."

She frowned. "What do you mean?"

"That I have solved your puzzle for you, Queen."

Puck said, "It was your arrow which killed Lysander."

"The arrow?"

"Lysander was killed at Delphi. His death was concealed, and the body smuggled back to Athens and placed in his house. My lady, when the house burned down *Lysander was already dead.*"

She frowned, staring at the arrow-head as if expecting it

to speak to her. "By what unholy magic can you know such things, sprite? Can you read the past?"

"No. But I have open eyes, Queen. When I touched Lysander's brow, where he had shaved away the hair he offered to the Oracle, I found smooth, cold skin. There was no stubble, for he died before the hair had a chance to grow back."

"And then there is the matter of the lamps."

"The lamps?"

"Did it not strike you as odd to find Lysander's oil lamps fixed to the wall of his burned-out house, intact, undamaged save for a little scorching?"

"Now that you mention it . . ." She toyed with the iron arrow-head. "The lamps would explode, scattering their oil, and so furthering the blaze – "

"No," said Puck. "A full lamp will not explode. Only a vessel which is half-empty, or less – the space filled with gases – contains the air to burn."

She shook her head. "What of it?"

"It is a further demonstration that Lysander was already dead, before the fire: that evening, his first after his return home, this great reader – by the testimony of his servant – did not light his lamps. That sad remnant of Lysander, with the iron arrow still lodged in his heart, sat in chill dark silence in the house that had been his home . . ."

"And then," Hippolyta said slowly, "someone crept to the house and torched it. And at the moment of eclipse, so that the gods themselves could be made suspect . . . But who?"

"Is it not obvious? The only man in Athens who *knew* the eclipse would occur in advance, for his patient astrological tables and charts told him so . . . The man who, with his intellect, controlled the moon itself, and used it to divert blame to the very gods . . . The man who hated poor Lysander for his theft of his daughter's affections – "

"Egeus," Hippolyta said, her voice full of wonder. "It was Egeus."

"You have your answer, Queen; I leave it to you and your Duke to ensure Athenian justice prevails over this cruel criminal."

"Not a spurned lover, not a jealous suitor. *Egeus*. The most rational man in Athens. How remarkable."

"Not so remarkable," said Puck sadly. "Egeus is tormented by the same passions which drive every human heart. What distinguishes him is the way he used his rationality, his logic and intelligence, to plot such a complex crime to satisfy those passions. Is this the future for you mortals? The minds of gods, acting out the whims of monkey hearts?"

She glared at him. "Do not presume to judge us, halfling."

Hippolyta escorted Puck from Athens. It was with relief that he left behind the city's rectilinear oppressiveness and returned to the soft green mouth of the wood.

"There is one thing I do not yet understand," said Puck.

She was sour and sarcastic. "Really?"

"Your interest, Queen. Why were you so concerned to unravel this mystery? And why involve me?"

"Because I tire of superstition. I tire of dread and dreams. I wanted to expose you, you demons of the woods, for the malignancy you are . . ."

"And you wanted me to see it."

She looked vaguely into the sky. "Monkey hearts? Perhaps. But one day we will run our monkey fingers through the cold soil of Egeus's Moon. The dream is over, and we are waking, sprite. Soon you will be gone from our lives, the empire of your father banished forever. For *we* control the moonlight."

He said softly, "My father?"

She looked startled; evidently she had not intended to reveal that. But she snapped: "Yes, halfling: I mean Oberon, King of the faeries, and you are his bastard son. Does that hurt you? Does it torment you to know that your cruel father has never spoken the truth to you?"

"He is not cruel," said Puck gently. "You were not seduced, Queen. I am sure he genuinely cared for you."

She looked shocked. "How do you know – what are you talking about?"

"I understand," he said.

She spat on the ground. "You understand nothing, halfling.

Our business is concluded. And I pray I will never see you again."

She turned, and stalked off towards the walls of the city.

"Goodbye, Mother," whispered Puck.

MUCH ADO ABOUT SOMETHING

Susan B. Kelly

Much Ado about Nothing *was probably written during the winter of 1598/99. In its day the plot of the play was fairly well known from other literary sources, though it is far from well known today. It is set in Sicily where Don Pedro of Arragon has defeated his half-brother Don John. The two becomes guests of Leonato, the Governor of Messina where Count Claudio, a nobleman in Don Pedro's service, falls in love with Hero, Leonato's daughter. Don John opposes the relationship and convinces Claudio that Hero has been unfaithful. He rejects her on their wedding day and Hero collapses and is believed dead. However the truth is uncovered by a rather bumbling constable of the watch, Dogberry, and all ends happily. There is a sub-plot involving the lovers Benedick and Beatrice where Benedick challenges Claudio to a duel for his treatment of Hero, though the fight becomes unnecessary when the truth is revealed. The play contains so much bluff and double-bluff, however, that it is tempting to place a different interpretation upon events, which is what Susan Kelly does in the following story.*

*   *   *

Messina 1 May

Dearest Mama,

Well, there's been a to-do here this last week and no mistake. I don't really know what to make of it so I shall set it all down exactly as I remember it and see what you think. Only what you might call the official version is all wrong, as far as I can see; it holds water the way a length of butter muslin does.

It all started when the Prince of Arragon, that's Don Pedro, came back from the wars after a mighty victory, with nobody important being killed at all. My Master, Signior Leonato, met him at the gates and welcomed him and said he must stay with us as long as he wanted. Well, the Prince thanked him and said he'd stay at least a month. You should have seen the Master's jaw drop! It's one thing to offer unlimited hospitality and quite another to have it accepted like that. Still, he bit the bullet and gave orders for rooms to be prepared and banquets set out and we didn't stop in the servants' hall that night until gone midnight and Sarah, the housekeeper, said she'd never known anything like it, the gentlefolk all drinking and carousing till dawn.

The Prince brought such a lot of people with him, you see, that the house was full to overflowing. There was his brother, Don John, that they call John the Bastard, which always seems a bit disrespectful to me but apparently it's all right to have natural sons when you're a prince, not like with the rest of us. He's a proud sort of man, though, with a nasty sneering way about him, much higher and mightier than Don Pedro himself.

Then there's Signior Benedick. You know, Mama, I've mentioned him before, the one that's always pinching the maids' bottoms and trying to put his hand up our skirts and down our bodices. He hasn't changed. You may remember how I told you a couple of years back that there was a bit of a thing between him and Miss Beatrice but how it all came to nothing in the end and now they haven't a civil word to say to each other. Sarah says they're still sweet together underneath it all but he called Miss Bea "Lady Disdain" in front of the whole household and asked if she was not dead yet, and if that's love, Mama, then you can keep it.

If ever there was a man with his eye on the main chance,
I should say it's Signior Benedick.

Then there was this Signior Claudio, that we'd heard so
much about. It seems the Prince has taken a fancy to him and
loaded him down with money and lands and titles which not
everyone is thrilled about, I suspect. He's not more than a
boy really, but old enough to be making sheep's eyes at Miss
Hero all the same. He looked at her like he'd never seen a
woman before although she is lovely, if I say so myself, all
little and dainty and that mass of black hair that looks like
a fine mist when it's brushed out in the morning. And she
knew he was looking at her all right, blushing away, which
looked right pretty against her porcelain skin and I said to
Sarah that we'd be laying out a wedding feast before Don
Pedro went away again and she said that that was as maybe
and meantime I could get on with stoking the fire.

I was right, though. Within three days Signior Claudio
had secured Miss Hero's hand; or rather he got the Prince
to do it for him which is not my idea of wooing, but then
the gentry is different to us as you've told me a thousand
times, Mama. And as for Signior Benedick and Miss Bea –
well, Sarah wasn't wrong, she seldom is. I was on my way
to the washhouse with the bedclothes and I saw them sitting
behind a hedge, all furtive, so I thought, "Two can play at that
game," I thought, and I hid behind the other side of the hedge
and listened and he was saying to her, "I love nothing in the
wide world so well as thee," which I thought was very pretty
and it made me a bit misty eyed for a minute but it didn't
stop him goosing me when he passed me in the passage on
the way to dinner that night. I nearly dropped my tray and
it wouldn't be him that got the rough edge of Sarah's tongue
if I had done, would it?

So there we were, working non-stop at preparing the
wedding feast for Miss Hero, and the ladies all excited
with cloth of gold and jewels and veils and presents. I
enjoyed the work and was whirling around singing that
fine new song I told you of – "Sing no more ladies,
for men were seducers ever," it goes – until Sarah told
me she could not stand any more of my warbling. Then

the wedding day dawned and that was when the real excitement began.

There was an odd thing happened that morning, though, which I'd better tell you about first. Sarah said that I might as well go and give Don John's room a good turn-out as he had upped and left at first light without a word to anyone and left his room like a pigsty to boot with wine spilt everywhere and other things I'd not like to examine too closely. So I did. And I was coming downstairs again into the front hall with my mop and bucket and there was a rat-a-tat-tat at the door and the Master himself came rushing to open it, so I made myself small against the staircase since I knew I shouldn't have come down the main stairs but it was the nearest way and we were that busy.

It was those two men from the Watch I told you about, Dogberry and Verges, that no one can ever understand a word they say. And they were going on and on to the Master about two men they'd arrested during the night they said were out-and-out villains and arrant knaves and the Master kept looking at his pocket watch and wishing they would get to the point. Then the big one, Dogberry, said something about treason and slander and the Master said rather abruptly that he had got a very busy day in front of him and could his two "kind neighbours" come back later when he would have the leisure to decipher them. Then he shooed them away without further ceremony.

Then he turned round muttering something like "Too early" or "Too soon", and saw me standing in the shadows and said, "Maria!" like he was very shocked to see me there. I curtsied and he said, "Well, well. This is a great day for the house, Maria. Here's for you to celebrate Miss Hero's good fortune," and gave me a coin which I put into my pocket without looking, thinking it to be a brass penny. So I thanked him and curtsied again and ran off with my bucket and mop back below stairs, but when I remembered to look at the coin, what do you think it was, Mama? A silver ducat!

The wedding was fixed for late morning to be followed by a feast going on all day and far into the night. Miss Hero looked so lovely in her white gown and veil, standing there waiting for her new lord. It's not just that she's beautiful either, Mama, she's so good and kind and not at all hoity toity the way Miss Bea can be when the mood takes her.

Only then, when the friar asked Signior Claudio if he took Hero for his wife he went and said, "No"! – just straight out like that. Then he called her a wanton and a common stale (excuse me, Mama, but I'm just repeating what I heard, however shocking) and said he had seen her with another man the night before, with her clothes all ruffled and her virtue gone and not for the first time either and the Prince backed him up and said he'd seen it too. Miss Hero fell to the ground in a dead faint and I thought the Master would have died of shame, wailing out that he wished he had never got a daughter and that it would be a kindness were somebody to stab him through the heart.

Signior Claudio, meanwhile, he turned on his heel and marched out saying there would be no wedding today, leaving the Master and Miss Bea and Signior Benedick to carry Miss Hero away senseless. We were all dismissed, of course, since the Master didn't want the whole world to witness his disgrace. Later, we were told that Miss Hero was dead indeed and that Signior Benedick had challenged Signior Claudio to a duel to the death. That would be Miss Bea making him, I think. I can't see him doing it of his own idea. Claudio and the Prince sat there looking all grave, but obviously thinking that dying was the only thing my lady could decently do in the circumstances.

I could hardly get on with my work what with crying over Miss Hero and the shame that had fallen on the household and Sarah told me if I didn't pull myself together, there'd be trouble. It seems it's only the gentry that's allowed any sensibility. After all, it's not as if someone like me would be able literally to die of shame like Miss Hero did.

Only then, late that afternoon, I was up in the apple loft sorting out some good ones from last year for baking, and that Dogberry and Verges turn up in the yard below, with two men in chains this time, men in the uniform of Don Pedro's army, and they tell the Master and the Prince and young Master Claudio that the whole thing was a put-up job – that what the Prince and Claudio had witnessed the previous night had been him – this man, I mean, in chains – with Mistress Margaret, Miss Hero's lady's maid – her I've always said was no better than she should be; well, haven't I? – and he calling her by Hero's name and her looking just like Miss Hero in the night, being small and dark-haired. He said that Don John had put him up to it because he hated Claudio because Don Pedro liked him better than his own brother and had given him all that money and stuff.

Well, Claudio was distrort (I do not think I have spelled that aright, Mama, but you will know what I mean). He talked of throwing himself on his sword and I wanted to run down and offer to hold it for him in case he should otherwise miss it, which I thought likely. Although after he'd got over that, he said something along the lines of "Anyone can make a mistake." But the Master just smiled kindly and said he could make amends by marrying his niece instead. First I thought he meant Miss Bea and I thought, "Here, hang on a minute", but he went on to say that he had another niece, the daughter of his brother Antonio, who looked just exactly like Mistress Hero.

Well, this was news to me. I remembered something I'd heard from one of the grooms, though, soon after I came to work here. He said as how the Master had a natural daughter he'd got on a serving maid nigh on twenty years ago and who was the spit and image of Miss Hero only not quite right in the head. He said they kept her lodged in the village where she was looked after kindly enough but not allowed out to be seen and talked about. When I mentioned this to Sarah at the time she flew right off the handle at me and told me it was not my place to go spreading gossip and slander and that she'd take the kitchen poker to me if I did it again. So I didn't talk about it any more and it went right out of my mind, until then.

The next thing is that someone turns up saying they've captured Don John who was behind all this deceit and they bring him in still all haughty and arrogant and sneering and the Master looked, I have to say it, a bit put about. Don Pedro is all for dealing with him right away and Don John looks very hard at Signior Leonato with that grim smile of his and the Master says quickly not to spoil the wedding festivities and that he will deal with Don John after the Prince has gone back to his old wars.

So, the next morning, Signior Claudio and the Prince turned up again in their dress uniforms and spurs just like before and they led a woman out, all veiled in white, and Claudio swore to marry her. Then they lifted the veil and he staggered back and started moaning, "Hero, my Hero. It is you, you're not dead after all," and stuff like that, except, mama, the thing is it wasn't Miss Hero although I admit it looked very like her, and perhaps it wasn't so very surprising that he should make such a mistake since he didn't really know Miss Hero at all well.

So they were married without further ado, her all smirking with lips which looked like Miss Hero's lips but weren't, and staring at him with what might have been eyes of rapturous love but just looked empty to me. Then Signior Benedick and Miss Bea were married too and they all stood around congratulating each other and looking mightily pleased with themselves and it was hardly my place to say anything, was it, Mama?

Do you ever get the feeling there's some secret which everybody knows except for you?

Anyway, the Prince had to go back to the wars earlier than he thought so the next morning they set off, with the whole household turning out to do them honour and Claudio's bride still smirking and simpering fit to bust and him looking perhaps just a little bit less full of himself than he had the day before, like he suspected there was something up but couldn't quite put his finger on it. Signior Benedick reckoned he had to stay behind – something about a lamed horse – and would catch up with them later.

So, I was standing there in my best apron like all the rest, waving, when I happened to glance up, and saw Miss Hero draw quickly away from a second-floor window where she'd been watching. I know it was her, but I said nothing. As soon as the Prince and his retinue were out of sight, they all burst out laughing, even Sarah. The Master was rubbing his hands with glee, and embracing Signior Benedick and saying it was a good day's work all told. "You'll not find me ungrateful, Signior," says he, "nor his lordship." Then he put his arm round Mistress Margaret too and told her she had done well instead of telling her to pack her things and be gone without a character or reference as I would have done, the trollop.

After supper one of the grooms comes into the kitchen and says that Don John has escaped. I'd like to know how since I'd have thought the dungeons here were impregnable but he's a cunning one, that Bastard, and may have a pact with the D— for all I know. He'll be miles away by now, having taken Signior Benedick's best horse, which has apparently recovered from its lameness. Lucio, the groom, says he doesn't think we will see Don Pedro alive again. Nor Signior Upstart Claudio for that matter, or if he does survive he won't dare show his face round here again with his idiot bastard of a wife. Then he says that Miss Hero will be the prettiest Princess of Arragon that ever was when she marries Don John. Of course, I asked him what he meant and he just laughed and said that Don John is the rising star now, and Sarah told him to hush up if he knew what was good for him and nodded her head in my direction rather meaningfully.

I went to the Master's room last thing with some hot water for his ewer and he came in while I was still there. I said, "A neat day's work, sir, by my troth," and he looked at me funny like and said, "You're a good girl, Maria, and a loyal one too, I'm sure, that knows what side her bread's buttered." Then he gave me another silver ducat and I went off back to my room and thought I would write you all about it while it was fresh in my mind and see what you –

What disturbed me there was a knock at the door. It was Sarah and she had a little silver tray with a goblet of the Master's best fortified wine that he saves for special occasions.

"The Master thought you might be wakeful after all the excitement of the day, Maria," says she, "and sent me with some of his wine to help you sleep."

You told me, Mama, when I was lucky enough to get this place, that I must be honest and loyal to my employer and then he would be good to me and you see how right you were.

Sarah saw the pen and paper on my night table and said, "Writing to your Mama again, Maria?" and I said I was and she said I was a good, dutiful daughter but that it was late now, my tallow was almost burnt down, and that I should drink my wine and get myself to bed.

"You can finish your letter in the morning," said she.

So that is what I shall do.

WHO KILLED MAMILLIUS?
or
Unconsidered Trifles

Amy Myers

The Winter's Tale *is another of Shakespeare's lesser known plays. It was written around 1609 or early 1610 and was based on* Pandosto, *a romance by Robert Greene, that would still have been known to Shakespeare's contemporaries. The play starts with a tale of jealousy. Leontes, the King of Sicilia, believes his wife Hermione has had an affair with his friend Polixenes, King of Bohemia. Polixenes escapes Leontes' wrath by returning to Bohemia, but Hermione is imprisoned. However, the newborn baby, Perdita, is smuggled away to safety by Lord Antigonus, who is subsequently killed by a bear. Although Hermione's faithfulness is proved, Leontes is too mad with jealousy to believe it and only recants after the death of Hermione and his own son, Mamillius. The play moves on sixteen years. Perdita, raised by a shepherd, has fallen in love with Polixenes' son, Florizel. The two return to Leontes' court where Perdita's true origins are revealed and all the characters are reunited, including Hermione, whose statue miraculously comes to life. All seems happily resolved except for the death of Mamillius.*

Amy Myers turns her not inconsiderable imagination to settle the matter.

"I tell thee true, Autolycus – " said he, slurping at his fifth gossips' cup of honest ale laced with white Ipocras – "'tis sixteen years since our noble king of Sicilia, Leontes, did falsely accuse his faithful Queen Hermione of shameless adultery with his dearest friend King Polixenes of Bohemia. Great Apollo declared her innocent, but too late, too late!"

He sobbed, which watering down the ale prompted me to take another bottle from a passing servant, for ale is the best story-teller. "Leontes believed her dead, but you'll scarce believe this, Hermione was hidden away by the Lady Paulina, who visited her twice or thrice daily for sixteen years before she came in likeness of her own statue before our noble king again. Poor lady. Aye me!"

He howled. "And her young son Mamillius dead of grief long since." His shoulders heaved. The tears ran from his eyes like a fool's money. "Have I told thee the tale of her babe exposed by her father's command on a barbarous shore? She who sixteen years after has been restored to us as the Princess Perdita?"

"Tell me again," said I, seeming all wonder as befitted a traveller from that "barbarous" Bohemia, and as though I hadn't heard the tale a thousand times 'ere now. I placed the new bottle before my prey. But today I drank in his words as fast as he his ale. This morning, in search of the comely wench who serves Paulina by day, and I would fain have serve me by night, I had come upon my master, Prince Florizel of Bohemia, son to Polixenes and betrothed to the Princess Perdita; he was in the withdrawing chamber, alone and out of sorts.

"Aye me," he groaned, as prenuptial gentlemen are wont to do, "the princess is sad and will not sport."

"And why's that, sir?"

"She grieves for her dead brother, Mamillius, who died

when she was but a babe. She would know more of him, but none will speak. 'Tis passing strange."

"He died of grief, sir, and *that* to me seems passing strange, for it is not an illness common in young lads."

"Find out more, good Autolycus." He staggered from the room in such a manner that were he Autolycus the rogue he would have made a merry income. I needs must remind myself I am now an honest man again. Cast out by my master in Bohemia, I rendered him such service in my next trade as a pedlar, that I was whisked once more into three-pile velvet, and into his employment.

So will I now do my master's bidding, for Florizel is honest, though he does not *tell* me so, which confirms he is honest and a worthy master for a reformed rogue such as I. Besides, as is well known, I was littered under Mercury and thus a snapper-up of unconsidered trifles. I sniffed a bad fish in the death of young Mamillius, and fain would out with it, for time hung heavy on my hands now my pedlar's garb is taken from me. I had forgot that honesty makes dull days, but a man must live so here sit I. Alas, here sit we *all* at the Sicilian court, until Apollo sets an auspicious date for the nuptials of Florizel and Perdita. In all the excitement no one thought to consult his oracle and only today does Cleomenes set sail once more for Delphos – and another twenty-three boring days 'ere he return. Yet more time for Leontes and Hermione to vanish to their bedchamber, my master and Princess Perdita to steal among the bushes where Apollo cannot spy, and the King and Queen's faithful emissaries, Lord Camillo and the Lady Paulina, to trot self-righteously to haul them out.

I had thought myself doomed to sit before this chessboard in the great chamber with my lord Diogenes, who when he did not send me to sleep while he slowly pondered each move as though it were to the gallows interminably related the sad tale of winter – a tale in which he modestly refers to himself as Second Gentleman. Alack, the lord Diogenes now slipped quietly to the floor. Had I poured him one of our Bohemian sleepy drinks I could understand it but this Sicilian brew –

It was then that I, a mere pawn, leapt the first two squares on my very own chessboard. Here was a game worthy even of my wit. *Had Mamillius been poisoned*? There were dark deeds in plenty at the Sicilian court sixteen years ago, and grief at his mother's disgrace seems a diagnosis that would pass few Justices.

At that very moment Cleomenes strolled in; he cast a scathing glance at my companion now lulled in the arms of Morpheus. "Does Florizel have any questions for Apollo before I leave for Delphos?"

"Funny you should ask that," I said brightly. Oh ho, the chess game was well begun indeed. "Prince Florizel was just telling me this morning that he had one. It's – "

"Give me the money first."

Gentlemen-born are always so suspicious. I called over the servant. "Have a pint of spiced spirit of wine on me, Cleomenes, while I count out what Florizel gave me." As he turned round to grab his goblet, I employed my skills and a fat purse was speedily removed from the Lord Diogenes' doublet and as quickly replaced minus twenty gold staters (as we "barbarians" call them in Bohemia). Apollo always seems to require money, despite his divine status. So his priest says.

"And the question?" Cleomenes was disposed to be amiable now business was concluded.

"Who killed Mamillius?"

Amiability vanished. "But – "

"Florizel is a prince, Cleomenes," I gently reminded him. "With a temper."

Mercury looks after rogues. You don't need scruples, just to be able to run fast to outpace trouble. I had twenty-three days to beat Apollo in my game of wits. Being a Mercury man, I've no great respect for Apollo, who spends more time chasing ladies than putting in time at the office delivering dubious oracular statements. After all, who was it pronounced Leontes a jealous tyrant when now he's as meek as a heifer being led around by the nose by Queen Hermione?

Next pawn's move: I went over to the Lord Diogenes peacefully snoring on the floor, and kicked him. He groaned and clambered back on to his chair.

"I will have that scurvy servant hanged for disturbing thy sleep," I roared. He blearily grinned his gratitude.

A rogue doesn't always have time for subtlety. "Where was Hermione when Mamillius was murdered?" I asked him cheerily.

"On trial for adultery, having come from prison."

He slipped back on to the floor and I kicked him again for the answer did not please me. He opened a pathetic eye: "But Mamillius was taken sick long before the trial, just after Hermione was taken to prison."

Having questioned him more, I retired to my truckle bed that night highly pleased (though alone, for my wench was a tease). Diogenes' indignant shouts after me still rang in my ears: "What do you mean, *murdered*?" Tomorrow, my part in the game would begin in earnest. Pawn I might be, but a quick-witted and fast pawn by reaching the far side of the board may become a queen – though that not being to my taste, a knight would suffice.

Hey nonny no, the trees are green
Set a pawn to catch a queen.

My ballad-making is not much required these days, save when Florizel has a mind to please Perdita with some pretty trifle. Why, I asked my wit, sing those words? Find out, my wit replied.

Although I am now a gentleman-clad, I must go softly. Can a pawn question a king and queen to discover whether they be white or red pieces on the board? No, so I considered my next move. I had it from Diogenes that Mamillius had been his usual pert obnoxious self (listening between his lines), getting on his mother's nerves and his sickness manifested itself shortly after his mother was taken to prison. He died twenty-three days later. First he grew lethargic, would not eat, later vomited with other sundry symptoms, became insensible and thus died.

For sure this could have been mandragora which we Bohemians do put in sleepy drinks to dull the sense, but which taken in great quantity brings about the longest sleep of all. Mamillius was probably given several doses, the last the heaviest. But who would wish to poison the King's son?

Not Leontes for sure. But his queen? Suppose Hermione were indeed false and sought to fly after King Polixenes, and Polixenes seeing some advantage in adding to his own kingdom if the King of Sicilia lacked an heir, persuaded her to it? I frighted even myself, for I spoke of my master's father, the King of Bohemia, and though of violent temper like Leontes himself, I quaked to think of him a murderer. Queen Hermione was in prison while her son sickened, but she had loyal supporters. Tush, what parent would murder their child? I asked indignantly of my wit. Medea, quoth my wit. Tantalus, it quoth again.

Set a pawn to catch a pawn. Emilia, lady-in-waiting to Hermione, was my first choice, so in the banqueting house that evening I contrived to come upon her as though by chance.

"They tell me, my lady," said I, offering her a plate of sugared gillyflowers, "you were with the Queen throughout that sad time sixteen years ago. I cannot believe it, for you must surely have been at your lessons."

Her wrinkled face brightened up, which is unusual for ladies of quality on seeing me. "They speak true, Autolycus." She puffed up like a partridge. "I saw everything with my own eyes. Who was it helped her in Perdita's birth? 'Twas I. Who was it never believed a word of ill against her? Who helped raise her from her swoon and place her in her coffin that Leontes might be deceived into thinking her dead? 'Twas I – and Paulina," she added offhandedly.

"And what of poor little Mamillius? The Queen must surely have grieved."

"Aye. With tears and lamentations over his sickness. She bid me go to him."

I grew cunning. "And bade you give the lad his food and drink, no doubt?"

"Any gentleman-in-waiting might do so, either in his chamber or at table with his father. But 'twas I gave his nightly posset into the hand of the serving men." My proud pawn suddenly became suspicious. "Why ask you this?"

"I feared it was his liquor or his food that made Mamillius ill, not grief and shame at his mother's dishonour, and I hoped that so reliable, so kind, so staunch a lady as yourself did care for him."

My lady preened her feathers. "His father sought to make a man of him by pressing him to take strong wine. Against my advice, mark you."

Aha, she sought to cast the blame elsewhere. Was she perchance more than a pawn on the chessboard of Mamillius's death?

"Saw you the Queen in those long lonely years, Lady Emilia?"

She couldn't wait to tell me. "I did not," she snapped. "My grand lady Paulina is jealous of anyone who comes near the Queen. Not for my precious lady's sake but her own. She came marching down to the prison, pretending to be interested in how the Queen had fared in childbed, but when I tried to tell her all she could ask was: Is it a boy? A daughter, I said, and promptly Madame Paulina insisted on taking her to Leontes in the hope of melting his heart. Well, it didn't, and Paulina blamed me. She never told me a word about my lady being alive. To think I was mourning her, and here she was all the time. Of course, you've got to make allowances. Paulina was never the same after her husband went. You ask her daughters."

Paulina's loyal husband, Lord Antigonus, I recalled, had been Leontes' choice to take the baby Perdita to the "barbarous" shore. Alas, a bear had taken a fancy to his maturer meat and left the babe unscathed.

Antigonus had long since been removed from the chessboard, but Paulina was still the Queen's rook, high in Hermione's favour. I could see no reason Paulina would herself wish to kill Mamillius, much as she hated Leontes, but of her devotion to the Queen there could be no doubt. Could she have been Hermione's emissary in this foul deed and delivered poison to Mamillius?

But a rogue must needs see the world for what it is, not as he would have it, and I was forced to admit that though compared with Tantalus's methods of boiling his son in a pot, the administration of mandragora seems a thoughtful act, on the whole it seemed unlikely Queen Hermione would take such a course.

So I abandoned that square, and pranced to the next. My

comely wench, softened by the gift of a pomander from my pack, was helpful here (skilfully avoiding where my hand would go next) and some days later I was bound for the countryside to see Mamillius's chambermaid. Everything of interest at court is undertaken by gentlemen but certain tasks like slops they have no objection to women undertaking. I donned my pedlar's garb once more, for a man is welcomed by his clothes and not by his face. The cottage lay but a league or two from the court and I begged a lift from a passing wagon. With spring's song upon us I enlivened the wagoner with some merry ballads until he threw me off, fortunately close to my destination.

"Who is it?" The door flew open and Mistress Audrey appeared, married to Master Ratcatcher and surrounded by young ratcatchers from twelve to an infant at her breast. I inserted one foot and leaned nonchalantly against the door.

"No pedlars," she snarled.

I thrust my tray with its knacks and trifles under her nose. "*Gloves as sweet as damask roses* – " I trilled.

She stamped on my foot. "Be off with you."

I groaned in agony. "I was treated better at the palace. Queen Hermione herself has taken one of my golden coifs."

"The palace?" Her foot clad in its heavy ratcatching boot paused half an inch away from another stamp. "I knows it."

"Then you too know the gracious Queen."

She spluttered slowly into life like a wet candle-wick. "She was a statue, so they say. For sixteen – "

"Yes, yes," I said hastily. "I had the whole story from Prince Florizel's man, a goodly gentleman who knows how to treat pedlars well."

In a trice I was by the fire with a hot bowl of nettle soup.

"Perchance you recall the young prince Mamillius?" I asked casually.

"Oh." She rocked back and forth, throwing her apron over her head to mop up the tears. "That I do." The apron came down to ensure I did not miss a single syllable of her story. "I emptied his slops, bless 'im. Always in the pot too."

"They say he was poisoned."

Her mouth fell open, displaying a fine set of black and brown teeth, give or take half a dozen or so. I thought of selling her a potion of burnt rosemary and alum, moistened with my very own spittle, and excellent for teeth cleaning, but decided not to distract her for she was well away. "I always thought there was something funny about the way the lad went. You should have seen his stools, poor lamb." She drew closer. "Who did it?" she hissed.

I hissed back, despite the foul odour. "The Prince has sent to the oracle, but Delphos is far away and I daresay there's many a tale a clever girl like you could tell."

She could. "I mind the day that the King and Queen were with the young Mamillius, and he came back to his chamber crying his heart out. No one wants me, he says. Then later after eating he fell quiet and then sickened. Poisoned, you say? Why I could have been killed too."

"Thank Olympus you weren't," I exclaimed piously. "Who could have done such a thing?"

"Any, sir, if they'd a mind. No doctor tended him, only the gentlemen. It did seem strange. He's grieving, poor lamb, says Lady Emilia. That's all. But he died, poor little love." She wiped her eyes. "Get out of that, you whoreson bawcock," she screamed at one of her own little loves, spotting him investigating my pack.

"Very helpful." I fumed. She saw she had disappointed me, and tried to make amends.

"The court was in such a taking. What days they were. There was Lord Camillo fled with King Polixenes, King Leontes in a rare carry-on about Queen Hermione, babes being born, babes being sent to their deaths, the trial, Apollo saying it was all a mistake, Paulina shouting at the King, brave soul, that the Queen is dead, and accusing him of ordering Lord Camillo to poison King Polixenes, and then she railed against him, by which I mean our King, noble Leontes, for having sent his baby daughter to her death, and crying that she and the King were both bereaved, he having lost his wife and son and she her husband. Then everyone had a good cry. Well, that was a time and no mistake."

I refrained from surreptitiously kicking the whoreson bawcock who was at it again, but only in gratitude to my hostess, for she had set my wit to work. Had Lord Camillo not left these shores before Mamillius was taken sick, I would have fain suspected him. Camillo and I, knowing each other of old, see no more eye to eye than a blind man sees Polyphemus. I weary of his honesty. Honest Camillo, they say, for not poisoning Polixenes at Leontes' request. Oh, honest Camillo, for fleeing with Polixenes to Bohemia, rather than serve under Leontes. Oh honest Camillo for accompanying Polixenes to spoil his son's spot of haymaking with his shepherdess. Oh honest Camillo, who persuades Florizel to come to Sicilia just because he fancies seeing his Sicilian home again, oh honest Camillo because, running into two Bohemian peasants (here in Sicilia by *my* good offices), he learned that Shepherdess Perdita is Leontes' long-lost daughter. Oh honest Camillo, who graciously settles his fat rump onto his cloud of glory on his private Mount Olympus. I say, distrust all such honest men.

No sooner was I back in my velvet than I met by chance the Lady Paulina, walking in the gallery. I was once again in pursuit of my comely wench, her maid, but the goddess Diana herself must be guarding her chastity, for Lady Paulina paused to talk to me. I bowed deep.

"I hear, Autolycus, you are strangely interested in the old stories. Would you make a ballad of us or a play for common players?" she jested.

I admire Paulina, whatever Emilia says. She told the King what she thought of him, brought up three daughters with but a single parent, her having no news of her husband since he disappeared, and has only now been given proof of his death. A hard life – but then so is a pedlar's.

"I could hear the tale of our gracious Queen and your loyalty a hundred times and tire not, lady."

"And the tale of Mamillius too, no doubt?"

Oh ho, so the hens have been a-chattering and the cocks a-crowing. If Apollo's oracle were to decree that Mamillius had not been murdered, my future looked to be either at the end of a boot or a rope.

WHO KILLED MAMILLIUS? 249

"Only that Florizel may soothe the heart of Princess Perdita," I tried hopefully.

Her face softened. "My little chick."

"Two little chicks," I pointed out bravely.

"Alas, Mamillius is lost to me for ever."

"Lost through a strange sickness, my lady. Did someone wish the King harm, or Sicilia heirless?"

She shot me a look like a Spartan archer. "Polixenes, you mean. As soon suspect my good Camillo, for they both fled 'ere Mamillius was taken sick."

"Perhaps they did not flee." My wit was inspired, and my sense could not stop it.

She laughed. "I trust you are a better pedlar than inquirer, Autolycus. They were seen to board their ships and the ships to set sail."

I was disappointed for the idea was growing on me. And, alack, on my wit, and it would speak. "Many people had opportunity to poison Mamillius: Emilia, yourself, Antigonus, all the gentlemen of the chamber – "

"Suspect me if you will, Autolycus, suspect even Queen Hermione if you must. But Antigonus is past your questions now, and who of the gentlemen would dare harm a hair of Mamillius's head, beloved as he was by his father? Only an enemy of Leontes."

"As you were, lady."

The puzzle made my wit overbold. I remembered only the chessboard and not with whom I was playing. Rooks have more power than pawns. Fortunately Paulina did not seem disposed to kick me from my square. Instead she smiled sadly: "Indeed. I hated him, but why should I kill my great joy, dear Mamillius, playmate of my young daughters? I had hoped one of them would some day wed Mamillius."

I kept my counsel, it being my theory that pedlars marry pedlars' daughters, riches marry riches, and most princes look out for a comely princess. Paulina had a point though. She had no reason to kill the prince and I had advanced no further.

That night I attended a merry jig in the servants' hall, for though I am more than a servant I am somewhat less than a courtier, for all my velvet, and thus a man could starve being welcome at neither table. Being born a rogue, I eat at both – and therefore must dance at both. At last, Aphrodite approved my courtship of my comely wench; it progressed finely, during the energetic country dances played on the Gentleman of the Kitchen's fiddle. Hand in hand we stole away and then a hand clapped me on the shoulder as we passed the great chamber.

"Ah, there you are, Autolycus." Florizel was all affability, being in his cups. "The masque draws to a close, come join us in their merry measure. And you, sweet maid." He chucked my wench under her chin, ogling her in a way I felt sure Perdita would hardly approve. There is more merriment in a wake than in most court dances, but a man in his cups is an opportunity not to be missed for a pawn seeking a knighthood. Though once more I felt myself in danger of being struck from the chessboard, a man grows more bold when he has nothing to lose but his life.

"Your good mother, sir, the late Queen of our native land. You never told me of her."

He promptly burst into tears and rested his head upon my shoulder, thereby doing great damage to my three-pile. "Alas no, she died when I was eight."

"Sixteen years ago or thereabouts." I am quick with my figures as behoves my trade. "Much about the time Queen Hermione had her spot of trouble. She died in childbed?"

"Of grief." He hiccuped.

Grief appears to have been a prevalent disease in those days.

"Having heard the false accusations of adultery against my father, King Polixenes," he wailed, "she died before news reached her that the Apollo's oracle declared him innocent."

"A tragedy, sir."

"It was indeed. That is the reason my father felt guilty – " My master stopped blubbing into my shoulder and seemed reluctant to finish his statement. Instead, he seized me by the shoulders and stared soulfully into my eyes. "Honest Camillo was my father and my mother too."

"Remarkable," I murmured.

"Honest Camillo always had my welfare at heart," he assured me. "He it was who persuaded me to come to Sicilia with him to gain Leontes' approval for my nuptials."

"Did you get it?"

"Not until Perdita turned out to be his daughter."

Of course I'd been listening behind a bush while all this persuasion was going on in Bohemia and knew full well Camillo wanted to leave the cod's roe and get back to the pasta for his own reasons.

I hopped a square forward in my eagerness. "Why should – er – honest Camillo have such love for your father, sir?"

"He didn't. He'd hinted often enough he feared for himself, if he poisoned Polixenes as Leontes wanted."

And what, I wondered, happened to the poison he was given to do the job with. Had he other uses for it? Oh ho, honest Camillo, I see thy schemes.

Had I not to dance a Lavolta with my wench I could have somersaulted over Mount Etna. *Camillo was my villainous red chessboard king.* He and Polixenes had left these shores, but how easy it would be for the ship to sail to Calabria or Syracusa or even anchor out at sea, from there to return by fishing boat for his foul purpose.

How now, Autolycus, says my wit, he would be recognized. Not so, wit, said I. He has but to don disguise as a gentleman of the kitchen – and where 200 sup who would mark him? – and add the foul potion to the Prince's bedtime posset.

Highly unlikely, observes my wit.

"A queen come to life disguised as a statue is highly unlikely too," replied I tartly. I heard that Duke Theseus of Athens once judged a case where four noble lovers lost in a wood were fairy-mazed. Puck (Fairy-King Oberon's Autolycus) put the magic drops into the wrong eyes, and many highly unlikely things occurred. When they awoke they saw the truth.

And so did I. *A queen come to life.* The words danced through my mind in a merry measure indeed.

My comely wench had grown bored, and I went in search of her for every pawn deserves encouragement along the path to knighthood. Alas, the hand that clasped my arm was not lily-white but sprouted black hairs.

"I want a word with you," growled my lord Diogenes.

He looked most grim, which puzzled me for I had forgotten my little lapse. "Is that servant who waited on us in the great chamber trustworthy?"

"Why?" I asked cautiously.

"Money disappeared from my purse."

"He's a rogue," I roared promptly. "Depend upon it, sir. I shall beat him black and blue."

"I'd rather have my money back."

"Twill be spent, sir. But he shall pay for it. I shall hang him like a side of roast beef, sir."

"Good of you," he grunted, somewhat appeased.

"While you're here, Diogenes, have a drink." I clapped him on the back. "Tell me that sad tale of winter again."

I listened even more carefully this time, though my spirits sank as fast as those in Diogenes' goblet. Verily this chessboard has more puzzles than old Minos's labyrinth. But a good rogue is a careful rogue, and dogs do not lightly let go their bone.

I sought out the Lady Paulina after her galliard with Leontes and boldly asked her to partner me in a pavane. "Lady," I hissed as we fleetingly passed, "I am told by Lord Diogenes that throughout those sad sixteen years you saw Queen Hermione twice or thrice daily."

"Daily," she repeated astounded, as our clasped hands brought us together once more. "How ridiculous. Only Lord Camillo knew the Queen's refuge, which was on the far-off isle of Lipari, and there is no horse save Pegasus could take me there. I saw her not above once every two or three years. It broke my heart. But Leontes is a clever man. His suspicions would have been aroused by frequent visits, had my lady remained in Sicilia."

So now were mine. I was jubilant again. Honest Camillo again. There was no doubt but that Hermione, willingly or not, was taken by our honest friend to Bohemia, and returned to see Paulina every two or three years in order not to arouse her suspicions. Oh honest Camillo would have won many a dishonest penny for that scheme from Polixenes. Mamillius's death was, I saw now, all part of a deeper chessgame played by Red King Camillo to serve his master Polixenes. 'Tis certain

Hermione was true to Leontes until he turned from her, and thus Perdita is his child, else Florizel would not be marrying the princess Perdita now –

But stay! –

Like the blast of Destiny's trump, I recalled that the oracle had not yet spoken. Suppose Apollo were to declare the union invalid because the happy pair are brother and sister? No. Destiny's trumpet quietly silenced itself. Polixenes would hardly countenance such a match. But how to prove Camillo's guilt? My eye fell on my comely wench. I could serve my master and myself at the same time. We stole away to an empty parlour, and there at last indulged in merry sport. Chaste goddess Diana must have been asleep. Afterwards: "Sweet chuck," I whispered, "I would fain ask your help."

Unfortunately she mistook my meaning and took my manhood once again, but it put her in good humour and once assured her lady was under no cloud, she offered me her services. 'Twas my turn to mistake her meaning, and when it was done it was too late to advance a further square.

A few days later, however, she came to me with a sweet blush and an ancient gentleman of the chamber, who had been a servant to the King sixteen years ago. His presence having been disregarded, he had a tale to tell of a conversation between the King and Camillo. "Oh you mark my words," he spluttered all over my three-pile, "it was Camillo first planted the idea of the Queen's unfaithfulness in Leontes' mind. He couldn't wait to point out to His Majesty that Hermione had been the one to press Polixenes to stay on longer."

I slid to another square. Suppose Camillo were merely Polixenes' tool, a rook and not a king? I recalled Florizel's "my father felt guilty – ". Was this because he had Hermione hidden away in Bohemia? Polixenes had urged Camillo to return, steal Hermione, and murder Mamillius.

Paulina suspected nothing, poor lady. Having three daughters and a house to run kept her busy most of the time. She couldn't forever be worrying about what was happening up in Lipari. My only puzzle was why Camillo was so anxious to get back to Sicilia this year.

Perhaps Hermione, over in Lipari on her three-yearly visit,

decided she'd had enough of Polixenes' temper, suggested my wit half-heartedly.

Oh yes? I replied sarcastically. How did that work? "I've a grand idea," says Hermione, thinking up some scheme whereby she can stroll back to Leontes' bed. "Why don't you say I'm a statue." "Pardon?" asks Paulina. No one would fall for that story, I informed my wit, speaking as a professional rogue. But gentlefolk are different, declares my wit.

I agreed, but only because I suddenly remembered Cleomenes would be back tomorrow. The pawn was trapped, for belatedly I asked myself how could I stand up in the great chamber and declare Mamillius had been poisoned by Camillo at the behest of Polixenes, only to have the oracle declare he died of grief? My head would be struck off my body, and yet if I speak not, after all the rumours flying around, I must steal from court.

Better steal oneself than have another steal one's head, so I packed my pedlar's gear ready to leave the moment I heard Cleomenes' dreary voice. Oracles can make mistakes, of course, but the point is that everyone *believes* them.

Why risk another night? asks my wit. Leave now. My self agrees. But other parts of Autolycus spoke stronger still, and I would bid farewell to my comely wench, not once but several times. I was occupied in pleasant ways, my head beneath my wench's skirts which were promptly thrown over her head, when her muffled voice said – to my annoyance at a delicate moment – "Camillo couldn't kill a sheep's fluke."

I lay awake bemoaning that tomorrow the stars would be my bedfellow and not my wench, and thought again of what she had said. She was right. Not everyone can be a rogue, not everyone can be a murderer. A man like Camillo, for example. If he couldn't kill Polixenes at Leontes' order for fear of retaliation, how could he kill Mamillius at Polixenes' command? His teeth chatter as soon as he sees a bush, let alone a bear, in this dark old world. *A bear*!

Chesspieces I had never considered sped through my mind, the whole board stretched out before me, and the path lay clear for this humble pawn to become ennobled. I sat up in my truckle bed and my wench fell out. I slapped her comely bottom. A man must take his chances in life, roared I. I would play my gambit, and make my declaration to the court.

Dinner was still in full progress when I begged leave to speak. Capon bones flew everywhere, pigeons were nestling in pots, dried neats' tongues were wagging.

"What ho, Autolycus," called Polixenes. "Have you written a ballad for us?"

"Nay, sir. A merry jest."

"It had better be," Leontes grunted. "News has reached me of your spreading rumours that my dear Mamillius was murdered."

"Indeed he was, sir."

The King frowned. "Have you proof, sirrah?"

"No, your Majesty. But the villain is dead."

"Who? And your reasons?" he barked.

"Antigonus!" A gasp ran round the court, and Paulina's face grew pale with shock.

"He it was who killed Mamillius, and you, sir, who in your infinite wisdom suspected and gave him a mission to flee the land, having arranged for him to be cast upon the shores of Bohemia, and a humble peasant to find the babe. Zeus in his mighty wisdom sent a bear to wreak the vengeance your merciful nature could not demand."

Leontes seemed bereft of breath, as well he might.

"Truly noble of you, sir," I added for good measure.

"Yes, yes," agreed the court. Even Camillo agreed, which in the circumstances was hardly surprising. Paulina moaned a little at hearing her late husband was a murderer, but it was a long time ago, and with a new husband in view the shock can't have been too great. Only Perdita – I hope my master isn't going to have trouble there – asked sharply: "Why?"

"In his grief, my lady, for the plight of the Queen."

As a reason it wasn't up to much, but everyone seemed satisfied. Having declared "stalemate!" on my chessboard, I was tactfully withdrawing with my pedlar's bag when Cleomenes came in, with the sealed letter from Apollo's priest.

"Aren't you going to wait?" he asked, surprised.

"A sudden desire to see the world." I picked up my

bag. "I've told everyone it was Antigonus anyway." I
fled.

It wasn't, of course. Honest red king Camillo had been
blackmailing his lady for years. It wasn't the powerless
king I should have sought, but his consort. He had indeed
stolen Hermione away to Bohemia (a fact Hermione might
not think it tactful to mention to Leontes) but who murdered
Mamillius? Had Emilia hoped to marry the King and beget
a child of him? She had told me of Paulina asking the sex of
the Queen's baby; had this been because Paulina suspected
Emilia of causing Mamillius's sickness, and thus feared for
the new baby were it a boy? Had Antigonus too suspected
Emilia and thus been sent to his death by a dancing bear
supplied by the lady to the captain of the ship that bore him
away? Did Emilia know all too well that Hermione lived, but
hoped to do away with her at her leisure? Did blackmailer
Camillo come rushing back to Sicilia because Hermione was
threatening to come back to court, and he was fearful Emilia
would kill her, and Polixenes would blame him if she were
murdered?

Emilia had made none of these moves, but all of them fitted
another. And only she could have known that Antigonus was
lost sixteen years before the official news came through, as the
ratcatcher's wife had informed me. Oh yes, my lady Paulina
was well matched to honest Camillo.

What's more, I think Hermione guessed the truth, and told
Leontes, and in a moment I'll tell you why.

But first you'll want to know what the oracle said. My
wench told me, having come to bid me back to court for the
wedding which Apollo orders for the morrow. Apparently
Apollo couldn't resist the chance to declare Autolycus a rogue,
but what's new in that? There's many a roguish knight, for
thus Florizel appoints me.

What did the oracle say about Mamillius? Nothing. The
priest had sent the money back. Fancy Diogenes having
counterfeit money in his purse. I found out why later –
he'd been given it by honest Camillo for agreeing to lie
about Paulina and the thrice-daily visits.

And what happened, you'll ask, to the red king and the lady I had formerly dubbed white queen's rook? Why, nothing, for Paulina and Camillo face a living death. If you recall, Leontes thoughtfully married them to each other.

Checkmate!

THIS IS ILLYRIA, LADY

Kim Newman

Like The Winter's Tale, Twelfth Night *is something of an extravaganza, not meant to be taken entirely seriously. Shakespeare wrote it several years earlier, probably in 1601. It is set in Illyria, the land opposite northern Italy, which in later years became Yugoslavia. Viola is shipwrecked on the Illyrian coast, and mourns the loss of her twin brother Sebastian. She disguises herself as a boy (Cesario) and enters the service of Duke Orsino. Orsino uses Cesario/Viola to take his messages of love to Olivia. She spurns Orsino but falls in love with Cesario/Viola, whilst Viola falls in love with Orsino. Unknown to Viola, Sebastian has survived. He and his friend Antonio arrive at the court and Olivia, believing him to be Cesario, marries him. Meanwhile, Orsino believes that it is Cesario/Viola who has stolen Olivia from him. It is not until all the characters meet up together that the Cesario/Viola/ Sebastian mystery is unravelled, and Orsino marries Viola. It is at this point, as the web of deceit and intrigue is finally unravelled, that the following story begins and takes us into the human psyche to explore the impact and lasting effect of such subterfuge in the not-altogether-real world of Illyria.*

*   *   *

Her deception was over, but they'd never trust her entirely. Not even – no, especially not – those who loved her. She was not a part of this place. Really, they didn't know her.

She was thinking of herself as a woman again. Provisionally, as usual. Since coming to these shores, she'd been in a flux. The Duke assumed the dissembling part of her life was finished, that this was the real woman. For the moment, it was and she was.

But only, she knew, for the moment.

It would be pleasing to settle.

But the deceiver never did. The *other* deceiver. It was her lot to follow wherever he led. Arrive with a shipwreck, depart with an exeunt of attendants. At first, she'd thought she could thwart him, save innocents, avert tragedies. But as cycles repeated, she knew that would never happen. Her purpose was to explore the human wreckage the deceiver left behind in his wake, to understand.

In her, deception was defence. In the other, attack.

He liked to taunt her with their similarities. The argument didn't wash and wouldn't hold.

She hurt no one but herself.

(She thought.)

All was for the best.

He had got away with it, of course. The deception had been seen as a joke that ran away with itself, and all the blame seemed shouldered by the fathead uncle, the drunken reprobate "punished" by marriage to a servant. The uncle was one of the comicals, as much deceived as deceiver, flattered and flattering, blustering through with his coterie of hangers-on, seizing on some scheme or other without thinking where the suggestion came from. There was real malice in jests, unappreciated by the beery conspirators.

Everybody in Illyria prized wit above all else.

But the flame of wit comes invariably from the spark of cruelty.

She knew she was looking for a wit.

Not a fool, a clown.

A whisperer.

This Illyria was a desert town of glass and stone and light, inland from a jagged coast. Its hostels and gambling dens rose in tiers above paved streets, thin white sand on thick black tar, fountains of water bursting around red or green lights. The hours of the clock meant little. The people slept in shifts. There was harsh music everywhere, and the wave-like crash of coins, fortunes turning over.

Her throat was always dry, the food always salted. Bottled water was precious.

There were hot outbursts at every intersection. Drawn swords, red slashes in tight shirts. Instant quarrels instantly settled, blooming and ending in death like accelerated desert flowers.

These were the squabbles and tantrums of children, nothing like the elegant schemes of the deceiver, which might end with sword-strokes but always began with whispered words, with ideas planted in minds and cultivated with care.

. . . are you sure your wife is faithful? . . . might you not be elevated to your true worth? . . . she says she loves you . . . would you not kill in a good cause?

She had walked here, from a muddy sea, salt-heavy skirts chafing her legs.

Now, she had her cooled penthouse and her Duke.

For the moment.

She had known at once that the deceiver was here. It was the sort of city he loved, the sort of people who appealed to him, whose chaotic interrelationships were like scattered puzzle-pieces he could break and fix together in a grotesque, cruel pattern.

They were always wary of each other.

She was not allowed to interfere, just rebuke.

As she found herself ensnared by her own deceptions, caught between the Duke and the Lady, separated from her male shadow self, she was lulled.

Story was always a trap.

Here, story grew and wound around them all. The deceiver slipped through the gaps, to work his own story, a sub-plot, to strike swiftly like an adder and pull back, uncaring, unpunished, at the end.

Madhouses were always the places to find his leavings.

No one could like the steward. She had mixed with him briefly, a tussle of words at a reception desk. He was in her way, refusing to help, citing the limitations of his job, using the rules to excuse a simple lack of fellow-feeling. He was the type common to everywhere, a petty obstruction. She saw self-importance, not self-deception.

Even now, she could not pity the broken man.

The Lady wished to take him back into her household, but there was no one to take back. A personality, puffed by feeble attempts at self-creation, had been expertly shredded away and trampled.

He was no one now.

She glimpsed the skeleton figure at four in the morning, at a crossroads at the edge of town, torn between all four streets. Talking with him was useless. He would most likely have no idea who did this to him, probably not quite realize that anything had been done. He might think on revenge, might even escalate the quarrel, murdering his persecutors real and imagined until he was himself brought down. It was not likely, though. The steward was not one of the great ones, nor ever could be even in his own self-deceptions.

In other countries, other cities, she had seen the deceiver's masterpieces, worlds skilfully woven around great men, worlds that superimposed upon their realities and drove them to self-destruction. The lesson he wished to teach was that all human personality was malleable, was what he could make of it. Kingdoms could be brought to ruins, but it was the men who were the victims.

The story was done, here.

She found the deceiver in the deserted lobby of a large hostel, in drab motley. Here, he was a clown. Without an audience, he was restless.

"My lady," he greeted her.

"Fool," she acknowledged.

He smiled, mocking the steward's rictus grin.

"You have to handle these people carefully," he said. "They break so easily. The game is often over too quickly for my taste."

"You still think of it as a game?"

He cocked his head.

"Don't you, my lord-or-lady? They can love as easily as hate."

"Can you?"

"I feel nothing. Just a mild interest. The essence of play is that it should be idle."

That was the difference between them.

(She thought.)

She was a part of her stories. She felt for people, she loved and hated. She bled and died.

The other puppeteered and passed on.

"This was just a diversion," he said, plucking banjo strings. "A what-you-will."

"You just pretend indifference. You are culpably cruel."

He shrugged.

She put a sword-point to his Adam's apple.

"Tell me why I do not end this now?"

He remained indifferent, even to the threat to his own life.

"You unpick your own question in the forming of it. You admit you will not end it, by your own choice. As to the why, that's for you to know."

"You could make me kill you."

He laughed, genuinely, shockingly.

"That would be novel. Perhaps, eventually, it will have to come to that. Often, I have included myself among my victims. I could as well be principle as player."

He was gone, and she was left behind.

She felt the pull. Soon she would doff her current mask and move on. This place would close down, street by street, waiting again.

Heigh-ho, the wind and the rain . . .

There was an attendant, as always. She had grown used to

seeing them in the corner of her eye, standing respectfully, rushing in or out with messages, listening.

"Why?" she asked. "This arbitrariness? This indulgence of cruelty? This acceptance of the casual smashing of one man by others? Why?"

The attendant shrugged.

"This is Illyria, lady."

It was as good an answer as any.

STAR-CROSSED

Patricia A. McKillip

Of all Shakespeare's plays, Romeo and Juliet *must be the best known and scarcely requires an introduction. The Montagues and the Capulets are two great rival families in the city of Verona. Romeo, a Montague, falls in love with Juliet, a Capulet, and the two are secretly wed with the help of their confessor, Friar Laurence and Juliet's nurse. Soon after, however, Romeo kills Tybalt, Juliet's cousin (who had killed Romeo's friend Mercutio), and is banished from Verona. Capulet, not knowing of their marriage, determines that Juliet shall marry Paris. Friar Laurence gives her a sleeping potion which will feign death and prevent the bigamous marriage. Her body is to be taken to the family vault where Romeo can meet her. Unfortunately Friar Laurence's message does not get to Romeo who learns only of Juliet's death. He visits her in the vaults, encounters Paris there, kills him and then takes the poison. Juliet awakes, sees Romeo dead and stabs herself. Now the big question: since all in the vault are dead, how did Friar Laurence know the real sequence of events and how each died? Was his version correct? That's what Patricia McKillip investigates.*

*   *   *

FIRST WATCH: Sovereign, here lies the County Paris
    slain;
  And Romeo dead; and Juliet, dead before,
  Warm and new-kill'd.
PRINCE: Search, seek, and know how this foul mur-
    der comes.
                Shakespeare, *Romeo and Juliet*, V, 3.

There were four bodies. The Prince did not count Tybalt, who
had been buried with Juliet, but who, unlike Juliet, had stayed
dead. The graveyard seemed frozen after the Prince spoke, in
one of those midnight moments when the owls are silent, and
the moon itself stops moving. The grass, and the Prince's
chain mail shirt, and the leaves in the great trees around
us caught light the color of bone. The vault yawned fire
from the torches; everything else shaped shadows alive and
coiled to spring. In the torchlight, the dead seemed to move,
gesturing and trying to speak, tell. But I couldn't hear them.
The Prince was still looking at me. An owl spoke, and then
so did I, the only thing I could say.

"Yes, my lord."

"There they all were," I told Beatrice later, next to her in
the rumpled sheets. "Dead. So young, all of them. Juliet –
a child. With a knife through her heart. And the Prince's
kinsman, Paris, who was to have married her. Blood still wet
from the wound in his belly. And Romeo, not a mark on him,
but lifeless, with Juliet crumpled on top of him. And Tybalt.
At least he was lying there quietly, without any mystery about
him except death. And we know how he died. Romeo killed
him, and the Prince banished Romeo. He should have been
in exile in Mantua, not killing people in a vault in Verona.
Especially people already dead."

"So you think Romeo killed Juliet?" Beatrice asked sleepily.
Her eyes, dark as moon-shadow and as mysterious, had that
distant, luminous look about them she got when she had us
both at both ends of the night: Antonio with the nightingale,
and me with the lark. I couldn't begrudge him: he was her
husband. I could only begrudge myself for knowing. He rose
with the dawn for the day watch, and left that hair like beaten

brass, those eyes you could crawl into and hide, those breasts the color of cream and scented with almonds. He left all that treasure alone, for anyone to plunder. For the likes of me, grimy and red-eyed from the night, to stagger home into her bed. I gave up asking how she could, why both of us, who did she love best – those things. She only ever laughed.

I could tell she wasn't listening carefully, but I had to speak anyway, to tell, so that the ghosts would rest in my own head, dwindle back into their deaths.

"He must have come back to dishonor the bodies," I said, puzzled because it was most reasonable and most unlikely. "Maddened by his exile. He stabs Juliet's body, and is discovered by Paris, who has come in sorrow to visit her grave. They fight; Romeo slays Paris. And then – " I stopped, because I could not see beyond. "Romeo dies. But how? Why?"

"I would think he would have attacked Tybalt's body first, since Tybalt was the cause of his exile."

"Romeo was young and could be fierce, but he was at heart a gentle man. I spoke with him, once or twice, when he roamed the streets and orchards at night, plagued to the heart by love of some fair Rosaline. I can't see him stabbing any woman, Capulet or no, dead or alive. But it was his knife."

"Maybe she tried to kill him, in grief for her cousin Tybalt's death – "

"But she was already dead!"

"Apparently," my mistress said with her charming laugh that was the clink of two gold coins, "not dead enough."

So it was, with what the Prince said to me, that day turned into night, and night to day. I had to catch sleep where I could, since I could hardly search and seek during my watch. After a too-brief morning in my mistress's arms, I went out and ate, and then met daylight head-on, bright and painful after such a night. I went to see the friar whose business it had been to bury Juliet and Tybalt in the Capulet's vault. He might remember a flickered eyelid, a sigh without a cause, that would tell us Juliet had not been entirely dead. She had not been, of course; she had bled when she was stabbed. So they had buried her alive, only for her to wake in that terrible vault to find the death she had eluded coming at her yet again, and this time no escape.

But I could not find the friar. He was not in his cell reading, nor in his chapel shriving, nor in his garden with his weeds and wildflowers he calls medicine. His door was latched; so was his gate. The sacristan I finally found in the chapel knew only that the friar had left for Mantua, the day before, but he did not know where or why.

So I went to the palace of the Capulets.

It was noon by then, and hot as a lion's breath. I saw my mistress's husband Antonio, still on watch and scowling like a bear. He caught my arm, but it was not what I thought. "Stephano," he said. "Come with me – there's a fight between servants on Weavers Street."

What we need, I thought wearily. More dead. "Montague and Capulet?" I guessed, as we began to run.

"Who else? They claim the very air that they both breathe. They blame one another for last night. The lordlings keep apart, only eyeing one another, waiting to pick their time. This quarrel shows which way the wind blows." He was panting as we rounded a corner. He was shorter than I, older, rounder, brown and furry beside my lanky bones and sun-whitened hair. I caught myself imagining him with her, snorting and huffing between her breasts, and I wondered in my own blank fury how she could? How? In my mind, she looked at me over his back, and lifted a finger to her lips and smiled.

Antonio gripped my arm again. "There." Still running, we watched two men chasing a third into an ale house. Another pair grappled on the ground, their livery, the red of one House, the blue of the other, slick with dust and muck tossed out the windows. Even as we came at them, someone emptied a pot from the second storey onto their heads. They sputtered, but never noticed much until we dragged them apart. Others of the day-watch had come to help; a couple, swords drawn, vanished into the ale house after the rest of the brawlers. Holding my dirty, bleeding catch by hair and arm, I yielded him to Antonio and his men.

"Thanks," Antonio said. "I'm glad I found you awake."

"I have to be," I explained. "I'm the one the Prince's eye fell on first, last night. Find out who did this, he said. So I'm up at noon, trying to make some sense out of a brawl among the dead in a burial vault."

He nodded. "I'll help," he offered. "These streets will run with blood, soon, if we don't untangle this. What can I do?"

I didn't hesitate. "Come with me. Talk to Lord Capulet, while I question Juliet's mother and her nurse. Women know things, sometimes, that men never see under their noses." I caught a whiff of myself then, having picked up the brawlers' perfume. "After I wash," I added ruefully, and we went together into the ale house.

Both women, I was told at the Capulet's palace, were prostrate with grief. But I waited, and they roused themselves to speak with me, to shape their horror into words, and to make sure I knew who must be to blame. They came together, the Lady Capulet with her fine face seamed with lines, her hair unbound, a new web of silver glittering over the dark, her eyes red-rimmed, sometimes dry with fury then spilling sorrow at a memory.

"That Romeo," she said between her teeth. "I should have sent poison to him in Mantua. I threatened to, because he killed our Tybalt. Juliet heard me – she said she would mix it for me." She told me this fiercely, without shame, without thinking. I did the thinking then. Poison might have killed Romeo in the vault, and never left a mark on him.

"Did you?" I asked her, since she brought it up. She stared at me. Her face crumpled then; she turned away, shaking her head.

"I wish I had," she whispered, weeping. "I wish I had."

I looked at the nurse, wondering if she, too, had considered poison. She was plump, doughy, pale as tallow; her eyes, fidgety as magpie's eyes, refused to meet mine. They spent much of their time hidden in a scrap of linen.

"Oh, sir," she wept. "Our treasure is dead, our precious duckling; all we had is so cruelly gone."

"Yes," I said as gently as I could. "But how? How did you

manage, as much as you all loved her, to put her in the vault alive?"

"She was dead!" the nurse cried out. "That morning she was to have married Paris – we found her dead in her bed! The pretty thing, with no more breath in her than a stone has, and no more life. So her wedding became her funeral."

"But she wasn't dead."

Her mother, sobbing into her skirts, turned to me again. "He killed her – that fiend Montague."

"That may be, but for him to kill her, she would have to be buried alive."

"You keep harping on that," she exclaimed angrily, while the nurse's sobs got louder and louder. "How could you think we would have done such a thing?"

"I don't know what to think," I answered, bracing myself stolidly in the full force of their gale. "A young woman about to be married dies mysteriously in her bed, and her bridegroom to be meets his death in her tomb." I could hardly hear my own voice over the nurse's noise. "Something was amiss. Perhaps she tried to poison herself?" I suggested at random, since the word was in the air around us. "She did not wish to be married?"

"She did!" the nurse cried out.

"She didn't," the Lady Capulet said at the same time. They looked at one another. The nurse resumed sobbing. "She didn't and then she did," Lady Capulet amended.

"She didn't at first?"

"I think she fretted – imagined things – the way girls will."

"The marriage bed." I guessed. The nurse had soaked her linen and begun on her apron.

"But she came to peace with the idea," Lady Capulet said.

"So she would not have poisoned herself, that morning, to avoid her marriage. Tried, and failed, I mean. And wakened later in the – "

They were both crying at me by then. It took me a moment to untangle their words, and then their meanings. "Married" they both said, and "marriage" but it wasn't until they finally met each other's eyes again, that we all realized the words they spoke meant wildly different things.

"My poor pet," the nurse was sobbing. Lady Capulet groped for a chair. I could have used one, too.

"What are you saying, Nurse." I half-expected Lady Capulet's voice, rasping harshly through her throat, to flame like a dragon's.

"She had no fear, my poor, proud duck, of marriage – she was no maid. She was a married lady when she died."

"Married." Lady Capulet had to stop to swallow. The nurse had hidden her face, trying to crawl into her apron, away, I sensed, from an impending explosion.

"To whom?" I asked quickly, before Lady Capulet found her breath again and scorched the nurse to cinders.

"Who else?" the nurse demanded of her apron. "Of course, to Romeo."

I tried to describe the ensuing chaos to my beloved, the next morning, but I did it badly. It made her laugh: the appalled and furious parents, the distraught nurse, the fury slowly giving way to bewilderment, and then fresh tears as they realized what their daughter had done and why.

"She loved him," I said. "That much. And he loved her. Enough for both to defy their Houses. They had some notion, the nurse said, that the marriage might bring peace between their families."

She had stopped laughing at the image of the Lord Capulet chasing the nurse around the room, brandishing a silver branch of candles, while Antonio and I stumbled over chairs trying to catch him. She was silent a moment, dropping kisses like soft petals down my chest until I could no longer think, and reached for her, and she lifted her head and said abruptly, "But it only answers a single question: Romeo did not kill Juliet. How did he die? How did she? Did she kill herself with his knife? Why? He came to her alive – She was still alive – "

"The nurse kept saying the friar's name – Friar Laurence, who married them in secret barely hours before Romeo killed Tybalt. But the friar has gone to Mantua." I stirred, puzzled by an echo. Coincidence.

"Why Mantua?" she asked, hearing the echo.

"I don't know ... Romeo had been exiled to Mantua, but ..."

But what she did then made me forget time and light and duty, until I stood in the streets again, smiling at nothing. Then time dragged at me, and light roared, and duty called, and I went home to sleep an hour or two before I faced them all again.

I met Antonio at noon, in the tavern where I had my breakfast. He sat with me, and gave me his news, which was little enough, after the previous day.

"I spoke to Lord Montague's nephew, Benvolio, who was Romeo's good friend," he said. "He knew nothing of any marriage. He was stunned by it. He thought Romeo was still brooding over some Rosalind. Walking the fields at night and babbling of love to the moon. It happened fast, his marriage to Juliet."

"Love does, when you're young."

"One advantage of age: It's a relief to be done with such stuff."

I looked at him, startled. "Surely you love. Your wife – "

"If I loved my wife," he said roundly, "I would be walking in Romeo's moon-calf paths. Love's as dangerous when you're older."

"Then what would you call it? What you feel – " I stopped to settle a crumb in my throat. "For one another."

"Use," he said comfortably. "Habit. Familiarity. She won't leave me, though she has her faults, and I have mine. She's beautiful, and I let her have what she wants. If she is sometimes restless, that's as it pleases her. She gives herself to me when I want, and she does so smiling. I don't ask about other things that catch her eye, and she doesn't tell. They don't matter."

"But – "

"We are content." He swallowed the last of his ale. "What should I do now?"

He was asking, I realized dimly, about our mystery. I was silent, remembering the open vault, the dead.

"Paris," I said finally. "It was his page who called the watch. Find the page and ask him what he knows."

"What will you do?"

"Break the news to Lord Montague," I said, rising, "of his son's unexpected marriage. Meet me here before my watch begins."

Lord Montague's palace seemed quiet, numbed with grief. He had lost both wife and son within days of one another: Lady Montague had died broken-hearted over Romeo's exile from Verona. Lord Montague, a tall, imposing man with hair whiter than I remembered, greeted me listlessly. He had been told, he said, of the marriage.

"By whom?" I asked.

His mouth tightened a little, eased. He sighed. "By my great enemies, the Capulets. We are left with very little to be angry about, and very much to grieve over. Our faults, especially. Our children might be alive, if we had – if we hadn't – " He stopped, his mouth twitching, then added, "I have made offers of peace to Lord Capulet. Our children tried to love. It seems wrong to war over that."

I bowed my head, relieved. But there were still questions. "Did Romeo go alone to his exile?"

He shook his head. "Balthasar went with him. His man. He was always faithful, very loyal to my son. Why?"

"May I speak to him? He might have been there in the graveyard with Romeo. He might be able to tell us how Romeo died. And why."

"He died –" He stopped again. "He died of love."

So it seemed. I touched my brow, where too little sleep, too many riddles, were beginning to brawl behind my eyes. "I am very sorry, my lord. He was a kind young man, and gentle, unless he was provoked. And then from all accounts brave, and true to his friends."

"Balthasar knows little," Lord Montague said, but sent a page for him. He added, while we waited, "My son was as good at killing as at loving. We taught him to do all things well. I suppose he killed Paris out of some kind of jealousy – "

"It seems unlikely. More likely that Paris attacked him, thinking that Romeo had come to dishonor the dead, in revenge for his exile."

"What was Paris doing there?"

"I'm not sure, yet. But he was young, in love. That's when I would meet Romeo, wandering alone at night, sighing over Rosalind."

"Rosalind." He snorted faintly, and then sighed himself. Better to have lived with a heart broken by Rosalind, than to have died for true love and Juliet.

Or was it better? I wondered.

Easier to think you love than to love.

Easier to tell yourself lies than truth.

"He took me with him to the graveyard, to help him open the vault, but he would not let me stay," Balthasar told us when I asked. He seemed a modest young man, neat and well spoken. Spidery lines ran across his brow; he blinked often, trying not to see, I guessed, not to remember. "He – he threatened me. That if I stayed he would kill me." He closed his eyes tightly, as if the light hurt them. "I didn't believe him. But he wanted so badly for me to leave – How could I not do what he wanted?"

"That's all you saw? The open vault, and Romeo entering? Where was Paris?"

"I don't know. I was running, by then. I never thought – never for a moment – I only thought he would take some comfort there, with her, and then leave. I thought – he had to see that she was dead, before he could live again." He ground the heel of his hand into one eye a moment, while we watched. Then he added tonelessly, "He gave me a letter for you, my lord."

"What?" we both demanded.

"I forgot about it. I think I lost it when I ran."

"What did it say? In heaven's name, boy – "

"I don't know, my lord," he answered wearily. "I never learned to read. I didn't know it might be important. I never use letters. He wrote it just before we left Mantua for Verona." He lifted his sad, winking eyes, to Lord Montague's face. "I expected that he would be alive to tell you."

I went to the Friar's cell again, to see if he had returned, but there was no sign of him, no word, the sacristan said. My steps led me through the graveyard then, back to the vault; I was seized with some vague, nightmarish notion that the dead had wakened again, and I would find the vault gaping open to show fresh horrors, more dead dead again, more mysteries. But it was closed, silent. Trees murmured around me in a hot summer breeze; doves cooed their sad, comforting song. I walked around the vault, searching the long grass, the bushes, looking for something. Anything. What I found was a crowbar one of them had dropped, which only perplexed me more. What had Romeo expected to find, if he had brought it to open the vault? A living Juliet? A shiver ran through me, even as I sweated. Was that what they had planned? That she should pretend to die, and he would come into her grave to rescue her? But why did he die, then? Had he not found her alive? She had been alive enough to kill herself at least, and fall over his lifeless body.

She had found him dead, then. And killed herself.

But how had he died? And why?

A beggar accosted me as I left the graveyard. A stranger to Verona, I thought; I did not recognize his face. He tried to speak to me, after I tossed him a coin, but I didn't listen; I couldn't hear him over the clamoring mystery in my brain. I went home again, to sleep a while before my watch. I woke at dusk, thick-headed and unrefreshed, still with nothing answered. I had hoped to shape my dreams into solutions, but all I dreamed was what I had seen: Juliet's face, lovely as a flower and ghostly pale, her blood seeping into Romeo's clothing; Paris lying against the wall, trying to coil himself around his wound; Romeo's staring eyes, his parted lips, as if in the end he had seen Juliet alive and tried to speak: great, waxen trumpets of lilies scattered everywhere.

As I ate my meal at dusk in the tavern, Antonio told me where the lilies had come from.

"Paris brought them, his page said." I nodded, unsurprised. "He told his page to keep watch, and whistle if he heard anyone coming."

"Did he bring a crowbar as well as flowers?" I asked.

"No. Why? Was there one?" He answered himself. "There would have to be."

"Then Romeo opened the vault himself. So the page is watching, and Paris is – "

"Strewing flowers in front of the vault and weeping – "

"And what then? Someone comes?"

"Romeo comes. They hide, Paris and his page, and watch Romeo order Balthasar away, and open the vault. So Paris – "

"Paris," I said, illumined, "thinks Romeo has come to defile the place. Of course. So he leaps to defend Juliet, and they fight."

"With some reluctance, it seems, on Romeo's part. The page said he spoke with a frantic courtesy, begging Paris to leave. But of course Paris would not. So he died there."

"And the page?"

"He left when they began to fight, and ran to get the watch."

Me. I grunted, and chewed a tasteless bite. I felt Antonio's eyes on me, watching, unblinking. I wondered if he knew where my steps led me, at every dawn after my watch. I met his eyes finally, found them smiling faintly, enigmatic. Amused? I pushed my chair back noisily, finishing my meal as I rose.

"What now?" he asked, intent as ever on the mystery. I shook my head.

"I don't know. If Friar Laurence does not return soon, I may have to ride to Mantua and look for him. I'll speak to the Prince tomorrow, tell him what he hasn't heard by now. But there are still those nagging questions. Did Juliet intend to kill herself on the morning of her marriage to Paris? Did Romeo come to the vault to mourn her death, or did he expect to find her alive? What killed him?"

"Poison, likely. He came to die beside her in the vault."

"But why was she still alive?"

He shook his head, baffled. "Star-crossed, maybe. They were never meant to live. Only to love."

He left me with that thought, as if the lovers had been more than human, nothing like us, who, older and growing tawdry with life, could no more have loved again than we could have cut new teeth. He went home to her; I went into the darkening streets.

Another beggar stopped me, just before dawn; I could not

see his face. Perhaps it was the same one. I could barely speak by then, with weariness; I only wanted to sleep. He tried to follow me, but I did not want him to see where I was going, and I spoke sharply to him. He faded away with the night. I dropped into my mistress's arms, which she held out to me as generously as ever. I tried to bury myself in her sweetness as in some warm, gently moving sea, but my thoughts kept tossing me onto a rocky shore.

"Do you love me?" I asked her once, without meaning to.

"Of course," she said. "Stephano. Of course."

The beggar was waiting for me when I left her.

I stopped when I saw him, angry and mystified. Maybe he thought to threaten me by telling Antonio what he had seen; maybe he had some notion that Antonio might care. He had started to speak even before I stopped; busy studying him, I didn't listen. He was tall and gaunt as some desert saint; his clothes hung loosely on him, where they weren't holding themselves together by a thread. His hair and brows were shaggy, iron-grey and white. His feet were bare and dusty, cracked, as if he had walked parched roads for some time.

He tried to fill my hand with gold, which is when I began to listen to him.

"He told me to buy food with it, but I found I could not eat his gold. Not with what I gave him. He would not hear 'no.' I pay your poverty, he said, not your will. I didn't have the will to refuse. Refuse to eat, refuse to live. Until I heard what happened to him. I came to give back his gold. I can't take back what I gave him, but I will not eat his death."

I closed my eyes, opened them, to see if he was still there, if his words made any better sense. "Who are you?" I asked, bewildered.

"A poor apothecary, from Mantua. I wept when I heard. He spoke so courteously to me. He was so young, so bright and vibrant with life. I could not believe he would really want to die. A young woman would smile at him, I thought, and he would wonder how he could have ever thought of dying – "

"Wait." I held up my hand. "Wait." My voice shook; I

had to swallow what it was he told me. "You're speaking of Romeo – "

"I didn't know his name," he said. "Until we heard the news in Mantua, about the strange deaths in Verona. Then I knew it must be him."

"He bought poison from you. To kill himself."

"Yes."

"It's death – " My voice rose, broke away from me. "It's death for you to tell me this – If I told them in Mantua what you sold – "

"I know." He peered at me, owl-like, from under his tufted brows, fearless, resigned. "I have done what I have done. And now you must."

I was silent, staring at him, piecing things together. Romeo must have heard of Juliet's death, and bought poison in Mantua to die beside her in that vault. I felt something push into my throat, some word, some noise. My eyes stung suddenly. They came alive for me, again: the two young lovers, wanting only time and room in the world to love. We had no time or room, in lives crowded with our empty passions, to give them.

I leaned back against the stone wall of my mistress's house, shaking, dry with sorrow, trying to hear some heartbeat in the stones. I heard only the clink of gold that was her laugh.

"You must take it," the apothecary said. I opened my eyes, stared down at the gold he had let fall into my hands. I moved finally, pushed myself away from the wall.

"Come with me," I said.

"What will you do with me?"

"Feed you. What else? And after that you will leave this city and I will never see your face again. Will I?"

"Why?" he asked me softly, his bird-eyes, weary and unblinking, holding mine.

"Because," I sighed, "neither you nor I nor the stars themselves could have kept that young man alive without his Juliet." I gave him back the gold. "Keep it. I would have to explain it otherwise. It is not from Romeo, but from me."

I walked him to the city gates, after we ate, to make sure that he did not linger. He seemed bewildered but not, on the whole, unhappy to be still alive. I had no desire to bring the issue up with the Prince. That Romeo took poison seemed obvious; he might have stolen it as easily as bought it. Juliet must have taken some herself, on her wedding morning; I had no idea where she had gotten that. Maybe, I thought, as I watched the apothecary become a shimmer of dust in the distance, we would never know.

But when I went to the Friar's cell that morning, his garden gate was open, and so was his door. I walked in. His lean face was harried and wan with grief, but unsurprised, as if he expected me.

"Stephano," he said, and pulled me down beside him. "I have been – "

"I know, in Mantua."

"No," he said, exasperated. "In Verona. I was leaving for Mantua to tell young Romeo that Juliet would only pretend to die – the letter I wrote him had gone astray. But I wound up quarantined along with my travelling companion, Friar John, who had been visiting the sick. Plague, we were told, but it was only measles. They finally let me out this morning. Only to be stricken with this news . . ."

"Friar Laurence, did you give Juliet the poison?"

"It was only to make her pretend to die! So that she would not have to go through that farce of a wedding." He pulled a dusty boot off and flung it across the room, then sat brooding at it a moment. "A foolish old man," he breathed. "Who did I think I was, to meddle with love? Blame me for everything. Let me find my sandals. Then take me to the Prince – I'll tell him – "

"I think we're all to blame," I said softly, and sat on one of his uncomfortable stools. "And maybe it was their destiny to bring Verona peace. Friar, will you shrive me before we go?"

His brows rose in surprise at my oddly timed request. But he only touched the crucifix on his breast and murmured, "Who will forgive me?"

THE BANISHED MEN

Keith Taylor

It has been suggested that The Two Gentlemen of Verona *was Shakespeare's first work for the stage, although the development of his plotting and structure implies he had already tested himself on earlier work. The first known performance of the play was in 1593 and it is unlikely that Shakespeare wrote it much earlier. Amongst his sources for the play was a long poem by Arthur Brooke,* The Tragical History of Romeus and Juliet *(1562), which shows that the two plays are closely related. They share the same setting of Verona. The two gentlemen of the title – Valentine and Proteus – are friends until they both fall in love with Silvia, the daughter of the Duke of Milan. Proteus betrays Valentine's intentions to the Duke (who plans to marry Silvia to the oafish Thurio) and Valentine is banished. Proteus is already beloved of Julia and Julia follows Proteus to Milan (disguised as a boy) and enters his service, discovering his love for Silvia. Silvia herself is sickened by these suits and runs away to find Valentine. She is captured by robbers, unaware that Valentine is the leader of the outlaws. Proteus rescues her, and Valentine witnesses Proteus's confession of his treachery. When Proteus asks for forgiveness Julia faints, revealing the ring Proteus had given her as a sign of his devotion. Somehow the couples all become reconciled: Valentine marries Silvia and Proteus marries Julia. In the following story, Keith Taylor succeeds in establishing the play in a precise historical setting (the year is 1534) and developing the adventures of Valentine amongst the outlaws.*

1

Well, sir, this gentleman is come to me,
With commendation from great potentates;
And here he means to spend his time awhile.
Shakespeare, *Two Gentlemen of Verona*, II, 4

Valentine was in a savage mood, a devil's potion mixed out of thwarted love, rage at a friend's betrayal, self-pity, quite reasonable fear for his own safety, and a blazing desire for revenge. His servant rode behind him in careful silence. He'd known Valentine for years, and seldom had to walk on eggshells around him, but this was such an occasion. He held his tongue.

Svelto did not in any case feel much urge to japes or drollery. This forest had an ill name. Bandits, sorcerers and devils all frequented it, by repute. The bandits were certain. Many travellers had been waylaid and robbed here, some never seen again, some seen only as corpses.

Pity that ever we left Verona, and worse pity that ever we came to Milan. To see the wonders of the world abroad, by God! My master should go home; we've seen enough.

Undergrowth rustled.

A flock of birds flew low across their path in a storm of wings. Valentine's horse curvetted. He swore. Then he shut his mouth, hard. Five men stood in his way, and they were armed. One held a crossbow aimed steadily at his chest.

"Stand, sir, and throw us that you have about you," the first called out. "If not, we'll make you sit, and rifle you!"

Bearded and corpulent, heavy with muscle under the fat, he

stood with fists on hips among slanting sunrays. His clothes were stained but splendid. He displayed a naked sword, and one of the others, a huge rawboned rogue in steel cap and studded leather vest, carried a pike. Valentine marked him; he and the crossbowman presented the most danger.

"Sir, we are undone!" Svelto said. "These are the villains that all the travellers do fear so much."

"Be quiet," Valentine said curtly. He was worried, particularly by that damned crossbow, but the situation did not seem hopelessly dire. The robber said nothing of murder, and he spoke like a gentleman. Maybe he had been. Valentine controlled his ire and replied courteously.

"My friends – "

"That's not so, sir," interjected another outlaw. "We are your enemies."

"Worthy bandits, then. Mercury's children and protégés of Saint Nicholas." Valentine dismounted without asking leave, young but experienced, tall, smiling and ready for mischief, a fencer, dancer and hell-for-leather horseman. He had black hair and very dark eyes. "I fear there's no profit for you with us. I have my clothes and this sword. You fellows are better equipped in that respect than I. Then there are these excuses for horseflesh." He jerked his thumb at the beasts. "Have them and welcome. Slain and buried, they might enrich someone's garden, but that aside, their usefulness is finite."

"And riding with one servant in these ill-omened parts?" This outlaw had a gentle face and melancholy hazel eyes. "I think you've been touched by adversity, sir."

"Touched? No." Valentine walked a few casual steps towards the bandits. "Lewdly fondled from neck to heels describes it better. I'm banished from Milan."

All five robbers laughed. The one with hazel eyes said amiably, "No malice intended, sir, but we are banished men ourselves. All but Georg there." He indicated the pikeman. "He's a Switzer mercenary last in the employ of Ferrara."

"Who didn't pay me," Georg said philosophically.

"Ettore is an exile from Pisa. Daniel, with the crossbow, has a sentence against him in Mantua, and I myself am banned from fair Verona. As for Teberigo – "

"Teberigo can declare for himself, if he wishes," said the bearded outlaw. "Benvolio, you always waste time in conversation with something to rob. By Bacchus! I'm not quite so ready to believe you have nothing, sir. Turn out your wallet and take off your gloves. Ettore, the saddle-bags."

"A moment," the hazel-eyed Benvolio said; softly, but he met burly Teberigo's sudden glare with equanimity. "This seems a proper man. He's banished, and a gentleman, and poor in goods, well qualified to join us. To offend his pride by turning him over like a sheep were to lose his sympathy."

"Who asks for it? Unglove, sir, or that must follow which will forfeit me your liking indeed."

He swaggered two hectoring steps nearer to Valentine. An experienced robber by now, he did not walk between his man and the crossbow, but one swift sideways movement by Valentine placed him there. Springing like a tiger, he swung his gloved fist to the side of Teberigo's head and staggered him. Swiftly, he spun Teberigo around, dragged his arm behind his back and ran him straight at the crossbowman, Daniel. Teberigo and Daniel crashed together. They went down in a heap. The crossbow bolt went high through the leaves of a cork oak.

Svelto, whose name meant the fast one, had dropped from his saddle the instant Valentine moved. He too assessed the Swiss pikeman as their second greatest peril. Svelto tackled him low and began a furious struggle, while Valentine brought his sword rasping out. His point touched Teberigo's throat.

"Are you certain you do not wish to discuss this?"

His dangerous mood now broke out of the constraint that crossbow had imposed. If Teberigo said no, Valentine was prepared to pin him to the sod and take his chances. Looking into his face, the robber saw that resolve.

"I think Benvolio's right. You're a proper man."

"Yes," Georg panted, "as I'm native to Bern!" He still grappled with Svelto for the pike. "Ease off there, lad. Hold! Peace! Or I'll break your head. I like your master. Proper? This fellow were a king for our wild faction!"

"Have a care." Ettore, lean, sinewy, vivid, and dark as a Moor, lifted an eyebrow. "The Captain would not like such talk. Will you join us, messire? Our chief must be the final judge of you."

"To outrage women, and murder poor passengers? Go to."

"None of that," Ettore answered. "We all detest such vile, base practices. The murders you have heard of were done by other companies. We've been at war with two, and made an end of them last month."

"For justice?" Valentine asked.

"More for their hoarded loot. But they smell sweeter dead. Why, sir, this noble, douce Benvolio of ours would ne'er be one of us if we did rape and wanton murder. He's nature's peacemaker, a child of God, a dove, straight from the sermon on the mount."

Benvolio grinned and made a crude gesture.

"Master, be one of them," Svelto urged. "It is an honourable kind of thievery."

"Peace, villain! Still, I'll go with you and see your chief. Has he a name, but Captain?"

"It's for him to tell it," Teberigo said. "Now let me rise. The camp's more than a league from here."

2

Treachery! Seek it out.
Shakespeare, *Hamlet*, V, 2

The bandit leader proved ready to tell his name, and loudly.

"Sforza!" he roared, ripping a baked duck apart. "Piero Sforza! I'm a grandson of old Duke Galeazzo Maria who was assassinated at Christmas sixty years ago, and my claim to rule Milan is better than that lackey of the Spaniards who sits there, sonless, now! So! My darling cousin banished you? Speaks eloquently in your favour. Come, though, for what cause?"

Seated in a massive chair beside Lake Garda, gorging and swilling, he bawled his queries at Valentine. The traveller quickly decided not to answer that last one truthfully. Sforza's response was likely to be mirthful and obscene, and Valentine knew he would reply with a sword-thrust through the man's gizzard. His own life would be short thereafter.

"I killed a man," he said. "I much repent his death, and yet I killed him face to face, without false vantage or base treachery."

"Don't trouble to repent, then," Sforza said cheerfully. "Did Francesco really banish you for such a minor crime?"

"He did. I reckon myself lucky."

"Hmm. Native to Milan?"

"No, Captain Sforza. I'm from Verona. I was returning there when your men waylaid me."

"Verona! Does everybody come from that bastard city, unfit for the habitation of men? Benvolio, Teberigo, Stefan there, now you! Bah! Were you in Milan long?"

"Sixteen months in service with the Duke, messire. Before that, I served the Doge's Serenity as a soldier, and fought the Turks in Cyprus and Illyria. Before that I did travel somewhat in the Empire . . . Innsbruck, Munich, Vienna. I've spent five years seeing the world."

"Have you the tongues?"

"My travels made me polyglot."

"A soldier, a courtier, and a linguist! Good! Now, have you secretarial skills? Except Benvolio, curse me if one of us can pen a decent ransom note."

"I studied in my youth, and practised it to some degree with Duke Francesco."

"No more of calling him the Duke! I'll be the Duke, once I amass sufficient wealth to pay an army! It's my right. He's merely my damned cousin! Remember it."

"Indeed," Valentine murmured. "Now, sir, I know I've heard of you. Captain Piero Sforza! You are the leader of condottiero whose badge was the ram's head! But gossip had you two years dead."

Sforza chuckled. "I think it lied. Yes, I'm that man."

"I'm honoured." Valentine bowed with courtly savoir-faire. In fact, he was not. Nothing he had heard of Sforza suggested special skill in war or great distinction, except as a brute butcher. If these curious outlaws did abstain from rape and careless murder, Valentine doubted it was by Sforza's command.

"Now, sir, your choice is, join us or die. I won't compel you. But before accepting you, I'll put you to the proof, of wit, resource and bravery! A traitor's in my band. Because of him we barely avoided fatal ambush Tuesday last, and before that, as I think, he tried to poison me with monkshood. My guts are still in turmoil. Find him, if you'd live."

Valentine bowed. "If that's my choice, I'll find him."

Leaving Sforza's presence was a delight. Valentine looked pensively across the blue lake and considered the task facing him. Despite his bluster, the captain was very likely correct. Every camp had its traitor, and this one would be no exception. Still, it wouldn't be easy to find the Judas among thirty men, all strangers, and Sforza had not impressed him as patient.

Valentine sought out Benvolio. He discovered that young man at his ease under a cypress tree, reading Petrarch. Catching his eye, Benvolio closed the volume and sat upright.

"Well, sir, felicitations! You are now one of us."

"Much upon conditions, and with a knife at my neck. The Captain told me you also have the honour of hailing from Verona."

"I *had* it," Benvolio said drily.

"Does one ask, here, about a man's past? I've observed that, excepting the Captain, all these men go by Christian names only. Thus I assume the answer's no."

"It's best not to ask if a man does not offer. Most of us hope for better times again, and would forget this as a dream if they come – but I at least don't mind. Yes, I'm Veronese, of the great house of Montague."

"Ah."

"Ah?" Benvolio repeated, as one who senses criticism.

"When I left, one could scarcely walk down the street but one found a Montague at sword-strokes with a Capulet."

"Conceded. And most tedious I found it. Well, the feud came to an end three years since, sir. Did you receive no letters from home that mentioned it?"

"Indeed, yes, my mother filled pages with the grievous story. By her account, Montague's son and Capulet's daughter loved, married in secret, and lost their lives to their parents' rage. Not only they. Lady Capulet's nephew Tybalt perished, and kinsmen of the Prince's."

"Alas, your mother wrote in fullest verity. Lord Montague's son Romeo was my kinsman and friend."

"I somewhat knew him. Nay, I was even acquainted with Tybalt, and trained at fence with him when we were boys. He'd quarrel with a cat for mewing."

"Yes. Tybalt slew Mercutio. Romeo slew Count Paris, fighting by Juliet's tomb. I think it was no murder, but fair fight. The Prince held otherwise, though Tybalt, Romeo, and most who were involved, lay far beyond his justice. 'Some shall be pardoned, and some punished,' said he, and the next thing my ears heard was sentence of exile – chiefly for being still available, and having been poor Romeo's heart-comrade." Tears gathered in Benvolio's eyes. "The fruit of love is death, as surely as the fruit of the tree of knowledge."

"I incline to agree." It had nearly been Valentine's, but he had told his tale of having been exiled for a killing, and he would look a fool to revise the story now. "And so you're here."

"And so I'm here. As exile's now my portion, I'll commit a crime or two that merits it. I have grown tired of being peaceful, mild Benvolio."

"Is Sforza the best leader you could find for your projected acts contra the law? He's bold, undaunted, with experience of war, yet appears somewhat, ah, somewhat – "

"Stupid?" Benvolio finished.

"I didn't think it would be polite if I said it."

"He's besotted," Benvolio declared. "He'll never rule Milan while the Emperor Charles supports his cousin. As for our operations, he brags of his great plans, but never has any; he always ends by taking Ettore's advice, or with due modesty, mine. Because we're valuable, we can restrain him."

"Do you believe the Duke of Milan has set a spy among you?"

"I don't know. But I would were I the Duke! That ambush of ours that nearly ended in disaster makes me think we were betrayed."

"The Captain talked of an attempt to poison him."

"Probably it wasn't. He'd been gorging, and may have eaten spoiled oysters or suspect pork. The symptoms were not those of monkshood poison. The Captain swears it was. He does not change a notion once lodged in his head."

"Then I'd better proceed on the principle that there is a traitor, good Benvolio."

The afternoon was warm. Absentmindedly, Valentine removed his gloves. The ring Silvia had given him flashed in the sun. Glancing at it, Benvolio whistled.

"It's well Teberigo did not see that before you were taken into the band! He'd have demanded it."

Valentine's smile held a flash of malevolence. "No doubt. And then there would have been a dispute more violent than the one we had. Messire Teberigo might have lost one or two of's light fingers."

"I infer it's a lady's love token."

"Well, yes, from one I love. And she was true. It was my closest friend proved false. Though promised to another, he conceived passion for my mistress, and deceived us both. We'd have successfully eloped if he had not betrayed our purpose. Fortune send I find her again, and be revenged on him! Meanwhile, I've other work before me. Walk through the camp with me, Benvolio, and make my new friends known."

3

The private wound is deepest. O time most accurst!
'Mongst all foes, that a friend should be the worst!
Shakespeare, *Two Gentlemen of Verona*, V, 4

They had waylaid a mule train bound for Mantua with leather, lace and soap. Nobody except Sforza, Ettore and Teberigo had even known where they were going until immediately before they set out. This policy of not letting the left hand know what the right hand did was Ettore's idea, and found ready acceptance with Sforza, who trusted no one. Perhaps because of it, the attack was a success. It involved riding swiftly in the dark and bringing men to the appointed place without a hitch. Valentine, with his experience against Turkish Spahis and Akinji, did his part ably. It was minor, but he thought he had proved he was worth his keep.

"You did well, sir," Ettore complimented him. "Many a man would have become lost at night in strange country like that. We often ride long distances to strike, you see. We'd be unwise to plague our own home region too much; the Duke's apt to send soldiers on a visit. It's why we rid ourselves of those too-bloody rivals."

"Sensible, indeed. What becomes of our haul?"

"We take it into Brescia and sell it. The law turns a blind eye. Brescia is a town working hard to prosper once again after French bombard and sack. You see young Luca there?"

Luca was a tall, fair-skinned youth, handsome as Narcissus, busy rubbing down a horse.

"He often goes into Brescia for days at a time," Ettore explained. "We don't mind because he brings back information, but what he really does these is serve as an artist's apprentice. A good one, too. Girolamo Romani's pupil Moretto. By God, Moretto's already better than his master, and he'd like to have Luca for his apprentice full time. An intoxicating compliment to the lad, no? And he's in love with one of Moretto's models besides. Naturaly he'd be glad to accept the maestro's offer, but the Captain says no."

Meaning that Luca could be the traitor. Remove Sforza, and he'd remove a major obstacle to his desires.

"Surely there are others here who go to Brescia?" He might as well, Valentine thought, hear the worst all at once.

"Surely, illustrious Valentine!" Ettore laughed, amused. "I do myself. I've a leman in the town, and not an artist's model. I leave such to cubs like Luca. No, she's a *cortigiana oneste** from Rome. Banished, like us, in her case for the flagrant immorality of declining to become a cardinal's mistress. A delightful woman. Perhaps you might enjoy dinner at her house with me some evening?"

---

* distinguished, cultured, stylish courtesan.

"With all my heart, sir! It's the noblest and most pleasant offer I've received since I saw this forest." He added, "Bacchus, but I see both the gentle and the common in this band make a good thing of their outlawry!"

Although sincere in his thanks, and eager to enjoy such a banquet, Valentine saw well that here was one more candidate for the traitor. This Roman courtesan could doubtless charm information from an oyster, and so deftly that the oyster would not even realize it was yielding any. She wouldn't like being consigned from Rome to a comparative backwater like Brescia. The vision of reward and favour from Duke Francesco of Milan would be like the golden fleece to her.

Well, then, who seemed *least* likely to stab his chief in the back? The three Frenchmen, Bernard, Raoul and Florian, had fought in Italy against the Spaniards. They didn't like the Emperor Charles or his puppet duke. Probably more to the point, they gained more in Sforza's band than they were likely to do by turning traitor. The same applied to the Swiss mercenary, Georg, and the Englishman, Christopher.

Counting Sforza and Valentine, there were ten Italian gentlemen among the outlaws. Sforza could not be the traitor, Valentine knew he was not, and unless a better actor than he seemed, the gentle, honourable Benvolio could be removed. Ettore? The man had fire, dash and ambition; he might well wish to be captain here or a courtier in Milan. A definite possibility. Teberigo? A boaster and brawler, crude, arrogant, forceful, he was a kindred spirit with Sforza and his closest boon companion – his friend, if Sforza possessed one. Not that Valentine put much faith in friendship after the way his own dearest friend had betrayed him.

That remembrance turned his thoughts aside into brooding. He and Proteus had been closer than most brothers since their childhood. Their only real disagreement was in their attitude to love. They had parted over it when they were both eighteen; Valentine to travel, seeking adventure and advancement, Proteus to remain in Verona and pursue his lovestruck suit with a noble girl named Julia. In Valentine's view, Julia didn't know her own mind, or the difference between what she thought was appropriate reticence in a maiden, and what she really wanted. It had probably been a good thing when old Antonio pushed Proteus out of the family nest, to travel, study and attend in foreign courts, after Valentine's example.

It had unquestionably been a bad thing when their paths crossed once more in Milan.

Valentine gritted his teeth, thinking of it. His fury doubled as he remembered the asinine way he had praised Proteus to the sky in the Duke's hearing, and been so filled with delight to see his friend arrive. Christ! What a trusting booby he had been to pour into Proteus's ear the tale of his ardent – and fully requited – love for the Duke's daughter Silvia, even to confess the details of their planned elopement! Within days of meeting Proteus again! Fatuous, trusting dolt!

Ha! Proteus turned out to be well named, changing his shape to suit the situation! He'd deserted his own mistress, the fair Julia, and once he set eyes on Silvia he conceived a blazing lust for her. Except for Valentine, there was no rival apart from the feeble Thurio, and it hadn't taken Proteus – the dog! – long to rid himself of Valentine. A word to Duke Francesco about the plan to fly with his daughter, and Valentine was banished, lucky not to be executed.

He lowered a burning gaze to the ring of his finger, Silvia's gift, thinking of her auburn-haired loveliness. It was torture to imagine that the Duke might give her to Proteus. *Hope that he doesn't, you obscenity villain, for if you marry her, by Saint Michael I'll widow her*!

False friend, true love. It had been a mistake to think on either, for now his mind so seethed with longing and vengefulness he could not give his fellow outlaws the cold assessment he must, to find the traitor. Stefan? Lorenzo? Moyses? Valerius? He didn't know enough about any of them, as yet, to hazard a guess.

"Valentine, your worship!"

"Svelto, you forward rogue! I vow you've taken to thievery as though it were your nature, and dress the part like a clown aping a ruffler. What, a dagger in your boot, another at your belt, a third strapped to your biceps and a cudgel in your hand? You are not a Titan, boy. You have but two arms."

"But I can juggle, sir, as well as I can fight."

"Better, to my knowledge. What is it?"

"Council, sir. A council of our kindred highwaymen. The Captain summons you to be there, and swears that no excuse will serve, and looks like thunder."

Valentine chuckled briefly. "His mortal thunder rattles empty. He's a poor imitation of great Jove. But I'll attend, since I am now a bandit, and hear what new lewd bit of reivery we're to commit."

4

What halloing, and what stir, is this today?
These are my mates, that make their wills their law,
Have some unhappy passenger in chase.
      Shakespeare, *Two Gentlemen of Verona*, V, 4

"It's a prize, a plum!" Teberigo insisted, his feet planted wide, his big hands gesticulating, fist smacking into palm. "The great merchant Zuppini, a Venetian ambassador, and a banker of the House of the Gorgon! All travelling together! Oh, fellows, smack your lips, taste the ransoms!"

"All travelling together, yes." Ettore agreed sardonically, "for protection from our sort, comrade! Their escort is a company of eighty lances led by Prembi. Look around, and count. There are thirty of us."

The Captain nodded grimly. "I know Prembi. He's no dunce. Now I'm game to encounter him, or Satan for that matter, and it's true he must pass through this forest, which we know down to the littlest twig – but who has a plan that can make such an ambush work?"

"Surprise attack at night!" Teberigo insisted. "A sudden, fierce descent and we'll have snatched the three before the guards rub sleep out of their ox's eyeballs!"

"It's brave," Benvolio said tactfully, "but will it work? They won't camp overnight in this forest, with its known dangers – us! – when they can leave Brescia early and travel hard all day. We'd have to ambush them awake and moving."

"Aye, Teberigo, and suppose we did take them asleep?"

the Englishman called out in his mangled Italian. "Besides Prembi's company of lances, there are the ambassador's retinue, the banker's and the merchant's, at least a hundred and fifty souls in all. How select the right men out of that many during a sudden night attack? With scant time to spare?"

"Christopher's right," growled a one-eyed rogue named Moyses. "By the rope that strangled Judas, if I were these rich men, passing through our country, I'd put a lackey in my tent and sleep on the ground concealed in a cheap cloak, among the soldiers!"

That got a laugh. Still, despite Teberigo's strenuous urging, the whole band felt his proposal was mad, and that any bandit force trying it with fewer than a hundred men would have no future. Teberigo swore at them for cowards and threw his hat on the ground, but even Sforza disagreed with him.

Valentine said nothing. However, he listened, and a wild, tingling excitement came to him along with an idea that promised success. He quelled his impulse to speak at once. The newest of the outlaws, his standing was low and precarious. He'd require backing from more respected men. Accordingly, he sought out Ettore and Benvolio. They listened, and by the end Ettore's black eyes were sparkling.

"It's a lunatic gamble, but with good chances," he said. "I love it! Valentine, you are a man!"

"It's daring, and we might win the main," Benvolio agreed, "but if the dice roll against us, there's nothing so likely as our utter destruction. I think we'd be stretching our arm further than our sleeve can reach."

The others worked on him, cajoling, urging. At last Benvolio gave in to their stronger wills, to the extent that he agreed to go with them and lay the plan before Sforza. The irascible captain was tempted, though hardly pleased to find the scheme was Valentine's.

"You, hey?" he sneered. "Most of us were brigands before you tore yourself out of your mother's arms, and you'll show us the way ransom victims should be taken? Ettore, Benvolio, why did you even bring him before me? It's a tyro's brainstorm!"

"Most noble captain, if it were my idea, you would be right," Valentine said. "I didn't have it, but stole it from another. When in Illyria serving 'gainst the Ottoman, I saw this done by an old brigand in the pay of Venice. He did effect it on a Turkish column that threefold outnumbered him, and with success. No tyro's brainstorm nor fool's luck in his case! He'd been a bandit more than thirty years, in a land where it's an honoured, sound profession. What he did, surely you and yours can do."

"Flattery!" Sforza barked. "Still – " Scowling, he sank chin on fist, the picture before him of a mighty triple ransom.

"We'll dare it!" he said at last. "Ettore, Benvolio, work out the details with me, then lay 'em before the rascals. But you!" He looked forbiddingly at Valentine. "This is not the work I set you. Unless you find the traitor who contrives against me, I'll give you nothing better than a formal burial. And be warned – I may not kill you first."

Valentine's eyes narrowed. He felt tempted to betray this shifty brute himself, but there was no way to square it with his gentleman's honour. Granting a certain bare, basic level of decency, one did not sell one's captain, even if he was captain of little but bombast, theft and throat-cutting.

Wakeful and watchful in his blanket that night, Valentine heard the sound of a man moving, and saw a burly figure rise from the ground, stealing away into the trees. Brass studs glittered on his leather tunic. Teberigo! And why would he wear such an uncomfortable garment to sleep, unless he did not mean to do much sleeping? There was nothing furtive in the way he moved; quite his usual bully swagger, and when he tripped he even cursed aloud, careless who heard. Valentine nearly turned over and resumed his own slumber, convinced that Teberigo was answering a call of nature. He could not have said why he rose and followed the man. Perhaps it was just that his nerves were on edge over the coming action and the Captain's threat.

Teberigo did relieve himself, but then he took a horse and rode eastward. Valentine followed on foot; along the forest's twisting game trails, he could actually move faster that way, and if he had saddled a horse himself, Teberigo

would soon have known there was someone behind him.
Valentine wondered why the devil he was going to this trouble.
Teberigo might be on some secret errand for the Captain. Still,
Valentine stayed obstinately with the slow-moving horseman.
The task made demands on all his rough-country experience
of hunting and war.

Beyond the forest, Teberigo raised a trot and came to a
little farm near Lake Garda. Valentine followed him running.
If this was a rendezvous with some agent of Milan, he'd found
the traitor. Would Sforza believe it, though?

Teberigo installed his horse in the barn as though he owned
the farm. (Valentine was later to learn that he did.) Then he
emerged, tossed a pebble at the back of the house, and waited
in the shadows. A figure scrambled out – a pleasant figure, so
far as Valentine could tell in the dark – and ran to Teberigo's
arms with a swaying of skirts.

Valentine struck the earth with his fist, mortified. An
assignation with a farm girl! Cross of Christ! He'd missed
sleep for this! Talk about a tyro's brainstorm! Probably he
couldn't even find his way to camp again, now, unless he
waited for Teberigo to finish with the wench and then
followed him back. He'd be dog-tired come morning, even
if his absence was not noted – and if Teberigo should see
him slinking behind, he might well sword him fatally. It
was certain the bravo remembered the way Valentine had
knocked him down the day they met, making a fool of him
in the process.

A superb finder of spies and discoverer of traitors he was!
Valentine settled down to wait, scalding with humiliation.
God grant he didn't have to explain this to Sforza. The
camp would rock with laughter if it were known.

5

*. . . the lion cannot defend himself against snares and the
fox cannot defend himself against wolves. Therefore, it
is necessary to be a fox to discover the snares and a lion
to terrify the wolves. Those who rely simply on the lion
do not understand what they are about.*

Machiavelli, *The Prince*, ch. 18

The days of the *condottieri* were done. Gian Prembi knew it. Never would his company be hired upon contract by any prestigious city or lord again. Jobs like this one, conveying rich men to the goal of their travels, were the best to be had these days. If fortune favoured him, Prembi would end his days as host of an inn somewhere, in reasonable comfort and a degree of funds. Otherwise, he might descend to a common brigand as Piero Sforza had done. Fortune had spurned that poor bastard and no mistake! At least Piero had not dared attack *him*.

Prembi listened to his men laughing, joking and bragging. There was relief wrapped in the bombast. They were all damned glad to be clear of the forest that was Sforza's special haunt. The bandit would have had an advantage there.

"Think you he might fall upon us here, in the open?" the Venetian ambassador asked. "The villain's men are well mounted, I hear, and cover a good deal of ground in their ravages. They ride as hard as Tartars."

"So they do, excellency. I'm posting a strong guard tonight. The entire company stays alert and sleeps – I should say dozes – fully equipped."

The ambassador sniffed. Clearly he regarded Prembi as a mere down-at-heel adventurer. The *condottieri* supposed he was. However, he viewed his excellency the ambassador as something worse – a long-eared, two-legged, and complete ass.

The dusk deepened, and several fires blazed in their camp, a sizeable one of 200 men. At its center stood the pavilion in which the merchant, ambassador and banker took their rest. Prembi walked around setting his guard, then examined the horse lines. All seemed well.

An eager aid approached him. "Captain Prembi! Something moves out there. Many hoofs. It could be a mounted force."

"Coming this way!" Prembi stood still, listening. Hearing several lovesick moos, he laughed harshly. "It's a herd of cows!"

The herd was large, though, more than a hundred beasts, and they blundered through the camp with idiot persistence. Prembi detailed a score of men to mount and disperse them.

"Drive 'em well away before they fill the camp with their turds, Salvatore. Our masters wouldn't like it."

With profane complaints, the riders herded the cattle together and forced them out to the plain. Before they knew it, other men galloped out of the darkness and were among them, striking with cudgels. Prembi's men went steadily down, to be tied like chickens for the oven. The outlaws bunched cattle and riderless horses together and turned their heads again, driving them back to Prembi's camp, in and through it, a good deal faster than their first entrance. Although Prembi's mercenaries still had the greater numbers, two to one, they were surprised afoot and trampled. Several were killed, two dozen wounded, before they cried quarter.

Valentine was among the leaders. "Throw down your weapons, and you shall live!" he shouted.

"Be damned to that!" came Teberigo's bass roar. "Let them all die! The captain's slain!"

Sforza? Dead? Valentine's first concern was to stop the raid from disintegrating into silly disaster because of this news. He countered Teberigo's roar with one even louder and more forceful.

"No killing if they yield! *No killing*! Before heaven, I'll murder with this sword the first three men who start it, and hang the rest afterwards! Ettore, Benvolio, stand by me and enforce!"

"I'm with you, sir," Benvolio said loudly.

"And I," Ettore seconded, "but let's settle quickly . . . I am wounded."

"Nay, kill them all!" Teberigo thundered. "Ignore those milksops, and avenge the Captain!"

Without hesitation, Valentine rode at him, swinging his sword. Teberigo called him a bastard, parried and slashed. Ettore rode behind Teberigo and struck him neatly down with a cudgel. The situation swayed wildly between control and chaos. Valentine and his allies found it touch and go to save their victory from disintegrating utterly. Ettore, dyed with his gore, barely had time to do his part before he fainted.

Valentine and Benvolio remained as the only functioning leaders. Blessing his experience as a soldier, Valentine had the captives rounded up and the *condottieri* pinioned. Next he identified the three captives for ransom, and had them placed under strong guard. Finally, he made sure their servants and attendants were all disarmed and safe.

"We've brought it off!" he said. "We're going to be richer for this night's work, camerados!"

"You're going to be racked to death!" the ambassador snarled. "All of you!"

"Malice is unworthy. Remember, signore, pray for them that despitefully use you . . . Moyses, are you there? Take ten men, and bring back those fellows we left on the plain, before any get free. Then attend me in the pavilion, yonder."

As he dismounted, he heard a shocked voice exclaim from among the captives, "Messire Valentine!"

Turning, he looked for the speaker. A fair-haired youth tried to duck out of sight. Valentine beckoned a torch-bearer and scanned the youngster's face.

"You know me?"

"I've seen you, sir. I too am from Verona. My name is Sebastian Liardini."

"Welcome," Valentine said, amused. "I'd be pleased to chat all night, Sebastian Liardini, but time is short and I've much to do."

He passed on. Thirty minutes later, he stood in the tent with his three main prisoners under guard, Ettore and Benvolio beside him, and Piero Sforza's body on a makeshift bier at his feet. The man was dead as Pontius Pilate; had fallen, it appeared, in the first moments of their assault on the camp.

Valentine was not aware of any shattering sorrow. Still, *dead* is a sobering, supernatural word, and he looked into Sforza's face with the chill knowledge that such might be his own fate tomorrow. Bending over the silent figure, he examined his death-wound for a moment, then crossed himself.

"I'm no soft-heart," he muttered, "but God spare him the pangs of hell."

6

For stony limits cannot hold love out:
And what love can do, that dares love attempt.
                Shakespeare, *Romeo and Juliet*, II, 2

Without armour, weapons or footgear, the *condottieri* milled together like sheep, doubting their fate. Valentine gathered their gazes to himself in the torchlight. Tall, bareheaded, fists planted on hips, he surveyed them a moment.

"Gentlemen," he said, "your wounded are having proper attention. We don't desire your lives, and except for the very best, do not even covet your horses; our own are superior. You may therefore go on to Milan. We have room in our band for ten recruits, if any of you care to join us instead. It's a good life, the world to rob. Benvolio there is the man to see if you are interested."

Valentine looked over the wounded mercenaries to be sure they were being fairly treated. One of the men salving and binding their wounds was the youth Sebastian. He worked gently, deftly, smiling and joking with his patients as he passed around.

He was pleasing to see, being clear-skinned and graceful. His yellow hair was twisted and coiled in several fantastic love-knots, and below his striped doublet a scarlet codpiece, boastfully padded, showed conspicuous in the torchlight. He moved with a bouncing strut. A dozen such green sprigs of fashion could be seen at any time in the streets of Verona. The late Tybalt had been just that kind. This Sebastian at any rate seemed good-natured, and he was doing a good job with the wounded.

He lifted his head. Valentine looked into a pair of candid grey eyes. They *were* familiar, like the level brown brows above them. Sebastian's face was rather square, with wide cheekbones and a short though delicate jaw. His forehead was somewhat out of proportion high. The sense of familiarity grew. Valentine and Tybalt had studied the art of fence with the same master as boys; might this have been some friend of Tybalt's? Or the younger brother of such a friend? But the name Liardini struck no chord at all.

"These men have cause to thank you, young sir," he said. "Would it suit you to join us in the forest?"

"The world to rob?" Sebastian smiled, but shook his head definitely. "No, sir, by your leave. I prefer to travel to Milan as I'd intended."

"As you wish."

By God, that smile was familiar, too. Scanning Sebastian's face, Valentine saw that he hadn't a whisker, not even a new one, unless that was a trick of the torchlight . . .

Then the heart slammed between his ribs. It couldn't be! It was.

"I know who you are now," he said with certainty, "and where it is I've seen you. Come to my tent when you have finished here." Sebastian looked as though he would protest. "That's a command. Georg, Perino – stay with this boy and bring him to me duly."

Sebastian turned pale. He was still pale when he came to the tent. He and Valentine were quite alone together.

"I'm amazed to see you," Valentine said frankly. "What's the cause of this masquerade? Lady Julia, have you gone mad?"

"No, sir," the disguised girl declared, "unless it be for love. I'm seeking Proteus."

"Hell!"

"Hell is where I have lived without him."

"Hell is where you will belike be plunged when you find him! You're arming scandal, courting infamy. Proteus isn't worth it."

"I thought he was your friend!"

"So, once, did I. No matter; what of you? I believed from our acquaintance in Verona you weren't so much inclined to favour Proteus's suit. I reckoned he was making himself foolish so to pursue a maid unwilling."

"Well, I was giddy then. I didn't know my own mind, sir, and also I believed I should be reticent – that it was less than seemly to receive his passion with open joy. So I blew hot and cold. It's not entirely his fault

that he left me. His father did command that he should
travel."

"Loving a lady enough to rave about it as Proteus did, I'd
resist even a father's dictum, were I bid to leave her on such
swift, arbitrary notice. Did he write letters?"

"Many, at first; then they grew few and ceased."

"You knew your own mind after he was gone?"

"Yes, when it was too late. *My* father called him shifting,
variable, not yet a constant or defined man, and wanted me
to marry someone else."

"Your sire's wise."

Julia laughed, not happily. "You should have seen the man
he chose! A drunken, gloomy fellow, twice my years, with wide
estates. If I married him I should soon be buried in a sad grave.
It's where two former wives of his have gone. Better outrage
propriety and chance great joy with Proteus."

"You formed that resolution slowly."

Valentine was determined to be cynical. Joy with Proteus
– God! It infuriated him to think of honest love being wasted
on such a traitor. He didn't deserve it. Besides, Julia was
desirable, and Valentine had lost his own sweet mistress due
to Proteus's treachery; to seduce Julia would be justice, in a
way, most fitting, sweet revenge on perjured Proteus.

"My time was not my own, sir," Julia rejoined. "My father
had me immured in a convent for forward refusal. I am not
bold by nature, no matter what you think of these my present
acts! I had to think, reflect, reach some firm resolution, then
find a way to 'scape those convent walls. My maid assisted
me. She gave advice, helped find me this disguise, and so at
last I made escape. Will you expose me?"

"Not to this company! We're surrounded by rascals who'd
consider you fair game if once they knew your sex." Valentine
smiled grimly. "I am an outlaw brigand now, myself, by force
of circumstance. It fits me to behave as one."

Julia took his meaning. Her grey eyes widened. "To me?"

Valentine folded his arms, deeply tempted. Forcing himself
to speak normally, he said, "Such risks go with leaving your
father's authority, the ward of law, and all usual standards of
woman's behaviour, Lady Julia. It's lucky we're not strangers,

and that I used to be a gentleman. Tell me, what brings you here? Why travel in particular to Milan?"

"A rumour came to me that Proteus is there."

The devil damn all honesty! Here goes my chance to turn her to my arms for desperate solace.

"I can assure it's more than airy rumour. He is there."

Julia seized his hand and kissed it.

For that cur! Valentine thought savagely. *Corpo di Cristo! You lovestruck unfortunate!*

"I'd heard as much. Bless you for telling me! I see you did not wish to. Noble Valentine, do not be cruel. Are you certain sure?"

"Most certain sure. I wish I weren't. Like an idiot, I recommended him to the Duke's grace, and now he's well in favour. We parted – just three weeks ago."

"Tell me," Julia said, lips dry.

"Proteus is well in favour at my expense. I love Silvia, the Duke's daughter. She returned my love and meant to run away with me. Our plans were set. Proteus betrayed us to the Duke and caused that scheme to fail completely. His reason? He's conceived a sudden love for Silvia himself."

"No! Oh, no! How could he? Such treachery to you, when once you were like brothers! I thought his love sincere, his thoughts immaculate! Valentine, say you've lied, and I'll forgive you."

"I have no means to prove it to you here. Take my advice; remain a boy, hide your woman's breasts inside a doublet still, and wear that codpiece . . . be Sebastian. Let Proteus think you male until you know how true my warnings are. Choose your course then."

"Impossible! Sir Valentine, *you* recognized me. What makes you think that Proteus won't?"

"He won't wish to. He's courting Silvia. Julia's presence would be inconvenient. Lady, when he came to Milan, he even told me you had died of fevers. Maybe he heard some insubstantial story you were ill – "

"I was, the winter before last."

"– and swift enlarged it in his fancy to your funeral. He was my friend. Like you, I thought him faithful, true of heart and mind. I know better now. He's shallow, false, and can believe whate'er he wishes to believe."

"No more." Tears were welling swiftly in Julia's eyes. "I'll proceed to Milan. I must. For now, though, sir, no more."

"No more, indeed. I've work to do. My robber comrades' lives and mine depend on it. I'm sorry, Lady Julia. It makes harsh news to hear, yet I could not but speak it."

She nodded, and fled. Valentine stood cursing himself. He should have lied, talked her out of Italy and seduced her there on the ground. Too late now. Well, perhaps it was for the best. God knew he did have work to do. Why did such a distraction have to come at such a time?

He poured a goblet of wine, swilled it, and banged down the cup. There was business to settle, of another order, but he couldn't settle it tonight. They had to return to the forest with their three captives and any mercenaries who decided to turn outlaw. After that, a few hours' sleep was called for, whether he felt like it or not, to restore his strength, and then – a reckoning with a certain dirty Judas who must think he was safe.

Valentine knew his identity now.

7

Say ay, and be the captain of us all.
We'll do thee homage, and be rul'd by thee,
Love thee as our commander, and our king.
Shakespeare, *Two Gentlemen of Verona*, IV, 1

The cork oaks and cypresses of the forest shadowed forty desperate men. The thirty outlaws Valentine had joined were now increased by ten disgruntled mercenaries, who had to be assimilated, taught to follow one man's orders and respect him – disciplined, in short. Now of all times it was not to be tolerated that the band should lack cohesion.

"We need a new commander," Benvolio said. "There's our old one, in his shroud. Whoever shall replace him must be brave, swift, cunning, someone we all trust. One who can plan and lead, or we are lost. I maintain there are only two with us who meet these stern requirements. Ettore and Valentine."

"Why, thanks," Teberigo laughed. "And what of me? I've been second in command among you half a year! Who says me nay?"

"I do." Valentine stepped forward. "Not because I seek the captaincy so much, but to discharge the task that Captain Sforza gave me. You all know what it was. To find the traitor in our midst. I know him now. The traitor murdered Captain Sforza yesternight, to earn his thirty pieces from his master, Francesco Maria, Duke of Milan."

"What tale's this?" demanded Teberigo. "Piero died in the first onslaught, by a mercenary's sword."

"Look at his wound!" Striding to the shrouded figure, Valentine drew back the winding-sheet dramatically. This must be carried off with dash. Right or wrong, let him display the slightest doubt or hesitation, and he would fail. Boldness, audacity, be his watchwords now.

"That's not a death-blow!" he continued, swinging round upon his audience. "Ettore was worse hurt, and he's still with us, fit for mischief later. This thrust into the groin, e'en if it did prove mortal, would not kill a man of Sforza's strength as quickly as he died."

"There is no other wound upon him, Valentine," Benvolio said, puzzled.

"One. This scratch upon his cheek. Look at its swollen, greenish edges, and tell me it's not poison."

"I don't know." Benvolio examined the inch-long rip. "He's been dead for hours. It could be due to that. We are not doctors or apothecaries."

"Aye, right you are!" Teberigo seized on that at once. "Poisoned? Who poisoned him?" He flung the words like a challenge. "He was healthy as a horse when he rode against Prembi's company last night. Healthy until he fell from an honest sword-cut!"

"You were beside him," Valentine said coldly. "You picked him up. You, brave and devoted, held off his attackers while the fight raged all around you. He would have lived. But one envenomed scratch from you made sure he died."

Teberigo cursed vilely. "I'll kill you for that lie. Draw!"

"In good time. Before we fight, I want the band to hear and judge. I think I can show proof."

"Proof!" Teberigo spat. "Why, you'd remove a rival for the captaincy! That's all your motive, bastard!"

"If the band desires, I'll stand down in favour of Ettore. But first I will be heard!" Valentine made his voice bite like a scourge. "The night before we rode, you left our camp and went towards Lake Garda."

Teberigo snorted. "Everyone knows that! I have a girl lives on a farm that way."

"A comely, useful pretext. I know it's where you went. I followed you. As you returned, you left a message in a hiding place where, I dare say, an agent of Milan comes to collect it. I have it here." From his wallet Valentine produced a folded sheet. "It says the perfect opportunity has come at last. You'll see that Sforza falls in his next action. As you did."

"Be damned! I don't know what the paper is! What if it does say what you claim? I never wrote it!"

"It's not signed with your name," Valentine conceded. "You wouldn't write it in your usual hand, either, I think, unless you're a complete fool."

"I say again, I never wrote it, not in my usual hand, nor any other! You have accused me falsely, and you'll pay."

Valentine pointed at Teberigo's belt. "The proof's with you. Sforza died of a little poisoned cut. The poison, I believe, is on your dagger-tip. We'll soon discover."

Teberigo stood still for a moment. Then a sneer of utter contempt crossed his face. Drawing his dagger, he pulled open his jacket and cut himself on the chest, nearest his heart. Blood trickled down.

"Witness, all of you, I use the point, that's steeped in fatal poison. Well! Can you believe it? I'm alive!" He turned a savage face on Valentine. "Now, shall we fight?"

Tossing the dagger to his left hand, he unsheathed his sword. Valentine drew his own sword and dagger. If he was dismayed, his face did not express it.

They both threw off their doublets, moving to the attack in linen shirts, the sunlight sprinkling through the leaves on white cloth and dazzling steel. Within a minute, Valentine knew he had hard work before him. His adversary had studied the modern art of fencing, too. It was thrust, parry, riposte, thrust again and remise, intensely fast, feet moving deftly in the grass and fallen leaves.

Valentine knew surely now that Teberigo was not what he pretended. This novel, jewel-precise skill was not something a thick bully would care to master. He attacked with force, using all the strength of heavy shoulders and massive legs, yet that power, channeled through the big-boned wrists and hairy, graceless fingers, directed his blades with skill precise as a surgeon's. Withal, he hid this skill from everyone but Valentine. To those watching, he made his swordplay *look* like a crude, swashing ruffler's.

He stayed consistent even when the other moved to the attack, pressing him hard. Maybe, Valentine thought, he had been mistaken about poison on the dagger, but not anything else. This *was* a crafty master dissembler he faced. He wasn't slipping from his assumed character, even under such deadly pressure. Actor . . . professional secret agent . . . assassin.

He fought faster, to meet Valentine's attack. Too fast. Lunging, with his point nearly level, he felt it beaten out of line. Valentine disengaged. His dagger grated on Teberigo's longer blade, while his sword twisted the big man's dagger free, to spin across the grass. Valentine drove his sword for the belly. Teberigo dropped low on the flat of his left hand, thrust neatly in return, and Valentine leaped backward while making a clumsy, desperate parry. Teberigo's edge drew blood from his hip. He scrambled to regain his dagger, but Valentine was before him. Teberigo faced him armed with sword alone.

Valentine's eyes narrowed. What was he up to? Surely he could have regained his dagger then. There was some trick. Teberigo defended, sword chiming, left hand raised shoulder-high, three huge garish rings flashing there.

Oh, Bacchus, the *rings*!

He wasn't defenceless after all. But he wished to seem so.

Teberigo retreated. Body to body fighting meant his finish now. The watchers all knew it. He parried, thrust, and stepped back, seeking a way past Valentine's guard. On his upraised left hand, the thumb moved across to press the side of a cabochon ring. Again, Valentine moved closer.

Teberigo allowed it. He parried, kicked at the younger man's knee so that he staggered, then swung a savage backhand smash at Valentine's face. Valentine, of course, would stab with his dagger . . .

He did not.

His sword came up in a blaze of light. Teberigo's empty, ringed left hand flew from the end of his arm, to follow his dagger into the leaves. Staring in disbelief, the assassin scarcely felt the thrust that ran him through from side to side, not even when he fell and perished.

Valentine, despite his soldier's service, was not a widely experienced killer. Pale, feeling giddy, no longer at peace with his last meal, he stood oblivious to the outlaws' praise. He needed a moment to master his gorge. Then he bent down and grasped the severed hand.

"The poison was not on his dagger-tip," he said hoarsely. "I was mistaken . . . it is here. This little, tainted spike that slides out of the cabochon. It scratched the Captain to death. He meant the same for me, but it had gone unnoticed, the way his three rings would have gouged my cheek. Examine it, my mates, but be careful."

"Venom, indeed," Benvolio said. "And this one beside it opens on a hinge. Traces of powder here, to be given in food or drink, I hazard."

"Maybe the Captain's sickness after eating *was* from poison," put in Raoul.

"Maybe." Valentine walked away from the corpse, trying to seem casual about it. "If so, the dose was insufficient, or the poison stale. That must have disappointed Teberigo. He'd taken so much trouble to become the Captain's bedfellow, and wished so badly to slay without suspicion. We are well rid of him."

The evidence of the poison rings convinced them all.

"Valentine for captain!" Christopher yelled.

Half a dozen voices echoed him. In the next breath twenty,

and then forty, raised the same cry. Benvolio clasped Valentine's hand. Raoul and Stefan clapped him on the back. The election was unanimous.

Valentine almost said, *the devil take your captaincy*. But only almost.

Epilogue

Who shall confirm my words with further deeds.
Marlowe, *Dido, Queen of Carthage*, I, 2.

Under the cliffs at the north end of Lake Garda lay a cave. Entered by twisting ways hard to negotiate, it held the outlaws' treasure. Velvet, satin, brocade and linen was there, a suit of gilded, inlaid armour, a chest of silver plate and vessels, a casket filled with gems and another crammed with gold.

"We'll quadruple this with our captives' ransoms," Valentine remarked, deeply satisfied. "That banker alone is worth it; the House of the Gorgon covers Europe."

"And has its name because kings turn to stone when it looks unpleasantly on them." Benvolio shook his head. "We must be cunning and cautious."

"We shall be. Friend, I'm glad you showed me this."

Pensive, he looked around, seeing the long cave's curtains of fretted stone, the limestone chandeliers and stalagmites, the disks of pale oolite that had grown for ages across a black pool's surface. Somehow it set things in proportion.

He thought of Julia, now, no doubt, safe in Milan. He remembered saying to her, "I've cherished dreams of being avenged on Proteus."

"I beg that you'll relinquish them for my sake."

"Relinquish?" Valentine had said incredulously. "I would be married to Silvia now, lady, and safely in Illyria if no other land would welcome us! Instead I'm thieving in the forest, and lucky to 'scape breaking on the wheel! These are grievous wrongs to overlook from one I held dear as a brother."

"I believe you are noble enough to forgive. Your conduct towards me shows it." Valentine had smiled crookedly. "Sir, if you slay Proteus, you slay my heart."

"God knows how men who ill deserve it gain the love of women such as you."

"His passion for the Lady Silvia, since it arose so suddenly, may be mere wilful fancy. May it not? I hope to win his heart again to me. Please. Let me try. Don't seek his life."

Valentine had faced her, struggling to control his anger. At last he said, "I wouldn't have you think that you must wed so poor a creature, to spare him swording. His life is safe from me. Take him or leave him, as you list."

"Sir Valentine, I thank you. May I take a message to your Silvia, to let her knew that you are safe, and that your heart's yet in her keeping?"

"No," he snapped. "Concern yourself with Proteus. Acting the go-between for me and Silvia would be too dangerous for you. I'll find some way to get word to her if I wish. Meanwhile, my course is to ensure that I can keep her like a duke's daughter, when she's mine."

"Will she feel proud that it was done by robbery?"

"The rule of states is mostly won in worse ways. No one complains of it in dukes and princes. Horace, lady, gave sound advice. *Si possis recte, si non, quocumque modo rem.*"*

It sounded glib and specious to him now, as he looked around the treasure cave once more prior to leaving. Silvia was a woman of upright character. She'd understand, though, surely. He'd first joined Sforza's band because they would have slain him otherwise. Now Sforza was slain, and Fate had all but thrust the role of outlaw king upon Valentine. He'd be pusillanimous to refuse it, and the chance it offered.

By Bacchus, he had earned it.

---

* If possible honestly, if not, somehow make money.

THE SHREWD TAMING
OF LORD THOMAS

Mary Monica Pulver

The Taming of the Shrew *is an early play, first performed around 1594 or possibly earlier. Many forget that it is actually two plays. The part that most of us remember, about how Petruchio seeks to woo and win the bad-tempered Katharina, is a play within a play. The frame within which it happens is more relevant to the following story. At the start of the play Christopher Sly, a tinker, falls drunkenly asleep and is taken in by a lord who is interested in seeing how a beggar would react if he were to wake up and discover himself living and dressed as a lord. Would the saying "clothes maketh the man" have any truth? But such a trick might rebound, and in so doing reveal a darker plot. That's the thread that Mary Monica Pulver now unravels.*

"Touch me and I'll do you!" growled Christopher Sly, staggering out of the mean little inn. It was still daylight; the beggar blinked into the sun's lowering red circle.

"I'll have you in the stocks, rogue!" shouted the innkeeper

– but from his doorway, not following Sly into the street. The beggar was a brawny sort.

Big with success – Sly had broken several glasses and was apparently not to be punished for it – he began to sing.

> *There were three ravens sat on a tree*
> *Down-a-down, hey down, hey down!*
> *There were three ravens sat on a tree,*
> *They were as black as they could be!*
> *With a down derry, derry, derry, derry, derry –*

He paused to count clumsily on his fingers. Was that too many derries? He tried again.

"*With a down derry, derry, derry, derry, down, down, down!*"

A suggestible fellow, Sly noticed a clean flat stone in front of a doorway and sat down on it. Was that still too many derries?

"*With a down derry, down derry, down derry, down!*"

He nodded. That was right, or nearly so.

But something about all those down, down, downs tempted him to put his own head down. Not in a state to resist temptation, he shifted back into the doorway and put his tangle-haired head tenderly to rest on the flat stone. He felt sleep overcoming him, but that was all right: it was only October, a man would not freeze to death in October with a belly full of stout English ale. "*Down, down . . . down a . . . down . . .*" Between one down and the next he was unconscious.

A ta-ta-tarooo of a horn sounded, and a pack of yelping black and tan hounds galloped down the street, followed by a plump little man in well-made but sweat-stained russet. By the fur trim on his doublet and the excellent quality of his boots, the man was a lord. Running to catch up and then pass his master was a huntsman in forest green. He was blowing the horn, a small one of bright silver.

The hounds, a pack of about a dozen, trotted noses down, tongues lolling. The lead hound's mouth was foaming from running and baying – it was the end of a long day in field and forest.

"Huntsman, see to Merriman, the poor cur is embossed," said the Lord Thomas Basset.

"I will, my lord." A tall, leggy man with large hands and a rawboned face that showed few of his thoughts, the huntsman ran to the front of the pack and took Merriman by his broad, studded collar, pulling a rag from his belt to wipe the dog's mouth. He tucked the rag away and stroked the dog's face, causing it to bound upwards and lick the huntsman's chin.

The lord stood admiring his hounds, who still trotted in circles, hunting even in town for the scent of game. "Harry, did you see how Silver picked up the scent at the corner of the hedge? I wouldn't sell him for twenty pounds!"

"Bellman is as good as Silver," grunted the huntsman, reaching for a deep-voiced dog who had come to collect a stroke of his own. "He twice picked up a scent the others couldn't find." He added, more softly, for his lord did not like to be disagreed with, "In fact, he is the better dog." He stroked Silver some more, and the hound wriggled with pleasure.

"He's swifter, that's all. Why if Echo were as fleet as Bellman, I'd trade a dozen of Bellman for another Echo. But take them all in and feed them. Check their feet and see their straw is deep and clean. I'll hunt again tomorrow – But hold, what's this? A dead man?"

The huntsman looked, and immediately waded knee-deep through the dogs to a form huddled in the doorway. "Nay, he breathes. What a stink! It's old Christopher Sly, the beggar, filthy as usual. But he's had a few pence, for it's ale that makes him sleep as soundly as if he were in a warm bed." The huntsman began to poke at the beggar, who did not stir. "Up, man! Up, begone!"

Lord Thomas came closer, a grin on his face the huntsman recognized with a sinking heart. "He thinks a cold doorway is a warm bed, does he? What then would he think if he were to wake and find himself indeed in a warm bed? A very fine bed, a *lord's* bed? And with rings on his fingers, and handsomely dressed servants to wait upon him? Would not he forget he is a beggar and think perhaps he was a lord?"

The huntsman forced a smile. "I think he would have no choice."

Lord Thomas laughed aloud. "Some believe clothes make the man, but I would set that notion to the proof! Summon my servants. We'll get them to carry him into my house, into my best chamber." He bent over the limp beggar, and his own nose wrinkled. "How like a swine he is! Tell them to wash that foul head and body before they dress him in silk." He straightened. "We'll have musicians for him when he wakes, and something delicious to eat. We'll have my servants address him in their most humble way. Oh, and a wife, he must have a wife!" Lord Thomas laughed again and rubbed his hands together, thinking out loud. "I'll get my ward Bartholomew. He's beardless yet; and did you see him the last time? He plays a very amusing lady. But no laughter from anyone, and he must appear to weep because her lord husband has been lunatic these seven years. When this Christopher protests he's a beggar, everyone must say it was his mad fancy. Ha, ha, this will be the best prank I have ever played! If everyone does his part properly, the beggar will be convinced, and not know this is a jest until I am ready to release him."

The huntsman bowed low, glad his part would be small, if any. Lord Thomas's pranks could be time-consuming, yet he did not want his servants to neglect their regular tasks. "I'm sure you will instruct them most carefully, my lord. He will believe he is no less than a lord until you tell him otherwise. With your permission, I will take the dogs to their kennels."

Lord Thomas stood awhile, staring at the unconscious beggar, amused at the thought of this simpleton faced with the conundrum of knowing he was a beggar while everyone around him told him he was a lord. And of course it would be a prank of sorts on poor Bartholomew as well, having to preen around again in women's skirts. Of all the many tricks Lord Thomas had played – and he was a notable trickster – this had every promise of being one of the merriest. He turned suddenly, impatient for the game to begin, and strode to his house to complete his preparations.

He woke the next morning under a beech tree in a meadow. By the sun it was hours past his usual rising time; the dew was already nearly off the grass. His head ached past bearing, and he groaned aloud. What had he been doing last?

Memories began to come. The prank with the beggar had been less merry than he'd hoped. The fellow had complained that it was a pity a lord in his own house couldn't get a nice cup of ale when he wanted it, but only sack, which had been amusing only the first five or six times. Bartholomew had played his role extremely well early on, then pretended to have some woman's complaint and vanished into "her" chamber. The group of players staying at Lord Thomas's house had put on an alleged comedy that was mostly noise and people pretending to be other than they were. The beggar hadn't liked it, nor had Lord Thomas, for reasons of his own.

Later, the beggar had shown signs of being a raucous, fall-down drunkard, so Lord Thomas had decided to go that way with his game, matching the beggar cup for cup and tempting him into comedic displays of ignorance.

And then . . . what?

The memory collapsed into a jumble of roistering which in the cool light of morning didn't seem very mirthful. And now Thomas was out of doors and Christopher Sly – Lord Thomas hastily looked around – was gone, thank heaven. Probably they had brought the beggar out to the road to hurry him on his way, and afterwards somehow Lord Thomas ended up going around his house instead of back into it, for now he recognized the tree and the meadow, just a little beyond his own cow byre.

But it still didn't make sense. Why hadn't one of his servants seen him safely back indoors? It wasn't as if this were the first time he'd been helpless with drink. What had been the matter with them?

He heard his dogs barking in their kennel, wondering where he was, why he had not come to lead them to the hunt. He rolled to his feet – he was nimble, as a short, stout man often is. His head roared as if he were

near a waterfall. He groaned and bent forward, prepared
to vomit.

But the impulse died when he saw he was dressed in old,
mismatched shoes and hose – wool on one leg and linen on
the other, and more holes than cloth. He wore something
unidentifiable in shape or color over his body. A ragged
patchwork that was meant to be a cloak swung clumsily to
the front of his neck.

The beggar's clothing.

A wordless cry of anger escaped his lips. What nonsense
was this?

He looked across the meadow, toward the back of his
house. He saw a milkmaid strolling from the barn toward his
back door, and other servants about their business. A weak,
early-autumn sun twinkled down on the roofs of his house, his
barn and sheds, his byre, his kennels, his stables. Smoke came
from the kitchen chimney. Suddenly he wanted to be within,
shouting for hot water so he could wash and dress, chaffing
Bartholomew about what a good wife he made, conferring
with his huntsman to see if they could still get into the fields,
scolding his valet for not seeing him to bed last night.

And maybe this evening, he thought as he strode toward
his house, he'd ask if anyone could tell him how he came to
be dressed in the beggar's clothing. What, had someone let
the fellow get away in the fine clothing they'd dressed him
in? Lord Thomas's mouth tightened, and the back of his neck
swelled. He took pride in his clothing and didn't like the idea
of it wandering off, especially on some dirty beggar's back.
A scolding wasn't enough; he minded to skin alive whoever
hadn't stopped him trading clothing – and also whoever had
let him sleep outdoors last night, by God's nails!

The milkmaid saw his approach and shouted a warning
towards the house. To his surprise, his ward Bartholomew
came out clothed as a steward, even to the highly polished
silver badge. In his hands he carried the thick staff Lord
Thomas had himself put into the hands of his own steward,
Nicholas Twosome.

Bartholomew brandished the staff in Lord Thomas's direction. "Be gone, beggar! We've nothing here for you! My master

pays his honest tithes to the church. Go bother the priest and leave us be!"

"What are you about, Bartholomew?" growled Lord Thomas. "Have you lost your senses? Use your eyes, 'tis I."

"I can see who you are, beggar. Who is Bartholomew?"

Thomas had never noticed before how tall Bartholomew had grown, and as Thomas continued his approach, Bartholomew waved the staff briskly.

Thomas said, "Fool, *you* are Bartholomew. Where is my true steward, Nicholas Twosome? Stand aside, let me into my house!"

"*Your* house?" crowed Bartholomew. "Listen to the fellow! A beggar dripping fleas and filth claims a lord's house! Sure as my name is *not* Bartholomew, nor is the steward of this place Nicholas One-some, Twosome, OR Three-some, this is not your house! Begone, before I give you the beating you deserve!"

There was jeering and sauciness from the onlookers, which enraged Lord Thomas. "Not Bartholomew? You are, and I'll make you sorry of it!"

"Ooooh, it sounds like a lord, all right," remarked another maid, whose open-work basket cooed against her skirts. Some in the neighborhood were angry with Lord Thomas because he had enlarged his dovecote – doves and pigeons ate grain right from the fields – but he outranked those who complained, and he was fond of pigeon pie. In fact, he had ordered it for his dinner.

The cowherd standing beside her sniggered.

Lord Thomas whirled on the two. "You're both dismissed!" he hissed. "Would it were winter, so turning you out would freeze your toes off!"

The maid with the pigeon basket looked skyward in an elaborate pantomime of not caring a button for his words. And Bartholomew laughed out loud.

Lord Thomas felt he would swoon with fury. He whirled and, as had happened to him before, he fell into sputtering. "You – you fool! Ruffian! You – you – you – bad, bad, bad – Have your eyes, guts, *head*!"

"He apes his betters in temper," remarked the maid with the basket, judiciously.

"But like the ape, he gibbers rather than speaks in sentences," replied Bartholomew.

At this, Lord Thomas lost his ability to speak altogether. He rushed at his ward, fists raised, and to his astonishment the fellow clouted him with the staff. Lord Thomas had not been struck since he grew out of childhood.

"Now go, before I strike again!" ordered Bartholomew brusquely, and raised the stick.

Lord Thomas scrambled backwards, not willing to see if the man would carry out his threat. He began reluctantly to go around the side of the house. The steward followed until Thomas had gone right around to the front and seemed headed for the street that led into town before, with a final brandish, he went away.

But then, with no watching eyes, Thomas slipped away to hide in the hayloft of his barn. He scratched his flea bites and tried to comprehend what had happened to him.

As his temper cooled, it occurred to him what he meant to say. "You, Bartholomew Stratford, are the basest knave I ever took in wardship! You peasant malt-house drudge! You whoreson, full of monstrous arrogance! Unconstant beetle-headed rascal, that would rob me of what is mine! I'll have your head set on a pole!"

That's what he should have said, and then he *and* that maid and cowherd would have been ashamed and humbled themselves, but would he have forgiven them? *No!* He tried to thump his fist, but lying half buried in hay all he did was stir up some dust, which made him sneeze thrice.

Which for some reason cooled his temper, and allowed him to more calmly try to reason out, first of all, why they were doing this to him. And why did they think they could succeed in stealing his land? Everyone knew who he was. Why, he had only to call on Sheriff Sir William Naps – no, hold a bit. Sir William was taking Lord Kevin's part over a prank involving a cross-eyed yeoman's wife Lord Thomas had hired to pretend to be Lord Kevin's leman, and further to say her idiot child was Lord Kevin's bastard. Lord Kevin was angry, because his daughter's prospective father-in-law had been at his house when the yeoman's wife came in. Well, how was Lord Thomas to know that? Still, Sir William had only to consider that this might be some kind of retaliatory hoodwinking . . .

Hmmm.

But Lord Kevin was up near the Scottish border.

Then played by whom? There were a number of people angry with him, Thomas admitted after a minute's thought, mostly because of jests he had played. But who among his victims was capable of persuading Thomas's steward to relinquish his staff and his badge of office?

Because Thomas had never found his steward to be anything but loyal and trustworthy.

Of course, Thomas's nephew and heir Henry Pimpernell had often warned him that he put too much trust in his steward, that he might be a thief or worse. And it was true that Thomas never paid much attention to the running of this place. It was enough that there was money to buy the new horse or new dog or new apparel whenever he wanted it, and plenty of good food to eat and good sack to drink.

At the thought of something to drink, he licked his lips and swallowed. His mouth felt lined with old wool, not uncommon when he had overindulged in drink. But first things first – and first he had to plumb the mystery of what had happened.

Perhaps Thomas had been wrong about Twosome; perhaps Bartholomew had persuaded his steward to take the manor from Thomas. But why? What grievance had Bartholomew? And was Twosome also unhappy, that he agreed to the robbery?

Thomas felt his temper begin to rise again at this notion of two who should be loyal collaborating against him. Before he could think more upon the why of it, he rose to stamp around a bit, waving his arms and kicking heaps of hay out of the loft. Unfaithful servant! Wicked ward!

"Who's up there?" came an angry voice.

Thomas froze in place. Was that Bartholomew? He didn't want to be smacked on the head again. It was hard to control his furious breathing, however; and every little movement toward a hiding place made the hay whisper in betrayal. He heard footsteps on the ladder coming up into the loft. He hastily backed behind a great heap of hay.

But of course in the open loft he was quickly found. Fortunately, it wasn't Bartholomew. Unfortunately, it was the brawniest fieldsman on his manor. Worse, he was carrying a pitchfork. Worst of all, Thomas could not remember his name. There was no way he could convince him he was master of this place.

"What are you doing up here?" demanded the laborer.

Rather to his surprise, but helpless against it, Thomas felt his voice rise to a whine. "I was just – cold – need to think – no harm!"

"Get out! Out w' ye, ye filthy old beggar!"

"I'm going, I'm going!" Thomas edged in as big a circle as the loft allowed around the angry man and his weapon, and hustled down the ladder. This time he left the manor and slunk into town. He wandered around awhile, trying to think what to do next.

Peculiar how just wearing the clothes of a beggar made one feel like a beggar. When Mistress Reedwell – to whom he had often given a friendly, condescending nod – gave him a hard look, he cringed.

This would never do. He needed a bath, a change of clothes, something to eat and drink, to restore the man. He was hollow as a bell, but even more thirsty. His tongue had gone from feeling like dry wool to feeling as if it were made of wood. If there had been a puddle in the street he would have lapped from it like a dog. So something for the inner man first.

But how?

Come, come, he told himself. You're a prankster, or so everyone says. Including yourself. There was an inn right across the way. There were always a few idlers about an inn, men who thought themselves sharp. But there were few so sharp as Thomas. Why only last month, he'd gulled an innkeeper out of a night's lodging. With a sly smile, Thomas went in.

"Hi, there!" shouted the innkeeper the moment he was inside. "What are you doing in here, you nasty old beggar!

Where's your money? Haven't a penny, have you? I won't have your sort in here bothering decent folk!" He came toward Thomas, hands curled into fists.

"Puh, pie, peace, innkeeper," Thomas implored, raising both hands, surprised at how his dry tongue tangled his speech.

But the man kept coming, and Thomas fled. Out the door and down the street he ran, overcoming the handicap of the mismatched shoes, feeling the rents in his stockings widening, and a chill breeze burrowing under the flapping cloak. He ducked into an alley between two houses, and ran to the end of it, then up another, narrower alley, where he found a deep doorway and collapsed into it. He drew the cloak close around him as if it would hide him from pursuers.

Who did not come.

When he got his breath back, he puzzled a bit. Why did everyone agree he was a beggar? This was beyond hoodwinking. Was it possible the beggar he'd played the prank on was not whom he had seemed? No, his huntsman had named him as Christopher Sly, before Thomas had decided to bring him home and dress him up as a lord.

And try to convince him he truly was a lord.

Had he driven him mad? So that now he thought, even dressed again in rags, that he was a lord? That he belonged in that beautiful manor house and owned those fine hunting dogs and played uproarious pranks on everyone in the neighborhood? When actually he was a low, mean beggar, who deserved to be kicked by everyone?

He tried to remember being a beggar in the summer, or back in the spring, sleeping out in flower-scented fields, stealing apples – and couldn't.

He tried to remember growing up in that manor house, and recalled his older brother, so tall and fine, who rode out with Father to collect rents or, one glorious time, to rid the neighborhood of the last of the wild pigs that came digging up a tenant's garden. They had brought home the still-sneering head of the old boar and he could remember trying his finger on the animal's curving tusks and admiring his brother's courage for going into the bushes against so fierce a creature. His brother had died in London the following year during a minor outbreak of plague, and his father had followed him a few months later, leaving Thomas in possession.

Was that but a story he'd heard around an evening fire in some grubby inn? Then why did his finger remember the feel of that boar's tusk, and why did his eyes recall the mud that fell in cakes from the boots his brother took off with a tired sigh?

His stomach growled at him. He grimaced, and felt his lips crack when they tightened.

Why, if he was a lord and this some sort of bad dream, did his lips hurt as if they were cracking from thirst?

No, he *was* Lord Thomas, a nobleman of considerable property, who lived in that lovely brick and timber house on the edge of town, who owned a pack of bell-voiced hounds and was known for his pranks.

But how to prove it?

That was going to take heavier thought. And it was impossible to think clearly at all when one was hungry and thirsty.

He went back to the main street of the town and sat himself down with his back to a wall. He had no hat and was ashamed of his filthy hands, and so made a pouch of a corner of his cloak and held it out to passers-by, at first wordlessly, then with a whine for mercy for a poor man who hadn't eaten since yesterday.

He looked up the street where another beggar was standing, hands upraised, head ducked shyly. He said something to a man who had passed Thomas by without even looking, and the man stopped. There was a brief exchange, and the man dropped a coin – something bigger than a penny, Thomas thought – into the beggar's upraised hands. The beggar's bow was so humble it was almost a crouch and the man went his way.

Thomas frowned. He had often tossed a coin to a beggar, but indifferently, without listening to why this one or that caught his eye. So he could not understand why that beggar had got a groat while he had got nothing.

He sidled up the street, staying near the buildings, to see

if he could overhear the beggar's plaint. When he got close
enough, he saw, with a start, that the beggar was Christopher
Sly. He was not dressed in the beautiful clothing Thomas had
put him into yesterday, but in something worn and faded – if
not quite so ragged as what Thomas had on.

Thomas did not say anything, but kept his distance and
watched. Soon a well-dressed yeoman carrying a rake came
up the street. Thomas slipped closer as Christopher began
to speak.

"A penny for a poor man, please you sir."

The yeoman jeered, "I'd sooner see a goose go barefoot
than a beggar weep," and paused to laugh at his own wit.

"Be liberal in thy lifetime, that thy name may shine before
men," whined Christopher.

"Better silent than saucy, beggar!" retorted the man, taking
a step or two on his way.

"Who is bold is favored by fortune," said Christopher
quickly. The yeoman turned back.

"As gold is tried in the furnace, so man by tribulation,"
said the yeoman, putting down his rake to lean on it. A man
on horseback pulled up to listen.

"Full belly believes none are empty." This came easily, but
Christopher was beginning to look desperate.

But the yeoman couldn't think of another proverb in retort,
either. "Aye, that's true enough," he said after some thought,
reaching for his pouch. "No man limps because another is
hurt." He reached in for a coin.

"Thank 'e, kind sir!" cried Christopher, catching it deftly
when it was tossed, and then tugging his forelock. "God bless
'e, sir!"

Thomas stepped up to Christopher. "Remember me,
Christopher Sly?" he said in his most noble tone of voice.

Christopher whirled, arms upraised defensively. Then he
looked between his elbows and saw what Thomas was
wearing. And he began to laugh. He laughed so hard
and long he had to lean against the building to support
himself, and then he laughed some more. Thomas would
have knocked him down, but he needed to learn what the
beggar could tell him.

When at last Christopher was able to control himself enough to wipe his eyes, Thomas said in a low voice, "You will take me to an inn, and you will buy me ale and bread enough to ease my pain, and then we shall talk."

That finished the beggar's good humor. "Yes, my lord, except we need to go up the street, as the innkeeper across the way won't allow beggars in his house." Thomas nodded condescendingly and did not see Christopher hide a smirk.

In a little while, sitting across a small table in a dark, mean inn, over cups of watery ale and bread that tasted of sawdust, Thomas demanded, "Tell me what part you played in all this!"

"All what, my lord? Or are you no longer my lord, but only a common beggar of this parish?"

He would have begun to laugh again, except Thomas grabbed him by the front of his patched but clean doublet and growled, "What happened to the fine clothing you were last wearing?"

Christopher whined, "They sent me out of the house so swift as they arrived, and dressed as I was. I was glad to be out of there alive. I sold your stuff, o' course, an' bought this. Wouldn't do for a beggar to be dressed so fine, who'd believe he was a beggar? I didn't get what it was worth, o' course, because I couldn't prove I come by it honest, but I got this and don't need to beg at all this week beside, except to keep me hand in."

"*Who* sent you out of my house?"

Christopher had to think. "I was a bit in me cups, but it was two lords I don't think I'd seen before. It was that fellow with the badge did the actual pushin'. Got a name like a number."

"Twosome?"

"Aye, that's him. You was – er, well, you'd had a long day, huntin' an' all, so you was lyin' on a bench with a book for a pillow an' you never stirred once when they come in shoutin'."

"Who?"

"I told you, sir, them two lords."

"What did they look like?"

Christopher had to think some more. "One was young, hardly more than a boy you'd think, except he was so tall, dressed very fine. And the other was not so many in years as your lordship, but all grown, and dressed even finer. Had a big brown beard and a way about him that made all the servants bow down to him."

"What were their names?"

Christopher thought, then shrugged. "I don't remember. The younger one seemed to know me and was not pleased to see me there, and the older one had his hand on his sword in an angry way. I was glad when all they wanted of me was to begone, so I up and went. They didn't give me my own clothes, and I didn't pause to ask for 'em." His eyes wandered up and down Thomas, but he kept his smirk to himself.

Thomas said, "Did Nicholas Twosome invite them in?"

"They come in without anyone's inviting, but Master Twosome was very polite to them; it was like he knew them, especially the young 'un. Or expected them, maybe."

Thomas ground his teeth. His nephew was right, he should not have trusted everything to his steward! This man betrayed him, helped a stranger take over his house, his property! He would go to his nephew, he would go to law, he would see them in the dock, he would have them hanged!

He stood and threw over the table, sending Christopher tumbling backward into the muck of the dirt floor. "Traitor!" he shouted. Almost gratefully he fell into a rage. "That ignorant beast – *cheat* – flap-eared thief – jolthead – sirrah – " Even these attempts at coherence failed and he lapsed into choking, angry noises.

A sharp, short roar brought his attention around.

Coming out of the darkest corner of the inn was a large dog with large, sharp teeth. Shouting and pointing to encourage it was the innkeeper, who wanted Thomas out before he did more damage.

Years of chasing after his own dogs lent the strength to Thomas's legs to get out of the inn door ahead of this dog, and stay ahead of it down the street, past the corner where he'd begged, and past the other, better inn. But only terror let him continue full speed past Mistress Reedwell's house, past the church, and along the brick wall that his father had built when the town stretched its limits to within a few yards of the manor.

Breathless with running, beyond thought, he sought the safety of home ground. The gate to the forecourt was never locked. He pushed it open and in one motion was inside, turned around, and pushing it shut on the open mouth of the ferocious dog.

The animal bit once on the wooden bar of the gate, sending chips flying, and Thomas, sincerely afraid it would eat its way into the courtyard, fled to the back of the house. There was no one about, for a wonder, and he flung himself behind the well's stone surround to gasp for air and let his heart slow down.

In a bit, his nose twitched. Someone in the kitchen had taken a cleaned rabbit and put it in a pottery jug along with an apple and an onion, stoppered the jug and buried it in the hot ashes of the fire that had cooked the dinner for the usurper lord of this place. It would be the servants' supper, he supposed; they ate their main meal in the evening. Thomas rarely ate so plain a meal as this, but after his meager "meal" of sawdust bread, the scent that drifted out of the half-open kitchen door now the stopper was removed was not a whit less heavenly than any feast he had ever delighted in.

He was determined to get hold of that rabbit and to eat it himself to the last morsel, and do it in the face of his erstwhile servants, and to their shame.

He could hear the faint sound of voices coming from the kitchen, whose door was ajar. Perhaps he could learn something of value. He slipped closer.

"He cares not whether the cowherd weans the calves too soon, he knows not whether his fields are in wheat or rye; he could not tell how many pigs he has if his life depended on it, nor how to choose which cows to keep over the winter; and as for the grasses we cut for hay, he doesn't know cat's tail from cock's foot!"

It was the voice of Nicholas Twosome. Of whom was he speaking? It might have been Thomas, but Thomas was no longer lord here, thanks to the traitorous Twosome. Was he now steward to the new lord, and already complaining?

A voice he did not recognize replied, "But does he, being so ignorant, nevertheless wish to make decisions in the running of his property?"

Grudgingly, "No. But for all he knows I am stealing him blind."

"Are you?" The voice was amused.

"No, my lord. I am become a prankster, but I am no thief." The steward's reply was very dry. No offence offered or taken. So the stranger's voice was doubtless that of the usurper. Twosome called him "my lord". Was he truly a lord or was Twosome only addressing him thus so he would not slip in company? Harry Pimpernell was more right than he knew about Twosome.

Thomas would have stayed to hear more, but the dogs in their kennel were trotting and whining. If they started to bark, someone would come out, and Thomas did not want to be run off again.

He went back to sit behind the well and think. Soon he rose, beaming, and went around to the front door, to smite it with his fist, shouting, "Where be my knavish servants? Nathaniel! Gregory! Philip!"

The door opened and three astonished serving men stood gaping.

When they did not bow, he demanded, "What, no attendance? No regard? No duty?"

He pushed his way into the house, and they fell back, possibly as much to avoid his soiled garments as because they were overawed by his shouting. "Go, you rascal," he said to the nearest, "go fetch my supper in! Food, food, food, food!" Genuine hunger lent sincerity to his loud demand.

"You, Gregory! Some warm water here, what ho! Philip, bring my three best hounds to me!"

The servants hastened out, whether to do his bidding or not, he did not know.

More hurried footsteps from a back room were followed by the appearance of Nicholas Twosome, once again in his steward's garb, and a tall stranger with a brown beard. The stranger's clothing was something Thomas aspired to. His gorgeous brown velvet doublet had a short, square-pleated skirt and close-fitting sleeves, all embroidered in gold and green. His very full breeches were of the same embroidered fabric, fastened below the knee with yellow, buff, and brown ribbons. His ruff was small, stiffened with yellow starch. His stockings were yellow, his shoes ornamented with big yellow-ribbon roses, the lace-edged cuffs of his sleeves were of translucent lawn.

"Who is this unmannered slave?" he demanded and Thomas nearly quailed before the authority in his voice. Surely this was no false lord.

But he straightened his own spine and said, "I am Lord Thomas, the rightful owner of this house, come to take possession. Who, may I ask, are you?"

"*You? You* are the owner of this place? I doubt that! Can you offer any proof?"

Thomas lifted his chin. "I can. There is an indifferent witness who can tell any who asks whether you or I am the rightful lord of this place. A witness incapable of lying."

"Who might that be?"

"Choose among several. I have sent for them."

To his relief Philip appeared, as if on cue, with three leashed hounds: Bellman, Silver, and Echo.

"I propose, my lord," said Thomas, "that you call whom you like as witness. Then you and I shall stand in opposite corners of this room and allow Philip to release any of those hounds you choose. I will let him set the hound facing you, if you like, to give you an advantage. Then we will both call him. The person he comes to and fawns upon is his master."

The dogs were already straining at their leashes to come to Thomas. Bellman, hoping he was yet to go hunting this day, was already baying in his deep, coarse voice. Silver's smooth, high-pitched cry joined in counterpoint. Only Echo fawned silently, crouched low to the ground, his whole back end wriggling hopefully, as he tried to lure his master closer.

"Cease your noise!" Thomas said, but fondly.

"Ha!" the stranger said to Twosome. "It appears we are undone."

"How is that, my lord cousin?" asked a new voice, and Thomas turned to see Bartholomew coming down the stairs.

"Lord Thomas has found a way to prove that this house and its attachments are his."

Lord Thomas smiled. At last he was addressed by his proper title!

"Doubtless you are wondering what has happened?" the stranger asked Lord Thomas.

"I am wondering how my faithless steward persuaded you that you might profit by depriving me of what is rightfully mine." Thomas could feel the back of his neck starting to heat up.

"Twosome?" The lord – by his dress he was at least a lord – turned to look at the steward, who was looking shocked and angry.

"My nephew Henry warned me about you!" shouted Thomas. "He said you were likely the worst thief that was ever made steward by a trusting lord. I'll have you on the gallows, you – you –!"

"Hold but one little while," said the stranger in a voice that did not brook disobedience. "It was not Master Twosome who summoned me. It was my cousin Bartholomew Stratford. I am Sir Philip Stratford."

Amazed, Lord Thomas bowed. When he had bought the wardship of Bartholomew, it had been to strike up an acquaintance with Sir Philip, who was exceedingly well connected. But the man for some reason had not been interested; and Lord Thomas had never actually met him, though he lived only a few miles away.

"*You* are the author of this – this game that has been played on me?" Lord Thomas asked Bartholomew, not daring to sharpen his tone too much in the presence of this more powerful personage.

But it was Sir Philip who replied, "*I* am. Though I have had considerable help. I must say, however, that it was inspired mostly by the game that you played on Christopher Sly. Our prank was of more consequence than the prank you played on the beggar, we hope. You pulled a beggar out of the world he knew, laughed at him for not understanding your world, and sent him on his way no wiser than when you began. I set out to teach you a lesson. I wonder if I have succeeded."

"What? What? You stirred up my, my whole household against me to – to *tell* me something? Why did you not merely send me a letter?" Lord Thomas was nearly beyond governance of his temper.

"Bart appeared on my doorstep dressed in clothing inappropriate to his sex, and claimed he was forced to it – and not for the first time – by his guardian. This was a dishonorable thing, and naturally your household agreed to help me remind you of that. Be grateful. My first idea was to run you through with a sword and toss you on a dung heap. The second was to cut you to pieces and feed you to your hounds."

There was real anger in the knight's voice and Lord Thomas suddenly found it easier to cap his own ire. "It – it was not my intention to dishonor Bartholomew, my lord."

"Yes, but that beggar will tell of the game played on him, and as the story spreads, people may think it was Bart's idea to play the woman. He may become a laughing stock, or worse. So I must not slay you after all, so that at every opportunity you will say it was entirely your idea, that Bartholomew objected strenuously to putting on women's gear, and that he made the most manly woman that ever was seen."

"As you wish." That story might be even more amusing, a stupid beggar entranced by a manly woman. "With pleasure, in fact."

Sir Philip went on. "I have heard of your many pranks, and laughed at some of them, for you are a witty man. But you must cease such nonsense."

Thomas wished strenuously to object. For one thing, Sir Philip had no authority to impose any rule on him. For another, Lord Thomas loved every manner of prank, jest, and trick and did not wish to be denied them.

"I beg your pardon – and his – for endangering Bartholomew's reputation," he said. "But surely you cannot object to my making a fool of a beggar? It was but sport."

"I am in earnest, Lord Thomas. If word reaches me that you have not obeyed me, I will summon my lawyers and wrap you and your property in such a web of lawsuits that it will be forty years before you are clear of them, and you will be bankrupt. You will fight the law alone, for your neighbors, who already speak ill of you, would be of no help."

Lord Thomas trembled at the thought of the law, but then allowed his ire to boil over. "How dare they speak ill of me?" he demanded. "Am I – blood – dare not rebuke me!"

Sir Philip said, "That ill temper of yours speaks more badly of you than your hoodwinks."

Astonished back into calm speech, Lord Thomas said, "But I am of noble birth! It is more than suitable, it is a requirement that my blood should rise when I am balked. Why, my ancestors were lords when William the First was the little-noted bastard of a tanner's daughter!"

"And what did your ancestors do when Lord William reached out with his two hands and took hold of this land? Did they splutter and shout and wave their arms harmlessly? Did they abandon their duty to go hunting? Did they try to hoodwink him?"

Thomas felt his rage swell – and then it died, for again there was a cold light in Sir Philip's eyes. This man was too powerful to quarrel with. Admit defeat, allow the knight to depart, then sort things out with his steward and his other servants. "What would you have me do?" he asked in a voice he forced to sound defeated.

"I'll tell you, my lord. I'd have you be sober, modest, and self-contained. Learn to be wise, and practice how to make your land thrive. Don't spend your money on every bauble that you fancy, or every foolish dog that bays on a new note. Don't come blazing into noble company in flashy clothing, lest a puff of scorn extinguish you. Don't spend more than you have, or talk braver than you are – don't let your sail be bigger than your boat. And especially do not stand so much on your gentility, which is a thing borrowed from dead men's bones and none of yours until you make it so and hold it. Do you understand?"

"Yes. Yes, I *do* understand, I really do." Lord Thomas bit his lip to hide the trickster's smile. "I – I feel like a man waked from an unpleasant dream of sloth, with a hard day's work ahead of him. I feel eager to start in, and will do so first thing tomorrow. For all it can be tedious, the labor of a nobleman is better than a beggar's." He essayed a smile to show he was being witty, not insolent.

"That was so well said," replied Sir Philip, "that I am encouraged to visit often, to see how my cousin Bartholomew does in this new school," Sir Philip smiled sardonically at Lord Thomas's swift change of countenance, and indeed Lord Thomas felt the dark folds of a better trickster's hood winking out his own prank. "Perhaps, when you learn that it is better to charm your friends than trick your neighbors, you may come to welcome my visits."

NOT WISELY,
BUT TOO WELL

Louise Cooper

Othello *is another of Shakespeare's Italian plays, based on a story in the Italian collection* The Hundred Tales *by Giambattista Giraldi (1504–73). The play revolves around trust and distrust. Othello is a Moor, serving as a general in the Venetian army. He has secretly married Desdemona, the daughter of the senator, Brabantio, who learns of the marriage through the treachery of Iago, Othello's trusted ensign, and Roderigo, a former suitor of Desdemona's. Othello and his associates (including Desdemona) are forced to leave for Cyprus which has been attacked by the Turks (which dates the events in the play to 1570). Iago continues to scheme against Othello to the point where Othello becomes convinced of Desdemona's adultery with Cassio, Othello's former lieutenant whom Iago despised because he had been promoted above Iago. The critical event is when Othello sees a handkerchief which he had given to Desdemona in the possession of Cassio's mistress, Bianca. Iago tries to get Roderigo to kill Cassio but Roderigo fails. In a mass of murder and recrimination, Iago kills Roderigo; Othello kills Desdemona; Emilia reveals Iago's guilt and is killed by Iago and Othello kills himself. Iago is captured and tortured to death. Only Cassio survives and takes over Othello's command as governor of Cyprus. And what of Bianca, Cassio's mistress? Louise Cooper tells her tale.*

"He is gone now, you see. It took a long time. But, finally, he is gone." Her gaze moved restlessly in the confines of the cubicle, then fixed on the filigree screen that separated her from the prioress as she tried but failed to make out some detail of the face beyond. "Dead." The word came hard and afterwards she licked her lips, as though to wipe the utterance away. "So I feel . . . I feel that I . . . can . . ."

"That you can speak." The screen was cleverly wrought, and the prioress could see the woman well. A beauty, yes; though time was beginning to take its toll of her youth and would not be kind to her for much longer. And the knowledge of her sin was weighing on her, like a cloak too heavy for her body to bear. A scent hung about her; not tangible, but in its own way as real as any sweet oil. In her years of service to Mother Church the prioress had learned to recognize scents such as this, and name them for what they were. Fear, passion, wrath, hunger – each one had its peculiar odour. And the guilt that Bianca wore like a perfume was, perhaps, the strongest of all.

She said: "Have courage, child. If your conscience is unquiet, it is better to be shriven than to endure in silence. Your secrets are known to Heaven, so what is to fear from me?"

Her voice was impassive, calm, and through the screen she saw the dim ember of hope ignite in Bianca's doubting eyes. She yearned to trust. She *needed* to trust, for she could not carry her burden alone any longer. Little surprise in that, the prioress thought. As yet she knew only a part of the story, but it was enough to have made her break with custom and grant this interview. That, and another imperative.

"So, then," she said, "Iago is dead."

A nod, quick, almost curt. "The torturers did their work well. He survived against all expectation."

"And suffered."

"Yes. Oh, yes. But did not speak. As he swore, as he promised, he did not speak, and so he died unconfessed and unsanctified." She paused. "They drew and quartered him at the last, and then hanged . . . what remained. I saw it done. I watched." A quick, ragged breath. "To be sure, lest I might not believe . . ."

"He *is* dead," said the prioress, who had known it long before this moment. "You may trust in that, if in nothing else."

There was silence for a time. At last, prompting, the prioress said again, "So, then."

"Yes. I . . . do not know where to begin. *How* to begin." Dear God, I am so afraid . . .

"It does not matter where or how. Tell me as you will, as you may. Only tell what is in your heart."

The second silence was far, far longer, and the prioress knew that Bianca was searching within herself for the courage she believed she lacked. A sad thing that a woman who knew so much of the world should have such scant knowledge of herself. But then, in Bianca's life and in the path she had chosen, the needs and desires of others had always been, of necessity, her first consideration.

Or almost always . . .

The words began at last, as the prioress had known they would. Haltingly, Bianca said: "Jealousy, mother, is a cruel and terrible thing."

The prioress made a soft sound of assent, in which sympathy leavened any suggestion of censure.

"It is, I think, a kind of madness . . ."

"That may well be so. Madness takes many forms."

"Yes . . . *He* was jealous. So jealous of the Moor, though from Othello's hand he had had nothing but kindness. And he was covetous. He coveted Othello's position, Othello's influence, Othello's wife . . ."

"His wife?"

"Oh, yes. I will not say he loved her, for I – I do not think him capable of love as I would term it. But he desired her; and the thought of her in the bed and the arms of her lawful husband made him . . . made him *hate*, with a depth that I cannot begin to convey." She hesitated, and a peculiar little smile caught at the edges of her mouth. "Jealousy, covetousness, hatred . . . So many sins in one soul. What right have I to lay them at his door, when I am no better?"

"As much right as any," said the prioress. "Your sin, I think, was not born of hatred, but of love."

"If I could believe that . . . ah, but what does the motive count? Sin is sin. Iago now burns in hell, and so shall I. So shall *I*."

"God is merciful, and even the vilest sins may be forgiven at the last. Iago did not repent. But you may, if you will."

"Oh, yes. Yes. Yet it is not of myself I am thinking . . ."

"I know; and that speaks much in your favour." The prioress waited a few moments, time enough for the unhappy woman's composure to return, before saying again, "So, then. He hated the Moor. He desired the Moor's wife. How did you come to know of this?"

Bianca shrugged, an odd gesture as though she were trying to shake off some unwelcome presence that had alighted on her shoulder. "I have eyes and ears. And then there was Emilia."

"Iago's wife?"

A nod. "We were not . . . friends, as such. But I believe she had some sympathy and kindness towards me." She uttered a peculiar little laugh. "She loved Iago – or had done, once – and she tried to be obedient and loyal and true to him, as a wife should. But when that loyalty was set against her loyalty to her mistress, Desdemona, she could not reconcile her conscience. She came to me, and she told me, frankly, what she knew of her husband's ambitions and what she feared might come of them." Her eyelashes flickered as she blinked rapidly. "She hoped that I would intercede for her with Cassio, and plead with him to make her man see reason. Or, if he could not, to warn the Moor that there was treachery afoot."

"Did you make that promise?" the prioress asked.

There was another long pause before Bianca replied. "Emilia was a good woman, but . . . gullible. Do I do her an injustice? I think not. She was as gullible as that poor fool Roderigo, who still harboured his fancies of being Desdemona's jilted swain. I made that promise, yes; and at the start I truly meant to keep it. But then I learned the truth – the *real* truth – and instead I turned the promise into a snare for Emilia. I lured and duped her, just as *he* lured Roderigo and duped so many others."

"And what was promised to you in return, Bianca? What meant so much to you that you were ready to break your oath?"

Bianca smiled sadly, obliquely. "I loved Michael Cassio, Mother. I still do. I wanted to see him happy. I wanted him to enjoy a place and position worthy of his talents and his nature. To then stand at his side and be acknowledged as his own would set a crown on my heart's desire. But even without that crown, to see *him* happy would have been enough."

"Ah," the prioress said, very gently. "I begin to understand."

"I think you do not, Mother. I think you *cannot*." Through the grille the prioress saw Bianca put one hand to her face. There was a handkerchief in her fingers; of fine fabric and, as far as its stained and crumpled state made it possible to judge, delicately and intricately embroidered. The prioress had not seen it before. But she thought she knew its significance.

As if reading her mind, Bianca clenched her fingers more tightly around the handkerchief, stared at it for a moment, then said, "This unlucky thing has left a trail of death in its wake. I have vowed to keep it with me always, to remind me of my guilt and his; and when I die – if I am judged fit for Christian burial – it shall be interred with me. Then its taint will be done with." Slowly, with a care that was almost obsessive, she started to smooth out the creases. "Emilia stole this. Or rather, she found it where her mistress had unwittingly let it fall. Iago had asked her time and again to procure it for him, and she suspected his motives."

"She was not, then, so foolish," the prioress interposed gently.

"Oh, she was foolish enough, for in good faith she gave the handkerchief to me. I told her that I would keep it safe, and assured her that if neither she nor Desdemona had possession of it, Iago could not use it for any mischief."

The prioress sighed. "Did that promise prove as hollow as the first?"

"Yes. I did not keep the handkerchief. Instead I gave it to Cassio."

"And Iago was contented."

"Yes. He was contented." Bianca's eyes took on a faraway look as she stared back into a past that only she could see. "I wish," she continued, "that I had understood the whole truth then. If I had, I might have found the courage to do what by all God's right and justice I should have done. And yet . . . I said that jealousy is a cruel and terrible thing. That's so. But I believe love is worse. When there is love, you see, one can always *justify*. 'I did this for love, and so can be forgiven.' Hate is more honest, for it doesn't deceive the conscience. Whatever the evil in it, hate at least is *clean*."

"But you did not hate," said the prioress.

"No. I did not hate the Moor, or his wife, or Iago, or Emilia, or any of those – innocents or fools or whatever else they were – who became embroiled in this. I had no *reason* for hatred. Yet I was a deadly enemy to them all." She laughed again, with an awful bitterness. "Or, all but one. It's strange to think it, but I believe that only one man emerged, at the last, with any semblance of honour. Only one, among so many. Isn't that so, Mother? Isn't it?"

"Yes, child. It is so." Silence again. Then the prioress asked quietly, "What did you do, Bianca? What did you do, out of love?"

She lowered her head. "I did what he wanted of me; no more and no less. It was so easy. And when he promised me . . . I believed him. I *wanted* to believe him." She looked up at the grille, striving to see through it, to find some true human contact with the shadowed face on the far side. For a few moments the only sound to break the quiet was the faint hush of the prioress's composed and steady breathing. Then: "I was the greatest fool of them all, Mother. I was the most gullible of them all, for I *believed* his promise to me . . ." For the first time her voice broke down. The lapse was small, and brought quickly under control, but the prioress noted it. She waited patiently, and after a second or two Bianca went on in a calmer tone. "Iago was clever. The finer points of the plot were all his own, and he was careful to arrange it so that anyone who might be in a position to betray him would have no chance to speak."

"All save for his wife," said the prioress.

"Oh, no. No, no, Mother; Emilia was *not* in that position. Not then. She thought I had kept my promise, and that her mistress was safe from Iago's scheming. That was how Iago planned it to be. It was only later – much later – that she realized what I had done. Realized that I had betrayed her trust, and that Cassio and Iago were . . . were . . ."

Her voice tailed off, and this time the quiet was complete. The prioress was holding her breath, holding it as she held back the words that wanted to form on her tongue. Now, she *did* understand, and all that was needed was Bianca's own word of affirmation. She understood, too, why Bianca was so afraid.

"Child," she said at last, and with a world of compassion in her voice, "do you truly want to tell me the rest?"

Bianca replied, "Yes. I think I must."

"I am only a woman; I cannot hear your confession and I cannot absolve you."

"I know."

"Yet you must confess, if your soul is to be saved."

"I know that, too. But if I were to make my confession to a holy priest, I could not find it in me to tell him . . . this . . . when I have never spoken of it to another living soul. Forgive me, Mother, but because you *are* a woman, I – I can speak more freely before you. And when I have told it once, the second time will be easier."

"Child – " the prioress began, but was interrupted.

"Please, Mother. *Please.* Hear me now, and let me go to confession with a freer heart."

A sense of defeat settled in the prioress's bones like the ache of fever. She had given the girl what chance she could, and tried obliquely to guide her. If she would not or could not listen, there was nothing more the prioress could – or dared – do to persuade her.

Aloud, she said, "Very well, dear child. Speak, then, and I will listen."

Bianca folded her hands as though praying. "I loved Cassio, and love him still. Love does not judge, does it? His loathing of the Moor had no just foundation, and his desire for Desdemona gave me pain. Yet when Emilia came to me with her plea for help, I went to him and told him all. I said, put aside your hatred for a better way. You are not like Iago; you have worth and honour, and can advance yourself by your own merits, not by deceit! Warn Othello, I begged him. See justice done . . ."

Abruptly the passion lost its grip on her voice and her shoulders slumped. "We quarrelled then," she continued. "Vile things were said on both sides before he ordered me out of his sight. But the next day he returned. He forgave my harsh words, as I forgave his – oh, I *always* forgave his – and when we were reconciled he told me that I had done him a great service by coming to him with Emilia's message. Emilia, he said, was right to suspect her husband's intentions, for Iago's loathing of the Moor made his own pale by comparison. Iago fully intended to do all Emilia feared, and more. So if evil was inevitable, Cassio said, it was surely better to turn it to some good account than to let it go unchecked. He had a plan of his own. And if I would be his co-conspirator . . ." For the second time her voice caught. "If I would do that, then he promised me I would have my heart's desire."

"To be acknowledged as his own." Softly the prioress repeated the words Bianca had spoken earlier, and had the bleak confirmation of a nod in reply. "That was the promise you believed."

"Yes. Fool that I am. Wretch that I am."

Greater fool than you, even now, the prioress thought, but kept her own counsel. It was too late to do anything else. "So," she said. "When yet another false promise was made . . . what then?"

Bianca raised both hands to her hair. She had let it loose to enter the cloister, as if to hide behind its veil, but now she drew it back and raised it, exposing her features and the curve of neck and shoulder. The gesture seemed to say: *this*

is myself, and there is nothing more. Then she let the hair
go again, a heavy cascade that brought the shadows back to
her face.

"The story of the Moor's downfall is known to all now,"
she said. "Even here, I think, it will have been told."

The prioress smiled drily. "We are not as secluded from
the world as many believe."

"Then you have heard how Iago brought the thing about. It
was all whispering, to begin with; hints and insinuations that
the pure Desdemona was not quite all she seemed. Then the
little evidences. Her sympathy towards Cassio when Othello
held him out of favour. Her plea on his behalf. It was for
my sake that Emilia urged her to present his case. She knew
I loved Cassio, and thought to do me a kindness in return for
what I had done for her. That, perhaps, was Desdemona's only
failing. She pleaded too extremely, and it seemed to confirm
Othello's suspicions. The bait was set, and the quarry was
taking it. It needed but one more morsel to spring the trap
. . . and so, again, we come to the handkerchief." Bianca
laughed, choked, wiped her mouth. "If women could be
actors, Cassio said, then my talent would be the talk of
Venice. I played my part very well, pretending pique and
anger as he gave me Desdemona's handkerchief while Othello
watched from hiding and Iago whispered poison in his ear. It
was that, I think, that sealed it. Oh, there was not enough
true evidence to reasonably condemn. How could there be?
She was innocent. But Cassio and Iago knew the Moor was
not entirely reasonable. They knew he would not wait to be
sure of his ground beyond any shadow of doubt. So Iago
persuaded him – it was not difficult, I understand – to
connive at Cassio's murder, using Roderigo as their pawn."
Bianca shivered slightly. "There are so many dead fools in
this tale. Roderigo was another. The attempt on Cassio's life
failed, of course, as it was meant to do, and Iago despatched
Roderigo and then wounded Cassio, not mortally but enough
to make the thing look plausible. As for the Moor . . . Iago
and Cassio had a strategy to finish him, but fate and his own
nature completed the work for them."

She was clutching her shoulders now, hands gripping,

knuckles almost white. "I did not think he would kill her. Beat her, yes; maybe put her away from him. But not *kill*." A tear dropped on to her lap, then another, catching the light briefly and glinting like shards of glass. "Emilia tried to stop it, but she came too late." She paused. "*Too late*. Don't you think, Mother, that those are the saddest words of all?"

"Yes," said the prioress, who had other and private reasons for agreeing. "I do."

"She also realized too late the significance of the handkerchief," Bianca went on. "She must have known, then, that I had played my part in the evil that was done. But before she could utter any word of condemnation against me, Iago stabbed her. His own wife. He killed his own wife, to protect me."

"Not only you," the prioress interjected softly.

"No. No, that's true. If I was implicated, it would have taken only one step from me to Cassio." Bianca brooded thoughtfully for a few moments. "I think they must have had some pact. Cassio and Iago. That if one was taken, he would protect the other. That is why Iago kept silent. I wonder . . ."

"Wonder?" the prioress prompted when her voice tailed off.

"I wonder if . . . if Cassio would have done the same for him? I suppose I shall never know the answer to that question. In any case, what does it matter now? Of all the players in this game, only two are left alive." A shrug, almost careless this time. "Cassio and Bianca. He is Lord Governor; she is discarded and forgotten."

I wish that that were true, the prioress thought. She was glad at this moment that Bianca could not see her face.

"So," Bianca continued, "I have told it all. All there is; all of any significance. I have put down my burden." Tears started to flow more freely, though she did not sob, only sat quietly, almost serenely, while they glittered on her cheeks.

The prioress said gently, "Will you make confession now, Bianca? Will you ask for God's forgiveness of your sins?"

"Bianca nodded. "I will do any penance. For all of my life, I will hope and pray for absolution . . ." Suddenly she looked up. "But what of Cassio, Mother? Do you think . . . that there might be hope of redemption for him?"

The prioress hesitated as compassion wrangled with honesty. Then compassion won and she replied, "Yes, my child. I think there is always hope." She rose to her feet. "Wait there, then. I will ask that a priest shall come to you."

Her back ached with sitting as she opened the door of the cubicle and went out. In the room beyond, which was richly furnished, a figure waited in the shadows.

"You did well, madam." The abbot was tall and lean, almost a shadow himself. It was hard to imagine that he had ever laughed.

"Thank you, holy father." The prioress's voice was bleak. "May I now be excused?"

"Not yet. You have one more service to perform, and then you may return to your women." He indicated a cup of wine that stood on a table between them, and something akin to terror flowered in the prioress's eyes.

"Father, I – "

He stopped what she might have said with a movement of one hand. You have won the woman's trust, and we can take no chances. You will give her the wine. You will see that she drinks it. It will not act immediately. There will be time for her to make her confession, and I myself will administer her last rites." He saw the prioress's expression and his manner unbent just a little. "It is best this way."

"She would never have betrayed him . . ." the prioress said miserably.

"Perhaps; or perhaps not. How can we know? Whatever the fact of it, we must do our duty."

"Our duty is to God!"

"But our survival depends on the goodwill of men."

It was true, and she had no ready answer. She cast her eyes down, and the abbot moved towards the outer door. Reaching it, he paused and looked back.

"I will await the woman in the confessional. Oh – and there is one final thing. You will be pleased to know that the lord governor intends to make an endowment – a *personal* endowment – to your convent. The sum is enough to build a chapel twice the size of your present edifice."

The prioress stared at him. He smiled. "And to furnish it in a manner that befits God's own house."

Or a whited sepulchre . . . With a tremendous effort the prioress found her voice. "The lord governor is . . . very generous, she said pallidly.

The smile faded from the abbot's face. "Not *too* generous, Mother. Never forget that."

The door closed behind him without the smallest sound. For perhaps half a minute the prioress stood motionless. Then she reached to the table, picked up the wine cup, and walked slowly back towards the room where Bianca waited.

MURDER AS YOU LIKE IT

F. Gwynplaine MacIntyre

As You Like It *was probably written in 1599. It's another of Shakespeare's romantic comedies. Frederick has deposed his brother Senior and usurped his duchy, banishing Senior to the Forest. To the court comes the bullying Oliver de Boys who has deprived his brother Orlando of his birthright and plans to have Orlando killed in a wrestling match. However Orlando wins, and falls madly in love with Rosalind, daughter of the deposed duke. Frederick will have none of this relationship. Rosalind is banished, and disguises herself as a boy, calling herself Ganymede. Orlando flees from the court, and all of them end up at the court of the deposed duke in the Forest of Arden. Frederick sends Oliver in search of his brother, but Oliver has a change of heart and we head towards the happily-ever-after multi-matchmaking finale. At the end of the play Duke Frederick also has a change of heart, restores his brother and seeks refuge in religion. But just what fate befell Frederick is not stated. F. Gwynplaine MacIntyre supposes a possible foul deed.*

Her breasts would bear no witness to this murder. She had tightly bound her ripening paps 'neath this borrowed doublet;

more perfectly to feign her made disguise. E'en now, as she restrung the yew-wood longbow, Rosalind was minded of the Amazons: the she-archers of old, who found their paps cumbersome when they drew back their bowstrings to loose their arrows. Within her treetop seat, she glanced down at herself now, and was pleased to see a flat masculine chest – firm, unbreasted – in the taut woollen tunic.

A man she was, and bent on a yeoman's task as truly as she bent her huntsman's bow. She had oft heard of hunters who disguised themselves as their own prey: who draped themselves in the cape and antlers of a stag, that they might draw near enough an honest stag to kill it unawares. Now a huntress was sworn to hunt a *man*, with man's weapons, and so she had costumed herself in the garb of her prey . . . as a man.

The guise was perfect. She had bartered one sex for the other, exchanging her maidenly graces for masculine form. Rosalind had practised counterfeiting a male swagger, taking long strides in leggings artfully padded to transform her slender girlish limbs into the muscular legs of a swain. The hem of her doublet hung unfashionably long, to conceal her wide maidenly hips. The doublet's sleeves were padded into the bargain, endowing Rosalind with the brawned shoulders and burgeoning arms of a yeoman. Her long chestnut-coloured tresses were pinned a-neath a huntsman's cap. Even the high leathern collar seemed to broaden her slim neck, concealing the fact that this daughter of Eve lacked the bulge of Adam's apple in her throat. As for that *other* man-bulge which she also lacked, Rosalind had attended to this: a codpiece, stuffed with linen handkerchiefs, gave her loins the full semblance of masculine pride. A boy's name – Ganymede – completed the translation of her gender.

She knew well the habits of her prey. In all the time she had lived in Duke Frederick's household, as kinswoman to his daughter Celia, Rosalind had observed that the duke was accustomed to walking in solitude at eventide, shortly ere sunset, at the meadow's edge where his stolen estate bordered the forest.

Rosalind's mouth was dry, with the excitement of a

murder-task to come. On either side of Ganymede's codpiece dangled two more male adornments: a wineskin and a bundle of arrows. Useful items, which any *man* might sport freely, yet which Rosalind's female identity had ere now denied her. "Come fill the cup, my Ganymede," she jested, while she unstoppered the wineskin to refresh herself. The vessel held pear-juice, not wine: Rosalind had no intention of fuddling her senses on this crucial occasion. She supped a long sweet drink, then let the empty skin a-dangle from her belt.

An oak-apple hung in front of her, confounding her aim. Rosalind shinnied higher up the tree, to have a clear view when her quarry should appear. It pleasured her: this unaccustomed feeling of stout wood between her thighs, as she straddled the oak. A lifetime spent in petticoats and skirts gives a maiden scant opportunity to sit boy-fashion, straddle-wise.

"I like this guise of Ganymede," the boy-clad girl decided in her thoughts. "When this murder is done, if no witness sees me fleeing in male guise, then I will save these garments for another time, and wear manhood whenever maiden's form wearies me. But if some witness attends the crime that Ganymede commits in my stead, then I must murder Ganymede as well: aye, bury doublet and tabard and all my other mannish fragments in some undiscovered place. Then I shall 'scape into the safety of a maiden's bodice and chemise, whilst the sheriffs and wardens seek the *man* who committed this crime."

Why had the duke not appeared? This wait was maddening. The boy Ganymede bent forward on his straddle-seat, while yet the mind of Rosalind felt once again the pleasant girl-sensation of the oaken limb a-tween her loins. Now she felt another urge: a less pleasant one. She had quaffed much pear-juice, and her bladder was beginning to announce itself.

Rosalind sighed wearily, and peered into the duke's grounds. No sentries came, no witnesses. She slung her bow across her shoulder, and slid down the smooth trunk of the oak tree to the ground. Quickly, she unfastened her male garments of doublet and hose, then slid the padded leggings to half-mast, so that she might empty her bladder.

"If I truly had a *man's hose* within this man's hose, I

could do this more easily," Rosalind grumbled. The youth Ganymede might sup his fill of drink with boyish haste, but the maid Rosalind must attend to the consequences . . . and in *maidenly* fashion.

Quickly, Rosalind crouched herself and made water. When she was finished, she snatched a handful of leaves to wipe her Venus-mound. There was another dampness in her loins, unauthored by her bladder, and she muttered an oath as she recognized it.

Her blooding had started: a bit earlier this month than the previous time. The wound of Eve that never heals had begun bleeding again. Fortunately, a-neath her Ganymede's garb, Rosalind had equipped herself with a napkin. Now she withdrew the linen: aye, it was full sodden with menstrual blood. And she had not a clean one! Then, of a sudden, she thought of a substitute . . . and she could not restrain herself from laughter.

"Ganymede must sacrifice his proud manhood to attend to fair Rosalind's maidenly needs," said the boy-disguised girl. She reached into her well-stuffed codpiece, taking one of the clean linen napkins which served to counterfeit Ganymede's rampant boy-bulge. Rosalind put this serviette to her loins, discarding the soiled napkin in favour of the fresh one. Then she garbed herself, donning male disguise again and climbing swiftly up the oak. Now the boy Ganymede was a trifle less proud of loin; all else was as before.

But soft! Now from her vantage in the treetop, Rosalind saw a figure below. His stride was familiar, his posture was cruel. Duke Frederick approached! The boy archer Ganymede drew two arrows from his bundle, nocked one, and drew back the bowstring while he carefully took aim. If the first arrow missed, the second would be nocked and fired in the instant . . .

"Ungentle nuncle," whispered Rosalind to her prey. "You stole the lands of my father your brother, usurped his dukedom, and did banish him . . . as you have lately banished *me*." She drew the bowstring taut, and aimed the fatal dart. "Now, mine uncle, I banish *thee* to a country from which no man ever returned . . . save Lazarus."

In the meadow beyond, Duke Frederick fancied that he heard a hissing sound. Whether it was the hiss of anger from his niece's lips, or the hiss of her arrow through the air, he never knew. But he turned towards the sound, and the oncoming arrow pierced his chest . . .

Oliver De Boys was the logical suspect, since Duke Frederick had lately seized his lands. The duke's bondmen arrested Oliver and dungeoned him, against the day when he could prove his innocence.

In prison, the eldest son of Sir Rowland De Boys had much time to think upon his fate. At first he railed 'gainst this injustice, for – though he was guilty of much – he was truly innocent of the duke's murder. But as time passed, and no rescue arrived, he turned his mind to other tasks. Oliver grew to admit that his imprisonment was full deserved, for – yet innocent of murder – he had fostered other sins. He had stolen the birthright of his youngest brother Orlando, cheated Orlando of his schooling, and e'en conspired Orlando's death.

"Cry providence, but free me from this cell," the prisoner wept, "and I'll amend my former life's offences."

Orlando, meantime, received word of his eldest brother's arrest from their mid-born brother Jaques. Orlando left the forest of Arden, and made haste to the duke's estate to acquit Oliver of this murderous charge.

A witness had seen all: the foppish LeBeau swore a summoner's oath, vowing that he had been nearby when an arrow sped forth from an oak and felled the duke. Moments later, the oak's foliage parted to reveal a male figure in doublet and tunic, who slid with girlish grace a-down the tree and fled into the woods with a longbow.

"Show me the place," Orlando bade.

The oak was some brief depth within the forest. Another investigator was already at the scene: a large raven, who pecked and heckled a rumpled bit of linen ensnared in some brambles 'neath the oak. "A moth may eat cloth, but ravens choose a ruddier diet," said Orlando. He snatched the cloth, unrumpled it, and found a red-brown stain within.

LeBeau crossed himself. *"Death's blood!"*

"No, *life's* blood." Orlando sniffed the ooze. "'Tis the red wine from Hymen's chalice, which doth pour but once each month."

"I witteth not thy metaphor, sirrah," returned LeBeau, who was evidently unschooled in matters menstrual.

Orlando tried again: "'Tis the sweet malmsey from the cask of Venus, and *this* . . ." – he brandished the bloodstained napkin – ". . . is the plug which stops her bunghole. Know you not a lady's blood-debt when you find it?"

LeBeau reddened, and one of the duke's warders spoke: "No woman could have entered this dense shrubbery."

"No person dressed in skirts and frocks, you mean," Orlando corrected him. "No petticoats nor panniers could pass a-tween these trees, but a woman clad in boyish garb could enter here with ease. Come, what's this?"

Behind the bush was a stain on the ground, which had aroused the attentions of the local flies. "Who among you are huntsmen?" asked Orlando. Most of the duke's men raised their hands, and Orlando gave a challenge: *Hart and hind their spoor doth leave; which is Adam, which is Eve?*"

All knew what he meant. A stag or a hart sprays the ground with his essence whilst standing erect; the spray strikes the ground with great force, from a height and at an angle. But a hind or a doe will squat herself to perform the same task; her essence trickles to earth from directly above, with less force. The two marks are distinctly unlike, and any skilled huntsman can distinguish he-puddle from she-piddle. "See, some daughter made her water in this spot before the slaughter," said Orlando.

The duke's yeoman seemed unconvinced. "A man may piddle woman-fashion. Mayhap the murderer – having need to relieve himself whilst awaiting his prey, but unwilling to stand up and attract attention – did sit-a-squat himself behind a bush to make his water, like a girl, so as not to be seen from the duke's estate."

"And wiped his handiwork afterwards?" Orlando asked mockingly. He pointed towards another clue: a shrub's branch torn bare of its leaves, and those same leaves on the ground nearby, slicked and damp. "See you: this wetness is witness to a *maiden's* piss-task."

"How not a man's?" asked the yeoman, and Orlando gave answer: "Because a maiden seeks to wipe herself afterward, *an' hath her way*, whereas a man *will shake his spear*."

Carefully pocketing the most important clue – the bloodied napkin – Orlando made his way back to the meadow, whilst the warders and courtiers followed. There was a maiden of Orlando's late acquaintance who was fond of wearing boyish garb . . . and who possessed full measure of motive for slaying her uncle Duke Frederick. But Orlando had his own motives for concealing her name from this company.

"'Tis clear what happened," said Orlando to the others. "Duke Frederick was slain by some person who dresses like a man, who kills like a man, but who lacks a man's proudest *weapon*." Orlando gestured towards his own bulging codpiece. "Furthermore, 'tis a killer who bleeds where a lady does, and who needs must piss as ladies do."

"Canst name the murderer, then?" asked the duke's chief warder.

"No, but I have proved my kinsman's innocence," said Orlando. "Duke Frederick was slain by some disgruntled *eunuch*. Bring forth my brother Oliver, and verify that he still has his man-baubles. Thus you will see it was not he who crouched to pee beneath yon tree."

There was joyful reunion of the sons of Sir Rowland De Boys. As soon as Oliver was freed from durance vile, and informed that he had his brother Orlando to thank for his release, the elder son made haste to earn his kinsman's forgiveness. "I will give thee thine inheritance and birthright," said Oliver to Orlando, while middle brother Jaques stood by as witness. "And thy neglected education shall be mended."

"We can discuss these things another time; I am late for an engagement," said Orlando impatiently.

Jaques remained behind, attending to the recovery of their family's estate and revenues from Duke Frederick's heirs. Meantime, Oliver and Orlando returned to the forest of

Arden. As they hastened forth, Orlando told his elder brother about the maiden whom he'd lately met and fallen full in love with. He made no mention of his knowledge that this selfsame wench was guilty of Duke Frederick's murder.

"Her name is Rosalind, and – when I met her at the duke's wrestling-match – I could not help but notice how delightfully she fills a well-laced bodice," said Orlando as he plunged through a stand of pine trees, not looking back to see if Oliver was keeping up with him. "'Tis fortunate that I noticed her maidenly attributes when first we met . . . for the next time I did see fair Rosalind, she was personating a *boy*."

Oliver spluttered through a mouthful of pine-needles. "A *boy*, say you?"

"Aye. For some reason it pleasures her to dress as a boy, to consort as a boy, to speak in mannish voice and call her boy-self Ganymede." Orlando shrugged. "Stranger still, this merry maid would seek a dalliance 'tween myself and the makeshift boy Ganymede . . . in which I must plight my love to the boy as if he were a *girl*."

Oliver spluttered again. "And you dance this galliard *willingly*, brother?"

"Hell, yes. *She* thinks I take her for a boy, and little does she wit that – when I embrace the sweet youth Ganymede – I know damned well that 'tis a *maiden* in my grasp." Orlando smiled at a fond memory, then shrugged again: "If it pleaseth her to counterfeit a boy . . . marry, both I and my codpiece will pierce her disguise, and we both shall rise to her occasion."

Just then the brothers entered a clearing in the forest, and Orlando of a sudden changed the subject: "Now, brother! I am late for my tryst with the boy Ganymede – I mean, the fair maid Rosalind – and I have need of some pretext to shrive my tardiness. Tell Rosalind that you fell asleep in this glade, and whilst you slumbered came a lioness . . ."

"A *lioness*?" Oliver spluttered once more. "We're in *Europe*, man! Lioncels, ounces and pards doth live in *Africa!*"

"Well, how could I know such things? You cheated me out of my education, remember?" said Orlando. "A lioness, a green and gilded snake; choose any beast that meets thy stratagem." Orlando reached into his jerkin, and unpocketed a certain bloodstained napkin, while nodding towards the scarf his brother wore. "Good thou, take this blooded napkin, and give me thy scarf to bind mine arm. Here is my plan: when you meet the fair Rosalind, I shall observe all from behind a nearby bamboo tree . . ."

"We haven't got *bamboo* in Europe, either," said Oliver. "Thine education is more beggared than I'd thought. But come tell me thy plan . . ."

Rosalind (in her disguise as Ganymede) and Celia (in her disguise as Aliena) had arranged to meet Orlando at two o'clock, yet he did not arrive. Now – at the hour's past quarter-mark – a wretched man, o'ergrown with hair, came in Orlando's stead. This was Oliver, his garments disheveled from his sojourn in the dungeon and his hastening through the forest. Upon the instant he clapped eyes on Rosalind in her doublet and hose, he knew her at once for a girl in boy's disguise. But, for Orlando's sake, Oliver pretended to be fooled. Rosalind, suspecting nothing, was full pleased that this man who looked upon her did in faith behold a *male*.

Although he held the bloodied napkin in his pocket, Oliver held no knowledge of this thing's significance. He had no notion that it was a clue to a murder; still less did Oliver suspect that the boy-clad girl who stood before him was the killer in disguise.

Remembering the speech he had rehearsed, Oliver bowed and announced that he came here in Orlando's name. From the pocket of his tabard, he withdrew a stained bit of cloth, and offered this on his brother's behalf. Rosalind glanced briefly at the rumpled object, and disdained to take it. Still Oliver yet held it forth, whilst unreeling his impromptu tale's embellishments. The tale itself was scarce believable: Oliver described how Orlando had come afoul of a serpent, or a lioness, or *some* damned beast, and fought it, and been wounded in his arm, and now Orlando sent this bloody napkin to Ganymede as his battle's souvenir . . .

From his vantage in the forest nearby, Orlando witnessed all. Midpoint through Oliver's soliloquy, Orlando saw Rosalind glance once more at the bloodied cloth in Oliver's hand. Of a sudden, she recognized the linen's weft . . . and Rosalind's boy-clad limbs stiffened whilst her girlish face went pale. She snatched the cloth, saw the bloodstain within, and knew it at once for her own. And knew, too, the message written invisibly in this napkin's return to her: *You dropped this. I know it is yours, and we both know where I found it and why you were hiding there. I have pierced thy boy-disguise: no boy thou art, nor guiltless maiden. Thou art murderess, and this attests thy guilt . . .*

Rosalind fainted.

"I would I were at home," were her first words, upon recovering . . . thinking not of the sylvan cottage where she now dwelt as Ganymede, but of her own sweet father's house where late she once had lived as daughter to the rightful duke. *Where am I?* Now she remembered.

The bloodied napkin! It was *gone!* Vanished in the brief interval of her swoon! Whoever had taken the napkin knew what she had done. As Oliver and Celia revived her, Rosalind glanced swiftly from one to the other, seeking some hidden knowledge in their eyes: *Does my cousin Celia know that I have slain her father? Does this man Oliver know my guilt, or does he merely bear the errand of another? Where is my tell-tale napkin?*

"Come, you look paler and paler," said Celia solicitously, helping Rosalind to stand and guiding her towards the cottage. Beside her, Oliver muttered some few words which Rosalind could not rightly discern. An accusation of murder?

"I shall devise something," said Rosalind then, and another few words. Then, anxious to 'scape prying eyes, and impatient to devise some strategy against a murder charge, she spoke once more to Oliver: "Will you go?"

There came no further mention of the deed. Still garbed as Ganymede, Rosalind trailed Oliver through the wood and found him conversant with Orlando. His arm was bound in a scarf as though wounded, yet Rosalind divined no blood against the cloth. Full confident that she had caught him in a lie, she was eager to press the subject. But two yokels arrived at an ill-chosen moment – the shepherd Silvius and his wench Phebe – and Rosalind was obliged to hold her tongue until they left again, and she was alone with Orlando. Then, mockingly, she touched his bandaged arm: "How come you to be wounded, yet not bleed?"

"Here's blood enough," Orlando answered, bringing forth the tell-tale napkin . . . which Oliver had given back to him before Rosalind's arrival. Rosalind stared full into Orlando's countenance, yet she found no friendly mercy in his eyes.

"So you know, then," she said.

"Yes, I know *all*. I know, young Ganymede, that thou art Rosalind . . . and I know that you did slay the duke your uncle. The duke's warders know that she who dropped this cloth performed the murder whilst garbed as a man. I have merely to speak a word in certain quarters, and thou'lt wear a hangman's hemp cord as thy wimple."

"What price to bribe thy silence?" fair Rosalind asked.

"Only this, lady: marry me, for I do love thee. This napkin – and my pledge of secrecy – will ensure the marriage be a happy one. If ever you feel urge to turn shrewish, remember that *my* tongue can wag as swift as thine, and – in this instance – cause more injury."

Rosalind nodded meekly, and lowered her eyes. "Is that your only demand?"

"I have another." Gently, Orlando kissed the boy Ganymede. "Have the goodness to discard thy boyish mode . . . for *I* shall wear the trousers in this marriage."

And so 'twas done. Meantime, Jaques – on behalf of himself and his brothers – had secured release of the estate and revenues of their deceased father Sir Rowland De Boys, lately seized by Duke Frederick before his cruel murder. Jaques arrived just in time for the double nuptials of his kinsmen: Oliver to Celia, Orlando to Rosalind. Having been forewarned that Celia was the late Duke Frederick's daughter, and being reluctant to ungentle the festivities with tidings of Frederick's death, Jaques invented a barely plausible excuse for the duke's permanent disappearance: something about the duke meeting an old monk, and undergoing religious conversion, and living henceforth as a hermit. In any event, the duke's vanishment had the happy effect of releasing from exile Frederick's brother – Rosalind's father – and restoring unto him his rightful dukedom.

Rosalind, for her part, married Orlando right gladly, for she loved him as full as he did her. "Still, it pleasured me to be the young man Ganymede for a time," Rosalind sighed regretfully, as she and Orlando made ready for their wedding-night. "I like not the notion of spending the rest of my days bound into a woman's stays and bodices."

Orlando kissed her lovingly. "Mayhap young Ganymede might yet return one day. Thou art Rosalind my bride, and thou wilt love me as a woman loves a man. Yet when I weary of a maiden's charms, then thou wilt turn the other cheek . . . and play the lad for me, as Ganymede."

Rosalind's brown eyes widened at this welcome news. "Then may I alternate 'twixt being female and male as I choose, playing shuttlecock as man and maid in turn?"

"Not *man*, perhaps," said Orlando. "I would not take a man to be my bride. But I have kept my father's name, which now I give to thee in marriage. And so long as you remain my wife, sweet Rosalind, you will always be . . . one of *De Boys*."

Exeunt omnes.

THE HOUSE OF RIMMON

Cherith Baldry

The Merchant of Venice *is known, if for no other reason, for Shylock demanding his pound of flesh. The story was not originally Shakespeare's. The core of it is based on an anonymous Italian story of the fourteenth century to which Shakespeare added his own embellishments. He completed the play around 1597, and it has remained one of his best known. It tells of Antonio, a Venetian merchant, who borrows a loan from Shylock, the Jewish money-lender, in order to grant the money to his friend Bassanio who requires it to help win the hand of Portia, a rich heiress. Shylock dislikes Antonio, who is openly generous and thus keeps down interest rates, and so Shylock demands a pound of flesh if Antonio defaults on the loan. Shylock is goaded further in his hatred of Christians when his daughter Jessica elopes with Bassanio's friend Lorenzo. Antonio's ships founder and he is unable to repay the money, and Shylock presses his claim before the courts. Portia, disguised as a male physician, along with her attendant Nerissa, defends Antonio and wins her case by agreeing that Shylock can have his pound of flesh but if he sheds one drop of blood then all his lands and goods will be confiscated. Shylock realizes he has been caught and gives in, but Portia presses home her claim and demands that since he had intended to claim the life of Antonio, he must*

now forfeit half of his fortune and also become a Christian.
For everyone except Shylock all ends happily. But then what
happened? That is where Cherith Baldry takes us.

"What news on the Rialto?"

At the sound of the voice, the account book in Antonio's
hands seemed to treble its weight. The meticulous columns
of figures danced before his eyes like dust motes in sunlight.
He closed the book and handed it back to the scrivener who
stood beside him.

"I thank you; it is well."

The man bowed and withdrew. Antonio turned. In the
doorway of the counting-house, Bassanio leant against the
doorframe, arms folded, laughter in his eyes. Antonio went
to him and caught him into an embrace; then he drew back
to look into his friend's face.

Wealth suited Bassanio. He was splendidly dressed, in a velvet
doublet laced with gold, and a silk-lined cloak, fastened with a
clasp like a sunburst. His hands flashed with rings. More, he
had lost the narrow, predatory look of the days of his poverty;
he was smiling, expansive.

"I didn't think to see you here in Venice," Antonio
said.

"We came this morning. Bag and baggage, lock, stock
and barrel, and pretty Nerissa's pretty kitten howling in a
handbasket. We're opening up the Palazzo Belmonte. We
mean to stay a month at least."

Warm happiness flooded over Antonio.

"What brings you here?"

"Oh, even the peace of Belmont can grow tedious," Bassanio
said carelessly. "Besides, Nerissa is near her time, and Gratiano
wants the best doctors of Venice for her."

"Gratiano a father!" Antonio said, marvelling. "What sort
will he make, do you think?" Bassanio laughed.

"You never saw a man so changed! All weighty sentences
and moral worth! And he treats Nerissa like a precious piece

of Murano glass." A shadow crossed his face. "They are very happy."

Antonio did not dare to ask the obvious next question. He took Bassanio's arm and led him out of the counting-house to the head of the stairs.

"Come and drink a cup of wine with me," he said.

"I may not stay." Bassanio disengaged himself. "I'm but a messenger."

"Oh? What message, then?"

"To bid you to our revels."

Antonio stared at him.

"What, tonight?"

"Indeed not!" Bassanio shook his head, mock-reproving, and pulled a sanctimonious face. "Tonight we keep our Friday fast, most religiously. But tomorrow – ah, tomorrow night we feast. With masquing and music and all the nonsense you most disapprove of, dear, grave Antonio!"

"And I'm bid to join you?" Antonio said, crushing down an obscure disappointment.

"Certainly, and more – to supper tonight, to help us plan our revels."

Antonio could not help smiling.

"I shall be honoured."

He escorted Bassanio downstairs and out across the wharf to where the boatman was waiting. Hand raised in farewell, he watched the gondola pull out into the Grand Canal, until it was lost among the other traffic on the water.

His mind was never wholly quiet, but now he was filled with surging agitation. He had thought he was finished with all that, a year ago when his friend had married, when he himself had escaped, almost miraculously, from the twin threats of death and destitution, saved by the lady who had become Bassanio's wife. They had been kind to him – very kind – but it was clearly time for a graceful retreat.

He would never belong in Belmont. He would not import the discords of Venice into its harmony. And he could have no part in Bassanio now, when he had given him – gladly, though his heart was torn in two – into the keeping of the lady Portia.

Before it all, he had seen the sidelong glances, heard the whispering. He knew there were those who thought his love for Bassanio was mortal sin. He shrugged, remembering. Mortal sin? He did not know himself if that was true. He did not know what he wanted, only that Bassanio had come like a shaft of sunlight into the dim warehouse of his life, and he had instinctively turned towards the warmth and the laughter. And he had known when the time had come to close the door against it.

Now the door stood wide open again. More sensible to refuse the invitation; but then, Antonio reflected, he had never been a sensible man, and he was too old to change now. Aware of something huge bearing down on him, like a wave ready to sweep him away, he bowed his head and murmured a prayer, there on the wharfside with the gondoliers calling to each other across the canal and the sailors unloading bales of silk from ships that at his command had spanned the world. Then he straightened his shoulders and went back to the counting-house.

The sun had gone down when Antonio left for the Palazzo Belmonte, but light still streaked the sky and was reflected pale in the surface of the canal. His gondola slid smoothly through the water; a cool breeze whispered against his face. Already lamps had been lit in the shrines along the waterside. From a pillared portico a lion looked gravely down, its paw on an open book. *Pax tibi, Marce, evangelista meus.*

His boat was loaded with gifts for Portia. A bolt of tabby silk from Cathay. Fat bundles of spices: cloves and saffron and cinnamon. An alabaster pot of Arabian perfume. He had brought no gift for Bassanio. *Pax tibi . . .* Not now, Antonio thought. Not here.

The boatman guided the gondola expertly alongside the Palazzo Belmonte's landing-stage, and moored it to a pole. A flight of steps led up to an arched loggia, in shadow now as night fell.

As he mounted the steps, Antonio saw movement beneath the arches, and glimpsed a flutter of scarlet silk. A fox mask snarled at him out of darkness, and then the masked reveller whisked away along the loggia and was lost in the shadows.

Unaccountably shaken, Antonio paused briefly and then beckoned to the boatman who was following, his arms laden with Portia's gifts. At the other side of the loggia the doors of the palazzo stood open, with no sign of a doorkeeper. Antonio stepped inside.

An archway led to the entrance hall. The lamps were unlit; the only light poured down from the landing above, showing the marble floor like a glimmering lake, and the sweep of a staircase.

Antonio had his boatman place his gifts on a side table, next to a rush basket full of apples. Then he dismissed him; as the boatman's footsteps died away he realized that he was not alone in the hall.

A man knelt at the foot of the stairs. Antonio took a few seconds to recognize Bassanio, and a little longer to realize that he crouched beside the body of another man.

"Bassanio?" he said.

Bassanio rose slowly to his feet. He held a knife; both hands were daubed with blood, and blood was smeared over his doublet.

"Bassanio, in God's name – "

"No!" Bassanio's voice was high-pitched, ready to break into hysteria. "It's none of my doing! God, you can't believe . . . I found him – here, like this, just now."

Antonio strode across the hall and looked down at the dead man. His dark hair fanned out over the marble floor. His face was very pale, the eyes staring. There was a ragged wound in his chest.

"Lorenzo," Antonio said.

"You cannot think I did it!"

Bassanio reached out to him, and checked, staring horrified at the blood on his hands. He let the knife fall.

"No – no, of course not," Antonio said.

He stooped and laid a hand against Lorenzo's face. It felt warm, as if he slept, but Antonio could not doubt that life had left him. The enormity of it swept over him. Someone had stabbed Lorenzo – Lorenzo, one of the most harmless men in

Venice – and only moments ago. And Bassanio stood there with blood on his hands. Antonio's heart contracted with fear for his friend.

A door opened at one side of the hall; Antonio heard laughter, and then Portia's voice.

"My lord Bassanio, are you – "

She broke off. Antonio rose to see her coming swiftly towards them, Gratiano and Nerissa just behind her. In the lighted doorway, Salerio and Solanio hovered nervously. Antonio repressed impatience. Those two had scarcely one respectable brain between them; they would not be much help now.

Portia stood looking down, silent, while Nerissa gave a little whimpering sound and hid her face against Gratiano's shoulder. He raised a hand to stroke her hair, his plump, cheerful face rigid with shock.

"In my house," Portia said. Her voice was low, pity and anger driving through it. "Jessica? Where is she? She must not see – "

A scream cut across her words. At the head of the stairs, Jessica, Lorenzo's wife, stood clinging to the balustrade. Nerissa was the first to move, slowly because of the weight of the child within her, but purposefully. Antonio remembered that she and Jessica had quickly become friends, when Lorenzo first took his bride to Belmont.

"I'll go to her, madam," Nerissa said.

"Thank you," said Portia. "Take her to her bedchamber. Send for restoratives – a doctor. Keep her away from here."

They watched as Nerissa intercepted Jessica and put her arms around her; Jessica seemed to struggle and then give in, leaning limply against her. The screaming changed to noisy sobs. Speaking soothingly, too softly for the watchers in the hall to hear, Nerissa led her away.

"Should we call for officers?" said Gratiano.

Bassanio let out a wordless protest.

"No," said Portia, seconding him. "For what will they see? My lord and husband, befouled with his friend's blood. The duke's officers are not subtle men."

Bassanio went white.

"They will put me to the rack."

"They will not," said Portia, "if we can show them who did this. Go and wash, and send servants with lights. I will have Lorenzo's body placed with all honour in our chapel here."

Bassanio almost ran out of the hall. A moment later, servants came with tapers, and as the lamps were lit Antonio reached down to retrieve the knife.

He never touched it. Darkness swirled over his eyes. He heard a roaring in his ears, and a voice rising out of it, soft and menacing: "Let him look to his bond."

"Antonio?" Portia said. "Antonio, are you ill?"

The darkness rolled back. He could see the knife again. The thin, curved blade, the ivory handle, clotted now with blood that might have been his own.

"Lady," he said, "this is the knife Shylock had, that day in court, when he claimed a pound of my flesh."

Gratiano exclaimed something, and came closer to peer at the knife. Salerio and Solanio crowded up behind him, their faces sharing shocked enjoyment. Solanio crossed himself vigorously.

"Are you sure?" Portia said. Antonio shivered.

"Lady, do you think I would not know?"

"Then Shylock did this?" Gratiano said.

Antonio heard a faint sighing, less than the rustle of wind in leaves, a relaxation as they all realized they could lay this hideous thing at the feet of another than Bassanio.

"I cannot believe it," he said.

Gratiano clapped him on the shoulder.

"So speaks Antonio, who would wish never to believe ill of anyone. But someone stabbed Lorenzo, and who better than Shylock? To kill the man who stole his daughter?"

"That was a year ago," said Portia.

"And is she any less stolen?"

Bassanio reappeared from the back of the hall and strode forward to stand beside his wife. He had washed the blood from his hands, and put on a fresh doublet.

"I can see that old villain," he said, "counting over his wrongs like a pile of ducats, waiting for the chance to be revenged. Don't they say revenge is a dish best eaten cold?"

Portia looked around the little group. Somehow they had

drawn around her as if, Antonio thought, they expected her
to discover the truth.

"Has anyone spoken with Shylock?" she asked. "Has anyone
heard him vow revenge?"

"I have seen him, lady," Antonio said. "He bought a
little house off the Campo Manin. He makes his living by
dealing in old books and manuscripts, and now and then a
painting. He – "

"Come to the point!" Gratiano interrupted.

"Forgive me. I go there from time to time, to render him
accounts of his investments, the income that was paid to
Lorenzo. We do not talk of personal matters."

Antonio remembered the blind wall of courtesy that Shylock
used to shut him out. He would have preferred spitting
hatred.

"He would hardly tell you if he had a mind to murder,"
Gratiano said.

"No matter if he did," said Bassanio. "Lorenzo was stabbed
with Shylock's knife. What more proof do we need? I'll call the
officers."

"No – wait."

Antonio caught Bassanio's arm as he moved towards the
doors. He almost flinched at the look of impatience – anger
almost – that his friend turned on him.

"What is it?"

"When Shylock became a Christian and left the Ghetto,"
Antonio began, trying to order his thoughts, "some of his goods
were put up for sale. The knife may have been among them. And
I know . . . I advanced Lorenzo money, to buy Jessica's clothes
and other things that she left behind when she fled from her
father's house."

Bassanio gripped his shoulders, his fingers digging in cruelly.
His face was hard.

"Are you telling me that Lorenzo bought the knife? In God's
name, Antonio, do you want to see me hanged?"

"Antonio is right," Portia broke in coolly. "Shylock
has been our enemy and we all have reason to mistrust
him. Maybe he is guilty, but we must be sure. If he is
condemned through our doing, our hands must be clean.

Could you sleep sound, my lord Bassanio, if it were other-wise?"

Bassanio released Antonio and stood looking sulkily at the floor. Portia began, "Jessica might know – " and broke off as Nerissa appeared on the landing. "Yes, Nerissa? How is she?"

Gratiano sprang up the stairs to his wife's side, and gave her his hand to come down. Nerissa smiled at him.

"I left Jessica with your old nurse, madam," she said to Portia. "She is brewing her a posset to make her sleep."

"Then we must wait to ask about the knife," said Portia. "But meanwhile, good Salerio –" Salerio stepped forward smartly and bowed – "go, I pray you, to Master Shylock's house. Do not let him see you, but speak with his servant. Ask whether Master Shylock was at home this evening, and if not, where he was. Bribe the servant if you must, and bribe him well." She nodded to Bassanio, who, still with a bad grace, fumbled a coin out of his purse and tossed it to Salerio. Meanwhile, Solanio, go you among the boatmen."

"At once, lady!" Solanio said enthusiastically, and added, "Why?"

"To find a man who delivered a passenger to the Palazzo Belmonte this evening. If you do, mark his name and where he plies his boat. Pay him, or if his news has weight, bring him straight here."

Solanio smirked, and held out a hand to Bassanio for money. Bassanio thrust the whole purse at him, and said, "For half a ducat you could bribe a boatman to say he brought Shylock here. For a whole ducat you could bribe him to say he brought his own grandmother."

"That I will not do," Portia said. "Gentlemen, you have your tasks. And do not gossip of this."

Salerio and Solanio bowed, kissed a hand each, and left. Portia watched them out of the doors, shaking her head slightly. She sighed.

"Signior Antonio, we invited you to supper, and you have had poor entertainment. I fear we – "

"Let us see to it," Gratiano interrupted, taking Nerissa's hand. "With your leave, lady."

The grin he gave her was a poor imitation of his usual cheerfulness, but he was trying hard. Portia nodded, and he drew Nerissa away.

"I would not trouble you, lady," Antonio said.

"No trouble, signior. We shall sit and eat, and instead of planning tomorrow's revels, we will plan what we must do, for I cannot long conceal this death."

She stood frowning thoughtfully, twisting a tress of her hair between her fingers. To Antonio's mind she was very beautiful, with a delicacy of line and distinction that almost missed being beauty at all. She wore a plain white dress with a narrow gold edging, and her golden hair was tied carelessly with a ribbon. Pure simplicity; yet no one could have doubted that she was a great lady.

Diffidently, Antonio said, "I brought you gifts, lady."

She smiled at him. "Antonio, you are all kindness." She moved over to the side table, and let her fingers stray over the silk. "So beautiful . . . and from so far away." Suddenly she glanced at him with a spark of amusement. "And a basket of apples?"

"No, lady. I lay no claim to the apples. Did you not bring them with you?"

"No." Portia's frown had returned. She took one of the apples from the basket, turned it between her fingers and sniffed it. It was a russet, brown and slightly wrinkled. "No, we grow none such at Belmont. Bassanio, who brought the apples?"

"How should I know?"

Portia was frowning still.

"You think . . . the murderer?" Antonio said. "Yes, I think I see. He came with a basket of apples, as a reason for coming at all. Perhaps to conceal the knife. Then he set down the apples here, killed Lorenzo, and left . . ." He drew in a painful, ragged breath. "Lady, I may have seen him!"

"What!" said Bassanio.

Antonio described his glimpse of the masked reveller as he was climbing the steps to the loggia. He understood now the danger he had sensed; if he was right, the man in the fox mask had just driven a knife into Lorenzo's breast.

"Then someone left this house," said Portia, "and went – where?"

"Down the loggia, to my left. There were no other boats at the landing-stage. He could have escaped along the alley between this house and the next."

Portia called to a servant who was crossing the hall, and told him to take a lantern, and a companion with him, and search the loggia and the alley. When he had gone, she said, "This does not answer. If this reveller wore a mask and domino, he did not carry a basket of apples. He would not need it, and he would look ridiculous."

"Just a minute," said Bassanio. "Suppose . . . look."

He flung open the lid of a wicker hamper standing close by. Following him, Antonio saw a jumble of silks and animal masks; a white owl stared fiercely up at him.

"These were for tomorrow's masquing," Bassanio said.

"Is anything missing?" Portia asked.

"I can't tell."

"Then perhaps he came with the apples," Antonio said slowly, trying to make sense of what he knew, "and disguised himself as he left. Perhaps to hide blood on his clothes . . ."

Bassanio shivered. He had recovered from the horror of the discovery, and from most of his ill-temper, but he still looked subdued.

"There was not much blood," he said. "The knife was still in the wound. I took it out to see if Lorenzo . . ."

He stumbled into silence. Portia laid a hand on his arm.

"Signior Antonio, what did you see of this masquer? Was he tall – fat?"

"I think not fat." Antonio closed his eyes, trying to recover the memory of a very swift impression. "Though the silks billowed . . . He moved gracefully, and fast. His height . . . I was standing below, on the steps. I cannot be sure."

"Shylock is a very tall man," Bassanio said.

"Yes. I – it may have been."

Bassanio snorted impatiently.

"What were the servants thinking of?" he said. "Why did no one see?"

"We came unexpectedly." Portia's explanation was for

Antonio. "The servants were busy opening the house, and preparing for tomorrow's feast."

"I sent that villain Launcelot Gobbo on ahead," said Bassanio. "But he dawdled on the way, to drink with his cronies, or chase some pretty – "

Portia shook her head at him, half smiling.

"We were not as orderly as I should like," she said.

At the foot of the stairs, servants were composing Lorenzo's body ready to bear it away. Antonio watched in silence, and almost unconsciously made the sign of the cross. Quietly, more seriously than usual, Bassanio said, "Who would murder Lorenzo?" He gave a stifled laugh. "No jealous husbands, no cast-off lovers. Lorenzo never looked at another woman but Jessica." His face grew harder. "It must have been Shylock. The old devil has planned his revenge all this time."

"Half his property is invested with me," Antonio said reluctantly, "for Lorenzo and Jessica to live on. And his will is made out in Lorenzo's favour. That is void now."

Portia was shaking her head, not in denial, but sadly.

"Perhaps he thought," she said, "that Jessica would return to him."

As supper began, the servants whom Portia had sent out to search returned. They displayed a scarlet domino and a fox mask, found stuffed into a cranny along the alley leading away from the waterside. The scarlet silk was spattered with stiffer, darker patches; Antonio lost what little appetite he had when he realized the streaks were dried blood.

He did not want to leave his friends until their trouble was resolved, and accepted Portia's invitation to stay the night. So he was there much later when Salerio came from speaking with Shylock's servant. The man had only just returned from an errand outside the city, that had occupied most of the day. He had no idea where Shylock had been at the time of the murder.

Salerio, with more intelligence than Antonio would have given him credit for, had asked questions in the taverns and on the street corners around the Campo Manin, but without success. No one had seen Shylock.

Solanio did not return until the following morning, looking green and shaky after a night spent drinking with every boatman between San Marco and Corpus Domini. He had found no one who admitted to bringing a passenger to the Palazzo Belmonte.

Antonio remained at the palazzo, but he felt restless. Portia explained nothing. She despatched servants with messages, but told no one, not even Bassanio, what they were.

Bassanio himself was even more restless, his temper fraying. Antonio suggested a game of chess, in the room that had been Portia's father's study, but before it was half over Bassanio thrust the table away so that the exquisite ivory and jade pieces rattled, and flung himself over to the window.

"This is damnable!" he said.

Antonio followed, and rested a hand on his friend's shoulder. Bassanio reached up and touched it, not looking at him. Awkwardly, Antonio said, "I will do all I can – "

"I know." Bassanio stared out of the window. "But if I am accused of this crime – "

"No one could believe . . ."

Antonio felt sick and inwardly shaking. A year ago he had willingly given Bassanio up to happiness; he could not endure losing him to the dungeons of the duke, from where so few men ever came back. His grip tightened as if pure physical strength could protect Bassanio, though he knew it could not. Nor all his merchandise . . . unless, perhaps, he could persuade Bassanio to take passage on a ship . . . But would his friend consent to give up his wealth, his position, to give up Portia?

Antonio was still confusedly forming plans when Bassanio tore away from him.

"I'll not endure this," he said. "I'll find her, and make her tell me what she means to do."

He strode out; Antonio followed anxiously, and caught him up in the hall, where Portia was talking with Launcelot Gobbo. As the two men approached, Portia handed Launcelot a purse; Launcelot ducked his head respectfully and left through the main doors.

"What's this?" Bassanio said petulantly. "Do you command my servant without telling me?"

Portia herself betrayed impatience, but she kept it under control.

"Launcelot has an important errand," she said. "You'll know all, in good time, my lord."

"In good time?" Bassanio said. "How long must we wait? We can't keep Lorenzo's death a secret for much longer. If we cancel our revels tonight the whole of Venice will know something is wrong, and if we hold them as we meant to do then all our guests will wonder why Lorenzo is not here."

Portia looked thoughtful. Then she said, "My lord Bassanio, call everyone to meet here this evening, at the same hour that Lorenzo died. Then I will tell you the truth."

"Tell me now!" Bassanio demanded, but Portia had already turned away.

At the time Portia commanded, all her household, along with Antonio, Salerio and Solanio, assembled in the hall where, the day before, Lorenzo had lain dead.

Jessica herself joined them, escorted gently downstairs by Nerissa. She wore black, with a veil, but when she was seated she drew it back from her face. She was pale, her eyes huge, and weariness shadowed her beauty, but she was calm.

As she settled herself, there came a pounding on the doors, and the doorkeepers, at their posts now, threw them open. In the doorway stood two of the duke's officers, enormous men in their resplendent uniforms. Antonio felt a stab of panic, and moved closer to Bassanio, but Portia went to meet the officers calmly, as if she had expected them. Antonio could not hear what she said, but watched as the two men bowed, and withdrew to stand beside the wall.

Portia returned to Antonio and her husband.

"Well?" Bassanio snapped. "We are all here. Why do we wait?"

"We are not all here, my lord," said Portia. Her manner had become more formal with the entry of the officers. "We wait for two more guests."

"Two more? Who?"

Before Portia could reply there was movement outside the

doors, which still stood open. A figure stalked into the hall. Shylock.

He halted and looked around. Antonio inclined his head as the cold gaze flickered over him. Recognition showed in Shylock's face of Bassanio and Gratiano, and a second's utter stillness as he saw Jessica. For all Antonio knew, this was the first time father and daughter had looked on each other since the events of a year ago.

Shylock's hesitation lasted only a moment. He paced forward again; his height commanded the room. He wore a plain black garment, like a cassock, with a silver pectoral cross; he might have been a priest. His face was a scimitar wrought of ivory, not steel. He laid a hand on his breast and bowed to Portia; there was a world of arrogance in his apparent humility.

"You sent for me, madam?"

"I asked you to come, Master Shylock," Portia said. "I thank you for your forbearance."

Her courtesy sounded unforced. Antonio felt sick. She was all honour, all truth; could she speak so to the man she had brought here to be trapped and condemned?

Shylock refused a seat, and stood waiting with massive calm for Portia to begin.

"I have grave news for you, sir," she said. "Yesterday, at about this time, here in my house, we found your son Lorenzo dead."

Shylock started, and his gaze became more intensely fixed on Portia. Antonio did not believe he could be guilty and look so, unless he was a superb actor. But of course he was; Antonio had proved that last year when he had been deceived by Shylock's offer of false friendship.

"Continue," Shylock said.

Portia described how Bassanio had found Lorenzo's body. She beckoned to a servant, and the man came forward with the knife laid across his palms.

"You know this knife, sir?" she asked Shylock.

For a moment Shylock hesitated. Then he said, "I do. I own that it was mine, once."

Although his expression was still guarded, there was

something about his stance which reminded Antonio of a wolf before the dog pack pulls it down.

He felt cold as Shylock's bright gaze focused on him. The old Jew's lips moved into a savage smile, his teeth bared.

"You think I did this?" he said.

Antonio could not answer; he did not have the courage. Only Portia was strong enough to stand against Shylock.

She said, "We know you hated Lorenzo – with some justice – for taking Jessica from you. And Lorenzo dead cannot inherit from you. You had cause, Master Shylock. You had cause."

"And who gave me cause?" He spat the words like filth at Antonio's feet. "You, with your Christian mercy."

"That has nothing to do with Lorenzo," Bassanio said.

"It has everything to do with Lorenzo," Shylock snarled. "Son, your lady called him. My son Lorenzo. Did I want him, would I own him, if I had been free? A Christian, a puling boy, a wastrel? Give me no more such sons."

"I thought to provide for him, and for your daughter, sir," Antonio said. "They were wed; would you have had them beg their bread in the streets?"

"I would have had them starve in the streets." In a fury more terrifying because it was quiet, he turned on Antonio, his words hissed out through his teeth. "You set my faith at nothing. You called me pagan, misbelieving dog. You spat on my rituals and my customs and the wisdom of my fathers. But this faith, this nothing, even this was too much to allow me. You stripped it from me, and flung me into the waters of your Christian baptism."

"Both your old faith and your new," said Portia, "tell you to do no murder."

"New faith?" said Shylock. Though he replied to Portia the intensity of his anger was for Antonio. "My new faith? Do you find faith in the sign of the cross or the wafer on the tongue or the bells and candles and the smoke of incense?" He beat a clenched fist upon his breast. "Faith is in the heart. In the heart, and you broke mine. With no faith to uphold me, what should I do but kill?"

He raised a hand and lashed it across Antonio's face. Antonio staggered from the force of the blow. He thought he would fall, and then Bassanio had an arm about him, tightly, bracing him. For a moment, to his shame, Antonio gave himself up to his strength, leaning against him.

"Don't touch him!" Bassanio spat out. "You had him in your power once, but never again. Don't try to shuffle off your own guilt on to him."

"No." Antonio drew away from his friend, forcing himself to speak coherently. "It's true. God help me, it is all true."

With blinding insight he saw how the crime was rooted in the events of a year ago, but not as he had thought at first. Not because of how Shylock's property had been disposed, but because he himself, with unconscious hypocrisy, had deprived Shylock of all he valued, in the name of mercy.

"I will repay the debt," he said, "if you will tell me how."

Shylock had withdrawn into immobility again, his passion veiled. He made no answer.

"Then all I am is forfeit," Antonio said.

"No." Portia touched his hand; her own felt cool. "Be at peace, Antonio. There is still mercy."

"I drove a man to kill – " he protested.

"Perhaps. If he had killed. But he did not. Shylock is innocent of this crime."

The silence in the hall broke up into a babble which Portia stilled with a single gesture. Only Shylock remained aloof, except for a flash of surprise which he hid almost at once beneath a mask of ironic inquiry.

"When Lorenzo was killed," Portia said, "the sun had already gone down. The Jewish Sabbath had begun. No Jew committed this crime."

"No Jew is accused," Bassanio said roughly. "Shylock has become a Christian."

Portia smiled faintly.

"A forced conversion is no conversion at all. You have heard him say so himself. And I do not believe that he has ever renounced the Jewish faith in his heart. Do I speak truth, Master Shylock?"

Shylock took his pectoral cross into his hand and contemplated it for a moment before letting it fall. Bowing his head, still with the look of ironic self-mockery, he said, "Truly, madam, although I have submitted myself to baptism, and worship most piously in San Marco, I will say with Naaman the Syrian, 'When I bow down myself in the house of Rimmon, the Lord pardon thy servant in this thing.'"

"Shylock still thinks as a Jew," Portia said, "and within the limits we Christians in our wisdom have laid down for him, he still acts as a Jew." She repeated, "No Jew committed this crime."

"Then in God's name, who did?" said Bassanio.

As he spoke, there was another disturbance near the hall doors. Antonio, almost faint with relief, could not see at first where it came from.

"I told you, my lord," Portia said, "that I was expecting two more guests. This, I think, is the second."

Through the doors beyond the archway Launcelot Gobbo appeared, leading someone with him – an old man, bent and whitehaired, wearing a leather cape and brown frieze breeches, and carrying a battered straw hat. The old man was reluctant, protesting, and grumbled to a halt just inside the hall, peering nervously at the duke's officers.

Launcelot grinned, and bowed.

"I brought him, lady," he said, tugging his forelock. "Hard work it was, on account of a pig that was just farrowing, but I told him, reckon old sow can manage for herself."

"Thank you, Launcelot," Portia said. "Now, Master Gobbo – "

"Eh, call me not Master Gobbo," said the old man bashfully, clapping the broadbrimmed hat across his breast and bowing.

"Master Gobbo, you came to visit me last night, did you not, about this time?"

Antonio suddenly began to understand.

"The basket of apples – "

"Then it was Old Gobbo who brought them!" Bassanio interrupted. "Are you telling us that he killed Lorenzo? This is lunacy!"

At the mention of killing, Old Gobbo made for the door, only to be hauled back by his son.

"Gently, my lord Bassanio," said Portia. "No, of course

Master Gobbo did not kill Lorenzo. But we have great need of him."

"Great need?" Bassanio said. "Why?"

Portia said, "He is a witness."

Bassanio gaped at her, and Antonio drew in breath painfully. He heard Gratiano mutter, "Of course!"

"Master Gobbo, you visited me last night and brought me a present of apples, did you not?"

"Best of the crop, mistress," the old man said.

"But you did not stay to speak with me, or my servants, or even your son Launcelot. Why did you not, Master Gobbo? What did you see?"

Old Gobbo shuffled further into the hall, and began peering at each of the company in turn. Antonio could not help reaching out to grip Bassanio's arm, not knowing whether he wanted to give reassurance or receive it.

Then Old Gobbo stopped.

"I seen her," he said, pointing straight at Jessica. "I seen her put on one o' they scarlet cloaks, and a mask like a fox. I seen her wi' a knife in her hand."

Into the leaden silence, Antonio breathed out, "You knew!"

Portia never took her eyes from Jessica, but her mouth twisted.

"Old lawyer's trick," she murmured. "Never ask a question without knowing the answer."

Nerissa began to sob quietly, and Gratiano took her into his arms.

"Good Master Gobbo," Portia said evenly, "what did you do then?"

"I run," the old man said. "Ladies wi' knives – I want naught to do wi' that."

"And left your basket of apples on the table there?"

The old man nodded.

"Thank you," said Portia. "Launcelot, take him to the kitchens and get him something to eat and drink."

No one spoke until Launcelot had led his father out. Then Jessica herself broke the silence, with angry laughter.

"Do you condemn me on the word of that old fool?"

Her face was ugly, sneering. "Everyone knows he's blind as a bat."

"Not so blind that he does not know what he saw," said Portia. "But there is more."

Antonio looked round at the company. The duke's men, still stolidly blank-faced, had moved up to stand close to Jessica. Salerio and Solanio were muttering together in a corner. Nerissa still wept, clinging to Gratiano. When Jessica was named, Bassanio had flushed scarlet, but now he looked white and miserable, as if he would rather be anywhere than here, listening to this. Antonio could not guess what he himself was revealing. Only Shylock had the self-command to move towards Portia, suddenly imperious.

"Go on," he said. "Make this good."

Portia stood her ground, but Antonio could see how this pained her. She had begun it only to save Bassanio, and then to save Shylock himself.

"When Signior Antonio arrived here last night," she said, "he met a masked reveller in the loggia. Later we found the mask and domino, spattered with blood, in the alley beside the house. We were all supposed to believe that someone had come here, killed Lorenzo, and left.

"But the house has a side door. One of us could have killed Lorenzo, gone out wearing the mask, abandoned the disguise in the alley, and returned through that door.

"Once I realized that, all became clearer. I did not consider the servants. Lorenzo treated them well, and they had no reason to want him dead. Earlier that evening, Signior Salerio and Signior Solanio visited us." At the mention of their names the two men bowed, uneasily. "I passed through the hall; it was empty then. After that, Signior Gratiano, Nerissa and I were together with our guests. The only people to be alone were my lord Bassanio, and Jessica.

"My lord Bassanio found the body, and was very much distressed. I did not believe he had killed his friend, and he could not have worn the fox mask, for there was no time for him to return to the house.

"And then Signior Antonio told me that the knife that stabbed Lorenzo was the one that Master Shylock used to threaten him in court last year. He also told me that Lorenzo himself had bought property from Shylock's house. He could have owned the knife.

"The only detail that I could not explain was the basket of apples, for it showed that someone had brought them, and gone away unseen. Then I remembered that Launcelot Gobbo was sent ahead to announce us to the servants here, but arrived late. When I questioned him, he admitted he had stopped to visit his parents. His father, good old man, knowing we were coming to Venice, brought a gift to welcome us, and saw . . . what you have heard, gentlemen."

She turned to Jessica, and held out a hand.

"Jessica, why?"

Jessica rose to her feet. Her eyes flashed; she laughed.

"You ask me that!" she said. Portia waited for an answer with patient gravity, to grow dismayed as Jessica pointed at Bassanio. "You should rather ask him!"

Portia looked at Bassanio. He could not meet her eyes, or see the pain there.

"He took me to his bed." Jessica's voice was defiant. "He told me he loved me. But for you, and Lorenzo, he would have wedded me."

Portia was shaking her head as if she wanted to deny what Antonio could see was true.

"Lorenzo loved you," she said.

Jessica made a sound of disgust.

"He prattled of stars and flowers, and turned my head when I was a girl in my father's house. But a woman needs more." Her voice dropped and her eyes went to Bassanio. "Your lord taught me that . . . more than Lorenzo ever could."

Antonio did not know where Portia found the courage to stand erect, steady, and go on probing for the truth before them all.

"Was I to be the next?" she said. "Was I to die so you and he could be together?"

"No!" Bassanio found his voice, outrage and fear warring in it. "Portia, I did not know!"

His wife said nothing to him. Instead, she gestured towards the duke's officers, who closed up on either side of Jessica and took her by the arms. She did not try to struggle; she gave them a look of scorching contempt, her head held high.

As they led her past Shylock, Antonio thought he saw a change in the man's face, as if he would have reached out to her. Jessica did not even look at him, but went out in silence.

The tension in the hall did not relax. Antonio knew that in finding the hand that had driven home the knife, Portia had solved only a tiny fraction of the problem.

At last Gratiano stumbled into speech.

"But you said no Jew committed the murder."

"She is no Jew," Shylock said. "Nor Christian, nor anything that is clean."

Antonio flinched from the condemnation, even though it was not now aimed at him. But Portia could bear it.

"Bassanio?" she said.

The tone was gentle, but the word pierced like a sword. Bassanio spread his arms.

"It was nothing," he said. "It meant nothing. One afternoon – there was wine, and sunlight . . . and she was willing, God knows! And you were playing the great lady, busy about your affairs . . ." He stammered to a close in a vast, listening silence, and made one final, pathetic effort to justify himself. "I never thought Jessica would take it seriously!"

"She lacked experience in her wantonness," Shylock said drily. "She thought when Christians take their pleasure, they mean marriage."

"And she has paid for it, as well as Lorenzo," Portia said. "I will do what I can for her."

Shylock bowed to her.

"You will excuse me, lady," he said. "I find myself . . . ill at ease, in this company."

Slowly, not looking back, he withdrew through the open doors. Portia watched him go; her face had grown flint hard.

"When you returned to me, my lord Bassanio, a year ago, without the ring you had sworn to me to keep, your friend Antonio pledged his soul for your good faith. What of his soul now, my lord? Who do you think will come and claim it at the last?"

Bassanio stared, and spun round to face Antonio. The handsome face was breaking up, the sunny confidence gone, leaving only a desperate need for refuge. His mouth was working, but no words came. He almost threw himself into Antonio's arms, and like a child gasped out, "Forgive me!"

Antonio held him in his embrace, feeling the sobs that shook him.

"He could be mine now," he thought. "I could take him away and he would stay with me because he has nothing else."

Unexpectedly he was confronted with the question of what he really wanted, and he did not know the answer, any more than he had known it twenty-four hours ago when he walked through the doors of the palazzo and found Bassanio with Lorenzo's blood on his hands. All he knew was that some prices are too high to pay.

He thrust Bassanio off to arm's length. Gripping his shoulders hard, he turned him to face Portia. He said, "Bassanio, you owe me nothing. That is where you must look for forgiveness."

Gently he thrust Bassanio forward. Bassanio stumbled, and fell to his knees. He reached out, groping blindly towards his wife's skirts.

Portia stood erect, white and staring at nothing. At her feet Bassanio crouched, sobbing, his face buried in his hands. Antonio took a step forward.

"Oh, lady – "

He could say no more. Portia turned her head, and her face lost that terrifying blankness as she focused on him. She said nothing, but she smiled; Antonio thought his heart would break at that smile, at the sweetness and the bitterness and the self-knowledge, as she reached out and laid her hand lightly on Bassanio's head.

Antonio was seized with a sudden urgency; one thing remained for him to do. He turned and almost ran out through the loggia, to where water lapped gently against the landing-stage.

The Grand Canal glittered under the stars. In the distance Antonio could hear the sound of a lute. Not far away a gondola filled with masked revellers was gliding towards the Palazzo Belmonte, its wake cutting the quiet waters like an arrow.

Shylock was about to get into his own boat. Hurriedly Antonio approached, stopped, gasped for air that suddenly seemed inadequate. He said, "Master Shylock – "

The old Jew paused. In that ivory countenance there was nothing to be read.

"Master Shylock," Antonio repeated, "I am sorry. I am so very sorry."

The words were pitiful. He wanted them to encompass so much: Jessica's guilt and Bassanio's part in it; the assumptions they had made; the way they had hoped to heap blame on the outsider and keep safe their own little world. He wanted to reach back across a year to the mistaken mercy at the end of the trial; to a father's loss of his only daughter; to his own careless pride and contempt. So few words to mean so much. He wanted to weep.

Shylock was still looking at him with that unreadable countenance. He bent his head with infinite dignity.

"Be at peace, Signior Antonio," he said. "For you too, I think, have bowed down in the house of Rimmon."

Antonio fought the ache in his throat. He did not know how to take his leave without offering more insult, or making a fool of himself. The silence was like a suffocating blanket. In the end, it was Shylock who spoke.

"Would it please you, Signior Antonio, to come and have supper with me? I have a cask of good wine, and a manuscript of Aristotle that might be worth your perusing."

Antonio stared at him. He had seen that face lit with savage mockery; he had seen it blandly ironic, and contorted with hatred. A few seconds ago he had seen it barricaded against him. He had never seen it, until now, friendly, with a touch of hesitancy.

The idea was, of course, impossible. He began to say so.

"I thank you, Master Shylock . . ."

He cast a glance over his shoulder. The windows of the palazzo blazed with light. The revellers had reached the landing-stage and were jostling their way through the loggia. Laughter spilled from them.

Antonio knew he should go back. Instead, he found himself

saying, "I thank you, Master Shylock. I should like that very much."

He turned away from the lighted windows and stepped down into the boat beside the Jew.

Epilogue 🖤

> Our last two stories are not based directly on Shakespeare's
> plays but on events and actions surrounding them. To
> reveal more would be to reveal too much. Suffice it to
> say that "An Ensuing Evil" relates directly to events
> arising at the first performance of Shakespeare's All is
> True (later printed as Henry the Eighth) on 29 June
> 1613, whilst "The Collaborator" brings together clues
> from all of Shakespeare's plays to reveal a much darker
> and deeper mystery.

AN ENSUING EVIL

Peter Tremayne

. . . yet I can give you inkling
Of an ensuing evil . . .
Shakespeare, *Famous History of the Life of King Henry
VIII*, II, I

"It's a body, Master Constable."

Master Hardy Drew, Constable of the Bankside Watch,
stared in distaste at the wherryman.

"I have eyes to see with," he replied sourly. "Just tell me
how you came by it."

The stocky boatman put a hand to the back of his head and scratched as if this action was necessary to the process of summoning up his memories.

"It were just as we turned mid-river to the quay here," the wherryman began. "We'd brought coal up from Greenwich. I was guiding the barge in when we spotted the body in the river and so we fished it out."

Master Drew glanced down to the body sprawled in a sodden mess on the dirty deck of the coal barge.

The finding of bodies floating in the Thames was not an unusual occurrence. London was a cesspool of suffering humanity, especially along these banks between London Bridge and Bankside. Master Drew had not been Constable of the Watch for three years without becoming accustomed to bodies being trawled out of this stretch of water whose southern bank came under his policing jurisdiction. Cut-throats, footpads and all manner of the criminal scum of the city found the river a convenient place to rid themselves of their victims. And it was not just those who had died violent deaths who were disposed of in the river but corpses of the poor, sick and diseased whose relatives couldn't afford a church burial. The pollution of the water had become so bad that this very year a water reservoir, claimed to be the first of its kind in all Europe, had been opened at Clerkenwell to supply fresh water for the city.

However, what marked this body out for the attention of the Constable, among the half-dozen or so that had been fished from the river this particular Saturday morning, was the fact that it was the body of a well-dressed young man. Despite the effects of his immersion, he bore the stamp of a gentleman. In addition he had not died of drowning for his throat had been expertly cut and no more than twelve hours previously by the condition of the body.

The Constable bent down and examined the features dispassionately. In life, the young man had been handsome, was well kempt. He had ginger hair, a splattering of freckles across the nose and a scar, which might have been the result of a knife or sword, across the forehead over the right eye. His age was no more than twenty-one or twenty-two years. Master Drew considered that he might be the son of a squire or someone in the professions – a parson's son, perhaps. The Constable's expert scrutiny had ruled out his being of higher quality for the clothes, while fashionable, were only of moderately good tailoring. Therefore, the young man had not been someone of flamboyant wealth.

The wherryman was peering over the Constable's shoulders and sniffed.

"Victim of a footpad most like?"

Master Drew did not answer but, keeping his leather gloves on, he took the hand of the young man and examined a large and ostentatious ring that was on it.

"Since when did a footpad leave jewellery on his victim?" he asked. He removed the ring carefully and held it up. "Ah!" he commented.

"What, Master Constable?" demanded the wherryman.

Drew had noticed that the ring, ostentatious though it was, was not really as valuable as first glance might suggest. It boasted no precious metals or stones, thus fitting the Constable's image of someone who wanted to convey a sense of style without the wealth to back it. He put it into his pocket.

There was a small leather purse on the man's belt. Its mouth was not well tied. He opened it without expecting to find anything, so was surprised when a few coins and a key fell out. They were as dry as the interior of the purse.

"A sixpenny piece and three strange copper coins," observed Master Drew.

He held up one of the copper coins.

"Marry! The new copper farthings. I have not seen any before this day."

"What's that?" replied the wherryman.

"These coins have just been issued to replace the silver farthings. Well, whatever the reason for his killing, robbery it was not."

Master Drew was about to stand up when he noticed a piece of paper tucked into the man's doublet. He drew it forth and tried to unfold it, sodden as it was.

"A theatre bill. For the Blackfriars Theatre. A performance of *The Maid's Tragedy*," he remarked.

He rose and waved to two men of the Watch who were waiting on the quay with a cart. They came down onto the barge and, in answer to Master Drew's gesture, manhandled the corpse up the stone steps to their cart.

"What now then, Constable?" demanded the old wherryman.

"Back to your work, man," replied Master Drew. "And I to mine. I have to discover who this young coxcomb is ... *was*, and the reason for his being in the river with his throat slit."

"Will there be a reward for finding him?" the wherryman asked slyly. "I have lost time in landing my cargo of coal."

Master Drew regarded the man without humour.

"When you examined the purse of the corpse, master wherryman, you neglected to retie it properly. If he had gone into the river with the purse open as it was, then the interior would not have been dry and neither would the coins."

The wherryman winced at the Constable's cold tone.

"i do not begrudge you a reward, which you have taken already, but, out of interest, how much was left in the purse when you found it?"

"By the faith, Master Constable ..." the wherryman protested.

"The truth now!" snapped Master Drew, his grey eyes glinting like wet slate.

"I took only a silver shilling, that is all. On my mother's honour."

"I will take charge of that money," replied the Constable, holding out his hand. "And I will forget what I have heard for theft is theft and the reward for a thief is a hemp rope. Remember that, and I'll leave you to your honest toil."

One of the watchmen was waiting eagerly for the Constable as he climbed up on to the quay.

"Master Drew, I do reckon I've seen this 'ere cove somewhere afore," he said, raising his knuckles to his forehead in salute.

Master Drew regarded the man dourly.

"Well, then? Where do you think you have seen him before?"

"I do be trying 'ard to think on't."

His companion was staring at the face of the corpse with a frown.

"'E be right. I do say 'e be one o' them actor fellows. Can't think where I see'd 'im."

Master Drew glanced sharply at him.

"An actor?"

He stared down at the theatre bill he still held in his gloved hand and pursed his lips thoughtfully.

"Take him up to the mortuary. I have business at the Blackfriars Theatre."

The Constable turned along the quay and found a solitary boatman soliciting for custom. The man looked awkward as the Constable approached.

"I need your services," Master Drew said shortly, putting the man a little at ease, for it was rare that the appearance of the Constable on the waterfront meant anything other than trouble. "Blackfriars Steps."

"Sculls then, Master Constable?" queried the man.

"Sculls it is," Master Drew agreed climbing into the small dinghy. The boatman sat at his oars and sent the dinghy dancing across the river to the north bank, across the choppy waters which were raised by an easterly wind.

As they crossed, Drew was not interested in the spectacle up to London Bridge, with its narrow arches where the tide ran fast because of the constriction of the crossing. Beyond it, he knew was the great port where ships from all parts of the world tied up, unloading cargoes under the shadow of the grim grey Tower. The north bank, where the city proper was sited, was not Constable Drew's jurisdiction. He was Constable on the south bank of the river but he was not perturbed about crossing out of his territory. He knew the City Watch well enough.

The boat rasped against the bottom of Blackfriars Steps. He flipped the man a halfpenny and walked with a measured tread up the street towards the tower of St Paul's rising above the city which was shrouded with the acrid stench of coal fires rising from a hundred thousand chimneys. It was not far to the Blackfriars Theatre.

He walked in and was at once hailed by a tall man who fluttered his hands nervously.

"I say, fellow! Away! Begone! The theatre is not open for another three hours yet."

Master Drew regarded the man humourlessly.

"I come not to see the play but to seek information."

He reached behind his jerkin and drew forth his seal of office.

"A Constable?" The man assumed a comical woebegone expression. "What do you seek here, good Constable? We have our papers in order, the licence from the Lord Chamberlain. What is there that is wrong?"

"To whom do I speak?" demanded Master Drew.

"Why, to Master Page Williams, the assistant manager of our company – Children of the Revel."

The man stuck out his chin proudly.

"And are any of your revelling children astray this afternoon?"

"Astray, good master? What do you mean?"

"I speak plainly. Are all your company of players accounted for today?"

"Indeed, they be. We are rehearsing our next performance which requires all our actors."

"Is there no one missing?"

"All are present. Why do you ask?"

Master Drew described the body of the young man that had been fished from the river. Master Page Williams looked unhappy.

"It seems that I know the youth. An impetuous youth, he was, who came to this theatre last night and claimed to be a playwright whose work had been stolen."

"Did he have a name?"

"Alas, I have forgotten it, if I were even told it. This youth, if it be one and the same, strutted in before the evening performance of our play and demanded to speak with the manager. I spoke with him."

"And what did he want?" pressed Master Drew.

"This youth accused our company of pirating a play that he claimed to be author of."

Constable Drew raised an eyebrow.

"Tell me, was there reason behind this encounter?"

"Good Master Constable, we are rehearsing a play whose author is one Bardolph Zenobia. He has written a great tragedy entitled *The Vow Breaker Delivered*. It is a magnificent drama . . ." He paused at the Constable's frown and then hastened on. "This youth, whom you describe, came to the theatre and claimed that this play was stolen from him and that he was the true author. As if a mere youth could have penned such a work. He claimed that he had assistance in the writing of it from the hand of some companion of his . . ."

"And you set no store by his claim, that this play was stolen from him?"

"None whatsoever. Master Zenobia is a true gentleman of the theatre. A serious gentleman. He has the air of quality about him . . ."

"So you know him well?"

"Not well," confessed Master Williams. "He has been to the theatre on diverse occasions following our acceptance of his work. I believe that he has rooms at the Groaning Cardinal Tavern in Clink Street . . ."

"Clink Street?"

It was across the river in his own Bankside jurisdiction.

"What age would you place this Master Zenobia at?"

"Fully forty years, with greying hair about the temples and a serene expression that would grace an archbishop."

Master Drew sniffed dourly. Theatre people were always given to flowery descriptions.

"So did the youth depart from the theatre?"

"Depart he did but not until I threatened to call the Watch. When I refused to countenance his demands, he shouted and threatened me. He said that if he did not recover the stolen play or get compensation, his life would be in danger."

"His life?" mused Master Drew. "Marry! But that is an odd thing to say. Are you sure he said it was *his* life in danger not the life of Master Zenobia? He did not mean this in the manner of a threat?"

"I have an ear for dialogue, good master," rebuked the man. "The youth soon betook himself off. It happened that

Master Zenobia was on stage, approving the costumes for his drama, and so I warned him to beware of the young man and his outrageous claims."

"What did he say?"

"He just replied that he would have a care and soon after departed."

"Is he here today?"

"No. He told me he would be unable to see the first performance of the play this afternoon but would come straightway to the theatre after the matinee."

"A curious attitude for an aspiring playwright," observed Master Drew. "Most of them would want to be witnesses to the first performance of their work."

"Indeed, they would. It seems odd that Master Zenobia only calls at our poor theatre outside the hours of our performances."

Constable Drew thanked the man and turned out of the theatre to walk back to the river. Instead of spending another halfpenny to cross, he decided to walk the short distance to the spanning wooden piles of London Bridge and walk across the busy thoroughfare with its sprawling lopsided constructions balanced precariously upon it. Master Drew knew the Watch on the bridge and spent a pleasant half-an-hour with the man, for it was midday and a pint of ale and pork pie at one of the grog shops crowded on the bridge was a needed diversion from the toil of the day. He bade farewell to the Watch and came off the bridge at the south bank turning west towards Clink Street.

The Groaning Cardinal Tavern was not an auspicious-looking inn. Its sign depicted a popish cardinal being burnt at the stake. It reminded Constable Drew, with a shudder, that only the previous year some heretics had been burnt at the stake in England. Fears of Catholic plots still abounded. Henry, the late Prince of Wales, had refused to marry a Catholic princess only weeks before his death and it was rumoured abroad by papists that this had been God's punishment on him. Protestants spoke of witchcraft.

Master Drew entered the tavern.

The innkeeper was a giant of a man, tall, broad-shouldered,

well-muscled and without a shirt but a short, leather, sleeveless jerkin over his hairy torso. He was sweating and it became evident that he was stacking ale barrels.

"Bardolph Zenobia, Master Constable?" He threw back his head and laughed. "Someone be telling you lies. Ain't no Master Zenobia here. He do sound like a foreigner."

Constable Drew had come to the realization that the name was probably a theatrical one for he knew that many in the theatre adopted such preposterous designations.

He repeated the description that Master Page Williams had given him and saw a glint of anxiety creep into the innkeeper's eyes.

"What be he done, Master Constable? 'E ain't wanted for debt?"

Master Drew shook his head.

"The man may yet settle his score with you. But I need information from this man, whoever he is."

The innkeeper sighed deeply.

"First floor, front right."

"And what name does this thespian reside under?"

"Master Tom Hawkins."

"That sounds more reasonable that Master Zenobia," observed the Constable.

"Them players are all the same, with high-sounding titles and names," agreed the innkeeper. "Few of them can match their name to a farthing. But Master Hawkins is different. He has been a steady guest here these last five years."

"He has his own recognizances?"

The man stared at him bewildered.

"I mean, does he have financial means other than the theatre?"

"He do pay his bills, that's all I do say, master," the innkeeper replied.

"But he is a player?"

"One of the King's Men."

Master Drew was surprised.

"At the Globe Theatre?"

"He is one of Master Burbage's players," confirmed the innkeeper.

Constable Drew mounted the stairs and knocked at the first floor, front right door. There was no answer. He did not hesitate but entered. The room was deserted. It was also untidy. Clothes and papers were strewn here and there. Master Drew peered through them. There were some play parts and a page or two on which the name "Bardolph Zenobia" was scrawled.

He took himself downstairs and saw the big innkeeper again.

"Maybe he has gone to the theatre?" suggested the man when he told him the room was deserted.

"It is still a while before the time of the matinee performance."

"They sometimes hold rehearsals before the performance," the innkeeper pointed out.

Master Drew was about to turn away when he realized it would not come amiss to ask if the innkeeper knew ought of the youth whose body had been discovered. He gave the man a description without informing him of his death. But his inquiry was received with a vehement shake of the head.

"I have not seen such a young man here nor do I know him."

Constable Drew walked to where the Globe Theatre dominated its surroundings in Bankside. Master Hardy Drew had been a boy when the Burbage brothers, Cuthbert and Richard, had built the theatre there fourteen years before. Since then the Globe had become an institution south of the river. It had first become the home of the Lord Chamberlain's Men who, on the succession of James VI of Scotland to the English throne ten years ago, had been given gracious permission to call themselves the King's Men. Master Drew knew Cuthbert Burbage slightly, for their paths had crossed several times. Cuthbert Burbage ran the business side of the theatre while his brother, Richard Burbage, was the principal actor and director of the plays which were performed there.

Master Drew entered the doors of the Globe Theatre. An elderly doorman came forward, recognized the Constable and halted nervously.

"Give you a good day, Master Jasper," Master Drew greeted him.

"Is ought amiss, good master?" grumbled the old man.

"Should there be?" the Constable smiled thinly.

"That I would not know for I keep myself to myself and do my job without offending God nor the King nor, I do pray, my fellow man."

Master Drew looked at him sourly before glancing around.

"Are the players gathered?"

"Not yet."

"Who is abroad in the theatre?"

Master Jasper looked suspicious.

"Master Richard Burbage is on stage."

The Constable walked through into the circular auditorium, leaving the old man staring anxiously after him, and climbed the wooden steps onto the stage.

A middle-aged man was kneeling on the stage appearing to be measuring something.

Master Drew coughed to announce his presence.

Richard Burbage was still a handsome man in spite of the obvious ravages of the pox. He glanced up with a frown.

"And who might you be, you rogue?" he grunted, still bending to his task.

Drew pursed his lips sourly and then suddenly smiled.

"No rogue, that's for sure. I might be the shade of Constable Dogberry come to demand amends for defamation of his character."

Burbage paused and turned to examine him closely.

"Are you a player, good master?"

"Not I," replied Drew, "and God be thanked for it."

"How make you freely with the name of Dogberry, then?"

"I have witnessed your plays, sir. I took offence to the pompous and comical portrayal of the Constable in Master Shakespeare's jotting. *Much Ado About Nothing* was its title and, indeed, Master Burbage, *Much Ado About Nothing* was a title never more truly given to such a work. 'Twas certainly *Much Ado About Nothing*."

Richard Burbage stood up and brushed himself down, frowning as he did so.

"Are you, then, a critic of the theatre, sir?"

"Not I. But I am a critic of the portrayal of a hard-working Constable and the Watch of this fair town of ours."

"How so, good master?"

"I judge because I am a Constable myself. Constable of Bankside in which this theatre is placed."

"Ar't come to imprison me for defaming the Watch then, sir?" asked Burbage stiffly.

Master Drew chuckled with good humour.

"Marry, sir, there be not enough prisons in the entire kingdom wherein to imprison everyone who makes jest of the Constable and his Watch."

"Then what . . .?"

"I am seeking one Tom Hawkins."

Burbage groaned aloud.

"What has he done? He is due on stage in an hour or so and I fear we have no competent understudy. Do not tell me that you mean to arrest him? On what grounds?"

"I come not to arrest anyone . . . yet. Where is Master Hawkins?"

"Not here as yet."

Master Drew looked round. There were a few people in corners of the theatre, apparently rehearsing lines.

"What play are you rehearsing?" he asked with interest.

"Will Shakespeare's *Famous History of the Life of King Henry VIII*."

"Ah, that is a play that I have not seen."

"Then you would be most welcome to stay . . ."

"Does Master Hawkins take part in this play?"

"He does for he is Cardinal Campeius," came Burbage's immediate response. "It is a part of medium tolerance, a few lines here and yonder."

The elderly harassed-looking doorman approached Burbage.

"I declare, Master Richard, that the fools have not sent us gunpowder. What shall I do?"

Burbage took an oath by God and his angels that all except himself were incompetent fools and idlers.

"Go directly to Master Glyn's gunsmithy across the street and take a bucket. Return it filled with gunpowder and tell Master Glyn that I will pay him after this evening's performance."

The old man went scurrying off.

"Gunpowder?" frowned Master Drew. "What part has gunpowder to do in your play?"

Burbage pointed to the back of the theatre.

"We have mounted a small cannon in one of the boxes on the second floor. The box will not be hired out during any performance."

"And what will this cannon do, except blow the players to kingdom come?" demanded the Constable wryly.

"Not so, not so. In act two, scene four, we have a grand scene with everyone on stage and the King and his entourage enters, with princes, dukes and cardinals. It is a grand entrance and Will Shakespeare calls for a sennet with divers trumpets and cornets. I thought to add to the spectacle by having a royal salute fired from a cannon. It will just be the ignition of the gunpowder, of course, but the combustion shall be explosive and startle our dreaming audience into concentration upon the action!"

Master Drew sniffed.

"I doubt it will do more than cause them to have deafness and perhaps start a riot out of panic for fear that the papists have attacked the theatre." He was about to settle down to wait for Tom Hawkins when he had a further thought. "In truth, turning to concentration reminds me that I would have you set your mind upon a youth whose description I shall presently give." He quickly sketched the description of the youth whose body they had fished out of the river.

Richard Burbage's reaction was immediate.

"God damn my eyes, Master Constable, I have been searching for that miscreant since this morning. He failed to turn up at the rehearsal and I have had to give his part to his friend. Where is the execrable young rogue?"

"Dead these past twelve hours, I fear."

Richard Burbage was shocked. He clapped his hand to his head. But the main reason for his perturbation was soon apparent.

"A player short! If ever the gods were frowning on me this day . . ."

"I would know more about this boy . . ." insisted the

Constable. Richard Burbage had turned to wave to a man who had just entered the theatre.

Master Drew recognized Richard Burbage's brother, Cuthbert, immediately.

"A good day to you, Master Constable. What is your business here this fine Saturday?" Cuthbert Burbage greeted him as he came forward. His brother raised his hands in a helpless gesture.

"Fine Saturday, indeed, brother! Tell him, Master Constable, while I am about my business. It lacks only an hour before the play begins."

He turned and scurried away.

Quickly, Master Drew told Cuthbert Burbage of what had passed.

"So, young Oliver is drowned, eh?"

"Oliver?"

"That was the lad's name, Oliver Rowe. Did he fall drunk into the river to drown?"

Master Drew shook his head.

"I said we hauled him from the river, not that he drowned. Young Oliver Rowe had his throat slit before he went into his watery grave. It was not for robbery either for he still had money in his purse and," he pulled out the ring from his pocket, "this ring on his finger."

Cuthbert let out an angry hiss.

"That, sir, is theatre property. No more than a simple actor's paste. A cheap imitation. I had wondered where it had gone. Damn Oliver . . ."

"He is damned already, Master Cuthbert," interrupted Master Drew.

Cuthbert hung his head contritely.

"Forgive me, I quite forgot. I was thinking of his making off with theatre property."

"Had this Oliver Rowe been long with you?"

"A year, no more"

"A good actor?"

"Hardly that, sir. He lacked experience and dedication. Though, I grant, he made up for his lack with a rare enthusiasm."

"Would anyone wish him ill?"

"You seek a reason for his murder?"

"I do."

"Then I have none to give you. He had no enemies but many friends, particularly of the fairer sex."

"And male friends?"

"Several within the company."

"Was Master Hawkins a particular friend of his?"

"Hardly. Tom Hawkins is twice his age and an actor of experience, though with too many airs and graces of late. He is a competent performer yet now he demands roles which are beyond his measure. We have told him several times to measure his cloth on his own body."

"Where did this Oliver Rowe reside?"

"But a step or two from here, Master Constable. He had rooms at Mrs Robat's house in the Skin Market."

A youth came hurriedly up, flush-faced, his words tumbling over themselves. Cuthbert Burbage held up a hand to silence him.

"Now, young Toby, tell me slowly what ails you?"

"Master Burbage, I have just discovered that there is no gunpowder for the cannon that I am supposed to fire. What is to be done?"

Master Drew pulled a face.

"If I may intervene, Master Burbage? Your brother has sent old Jasper across to the gunsmithy to purchase this same gunpowder."

The youth gave Drew a suspicious glance and then left with equal hastiness.

"I will ascertain if this be so," he called across his shoulder.

Cuthbert Burbage sighed.

"Ah, Master Constable, the play's the thing! The player is dead, long live the play. Life goes on in the theatre. Let us know what the result of your investigation is, good master. We poor players tend to band together in adversity. I know young Rowe was impecunious and a stranger to London, so it will be down to us thespians to ensure him a decent burial."

"I will remember, Master Cuthbert," the Constable agreed before he exited the theatre.

It took hardly any time to get to the Skin Market, with its busy and noisome trade in animal furs and skins. A stall holder pointed to Mrs Robat's house in a corner of the market square. Mrs Robat was a large, rotund woman with fair skin and dark hair. She opened the door and smiled at him.

"*Shw mae. Mae hi'n braf, wir!*"

Constable Drew glowered at her ingenuous features.

"I speak not your Welsh tongue, woman, and you have surely been long enough in London to speak in good, honest English?"

The woman continued to smile blandly at him, not understanding.

"*Yr wyf yn deal ychydig, ond ni allaf ei siarad.*"

A thin-faced man tugged the woman from the door and jerked his head in greeting to the Constable.

"I am sorry, sir, my wife, Megan, has no English."

Master Drew showed him his seal of office.

"I am the Constable of the Watch. I want to see the room of Master Oliver Rowe."

Master Robat raised his furtive eyebrows in surprise.

"Is anything amiss?"

"He is dead."

The man spoke rapidly to his wife in Welsh. She turned pale. Then he motioned Master Drew into the house adding to his wife: "*Arhoswch yma!*"

The Constable followed the man up the stairs for five flights to a small attic room.

"Was there an accident, sir?" prompted the man, nervously.

"Master Rowe was murdered."

"*Diw! Diw!*"

"I have no understanding of your Welshry," muttered the Constable.

"Ah, the loss is yours, sir. Didn't Master Shakespeare give these words to Mortimer in his tale of *Henry the Fourth* . . .?" The man struck a ridiculous pose. "I will never be a truant, love, till I have learn'd thy language; for thy tongue makes Welsh as sweet as ditties highly penn'd . . ."

Master Drew decided to put an end to the man's theatrical eloquence.

"I come not to discuss the merits of a scribbling word-seller nor his thoughts on your skimble-skamble tongue," snapped the Constable turning to survey the room.

There were three beds in the room. Two of them untidy and there were many clothes heaped upon the third. There were similarities to the mess he had observed in Hawkins's room. A similar pile of untidy papers. He picked them up. Play scripts again. He began to go through the cupboards and found another sheaf of papers there. One of them, he observed, was a draft of a play – *Falsehood Liberated*. The name on the title page was "Teazle Rowe".

"What was Master Rowe's first name?" he asked the Welshman. He had thought the Burbages had called Rowe by the first name of Oliver.

"Why, sir," confirmed the man, "it was Oliver."

"Did he have another name?"

"No, sir."

"Can you read, man?"

The Welshman drew himself up.

"I can read in both Welsh and English."

"Then who is *Teazle* Rowe?"

"Oh, you mean Master Teazle, sir. He is the other young gentleman who shares this room with Master Rowe."

Constable Drew groaned inwardly.

He had suddenly remembered what Page Williams, at the Blackfriars Theatre, had said. What was it? Rowe had complained that Bardolph Zenobia had stolen a play written by Rowe with the help of his friend.

"And where is this Master Teazle now?"

"He is out, sir. I don't suppose he will return until late tonight."

"You have no idea where I will find him?"

"Why, of course. He is doubtless at the theatre, sir."

"The theatre? Which one, in the name of . . .!"

"The Globe, sir. He is one of Master Burbage's company. Both Master Rowe and Master Teazle are King's Men."

Master Drew let out an exasperated sigh.

So both Rowe and his friend Teazle were members of the same company as Hawkins, alias Bardolph Zenobia?

Rowe had accused Hawkins of stealing a play that both he and Teazle had written and of selling it to the Blackfriars Theatre. A pattern was finally emerging.

"When did you last see Master Rowe?"

"Last night, sir," the reply came back without hesitation.

"Last night? At what hour?"

"Indeed, after the bell had sounded the midnight hour. I was forced to come up here and tell the young gentlemen to be quiet as they were disturbing the rest of our guests."

"Disturbing them? In what way?"

"They were having a most terrible argument, sir. The young gentlemen were quite savage with each other. 'Thief' and 'traitor' were the more repeatable titles that passed between them."

"And after you told them to be quiet?"

"They took themselves to quietness and all was well, thanks be to God. Sometimes Master Teazle has a rare temper and I swear I would not like to go against him."

"But, after this, you saw Master Rowe no more?"

The man's eyes went wide.

"I did not. And you do tell me that Master Rowe is dead? Are you saying that . . .?"

"I am saying nothing, Master Robat. But you shall hear from me again."

The play had already started by the time the Constable reached the Globe again.

He marched in past the sullen old doorman and examined the auditorium. The theatre was not crowded. It being a bright summer Saturday afternoon, many Londoners were about other tasks than spending time in a playhouse. But there was a fair number of people filling several of the boxes and a small crowd clustering around the area directly in front of the stage. He noticed, in disapproval, the harlots plying their wares from box to box, mixing with fruit sellers and other traders, from bakers' boys and those selling all kinds of beverages.

Master Drew saw a worried-looking Cuthbert Burbage coming towards him.

"Where is Master Hawkins?" he demanded.

"Preparing for the second act," replied the man in apprehension. "Master Constable, swear to me that you will not interrupt the play by arresting him, if he be in trouble?"

"I am no prophet, Master Burbage," returned the Constable, moving towards the area where the actors were preparing themselves to take their part upon the stage. He looked at them. What was the part that Hawkins was said to be playing – a cardinal? He picked out a man dressed in scarlet robes.

"Are you Master Hawkins?"

The actor raised a solemnly face and grimaced with contempt.

"I am not, sir. I play Cardinal Wolsey. You will find Cardinal Campeius at the far end."

This time there was no mistake.

"Master Thomas Hawkins?"

The distinguished-looking cleric bowed his head.

"I am yours to command, good sir."

"And are you also Master Bardolph Zenobia?"

The actor's face coloured slightly. He shifted uneasily.

"I admit to being the same man, sir."

Master Drew introduced himself.

"Did you know that Master Oliver Rowe has been discovered murdered?"

There was just a slight flicker in the eyes.

"It is already whispered around the theatre from your earlier visit, Master Constable."

"When did you first learn of it?"

"Less than half-an-hour ago when I came to the theatre."

"When did you last see Master Rowe?"

"Last evening."

"Here, at this theatre?"

"I was not in last night's performance. I went to stay with . . . with a lady in Eastcheap. I have only just returned from that assignation."

"And, of course," sneered the Constable, "you would have no difficulty in supplying me the lady's name?"

"None, good master. The lady and I mean to be married."

"And she will be able to tell me that you were with her all night?"

"If that is what you require. But not just the lady but her father and mother, for she lives with them. They own the Boar's Head in Eastcheap and are well respected."

Master Drew swallowed hard. The alibi of a lady on her own was one thing but the alibi of an entire respectable family could hardly be faulted.

"When last did you see Master Rowe?"

"It was after yesterday afternoon's performance. Rowe asked me to go with him to a waterside tavern after the matinee performance. I had an appointment across the river before I went on to Eastcheap and could not long delay. But Rowe was insistent. We wound up by having an argument and I left him."

"What was the argument about?"

Hawkins' colour deepened.

"A private matter."

"A matter concerning Master Bardolph Zenobia's literary endeavours?"

Hawkins shrugged.

"I will tell you the truth. Rowe and a friend of his had written a pretty story. Rowe wanted help in finding a theatre to stage it."

"Why did he not take it to Burbage?"

"Sir, we are the King's Men here. We have a programme of plays of surpassing quality for the next several years from many renowned masters of their art, Master Shakespeare, Jonson, Beaumont, Fletcher and the like. Master Burbage would not look at anything by a nameless newcomer. Rowe knew I had contacts with other theatres and gave me the script to read. The basic tale was commendable but so much work needed to be done to revise it into something presentable. I spent much time on it. In the end the work was mine, not Rowe's nor that of his friend."

"I suppose by 'his friend', you mean Teazle?"

"Yes, Teazle."

"So you felt that the play was your own to do with as you liked?"

"It *was* mine. I wrote it. I will show you the original and my alterations. At first, I asked only to be made a full partner in the endeavour. When Rowe refused, saying the work was his and his friend's alone, I put the name of Zenobia on it and took it to Blackfriars. I told Rowe after I had sold it and offered to give him a guinea for the plot. I did not wish to be ungenerous. He refused. Rowe found out which theatre I had sold it to and even went to the theatre after I had left him last night, claiming that I had stolen the work.

"But from what was said yesterday afternoon, I had the impression that Rowe might have accepted the money if Teazle had not refused his share of the guinea. Rowe told me that Teazle thought him to be in some plot with me to cheat him and share more money after the play was produced. I told Rowe that it was up to him to make his peace with Teazle. I think a guinea was a fair sum to pay for the idea which I had to turn into literature."

"I doubt whether a magistrate would agree with your liberal interpretation of the law," Master Drew replied drily. "Has Master Teazle spoken to you of this business? Where is he now?"

Hawkins gestured disdainfully.

"Somewhere about the theatre. I avoid him. He has a childish temper and believes himself to be some great artist against whom the whole world is plotting. Anyway, I can prove that I am not concerned in the death of young Rowe. I have robbed no one."

"That remains to be seen."

Master Drew left him and went to the side of the stage. The third scene of the second act was closing. The characters of Anne Bullen and an Old Lady were on stage. Anne was saying:

> – *Would I had no being,*
> *If this salute my blood a jot; it faints me,*
> *to think what follows.*
> *The queen is comfortless, and we forgetful*
> *In our long absence: pray, do not deliver*
> *What here you've heard to her.*

The old lady replied, indignantly: "What do you think me?" And both made their exit.

All was now being prepared for the next scene.

Master Drew glanced around, wondering which of the players was Teazle.

Something drew his eye across the auditorium to the box on the second storey in front of the stage. Someone was standing bending over the small cannon which had been pointed out to the Constable earlier. Master Richard Burbage had explained that the cannon would herald the scene with a royal salute, followed by trumpets and cornets, and then the King and his Cardinals would lead a procession onto the stage.

The muzzle of the cannon appeared to be pointing rather low.

The Constable turned to find Master Cuthbert Burbage at his shoulder.

"That is going to stir things a little," grinned the business manager of the theatre who had observed Master Drew's examination.

"Your brother has already explained it to me," the Constable replied. "The cannon will be fired to herald the entrance of the procession in the next act but isn't the muzzle pointing directly at the stage?"

"No harm. It is only a charge of gunpowder which creates the explosion. There is no ball to do damage. Take no alarm; young Toby Teazle has done this oft times before."

Master Drew started uneasily.

"That is Master Teazle up there with the cannon?"

A cold feeling of apprehension began to grip him as he stared at the muzzle of the cannon. Then he began to move hurriedly towards the stairs on the far side of the auditorium, pushing protesting spectators out of his way in his haste. He was aware of Cuthbert Burbage shouting something to him.

By the time he reached the second floor he was aware of the actors moving onto the stage in the grand procession. He heard a voice he recognized as the actor playing Wolsey. "Whilst our commission from Rome is read, let silence be commanded." Then Richard Burbage's voice cried: "What's the need? It hath already publicly been read, and on all sides the authority allow'd; you may then spare that time." Wolsey replied: "Be't so. Proceed."

The cacophony of the trumpet and cornets sounded.

Drew burst into the small box and saw the young man bending with the lighted taper to the touch hole. On stage he was aware that the figures of Burbage's King, and the actors playing Cardinal Wolsey and Cardinal Campeius, the urbane figure of Hawkins, had come to the front of the stage and were staring up at the cannoneer, waiting. The Constable did not pause to think but leapt across the floor, kicking at the muzzle of the small cannon. It jerked upwards just as it exploded. The recoil showed that it had been loaded with ball; its muzzle had been pointed directly at the figure of Cardinal Campeius. The hot metal crashed across the interior of the theatre and fell into the thatch above the stage area.

There were cries of shocked surprise and some applause but then the noise of the crackle of flames where the hot metal landed on the dry thatch became apparent. Cries of "Fire!" rose on all sides.

Master Drew swung round only to find the fist of the young man, Toby Teazle, impacting on his nose. He went staggering backwards and almost fell over the wooden balustrade into the crowds below as they streamed for the exits of the theatre.

By the time the Constable had recovered the young man was away, leaping down the stairs and was soon lost in the scuffling fray.

Master Drew, recovering his poise, hastened down the steps as best he could. The actors, with Cuthbert Burbage, were pushing people to the exits. The dry thatch and tinder of the Globe was like straw before the angry flames. The theatre was becoming a blazing inferno.

Master Drew groaned in anguish as he realized that the young man was lost among the crowds now and never a hope in catching him.

It was over nine months later, in the spring of the following year, 1614, that the new Globe Theatre eventually rose from the ashes. This time it was erected as an octagonal building with a tiled roof replacing the thatch. Fortunately no one had been injured in the fire and all the costumes and properties had been saved thanks to the quick wit of the actors and all the manuscripts of the plays had been stored elsewhere, so the loss was negligible.

Apart from Master Oliver Rowe, two other players were not present to see the magnificent new Globe Theatre. Master Tom Hawkins was languishing in Newgate Gaol. However, he was not imprisoned for the fraudulent misuse of another playwright's work. In fact, *The Vow Breaker Delivered* had been taken off on the third night and had made a loss for the Blackfriars Theatre. No, Master Hawkins was imprisoned for breach of promise to the young lady who lived at the Boar's Head Tavern in Eastcheap. As Constable Hardy Drew remarked, *The Vow Breaker Delivered* had been an inspired prophetic title, as apt a title as could have been chosen by Master Bardolph Zenobia.

The other missing player was Master Toby Teazle.

It was the very day after the new Globe Theatre had opened that Constable Drew was able to conclude the case of the murder of Master Oliver Rowe, sometime one of the King's Men. Master Cuthbert Burbage asked Constable Drew to accompany him to The Hospital of St Mary of Bethlehem. Drew was mildly surprised at the request.

"That is the hospital for the insane," he pointed out. Most Londoners knew of Bedlam, for as such the name had been contracted.

"Indeed it is, but I think you will want to see this. I have been asked to identify someone."

An attendant took them into the grey walled building which was more of a prison than a hospital. The stench of human excrement and the noise arising from the afflicted sufferers was unbelievable. The attendant took them to a small cell door and opened it.

A young man crouched inside in the darkness, was bent industriously over a rough wooden table. There was nothing on it, yet he appeared to be in the act of writing in the blackness. His right hand held an invisible pen, moving it across unseen sheets of paper.

The attendant grinned.

"There he is, good sirs. He says he's a famous actor and playwright. Says he is a King's player from the Globe Theatre. That's why you were asked here, good master Burbage, just in case there might be truth in it."

The young man heard his voice and raised his matted head, the eyes blazing, the mouth grinning vacuously. He paused in his act of writing.

It was Toby Teazle.

"Ah, sirs," he said quietly, calmly regarding them. "You come not a moment too soon. I have penn'd a wondrous entertainment, a magnificent play, I call it *The Friend's Betrayal*. I will allow you to perform it but only if my name should go upon the handbill. My name and no other." He stared at them, each in turn, and then began to recite.

> *'Tis ten to one this play can never please*
> *All that are here; some come to take their ease*
> *And sleep an act or two; but those, we fear,*
> *We have frightened with our cannon; so, 'tis clear,*
> *They'll say, 'tis naught . . . naught . . .*

He hesitated and frowned.

"Is this all it is? Naught?"

He stared suddenly at the empty table before him and started to chuckle hysterically.

As Constable Drew and Master Cuthbert Burbage were walking back towards Bankside, Drew asked: "Were those his own lines which he was quoting with such emotion?"

Master Burbage shook his head sadly.

"No, that was the epilogue from *Henry VIII*. At least, most of it was. The poor fellow is but a poor lunatic."

Master Drew smiled wryly. "Didn't Will Shakespeare once say that the lunatic, the lover and the poet are of imagination all compact?"

THE COLLABORATOR

Rosemary Aitken

It was a dreadful night. Robert Bullen picked his way down to the shingle spit under the arch of the bridge, his heart thudding so hard it sounded like horse-hooves in his ears. Why, in all London, pick a spot like this, and on such a night too? He huddled his thick cloak closer around him and strained his eyes and ears against the muffling gloom. In vain. Thick ugly mist rose from the river and mingled with the smoke from chimneys. It was pitch dark besides – the ruddy candles in the shadowy houses no more than glimmering pinpricks, too weak to pierce the swirling folds of that engulfing dark.

He was scared, more scared than he had ever been in all his eighteen years, but he was excited too. It was thrilling: a cause – to clear his family's name – a chance to be a man among real men. He had been proposed by his cousin, watched – he knew – by unseen eyes, and now he was judged worthy. Tonight was to be his first real errand. Part of the test, perhaps, was the keeping of this tryst. That in itself was dangerous. Since the fall of the Earl of Essex the city was full of spies.

Suppose he were betrayed? He could not deceive himself – it was possible. Gold, or fear, could loosen many a tongue. And then? His enemies would find some pretext to haul him to the Tower, and he would lose his head, as his kinswoman – the Lady Anne – had once lost hers. Rank and fortune would not save him. It had happened already to wealthier, worthier men than himself.

He thought of the bloodstained block and heavy axe, and shivered. Partly in fear but also with bitter cold. Cold to pinch the sharp noses of the rats, scuffling at unspeakable things by the river's edge. Cold to creak the timbers of the boats which loomed in the darkness – mere grey wraiths, their rigging muffled in mist. Every sound, every movement turned his veins to ice, but though his senses were stretched to aching he could distinguish nothing – only the sigh of the water, the slithering scrabble of a rat.

A touch on his shoulder almost made him cry aloud.

He whirled round, one hand on his dagger, then sagged in relief. "Hawke, how you startled me! I almost ran you through." He was ashamed to hear his voice tremble.

"Hush!" The newcomer said sharply. "The night has ears. You found the place?"

Bullen thought of saying "Clearly, since you find me here," but said nothing. It was a reasonable question. In the web of suspicion that was London, passing a message was no easy task. There were court spies everywhere. It was no secret that Hawke had dined with Essex, more than once. He would be closely watched.

Hawke was uneasy now. "Did any see you come?"

Robert shook his head.

"Good. Then listen well. There is no time to lose. We need a messenger."

Bullen felt that rush of thrilling fear again. "Send me. Where must I go?" His mind was painting a thousand visions – France perhaps, or Italy.

"The playhouse."

Bullen gasped, almost, with disappointment. But the playhouse was a public place. Easy there to make casual contact with a stranger. A mere moment, a brush of the hand, and anything might be exchanged. "I have been once or twice, to the comedies. The Chamberlain's Men. I would gladly go again. And there, what should I do?"

"Why – watch the play."

"The play!" He could not restrain his tongue. "You mock me," he said bitterly.

Will Hawke shook his head. "No. Did you not hear, when

Essex raised his rebellion, that the Globe players staged *Richard the Third*, about overthrowing a monarch? A message to the populace, some said. The Earl of Southampton was the playwright's patron, and he was imprisoned for it."

"But what is that to us? Our cause is different."

"It is the same device. We have a hidden friend within the company. He is our eyes and ears, where we ourselves cannot hope to venture. He tells us much. But I have been too often to the plays. I dare not go again."

Bullen shook his head stubbornly.

"You doubt it? You went to the comedies, you say. What did you see?"

"*Love's Labours Lost*," Bullen began, "*All's Well that . . .*"

"No, no." Hawke said impatiently. "Tell me the substance of the plays?"

The young man glanced at him in disbelief. Here, in this cold and loathsome place? "It was a mere nothing," he said. "An entertainment that is all. A young woman is falsely accused . . ." he stopped. "You mean, this is related to our cause? The Lady Anne . . ."

"Hush! We will be heard."

Bullen's mind was racing. Queen Anne Bullen, his distant kinswoman, had been falsely accused. Beloved wife of the King – until she miscarried of her second child. Then, all at once she was accused of adultery with her music-master. It was a lie, the family knew it, but the man confessed, and there were witnesses to swear that the two had been seen together. And, Bullen thought suddenly – there had been tokens produced to prove the matter. A letter, a ring – a gift from the King – just like the story of the plays.

Hawke looked at him grimly. "I see you understand. And the others? *A Comedy of Errors, Two Gentlemen of Verona, Twelfth Night*. You have seen them too?"

Bullen nodded. "There are two young men in the company who look much alike, and the joke of all the plays was that their lovers and friends mistook one for the other . . ." He stopped and stared at Hawke.

"My grandmother was attendant to the Queen," the older man said. "She went to her deathbed swearing that she was with the Queen that day, in Windsor – while Anne was supposed to be in London disporting with her lover."

"So that was it?" Bullen cried. "There was not one Anne Boleyn but two. Another woman so like the Queen that people swore they had seen Anne with her lover – and believed it too. My God, it answers everything. It has to be so – it was not in her nature to play the King false." He stopped. "There must have been a powerful enemy to play so cruel – and difficult – a trick."

Hawke sighed. "Not difficult. One might find someone very like the Queen, if one had motive and means enough to search all England. The cut of the hair, the turn of the hand, the clothes – with a little acting the thing is easily done."

"But the music master must have known."

"Perhaps he did. He swore he never touched the Queen – until the torturers had him. In their hands a man will confess to anything."

"But who would plot it?"

Hawke shook his head. "The plays will tell us. Will you go?" Then, as Bullen nodded, "The new play, then, next Friday. Till then, farewell. We must not loiter here. Now, do not follow me direct. Wait a few moments more before you go."

He wrapped his cloak about him and vanished into the mist.

Bullen shivered again. The night, which had seemed dreadful before, seemed still more fearful now. He waited, moments that seemed like hours. When he did dare to move, his foot fell on something soft and yielding – a dead rat, rotting by the water's edge. He yelped and scrambled up the bank and home, forgetting all caution.

Even there, with the fire made up and a dozen candles to ward off shadows, he could hardly sleep. He tossed all night, the bed-curtains tightly drawn and a poker handy beside his pillow. Who was Anne's enemy? But he found no answer.

All week he spent sleepless, revolving again and again the events of that evening, and he awaited a message from Hawke more eagerly than a love-letter. None came, and

Robert presented himself at the new play in an tense state of anxious anticipation.

At first he was doubtful. The play concerned the King of Denmark, which hardly fitted the case. But suddenly – "My oath!" he exclaimed aloud. He had it!

Who married the dead King's widow with unseemly haste? Thomas Seymour. He had wed the widowed Catherine Parr before the King's corpse was fairly cold. The Prince's uncle, besides. That would fit, too. Jane Seymour had a young prince that died. Jane Seymour, Thomas's sister, who married the King only eleven days after Anne Bullen's execution.

Who benefited from the fall of Anne? The Seymours. Jane had been Queen. Edward had been Protector of the Realm. But it was said that Thomas was the most ambitious of them all. He too longed to rule the realm. Closest to his sister, he had wielded power with her. He had shared his brother's rise, and yet survived his fall. And he had married Catherine Parr! If she had been with child when Henry died – a son perhaps – who would be Regent then?

Excited, Robert dragged his thoughts back to the play. There was a dumbshow, in which poison was poured in the King's ear. That was absurd. No one was ever murdered by such means. But pouring poison in the ear, Bullen thought, might mean malicious slander. Which was, of course, exactly the matter of it. Seymour had poisoned Henry's ear.

He came out of the playhouse with his head awhirl. Where was Hawke? He loitered for a long time, but nothing happened, and at last, feeling awkward and confused he made his way home.

"Ah! You are here are last!" William Hawke was sitting on the wooden settle in front of the fire with a bearded swarthy man, drinking Bullen's brandy as though they owned the place and this meeting was a nightly occurrence. "What have you to tell us?"

Bullen, who until that moment had not the slightest notion that there was anyone in the house – since he had secured the door and carried the key himself – almost dropped dead of fright, but he governed himself sufficiently to give some account of the evening. "So," he finished at last, "Everything points to Seymour."

"You have done well," Hawke looked at him." And there is more you may not know. The present Queen was once a ward of the Seymours. Edward kept her in the Tower, but gossip said that Thomas dallied with her, and might have married her, despite the years between them – except he had a wife. Poor Catherine: it was whispered he tried to poison her once. If he had wed Elizabeth, he would have ruled the realm, indeed. Yes, it makes sense. Seymour was ambitious. And he studied potions too." He looked at the swarthy man. "We should tell him, do you think?" The man nodded.

"Then," Hawke said, drawing his sword, "Swear on this sword, that what you hear shall never be revealed." It was so like the play that Robert almost smiled, but Hawke repeated "Swear!" so forcefully that he laid his hand on the hilt and made the oath.

"You have heard," Hawke continued, "rumours that the Queen had a child once?"

Bullen nodded. "One of a thousand rumours. Hidden in a warming-pan, they say."

"The tales are true. There was such a child. Only it was not Elizabeth's, it was the Lady Anne's. A true sister to the Queen. King Henry's child."

"But Anne miscarried of her second child . . ."

Hawke shook his head. "Untimely born. Anne's enemies were clever. A waiting-maid brought her a potion 'to soothe the back-ache' and her pains began. We know now, I think, who that serving-woman was. Jane Seymour was lady-in-waiting to the Queen, and, as I say, Seymour was skilled with potions. But the child lived. My grandmother attended her, and fearing for the child's life smuggled it out. The child – an ageing woman now – still lives, in France, where she was sent for safety. So like her mother, they say, that you would think it was the Lady Anne alive and grown old. She does not know her own story. There are proofs – letters, an embroidered wrap. You see our cause? Elizabeth is ill, dying perhaps, and leaves no heir. The crown will go to the Scottish monarch, James, if we do not act. But the King's own daughter lives."

"What should we do, proclaim the truth? Have you informed the Queen?"

Hawke shook his head. "We did not dare. See how she treated her cousin of Scots. She would have suspected a plot against her – I was a friend of Essex. Besides, we did not know our enemy till now. We are not safe yet, there are Seymours still at court. But Thomas Seymour himself is long since dead, and the time has come for action. I will go to France, where the lady is hidden."

"I might crave an audience with the Queen. I am a Bullen, still."

Hawke shook his head. "No, Seymour is dead, but there are new enemies. You stay here and keep watch of the plays. Say nothing to anyone till you hear from me. God send we are in time." He gripped Robert's hand. "Now, we must go."

He and the swarthy man slipped into the dark and deserted street, and were gone.

The next months were a torment. The climate of suspicion grew denser every day. More friends of Essex followed their leader to the block. There was no word from Hawke. Bullen even joined the jeering crowds, fearing the worst, but none of the bloodstained heads displayed on spikes had a familiar face. There were no new plays, either. Bullen ached with the secret that he carried, but nothing happened.

Then the Queen died. There was still no word. Some of the prisoners in the Tower were freed, including Southampton, patron of the playwright. But there was no message. James was proclaimed King. Bullen felt sick at heart. Something must have befallen Hawke. The cause had failed.

Then suddenly, there was a new play. He went, not knowing what to think, but to his surprise the message was unchanged. It was Anne's story still. It was called a comedy, *Measure for Measure* – how a virtuous woman was supposed to have sinned – but her place was taken by another. And, the play said, there were some who could swear to her innocence.

He went home in a turmoil. Surely the cause was over now? Why did the messages remain? The next play was not long coming, and its message was plainer still. He went home from the playhouse to find Hawke awaiting him.

"What news?" he cried eagerly.

"The play first."

He could hardly wait to tell it. "It is called *Othello*, but it is the very story of Anne's fall. A virtuous wife, brought down by lies and half-truths, until her husband kills her. And it is clear too, how the trick was played. The villain has one of her maid-servants steal a precious handkerchief and makes it seem she gave it to her lover. The same was said of Anne. I think we could give a true name to the villain, and to the waiting-woman too."

Hawke smiled grimly. "More evidence! Good. Now, we must act."

"Act, how? King James is crowned. The chance is lost."

The smile grew broader. "It is all arranged. We wait until the so-called King goes to the Parliament. Then when the lords are all gathered, we shall burst out from below, break down the doors with dynamite and make our claim before the whole assembly. It is the only way. If we take them piece-meal we shall fail. Now, you are a kinsman of the Lady Anne. Will you come with us, and set forth her cause?"

Bullen swallowed. It was one thing to be a messenger, another to lie in wait under the Parliament with gunpowder. But he found his voice. "I will. What of the plays?"

"We hope for one more before that day. Go and be sure our cause is safe."

For the rest of his life Bullen never knew how he passed the next few months. Food, sleep, friends – nothing was of importance, but the plan. He grew gaunt and hollow-eyed, distrusting strangers and suspicious of friends, and in his room, alone, paced the floor restlessly for hours.

At last the playbills promised a new play. It was almost past his capacity to go – weakness, sweating and fear almost undid him, but he braved it in the end. He watched the action with unbelieving eyes. When the play ended and the mad King held dead Cordelia in his arms, he could scarcely prevent himself from weeping openly.

"Midnight", said a soft voice in his ear. He whirled. Will

Hawke was standing at his shoulder. "Under the bridge," Hawke said, and disappeared into the crowd.

It was dreadful to return to that appalling place. He was horribly aware of the noise he made scrabbling down the bank and across the stones – but he no longer cared.

Hawke was there first, and amazingly, he was smiling. "Three daughters of the King. Two who ruled, the third in France – returned and recognized at last. We move!"

"No," Robert said, appalled. "That was not the message. Did you not understand? The recognition comes too late, the play said! The conspiracy is betrayed by a letter. All that follows is madness and despair."

"Nonsense man. Courage! It is a bold venture, but we shall succeed."

Bullen shook his head, seized by conviction. "No," he said firmly. "Do not say 'we'. I think I read the spirit of the play. Ignore it at your peril. We are betrayed. Send word and ask the fellow outright, if you must. It is dangerous, but so much is at stake."

"What, in the court and have us all betrayed? No!" Hawke shook his head. "The way is clear. It is all prepared. If you will not come I shall ask Fawkes to do it – the swarthy man you saw. He has not your wit, but he has a stout heart."

Bullen's cheeks flamed at the rebuke, but he said stubbornly, "I am with you in everything but this. I shall go to the plays, still."

Hawke's face was steely. "As you will. Once this is over, they are simply plays."

"And you, will you go to the Parliament? I beg you, don't. Stay with the lady."

"What is that to you? Go now – we shall not meet again."

That sudden cool rush of courage again. "You do not fear that I'll betray you all?"

Hawke looked at him coldly. "I do not think you have the mettle for it."

There was a long silence, and then Bullen turned and walked away. He did not look back, although he expected a dagger in his ribs at every step. It was the bleakest, loneliest hour of his life.

Nothing surprised him. The conspirators were caught – betrayed by a letter, as the play said. One man was killed and Fawkes was captured: half-hanged, cut down, drawn and quartered for endangering the King. But whatever they did to Fawkes, he did not betray the secret. Bullen knew that he himself could not have been so brave.

He did go to the plays, as he had promised, and it wrung his heart to do so. They were turbulent, angry. A wild drama of a Scottish King who usurped the crown (dangerous, he thought, with James I on the throne) until an heir came who was "untimely born". Coriolanus losing all because he would not plead his cause. After that, play after play showing a hidden heir returned. *Pericles, Cymbeline, The Winter's Tale* – the last so poignant in its imagery – the jealous king, the cast-off wife, the long-lost daughter found – that Bullen was amazed the whole theatre could not see it.

As for the story of Cleopatra, it might make you weep. The lovely Queen, the second love of her lord, losing everything to an ambitious man who married that lord to his own sister. Even a music-master, and a sooth-sayer promising advancement to the serving-maid. Caesar and Seymour – spoken aloud, even the names were close.

It was sad, hopeless, this faithful stream of messages in support of a cause long dead. But there was no word from Hawke. Bullen took up the stream of his life again. There was a girl – a pretty girl – who had a smile for him and little by little he began to notice her. He was a young man still, and his blood was warm. He rediscovered the pleasures of food and drink and when he woke now, sweating in the night, he could turn in his bed and tell himself it was all over.

But it was not over, quite. He had been so busy with his amours that he almost missed the first public performance of the new play. He arrived late – just before the performance, and there was Hawke, pale, strained, defeated, looking an old man among the crowd. Robert elbowed his way towards him. "William?"

Hawke glanced up and looked away. He did not speak.

Bullen dropped his voice, "How goes ... our former business?"

Hawke did raise his eyes then, and they were tired and pained. "It is all lost. All our supporters, and our money too – you saw the play of Timon? Well, it is true. All lost."

"And ... the lady?"

"She wishes to leave this island. She has met a man, at last, and hopes to marry – though it is late, for her. Still, I should wish her happy – poor blighted girl. She has known no life, thanks to us. When she was young, her so-called father kept her hidden from the world. Partly to protect her from her enemies, and because it would not do for her to wed a common man. It was all in vain, I see. Though it was intended for the best."

"Perhaps, it is not too late? She is as much the heir as ever, and the proofs still stand. The plays say so."

Hawke shook his head. "Poor fool. He cannot believe the cause is lost."

The play began. He was amazing, that "poor fool" who wrote it. The play echoed Hawke's story of the lady as closely as if the author had listened at their shoulder.

"Yes," Bullen said at last, and there were tears in his eyes, "it is over. For him as well as you. Did you hear the last words? '*As you from crimes would pardoned be, Let your indulgence set me free.*' He wants to stop writing these plays for you."

Hawke nodded. "And he shall. There is a little money, enough to let him retire. He has earned it handsomely."

"He has." Bullen hesitated. "I have often wondered – how did he learn all this?"

Hawke shrugged. "Who knows? His patron, perhaps? Southampton knew a great deal about court intrigue. And then, his own home is in the Avon Vale. Scarcely twenty miles from Thomas Seymour's estate at Sudeley. There are those still alive who served there – and who knows what secrets they possess? A man can conceal things from his King and colleagues that are common gossip to his servants." He sighed. "Our friend wants to return to Stratford and retire. Well, let him do so. My dreams are in ruins."

Robert looked at him intently. "May I go with you when you deliver the money? I should like to meet the man at last. There is something else I find in the plays. I should like to ask him about it."

"Another message?" Hawke said wearily, "Have there not been enough?"

"I think there is another secret," Bullen said. "Even more fearful. How often in the plays is the true King murdered? In *Hamlet*, the usurper poisons the King to marry his widow. Hamlet talks of 'fishmongers' and Kent – in *Lear* – declares he'll 'eat no fish'. Does it not strike you strange that King Henry died from a surfeit of lampreys? The man ate like a lion – why should a few fishes kill him?"

Hawke looked at him, his face alive again, his eyes shining. "Unless . . .? Seymour, you know, was skilled with potions. And, after all, he married the widow. Do you suppose . . .?"

The Tempest was the last undisputed play Shakespeare wrote. Soon after, he retired to Stratford. A later play which bore his name was almost certainly a collaboration. It is called Henry VIII *and is chiefly in praise of Anne Boleyn.*

THE CONTRIBUTORS

Rosemary Aitken "The Collaborator". Rosemary Aitken is the author of a series of historical novels set in turn-of-the-century Cornwall which explores the trials and tribulations of the tin miners. The series began with *The Girl from Penvarris*. She has also written many highly regarded textbooks on the subject of language and communication, and her knowledge of this field comes through in her story on the interpretation of Shakespeare's plays.

John T. Aquino "When the Dead Rise Up". John Aquino (b. 1949) is an American author with a special interest in the Elizabethan period, especially its relationship with the death of the elder world of faery. He has written a series of stories about Merlin, tracing him through time. The first of these stories, "The Sad Wizard", was included in my anthology *The Camelot Chronicles*. His wife Deborah Curren-Aquino is a Shakespeare scholar of note. She has compiled both a detailed annotated bibliography and a volume of essays about the play *King John*.

Cherith Baldry "The House of Rimmon". Cherith Baldry (b. 1947), a former teacher and librarian, is best known for her children's books, particularly the Saga of the Six Worlds, starting with *The Book and the Phoenix* (published in America as *Cradoc's Quest*), which is set on a distant binary star system whose settlers have long since forgotten Earth. She is also a noted Arthurian scholar, and in a series has set out to redeem the character of Sir Kay. She does something similar for Shylock in her contribution to this anthology.

Paul Barnett "Imogen". Paul Barnett (b. 1949) is a Scottish writer and editor who also writes under the names John Grant and Eve

Devereux. He is perhaps best known for his novels of science fiction and fantasy, in particular *Albion, The World* and the more recent series of *Strider's Galaxy*. His profound knowledge of cinema is evident in his *Encyclopedia of Walt Disney's Animated Characters* and in his many entries for *The Encyclopedia of Fantasy* of which he is joint editor.

Stephen Baxter "A Midsummer Eclipse". Since his first novel, *Raft*, in 1991, Stephen Baxter (b. 1957) has established himself in the front rank of British writers of science fiction. His related novels include *Timelike Infinity, Flux, Ring* and the collection *Vacuum Diagrams*. One of his most popular books was *The Time Ships*, a sequel to H.G. Wells's *The Time Machine*.

Molly Brown "Mother of Rome". Chicago-born and now London resident, Molly Brown has rapidly established herself as a writer of science fiction, fantasy and thrillers. She has written the historical mystery novel, *Invitation to a Funeral*, in which Aphra Behn and Nell Gwyn feature as investigators. This novel grew out of Molly's short story, "The Lemon Juice Plot" in the anthology *Royal Crimes* edited by Maxim Jakubowski and Martin H. Greenberg, and she has now become something of an expert on Restoration London, developing her own website on the Internet (http://www.okima.com/) where you can explore late seventeenth-century London. Her other books include a novelization of the TV series *Cracker, To Say I Love You*, and a science-fiction thriller for children, *Virus*.

Louise Cooper Not Wisely, But Too Well". Cooper (b. 1952) has been a writer of fantasy since her first novel, *The Book of Paradox* in 1973. She subsequently developed the plot and characters of her second novel, *Lord of No Time*, about the opposing factions of Chaos and Order, to form the popular Time Master series, which has also incorporated the Chaos Gate and the Star Shadow trilogies. Her other long-running series is Indigo, which began with *Nemesis* in 1988, and in which the heroine must track down and destroy the various demons she has unwittingly released. Cooper has also written several horror novels plus fantasies for younger readers.

Martin Edwards "Serpent's Tooth". Martin Edwards (b. 1955) is a practising solicitor, and has used his experience as the background for his series of novels about Liverpool solicitor and amateur detective Harry Devlin. The series began with *All the Lonely People* in 1992 and there's been a novel a year ever since. Edwards has also edited the crime anthology *Northern Blood* and others in a regionally related series.

Margaret Frazer "The Death of Kings". The Margaret Frazer alias originally hid the identity of two writers, Gail Frazer and Mary Monica Pulver, who between them produced the popular series of Dame Frevisse novels, which began with *The Novice's Tale* in 1992. Their stories also appeared in *The Mammoth Book of Historical Whodunnits* and *The Mammoth Book of Historical Detectives*. Although of late Mary Pulver has gone her own way (after an amicable parting), Gail is continuing the Dame Frevisse series on her own, but keeping the pseudonym. Gail Frazer came to Shakespeare and medieval England through seeing a production of *Richard II* and, since then, besides researching and writing about medieval England, she has been in more than a dozen productions of Shakespeare's plays, both amateur and professional.

Peter T. Garratt "Buried Fortune". Peter Garratt (b. 1949) is a lecturer and a regular writer of science-fiction and fantasy. Much of his work has appeared in the British magazine *Interzone*. He has a particular fascination for Arthurian fiction and has contributed to the anthologies *The Chronicles of the Holy Grail* and *The Chronicles of the Round Table*.

Susanna Gregory "A Villainous Company". Susanna Gregory (b. 1958), has written historical mystery novels about Matthew Bartholomew, a teacher of medicine at Michaelhouse, part of the fledgling University of Cambridge, in the mid-fourteenth century. The series began with *A Plague on Both Your Houses* in 1996. When not writing she conducts research into marine biology and pollution with particular interest in the Antarctic. She previously worked in a coroner's office, which gave her a special insight into criminal behaviour.

Edward D. Hoch "Toil and Trouble". Edward Hoch (b. 1930) is a phenomenally prolific American short-story writer with over seven hundred to his credit. He has created many fascinating detectives, including Captain Leopold, Dr Sam Hawthorne, Nick Velvet, Ben Snow and Simon Ark. His stories appear regularly in *Ellery Queen's Mystery Magazine* and *Alfred Hitchcock's Mystery Magazine* but only a small percentage has made it into individual story collections. Well worth tracking down is his Captain Leopold volume, *Leopold's Way*, his Simon Ark series, *The Judges of Hades, City of Brass* and *The Quests of Simon Ark*, the Nick Velvet books *The Spy and the Thief* and *The Thefts of Nick Velvet*, whilst a few of his Sam Hawthorne stories have been collected as *Diagnosis: Impossible*. His more general mystery fiction will be found in *The Night My Friend*.

Tom Holt "Cinna the Poet". Tom Holt (b. 1961) is best known for his immensely popular comic fantasy novels, which began with *Expecting Someone Taller* in 1987 and include *Who's Afraid of Beowulf?*, *Ye Gods!*, and *Faust Among Equals*. He had earlier written two sequels to E.F. Benson's series of books about those small-town busybodies Mapp and Lucia, *Lucia in Wartime* and *Lucia Triumphant*. A lesser-known fact is that Holt is an expert on ancient Greece and Rome and has written two novels set in classical Greece, *Goatsong* and *The Walled Orchard*. He jumped at the chance of returning to his favourite period in this anthology.

Susan B. Kelly "Much Ado About Something". Susan Kelly was born in the Chilterns. After reading French at London University she worked as a freelance computer consultant during the eighties before turning to writing full time. Her short stories have appeared in magazines and anthologies in both Britain and America and have been broadcast on BBC Radio 4. She is the author of the Hope series of novels featuring Chief Inspector Nick Trevellyan and businesswoman Alison Hope, which began with *Hope Against Hope* in 1990. She should not be confused with her American namesake who is the author of the series about Detective Jack Lingemann.

Steve Lockley "A Sea of Troubles". Steve Lockley (b. 1958) is an English writer, now resident in Wales. He is the editor (with Paul Lewis) of the *Cold Cuts* series of horror fiction anthologies. He has recently completed a children's novel and is working on an adaptation of the legends of Twm Siôn Catti, the Welsh Robin Hood.

F. Gwynplaine MacIntyre "Murder as You Like It". F. Gwynplaine MacIntyre (b. 1948) is the Scottish-born, Australian-raised, American-resident author of the Victorian-SF novel *The Woman Between the Worlds*, as well as several pseudonymous novels and many stories for the science-fiction magazines.

Patricia McKillip "Star-Crossed". Patricia McKillip (b. 1948) is a much respected writer of fantasy fiction whose work began with the novels for children, *The House on Parchment Street* and *The Throme of the Erril of Sherill*, both in 1973, and continued with the highly regarded *The Forgotten Beasts of Eld* in 1974 and the Chronicles of Morgon trilogy, *The Riddle-Master of Hed*, *Heir of Sea and Fire* and *Harpist in the Wind* published in 1978 and 1979. She has written many SF and fantasy novels since including *The Changeling Sea*, *The Sorceress and the Cygnet*, its sequel *The Cygnet and the Firebird*, and *Winter Rose*.

Amy Myers "Who Killed Mamillius?". Amy Myers is best known for her books featuring the Victorian/Edwardian master-chef with the remarkable detective powers, Auguste Didier who first appeared in *Murder in Pug's Parlour* in 1987 and has built up a dedicated following. She was previously an editor for the publisher William Kimber for whom she edited the *After Midnight Stories* series of anthologies. She has also written a series of novels under the name Harriet Hudson, including *The Wooing of Katie May*, *The Sun in Glory* and *Look for me By Moonlight*.

Kim Newman "This is Illyria, *Lady*". Kim Newman (b. 1959) is a prolific writer, broadcaster and film critic whose first book, *Nightmare Movies* in 1984, was a critical study of recent horror films. He has written a fascinating series of avant-garde science-fiction and fantasy novels heavily influenced by the film, detective and comic-book media. These include *The Night Mayor*, *Jago*, *The Quorum*, and his vampire sequence *Anno Dracula* and *The Bloody Red Baron*. Some of his shorter stories will be found in *The Original Dr Shade*. He has brought that same other-worldly unreality to his thinking on *Twelfth Night*.

Mary Monica Pulver "The Shrewd Taming of Lord Thomas". Mary Pulver (b. 1943) was, until recently, one half of the Margaret Frazer writing team, and co-author of the Dame Frevisse series of historical mystery novels. Under her own name she has produced a series about mid-west cop Sergeant Peter Brichter, starting with *Murder at the War* in 1987.

Mary Reed and Eric Mayer "A Shadow That Dies". Mary Reed and Eric Mayer are a husband-and-wife writing team whose short stories include a series about John the Eunuch who investigates crimes in the early days of the Byzantine Empire, and the stories about Inspector Dorj of the Mongolian Police. In their own right they have each written a number of books and articles on a remarkable assortment of esoteric subjects, ranging from Mary's items on weather lore and fruits and nuts, to Eric's articles on marathon running.

Darrell Schweitzer "The Death of Falstaff". Darrell Schweitzer (b. 1952) is a prolific American critic, editor and writer, mostly of fantasy, including the novels *The Shattered Goddess*, *The White Isle* and *The Mask of the Sorcerer*, and the short story volumes *We Are All Legends*, *Tom O'Bedlam's Night Out* and *Transients and Other Disquieting Stories*.

Keith Taylor "The Banished Men". Taylor (b. 1946) is an Australian writer who has a fascination for Celtic history and myth. He has written a series of historical fantasy novels set at the time of the downfall of the Roman Empire in Britain which runs *Bard*, *The First Longship*, *The Wild Sea*, *Ravens' Gathering* and *Felimid's Homecoming*, plus another series set in mythical Ireland, which runs *The Sorcerer's Sacred Isle*, *The Cauldron of Plenty* and *Search for the Starblade*.

Peter Tremayne "An Ensuing Evil". Peter Tremayne (b. 1943) is the pseudonym of Celtic scholar and historian Peter Berresford Ellis who, under his own name, has written many books tracing the history and myth of the Celts, including *The Celtic Empire*, *Celt and Saxon* and *Celt and Greek*. In the fiction field he established an early reputation for his books of horror and fantasy, particularly his Dracula series collected in the omnibus *Dracula Lives!*, and his Lan-Kern series based on Cornish mythology, which began with *The Fires of Lan-Kern*. He has written thrillers as Peter MacAlan and also wrote a new novel featuring E.W. Hornung's rogue detective Raffles in *The Return of Raffles*. He is perhaps now best known for his series of historical mysteries featuring the seventh-century Irish Advocate, Sister Fidelma, in the books *Absolution by Murder*, *Shroud for an Archbishop*, *Suffer Little Children*, *The Subtle Serpent* and *The Spider's Web*.

Derek Wilson "A Serious Matter". Derek Wilson has written over thirty books of history, biography and fiction, including the acclaimed family biographies, *Rothschild: A Story of Wealth and Power* and *The Astors 1763–1922: Landscape with Millionaires*. He also written two fascinating books on the circumnavigation of the globe, *The World Encompassed – Drake's Voyage 1577–1580* and *The Circumnavigators*. In the world of mystery fiction he has created the character of Tim Lacy, international art connoisseur and investigator whose cases have been chronicled in *The Triarchs*, *The Dresden Text* and *The Hellfire Papers*.